Homo Temporalis

signale
modern german letters, cultures, and thought

Series Editor: Paul Fleming, Cornell University
Peter Uwe Hohendahl, Founding Editor

Signale: Modern German Letters, Cultures, and Thought publishes new English language books in literary studies, criticism, cultural studies, and intellectual history pertaining to the German-speaking world, as well as translations of important German-language works. Signale construes "modern" in the broadest terms: the series covers topics ranging from the early modern period to the present. Signale books are published under a joint imprint of Cornell University Press and Cornell University Library in electronic and print formats. Please see http://signale.cornell.edu/.

HOMO TEMPORALIS

German Jewish Thinkers on Time

NITZAN LEBOVIC

A Signale Book

CORNELL UNIVERSITY PRESS AND CORNELL UNIVERSITY LIBRARY
ITHACA AND LONDON

Cornell University Press and Cornell University Library gratefully acknowledge the College of Arts & Sciences, Cornell University, for support of the Signale series.

Copyright © 2024 by Nitzan Lebovic

All rights reserved. Except for brief quotations in a review, this book, or parts thereof, must not be reproduced in any form without permission in writing from the publisher. For information, address Cornell University Press, Sage House, 512 East State Street, Ithaca, New York 14850.

First published 2024 by Cornell University Press and Cornell University Library

Library of Congress Cataloging-in-Publication Data

Names: Lebovic, Nitzan, 1970- author.
Title: Homo temporalis : German Jewish thinkers on time / Nitzan Lebovic.
Description: Ithaca : Cornell University Press, 2024. | Series: Signale: modern German letters, cultures, and thought | Includes bibliographical references and index.
Identifiers: LCCN 2024020241 (print) | LCCN 2024020242 (ebook) | ISBN 9781501779558 (hardcover) | ISBN 9781501779565 (paperback) | ISBN 9781501779589 (epub) | ISBN 9781501779572 (pdf)
Subjects: LCSH: Buber, Martin, 1878-1965. | Benjamin, Walter, 1892–1940. | Arendt, Hannah, 1906-1975. | Celan, Paul. | Time—Religious aspects—Judaism. | Time—Philosophy—History—20th century. | Time in literature. | Jewish philosophy—Germany—20th century.
Classification: LCC BM729.T55 L43 2024 (print) | LCC BM729.T55 (ebook) | DDC 181/.06—dc23/eng/20240706
LC record available at https://lccn.loc.gov/2024020241
LC ebook record available at https://lccn.loc.gov/2024020242

For Avigail, Asaf, and Yael

Contents

Acknowledgments	ix
Introduction: Time and Rupture	1
1. A Temporal Turn: Time Out of Joint	17
2. Martin Buber: A Time for Theopolitics	44
3. Walter Benjamin: The Rhythm of Time	107
4. Against Self-Referentiality: Hannah Arendt Reads Augustine	158
5. Paul Celan: The Syntax of Time	216
6. Life-Form: After the Turn	254
Bibliography	289
Index	323

Acknowledgments

"An afterword should leave the skin quickly, like an alcohol rub," Anne Carson writes. An academic acknowledgement may feel like an alcohol rub, but it is meant to do the opposite: not sting, but lure in, not evaporate, but remain on it, like honey. An acknowledgment is where academics admit that we are part of what the early modern *philosophes* depict as a busy beehive. We are writing for a community of peers engaging with similar ideas, and aim to give our subjects the intellectual treatment they deserve. We are also writing within and for the context of our time. The philosophes wrote during the age of liberal revolution; I'm writing in a time that has witnessed mass violence—my country of origin included—the collapse of liberal institutions, and unprecedented environmental crisis.

The German Jewish intellectuals discussed in this book dealt with similar issues in their own time, and chose to wrestle with them by thinking about fundamental forms of equality: the equality of life, devoid of status and identity, beyond method. They used concepts of time, the time of life, as the starting point for understanding every political, social, and economic system. They chose the language of temporal existence as a measure against which no institution can claim victory. This is what I depict in this book as an ontological equality of life, or non-anthropocentric humanism. It is the irony of history that, with time, their own critical systems were institutionalized as well, and became a matter of (academic) status. Honey indeed, but a tad too sticky and sweet. Considering that a century has passed since they began publishing their work, it is not surprising that the fault lines of their systems are becoming apparent and that the questions they asked must now be reformulated. Still, these thinkers remain a source of inspiration for those of us who want to think (and feel) with the vanquished, the underrepresented, and the "unworthy of life."

The people and institutions I mention below have inspired my own thinking for longer than I can recall. It is a group of people whose lively intellectual cross-pollination inspired not just ideas, but an intellectual ethos I am grateful for. In other words, this acknowledgment expresses a debt much greater and longer than for this specific book. My colleagues at Lehigh University were helpful in giving me the time to complete this book with several grants and leaves that supported the work. I am deeply grateful to William Bulman and Robert Flowers for their profound institutional and personal support. Taieb Berrada and Chad Kautzer shared ongoing conversations with me about these and other topics. The Berman Center for Jewish Studies, especially Jodi Eichler-Levin and Hartley Lachter, gave unreserved support to the project. John Savage and the late John Pettegrew—dearly and painfully missed—challenged me in different, though always affectionate, ways.

I was lucky to present parts of the book in various prestigious forums, which opened new worlds of knowledge to me. Sylvie Anne Goldberg invited me to the École des hautes études (EHESS) for a monthlong seminar where I was able to present the different chapters of the book. Na'ama Rokem invited me to serve as the Greenberg Visiting Professor at the University of Chicago in the fall of 2022, where I presented the key arguments of the book to a forum that included, to my utter delight, Dipesh Chakrabarty, François

Hartog, Orit Bashkin, Michael Geyer, and Kenneth Moss. All of them became close compatriots in the fight over (the history of) time. I was lucky to win fellowships at the Katz Center for Advanced Judaic Studies (UPenn) and the Remarque Institute (NYU), where I met intellectuals I came to deeply care about. I continue to connect and share ideas and work with many of them.

Many friends offered their unwavering support during the process: I was repeatedly astounded by the generosity and never-ending patience of Ethan Kleinberg and Zvi Ben-Dor Benite. Alys George, Karin Loevy, Galili Shahar, and Eugene Sheppard, allowed me to test out ideas on them and gave helpful recommendations. Frances Tanzer read essays and parts of the final manuscript, gave me sage advice, and drew striking images that I integrated into my work. David N. Myers was not just a source of intellectual inspiration but also a personal mentor who never failed to offer support and a warm, encouraging word. In Berlin I met with Evelyn Annus, Eva Horn, Martin Treml, Arnd Wedemeyer, and Daniel Weidner, who became, to my great joy, close personal friends. The Leibniz-Zentrum für Literatur und Kulturforschung (ZfL, Berlin) became an intellectual home, and I am grateful to Sigrid Weigel and Eva Geulen for their support. I consider Saul Friedlaender, Anson Rabinbach, Vivian Liska, and Enzo Traverso my spiritual and intellectual guides. Over the years, they heard much about this project and supported it in different ways.

I owe a great debt to the editors and commentators whose work deserves recognition: the brilliant Michael Lesley and Sophie Duvernoy helped me turn this incredibly dense intertextual universe into a comprehensible one. Andrea Dara Cooper, Ethan Kleinberg, and Patchen Markell were ideal readers for the manuscript, gave careful reflections on the conceptual framework, and valuable notes and recommendations. At Signale, Paul Fleming, Mahinder Kingra, and Kizer Walker embraced the manuscript with open arms, and then worked to bring it through the revision and production process swiftly and generously.

Earlier, and considerably different, versions of sections of this book have appeared in the following places: the Bachofen section in chapter 3 supported a different argument in my first book, *The*

Philosophy of Life and Death: Ludwig Klages and the Rise of a Nazi Biopolitics (New York: Palgrave Macmillan, 2013); the argument connecting Benjamin's analysis of human time to the Anthropocene was developed in "Benjamin and the Anthropocene," in *Forces of Education: Walter Benjamin and the Politics of Pedagogy*, ed. Dominik Zechner and Dennis Johanssen (New York: Bloomsbury, 2022), 211–224. The brief reference to Paul Celan's poem "Close, in the Aorta's Arch" was the focus of a close reading in "Near the End: Celan between Scholem and Heidegger," *German Quarterly* 83, no. 4 (Fall 2010): 465–484. I thank the editors and reviewers who read those earlier essays for their careful work.

Finally, while writing this book I never ceased to think about my children, Asaf and Yael, and my partner of three decades, Avigail. I cannot think about time, life, and what it means to love these two things, without them. It makes no sense to thank someone for who they are, but I know that I owe all I do to them. This book is dedicated to them. They, and the critical intellectuals I mention above, give me the courage to adopt the motto that concludes this book: *to not build on the good old days, but on the bad new ones.*[1]

---

1. Walter Benjamin, "Conversations with Brecht," in *Reflections: Essays, Aphorisms, Autobiographical Writings*, ed. Peter Demetz, trans. Edmund Jephcott (New York: Harcourt Brace Jovanovich, 1978), 219.

Homo Temporalis

Introduction

Time and Rupture

Shortly after the end of World War II, the German Jewish thinkers Jacob Taubes and Abraham J. Heschel concluded in separate studies that Israel is "a people of time" (*Volk der Zeit*) and that "Judaism is a religion of time."[1] They were joining a decades-old lineage of German Jewish intellectuals for whom the concept of time was key to their philosophical systems. In this book I examine the commitment of twentieth-century German Jewish thinkers to the concept of time, bringing into dialogue key figures such as the philosopher of religion Martin Buber, the critical theorist Walter Benjamin, the political theorist Hannah Arendt, and the poet Paul Celan, along with many of their contemporaries.

---

1. Jacob Taubes, *Occidental Eschatology*, trans. David Ratmoko (Stanford, CA: Stanford University Press, 2009), 12; A. J. Heschel, *The Sabbath: Its Meaning for Modern Man* (New York: Farrar, Straus and Giroux, 1951), 8. Taubes's work derived from his dissertation from 1947. Heschel made his claim in 1951.

Despite their varied intellectual backgrounds, these figures were united in choosing the concept of time, rather than space, as the key to theorizing their individual and collective experience.[2] Indeed, Taubes proposed that "Israel [was] able to become a people without space" (*Volk ohne Raum*).[3] Instead of spatial categories such as borders, territory, or national origins, German Jewish thinkers proposed critical temporal concepts such as human finality, contemporaneity, natality, and life as responses to the political crises of the early 1900s, World War I, the collapse of the Weimar Republic, and the Holocaust. Temporality shook off the constraints of national identity and instead proposed a vision of existence shaped by equality. This focus on life, or lived experience, enabled a new form of egalitarian politics. Having written this book in a contemporary moment that shares unwelcome features with the early 1900s, I have attempted to link current critical thought to a political commitment that is directed beyond borders and disciplinary systems.

Many works have been dedicated to each of the four thinkers central to this book, but none have brought them together to explore the critical impetus they share: a reconsideration of temporality in response to modern dilemmas. Few scholars have considered these four intellectuals' stress on temporality to be a significant starting point for their philosophy and politics, perhaps because each of the four framed it differently. Concentrating on time, rather than space and ideology, reveals that Buber adopted Nietzsche's *Kulturkritik* (cultural critique) to develop an account of Jewish "renewal" and "lived experience."[4]

---

2. Many scholars have argued the opposite. I instead argue that what Buber, Benjamin, Arendt, and Celan call "space" is defined by temporal concepts and the life, dynamic, and rhythm of movement within a particular space. This does not mean that space is unimportant; instead it means that space is defined differently and against static terminology. For a contrary perspective, see, for example, Martin Shuster's identification of anachronism with a measured space. Shuster, *How to Measure a World? A Philosophy of Judaism* (Bloomington: Indiana University Press, 2021).

3. Taubes, *Occidental Eschatology*, 12.

4. Ever since Buber's biographer Maurice Friedman pointed out Nietzsche's influence on young Buber, most of the scholarship on Nietzsche and Buber has been dedicated to Nietzsche's ideological and philosophical influence on Buber. See Friedman, *Martin Buber's Life and Work: The Early Years, 1878–1923* (Detroit: Wayne State University Press, 1988), 143.

Benjamin and his friend Gershom Scholem invoked the terms "standstill" and "deferral" in response to Buber's push for Jewish realization. Arendt, on the other hand, painted the whole generation of "German-Jewish intellectuals" as living "in dark times," and pleaded for a republican "rebirth" of universal values. Last, Paul Celan focused on the poetic concept of the literary caesura and the status of "in-betweenness," a term Buber popularized before the rise of fascism.

Even though none of these thinkers shared the same temporal concepts, the focus on time itself formed a condition of dialogue among their works. But the drama was not just intellectual and interpersonal: it was historical, too. These German Jewish thinkers reacted to the rise of nationalism, antisemitism, and to the emergence of the social-Darwinist "struggle for life" in the early 1900s. Their response had three main features: first, in the early 1900s, a critical engagement with the concept of life and a post-Nietzschean life philosophy (*Lebensphilosophie*), or a phenomenological engagement with the "life-time" (*Lebenszeit*) and "life-world" (*Lebenswelt*), or life-form (*Lebensform*); second, during the 1920s and 1930s, a process of working through the "Christian regime of historicity" and the internal tension between a Christian and a Jewish notion of "betweenness";[5] third, before and after the Holocaust, a critical response to Martin Heidegger's philosophy of time and its interpretations of both life philosophy and Judeo-Christian metaphysics.

The three responses build the core chronology of my narrative, but they also reflect my own intellectual development. In my first book, *The Philosophy of Life and Death: Ludwig Klages and the Rise of a Nazi Biopolitics*, I focused on radical right-wing German life philosophers of the early 1900s who aestheticized the circular and recurrent flow of blood to develop a new cultural narrative surrounding life.[6] In this book I begin with the same period but adopt

---

5. François Hartog defines the "Christian regime of historicity" as "a time, bookended by the incarnation and the *parousia* [second coming], that has no duration. [It is] an interval . . . [that] exists as the permanent present of the new covenant." Hartog, *Chronos: The West Confronts Time*, trans. S. R. Gilbert (New York: Columbia University Press, 2022), 49.

6. Nitzan Lebovic, *The Philosophy of Life and Death: Ludwig Klages and the Rise of a Nazi Biopolitics* (New York: Palgrave Macmillan, 2013).

an opposing lens. Although right-wing German thinkers championed the circulation of Aryan blood and the eternal existence of Germanic soil, German Jewish thinkers interpreted the life-form or "stream of life" in more egalitarian, temporal ways. Their understanding of the self and its surrounding community starkly contrasts with right-wing calls for "living space" (*Lebensraum*) and an absolute sovereign. As Steven Aschheim explains, this group of German Jewish intellectuals belonged to the Nietzscheans of the early 1900s who aligned themselves with radicalism, the avant-garde, and cultural critique.[7] In *Zionism and Melancholy: The Short Life of Israel Zarchi*, I followed the melancholy of Zionist socialists, many of them admirers of Nietzsche, who settled a collective biblical homeland but found themselves severed from their own past, home, and culture. In this book I follow German Jewish thinkers, most of them stateless, who opposed the territorial and demographic language of Zionist settlers and advocated instead for a confederative and pluralist solution. Writing in an era of economic and political upheaval, wars, and genocide, they wanted to develop a vision of life that was humanistic but not anthropocentric. To address the intellectual and historical challenges posed by the twentieth century, this group of thinkers elaborated various theories of "temporal egalitarianism": the notion that living time is the first and most fundamental equalizer among all forms of life because of the biological and existential condition of being subject to time. Buber and Benjamin stressed the "creaturely" in their emphasis on the sacredness of life, while Arendt and Celan took up the language of "creation" and "natality." New conceptions of time—a "temporal turn" in the eyes of contemporary scholars—offered a context for the vision that contrasted the late nineteenth-century creaturely life with the modern Christian state, on the one hand, and the

---

7. Steven E. Aschheim, *The Nietzsche Legacy in Germany: 1890–1990* (Berkeley: University of California Press, 1992), 6–7. Following Aschheim, Scott Spector points out that Scholem's "self-certitude" emerges out of a deep engagement with German culture, "especially Nietzsche, . . . with the panoply of German vitalism (*Lebensphilosophie*), and with pronounced strains of *völkisch* nationalism." See Spector, *Modernism without Jews? German-Jewish Subjects and Histories* (Bloomington: Indiana University Press, 2017), 14.

inherent "in-betweenness" of all life, with the racial "unworthy of living," on the other hand.[8]

In this introduction I explain the conditions for the three temporal turns of the twentieth century, which itself became the source for two later turns: the failure of assimilation, the industrialized annihilation of the Jews, and what we, in the present, experience as a recent turn toward the end of time. While the first turn witnessed the rise of secularized and racialized discourses, the latter two turns drew much of their language from early 1900s political theologies. In his autobiographical text about his friendship with Walter Benjamin, Gershom Scholem wrote how "German Jewry . . . *wanted* to believe in assimilation with, and integration into, an environment that by and large viewed the Jews at best with indifference and at worst with malevolence."[9] As Scholem and other intellectuals testified, nationalism and antisemitism were accompanied by a tense discussion of Jewish and German origins. During the early twentieth century, Protestant theologians identified with "crisis theology" or "dialectical theology," such as Karl Barth, cultivated an eschatological terminology that broke from centuries of ecclesiastic authority and political stability.[10] German Jewish conceptions arose that countered the eschatological "already but not-yet" of Christian resurrection with a model of in-betweenness: an "already-not and not-yet" (*schon nicht und noch nicht*).[11] Seemingly a minor change, the stress

---

8. Christopher Clark, *Time and Power: Visions of History in German Politics, from the Thirty Years' War to the Third Reich* (Princeton, NJ: Princeton University Press, 2019), 16. For a discussion of the "lives unworthy of living" as a modern *homo sacer*, see Giorgio Agamben, *Homo Sacer: Sovereign Power and Bare Life*, trans. Daniel Heller-Roazen (Stanford, CA: Stanford University Press, 1998), 138.

9. Gershom Scholem, *From Berlin to Jerusalem: Memories of My Youth*, trans. Harry Zohn (Philadelphia: Paul Dry Books, 2012), 27. Emphasis in the original.

10. Thomas Albert Howard, *Protestant Theology and the Making of the Modern German University* (New York: Oxford University Press, 2006), 303.

11. For a discussion of the Christian—mostly Protestant—model, see Christopher Frey, "Eschatology and Ethics: Their Relation in Recent Continental Protestantism," in *Eschatology in the Bible in Jewish and Christian Tradition*, ed. Henning Graf Reventlow (Sheffield: Sheffield Academic, 1997), 62–74; Susannah Heschel, *The Aryan Jesus: Christian Theologians and the Bible in Nazi Germany* (Princeton, NJ: Princeton University Press, 2021), 13; Daniel Weidner, "The Political Theology of Ethical Monotheism," in *Judaism, Liberalism, and Political Theology*, ed. Randi

on the "already-not" ensures a clear distinction between past and present, history and interpretation. The reason for this insistence among Jewish thinkers has to do with centuries of living among Christians, being defined negatively by them, and, as a result, suffering "the hatred of one's own imperfection, one's own Not-Yet."[12]

In the same time period, Jewish thinkers were forced to reckon with both Paulinian and Augustinian doctrines concerning the possibility of coexistence between Jews and Christians in the face of modernization, (ostensible) secularization, incomplete emancipation, and the rise of modern antisemitism. Augustine's conception of Christianity had, for two millennia, propagated the idea among Christians that Jews were a living testament—witnesses—to the victory of Christ. While Christians live within the timeline of Jesus's messianic arrival as an "already," Jews are left behind as "already-not" of the past, and eternally "not-yet" of the future. The Augustinian witness doctrine thus categorized Jews as a political minority and theological exception in a homogeneous Christian society by keeping them in an inferior position. At the same time, this view historically helped protect Jews from persecution.[13] Augustine's doc-

---

Rashkover and Martin Kavka (Bloomington: Indiana University Press, 2014), 178–96.

12. Leora Batnitzky, *Idolatry and Representation: The Philosophy of Franz Rosenzweig Reconsidered* (Princeton, NJ: Princeton University Press, 2000), 89.

13. The witness doctrine allowed for the presence of Jews within Christian communities as a testimony to the Christian narrative of transfiguration from the Old to the New Testament and from the Old Israel to the new "Israel of the spirit." Jeremy Cohen and Paula Fredriksen explain that Jews and Christians in the Augustinian era fought against a common pagan world, and that in this context Augustine "reimagined the relationship of God and Israel, and thus he reimagined as well the relationship of his church, past and present, to the Jews." Paula Fredriksen, *Augustine and the Jews: A Christian Defense of Jews and Judaism* (New York: Doubleday, 2008), 211. Although Fredriksen sees the doctrine as a question of "theological imagination," Cohen identifies it with Augustine's practical interest in both theology and politics. See Jeremy Cohen, *Living Letters of the Law: Ideas of the Jew in Medieval Christianity* (Berkeley: University of California Press, 1999); and Cohen, "Revisiting Augustine's Doctrine of Jewish Witness," *Journal of Religion* 89, no. 4 (2009): 564–78. In contrast to both Cohen and Fredriksen, David Nirenberg explains the doctrine from the opposite ideological end as part of Christian anti-Judaism: "Within Augustine's historical approach, those who lived as Jews in a Christian age played an important role as 'witness.' Like fossils for the naturalist, their survival provided the best

trine was itself a response to Paulinian anti-Judaism; in contrast to Augustine's demand to preserve the Jew as a relic, Paul called for the obliteration of Jewish law, warned of the danger of "Judaization," and longed for the second coming of Christ (*parousia*).[14]

Around the year 1900, Jewish thinkers were forced to reassess the value of Augustine's witness doctrine and Paul's abolition of Jewish law as a political and existential principle. When anti-Jewish rhetoric rejected Augustine's position in favor of Paul's eschatological anti-Jewish rhetoric, German Jewish thinkers engaged critically with Paul. The fact that Martin Heidegger, the doctoral adviser of many German Jewish thinkers, used Paul to counter Augustine only made their task more urgent.[15] In the eyes of German Jewish thinkers, Augustine's recognition of the continuity between Jews and Christians, his stress on duration, linking past, present, and future, and on memory, helped offer an alternative vision of coexistence between creation and eschatology, origin and end. As will be shown in the chapters of this book, German Jewish thinkers revisited the prophecy of destruction and the late Jewish prophets by invoking the eschatologies of Paul and Augustine, and they dedicated plays, as well as philosophical and literary pieces, to the topic. The point of the political theology practiced by German Jewish thinkers was to make a historical-theological claim for equality.

---

evidence for the transformation of God's promise in the distant past.... [The Jews] were milestones, mirrors, vessels, desks for the Christians." Nirenberg, *Anti-Judaism: The Western Tradition* (New York: W. W. Norton, 2013), 254–55.

14. Regarding Paul's warning against the danger of "Judaization," and the Paulinian anti-Jewish rhetoric, see the second chapter of Nirenberg, *Anti-Judaism*, 48–86.

15. Ryan Coyne shows that "the route Heidegger takes to isolate the function of the *katechon* is a circuitous one" [Carl Schmitt, taking inspiration from Paul, used the term *katechon* to denote the sovereign who withholds or suspends the time of the end—N. L.] and depends on "the ability of the Christian to recognize the Antichrist" and the ability to "await the *parousia*." Heidegger explains this theological-political structure, later building the heart of Carl Schmitt's interpretation of the friend–enemy distinction, by referring to "how eschatological time illuminates the essence of history... the critical time or *kairos* has grown short for Paul." Coyne, *Heidegger's Confessions: The Remains of Saint Augustine in Being and Time and Beyond* (Chicago: University of Chicago Press, 2015), 41.

In the four intellectual portraits in this book, I trace this new conception of time through biographies and disciplines. The philosophy of religion would not be what it is today without Buber's early emphasis on immediacy and lived experience (*Erlebnis*) or his later analysis of dialogical philosophy as a form of temporal betweenness. Critical theory was deeply shaped by Walter Benjamin's angel of history, "nowness" (*Jetztzeit*), and his contrast between lived experience and practical experience (*Erfahrung*). Hannah Arendt's understanding of democracy as natality or "permanent revolution," as well as her emphasis on nowness, the present "between past and future," has made a significant contribution to political philosophy. Finally, there can be no "poetry after Auschwitz," to use Theodor Adorno's dictum, without Paul Celan's understanding of "nearness" as the point in time—not space—which Celan equates with the breath-turn (*Atemwende*) or the moment between life and death. The poem, he argued in his "Meridian" speech (1961), "ceaselessly calls and hauls itself back . . . from its now no-longer into its still-now" (*es ruft und holt sich . . . unausgesetzt aus seinem Schon-nicht-mehr in sein Immer-noch zurück*).[16] In other words, German Jewish thinkers saw the temporality of life as the primary force that could overcome difference and distinct identities. By separating the temporality of life from a spatial and normative sense of belonging, those thinkers worked against an absolute principle of sovereignty, and its capacity to turn the exception, violence, into the norm. They suggested, instead, to normalize another exception: transforming the stranger, the immigrant, the Jew, the pariah, the minority into a dynamic principle for political reform.

Previous research on these thinkers has tended to emphasize the discrete contributions of each of these authors, either for disciplinary reasons or because they are taken to be parts of different ideological discourses. Buber is generally considered the father of cultural Zionism, Benjamin a critical opponent of nationalism, Arendt

---

16. Paul Celan, *The Meridian: Final Version—Drafts—Materials*, ed. Bernhard Böschenstein and Heino Schmull, trans. Pierre Joris (Stanford, CA: Stanford University Press, 2011), 9.

a supporter of constitutional democracy, and Celan a lyrical poet-philosopher. By working across intellectual history, political philosophy, and literature, I propose to correct these myopic and overspecialized readings in two ways. First, I show that their development and use of temporal concepts—rather than spatial or biologically determinist ideas—connects them not only with one another but with the shared project of life and political-theological reform. Before a person enters into any individual or communal form of existence, the inescapability of life and death, being born into the world and leaving it, does not allow for discrimination on the basis of race, nationality, religion, class, gender, or personal trait. Second, I mean to counteract the inclination to treat various disciplinary foci as unrelated—reading Buber's philosophy of religion in isolation from his politics, for example, or Celan's syntax separate from his thoughts on culture and memory.

All four of these figures employed the terminology of post-Nietzschean life philosophy and Heideggerian phenomenology, and all offered a radical vision of change to encourage dissent and critique in political and disciplinary terms. In that respect, in this book I explore and challenge views of German Jewish history that identify it with political compromise and *Bildung* (acculturation, education), a "dual identity" between the German and the Jew, a deterritorialized in-betweenness, or the transcendence of borders.[17] Such acclaimed works on German Jews frame the German Jewish experience in terms of liberalism, pluralism, moderation, and spatiality. They focus on issues of origins, identity, and boundaries, even while recognizing that the thinkers they discuss rejected such categories. Historians of German Jewish modernity have noticed the widening

---

17. For *Bildung*, see George L. Mosse, *German Jews beyond Judaism* (Bloomington: Indiana University Press, 1985); for dual identity, see Paul Mendes-Flohr, *German Jews: A Dual Identity* (New Haven, CT: Yale University Press, 1999); for deterritorialized in-betweenness, see Scott Spector, *Prague Territories: National Conflict and Cultural Innovation in Franz Kafka's Fin de Siècle* (Berkeley: University of California Press, 2000); and for the transcendence of borders, see Steven E. Aschheim, *Beyond the Border: The German-Jewish Legacy Abroad* (Princeton, NJ: Princeton University Press, 2007).

gap between the private Jewish home and German public acculturation, but these historians have used identitarian terms, rather than temporal ones, to explain it.[18]

The story of this work is particularly German Jewish, or European, yet it is also critical of identity as a defining category. Stressing temporality enabled German Jewish thinkers to avoid both nationalist redemptive stories and defeatist narratives about futurelessness.[19] I

---

18. Alexander Altmann presents Moses Mendelssohn as living under the "dual aspect" of secular Enlightenment and rabbinic Judaism; see Altmann, *Moses Mendelssohn: A Biographical Study* (Tuscaloosa: University of Alabama Press, 1973), 605. George Mosse describes German Jews as forming "beyond Judaism"; Anson Rabinbach's *In the Shadow of Catastrophe*, David Myers's *Resisting History*, Peter Gordon's *Continental Divide*, and Barbara Hahn's *The Jewess Pallas Athena* all discuss the complexity of living and thinking with and among the democratic "Athena" of Christian Europe. See Mosse, *Germans and Jews: The Right, the Left, and the Search for a "Third Force" in Pre-Nazi Germany* (Detroit: Wayne State University, 1987); Rabinbach, *In the Shadow of Catastrophe: German Intellectuals between Apocalypse and Enlightenment* (Berkeley: University of California Press, 1997); Myers, *Resisting History: Historicism and Its Discontents in German-Jewish Thought* (Princeton, NJ: Princeton University Press, 2003); Gordon, *Continental Divide: Heidegger, Cassirer, Davos* (Cambridge, MA: Harvard University Press, 2010); and Hahn, *The Jewess Pallas Athena: This Too a Theory of Modernity*, trans. James McFarland (Princeton, NJ: Princeton University Press, 2002). Literary and philosophical interpretations tend to be more interdisciplinary but also return to spatial boundaries as a framework. Scott Spector, in *Prague Territories*, beautifully depicts the deterritorialization and in-betweenness of German Jewish life in Prague. Stéphane Mosès's *Angel of History*, Michael Levine's *Weak Messianic Power*, Amir Eshel's *Futurity*, and most recently Vivian Liska's *German-Jewish Thought and Its Afterlife* emphasize specific aspects of temporality considered, usually, in relation to a particular disciplinary focus. See Mosès, *The Angel of History: Rosenzweig, Benjamin, Scholem* (Stanford, CA: Stanford University Press, 2009); Levine, *A Weak Messianic Power: Figures of a Time to Come in Benjamin, Derrida, and Celan* (New York: Fordham University Press, 2014); Eshel, *Futurity: Contemporary Literature and the Quest for the Past* (Chicago: Chicago University Press, 2013); and Liska, *German-Jewish Thought and Its Afterlife: A Tenuous Legacy* (Bloomington: University of Indiana Press, 2018). For more on these topics, see Aschheim, *Beyond the Border*; Peter Eli Gordon, *Rosenzweig and Heidegger: Between Judaism and German Philosophy* (Berkeley: University of California Press, 2003); Hillel Keval, *Languages of Community: The Jewish Experience in the Czech Lands* (Berkeley: University of California, 2000); and Mendes-Flohr, *German Jews*.

19. For examples of each, see Yael Zerubavel, *Recovered Roots: Collective Memory and the Making of Israeli National Identity* (Chicago: Chicago University Press, 1995), 220; and Kenneth E. Moss, *An Unchosen People: Jewish Political Reckoning in Interwar Poland* (Cambridge, MA: Harvard University Press, 2021).

argue that all four thinkers shared an unequivocal belief in life and living time beyond national borders. In criticizing the Judeo-Christian anthropocentric or idealist approach, the German Jewish thinkers also responded to the conditions of their time. This response is also where all four projects meet their anthropogenic limit.

The four thinkers in this book considered not just the physical limitations of existence, but the linguistic and cultural ones as well. Here again, they worked within a broad context: Max Brod fashioned in-betweenness as the aesthetics of "indifferentism"; Fritz Mauthner talked about the "poetic language lacking the highest and deepest: the earth"; Kafka himself advocated "a language that is in continuous flux"; Karl Kraus identified this in-betweenness with the *Mauschel*—a derogatory reference to "Jew talk" (Kafka and Celan both borrowed this term); Franz Werfel identified it as *Erdentelologie* (earth teleology), and so on.[20] Scott Spector writes that German Jews occupied "the uniquely charged spaces between identities."[21] According to most of the literature on German Jews, though, this space between identities gradually became the very definition of identity, and its critique a form of affirmation.[22] Indeed, Arendt used the concept of betweenness, or being between (*Dazwischen* or *Dazwischensein*), along the lines of Buber's betweenness (*das Zwischen*) and Benjamin's interval (*Abstand*) against Heidegger's stress on destruction, finality, and anxiety.

German Jewish thought about time asks us, as denizens of the twenty-first century, to consider not only that Jews, Muslims, or Christians might constitute a social and cultural minority, but that "*Homo sapiens* are a minority form of life."[23] Historian Dipesh Chakrabarty has recently pleaded for this minoritarian perspective in

---

20. Spector, *Prague Territories*, 61, 79, 88, 90–91, 97.
21. Spector, *Prague Territories*, 5.
22. The standard literature on German Jews supports this evaluation. George Mosse describes German Jews as forming the "third force." Paul Mendes-Flohr refers to their "dual identity." Steven Aschheim refers to "German-speaking Jewish intellectuals beyond their borders." From a different angle, the affirmative tone of many academic societies and centers allows little, if any, critique of their German Jewish protagonists, and these groups usually resist any critical application of their ideas.
23. Dipesh Chakrabarty, *One Planet, Many Worlds: The Climate Parallax* (Waltham, MA: Brandeis University Press, 2023), 38.

view of the many forms of life beyond the anthropocentric: "Is it possible for humanity as a whole to look on themselves as a 'minor' form of life and work toward minoritarian forms of political thought, of the kind that Arendt or Deleuze on Kafka have educated us in, though that would avoid 'majoritarian' ... dreams of domination?"[24]

The scope of this book has broad political and methodological implications. When contemporary thinkers discuss innovative approaches to politics, they often draw on German Jewish in-betweenness. When the postcolonial thinker Homi K. Bhabha "unpacks [his] library again"—a clear allusion to Walter Benjamin and Jacques Derrida's essay on Benjamin—he finds there a "Jewishness [that] stands for a form of historical and racial in-betweenness."[25] When Giorgio Agamben considers the "interim character" "between the present eon and the future eon," he thinks again about Benjamin's "weak messianic force" at the core of his biopolitical critique.[26] When Achille Mbembe points to necropolitics, "the postcolony," and biopolitics, he grounds his analysis of exclusion in Arendt's "otherness."[27] As I show in chapter 6, the fascination with German Jewish in-betweenness began with critiques of modernity in the early 1900s, transitioned in response to

---

24. Chakrabarty, *One Planet, Many Worlds*, 39. Recent histories demonstrate that majoritarian decision-making is following closely the forming of a consensual and procedural discourse. See William Bulman, *The Rise of Majority Rule in Britain and Its Empire* (Cambridge: Cambridge University Press, 2021), 18.

25. Homi K. Bhabha, "Unpacking My Library Again," *Journal of the Midwest Modern Language Association* 28, no. 1 (Spring 1995): 14. Lila Berman suggests "a critical constructive approach" that "offers a nonfoundational vision for freeing Jewishness and Jewish history from tests of individual, group, or nationalist verifiability and, instead, reconceiving Jewishness as a structuring mode that can affect how a broad range of subjects have operated within history." Lila Corwin Berman, "Jewish History beyond the Jewish People," *AJS Review* (2018): 1–24. See also David Shraub, "White Jews: An Intersectional Approach," *AJS Review* 43, no. 2 (2019): 379–407.

26. Giorgio Agamben, "The Messiah and the Sovereign: The Problem of Law in Walter Benjamin," in *Potentialities*, trans. Daniel Heller-Roazen (Stanford, CA: Stanford University Press, 1999), 168.

27. In *On the Postcolony* Mbembe builds on Arendt's understanding of bureaucracy in his analysis of "the banality of power." In *Necropolitics*, he relies on her analysis of genocidal acts in "traditional imperialism" and the concentration camp. See Achille Mbembe, *On the Postcolony* (Berkeley: University of California Press, 2001), 3; Mbembe, *Necropolitics*, trans. Steve Corcoran (Durham, NC: Duke University Press, 2019), 200n40.

fascism and racism, and reached its most recent form of cultural critique in environmental studies.

Chapter 1 begins by offering a cultural and political history of German Jewry in the early twentieth century before considering in detail its intellectual protagonists and their critique of national and communal identity, and it closes with the reception of German Jewish thought after 1945, when Paul Celan wove it into a new (poetic) language. I conclude this book, in chapter 6, with a methodological and theoretical discussion that revisits the temporal concepts of the early 1900s through the lens of the Anthropocene, or what I call the third temporal turn.

The chapters are ordered chronologically. Chapter 2 begins in the early 1900s with Martin Buber's work in Berlin with his mentor, the sociologist Georg Simmel, who had himself taken up Nietzsche and Stefan George's life philosophy. Simmel, Buber, and later Buber's close friends, Gustav Landauer, Franz Rosenzweig, and Hugo Bergmann, all developed influential theories of life and lived temporality. Focusing on the immediacy of lived experience allowed them to look beyond social norms, affirmative notions of self, and political institutions in favor of dialogism.

Chapter 3 explores Walter Benjamin's critique of Buber's "realization" (*Verwirklichung*) of lived experience, alongside Heidegger's understanding of historical time. While acknowledging the relevance of immediacy and other temporal forms to critical thought, Benjamin and Scholem saw Buber's stress on realization as teleological and conservative. For them, as well as for Buber's close allies Franz Rosenzweig and Hans Kohn, Buber's use of blood symbols, "which he feels to be the antecedents of his I," were anchored in the treacherous waters of a biological *Lebensphilosophie*.[28] In the early 1910s Benjamin began to develop an anti-teleological and anti-linear philosophy that criticized all forms of immediacy and realization. During the later 1920s and early 1930s he developed a complex understanding

---

28. Laurence J. Silberstein, *Martin Buber's Social and Religious Thought: Alienation and the Quest for Meaning* (New York: NYU Press, 1990), 89. For an excellent close reading of the debate on blood symbols, see Adi Gordon, *Toward an Intellectual Biography of Hans Kohn* (Waltham, MA: Brandeis University Press, 2017), 36–52.

of "nowness" and "dialectics at a standstill" that wrestled with Heidegger's stress on being. "I expect sparks will fly from the shock of the confrontation between our two very different ways of looking at history," he wrote to Scholem.[29] Starting the historical timeline from nowness, standstill, or a "flash of recognition" enabled him to escape the pitfalls of essentialism, anachronism, and teleology.

Chapter 4 is dedicated to the work of Hannah Arendt, both with and against Heidegger. In private notes and letters, some of them still unpublished, Arendt reflected on her interpretation of Heidegger in relation to her lifelong work on Augustine's temporal concepts and her analysis of time and memory. Starting with her dissertation in 1928, this preoccupation with change and duration, immediacy and memory, was the basis of her interpretation of totalitarianism, revolution, and Augustine's "new order of the ages." Interestingly, in different works she linked Franz Kafka, Walter Benjamin, and Hermann Broch with the principles of "*homo temporalis*"—the human who is "inserted into time"—as a corrective to Heidegger's solipsism and Scholem's Zionism. Out of this dense network of interwoven concepts, Arendt developed her own vision of natality as a defining characteristic of humanity: that the fact of being born involves the ability to begin anew.

Chapter 5 follows Paul Celan's readings of Buber, Benjamin, and Heidegger with the intent to understand Celan's interpretation of the language of time after 1945. Like many other German Jewish thinkers, Celan built a new, postwar language that stressed caesura as a primary form of lived temporality.[30] Celan's poetry integrated and adapted various concepts of temporality borrowed from his German Jewish colleagues, as well as from Augustine and Heidegger. In contrast to the latter, and in agreement with the earlier, he considered the fissure of time as the starting point for any notion of an orphaned self and her broken language.

---

29. Walter Benjamin to Gershom Scholem, January 20, 1930, in *The Correspondence of Walter Benjamin*, trans. Manfred R. Jacobson and Evelyn M. Jacobson (Chicago: Chicago University Press, 1994), 360.

30. Werner Hamacher, "'Now': Benjamin on Historical Time," in *The Moment: Time and Rupture in Modern Thought*, ed. Heidrun Friese (Liverpool: Liverpool University Press, 2001), 168.

Chapter 6, the final chapter, looks at German Jewish time from the turn of the twentieth century, its post-1945 reception by theorists of deconstruction and biopolitical critique, and current thinkers engaging with the age of the Anthropocene. Grounding much of the earlier critical strands in German Jewish understanding of life, Jacques Derrida explains that "the principle of life (*torat ha'ayim*) remains a great intangible Judaic principle."[31] Giorgio Agamben's attempt to revive a Paulinian-Benjaminian understanding of now-time (*ho nyn kairos* or *Jetztzeit*) as a "recapitulation of the vocabulary of messianism" grounds itself in Benjamin and Scholem's understanding of deferral: "Deconstruction is a thwarted messianism, a suspension of the messianic."[32] More recently, Agata Bielik-Robson turns the principle of deferral into a general principle, informing both her understanding of Derrida and her own thought by contrasting modern Jewish thinkers with the vitalism of Nietzschean life philosophy and Heidegger's being-toward-death.[33] Elizabeth Povinelli draws on these concepts in her call to move beyond old dichotomies between life and nonlife into the era of planetary afterlife that is "after finitude."[34]

Chapter 6 helps us understand the stakes involved, not just for the past but for the present and future of planetary thought as well. I demonstrate that contemporary environmental theorists have begun to unpack the angel of history to cast its gaze upon a new age of catastrophes. In short, a post-1945 German Jewish interpretation of life concerns not only the lived experience of catastrophe and the exclusion of specific life-forms, but also the first open discussion of the environmental destruction of our planet. Specifically, Günther Anders, Benjamin's cousin and Arendt's first husband, and Hans Jonas, Arendt's lifelong friend and colleague, explored the notion of

---

31. Jacques Derrida, *The Animal That Therefore I Am*, trans. Marie-Louise Mallet (New York: Fordham University Press, 2008), 112. Derrida refers to the principle as a legacy left by Emmanuel Levinas.

32. Agamben, *The Time That Remains*, 6, 103.

33. Agata Bielik-Robson, *Another Finitude: Messianic Vitalism and Philosophy* (New York: Bloomsbury Academic, 2019), 25.

34. Here Povinelli follows the work of Eugene Thacker and Quentin Meillasoux. See Elizabeth A. Povinelli, *Geontologies: A Requiem to Late Liberalism* (Durham, NC: Duke University Press, 2016), 51–53, 71–75.

"not yet being nonexisting," which we have recently come to identify with the age of the Anthropocene.[35] When Dipesh Chakrabarty and François Hartog build their analyses of the "empty time" of the present on the work of Benjamin, Arendt, Derrida, and Agamben, they warn us against both metaphysical and anti-metaphysical understandings of temporality, for the time of the earth is embedded in the interim of no-longer and not-yet that belongs no longer to earthly time but to planetary time.

In this book, thus, I have two aims: to explain the impact of three temporal turns—in the early 1900s, in the midcentury (1945), and in the past two decades (the early 2000s)—and to clarify how the work of German Jews helped bring Jews back into focus in a way that revolutionized minoritarian thinking about time and politics as a whole. In the conclusion I consider the limitations of this revolutionary thinking for the present, as we consider the third turn.

---

35. Günther Anders held a two-day seminar on this topic at the Free University in Berlin, in February 1959, which he later published as a short text. See Anders, "Theses on the Atomic Age," *Massachusetts Review* 3, no. 3 (1962): 493. For the plea to reconsider our temporal and historical terminology in the age of the Anthropocene, see Dipesh Chakrabarty, "The Climate of History: Four Theses," *Critical Inquiry* 35, no. 2 (2009): 197–222.

1

A Temporal Turn

Time Out of Joint

Issues of time and temporality gained significant traction in political and social thought in the early twentieth century, and they continue to be important in our time. Recent histories describe both the early twentieth century and the early twenty-first century in terms of "temporal turns" and as times of emergency or catastrophe. According to the historian Christopher Clark, the temporal turn of the early 1900s "broke with all ... precedents, rejecting the very idea of a history."[1] Alun Munslow writes of a modern "temporal turn from 'real time' as it is culturally understood and 'narrated history time.'"[2]

---

1. Christopher Clark, *Time and Power: Visions of History in German Politics, from the Thirty Years' War to the Third Reich* (Princeton, NJ: Princeton University Press, 2019), 16.
2. "Though normally conceived of in terms of centuries, decades, years, seasons and days, real time is also perceived to be both cyclical (weeks, seasons, genealogical) and ... linear as with a life, a presidency, a Royal House or a dictatorship. Historians do not only have to do justice to the referential nature of the past chronologically, but

Scholars of Judaism have identified a recent temporal turn in Jewish studies with a "'re-turn' to areas of research that had been of interest to previous generations of . . . Jewish studies scholars"; those areas of research have gained momentum from the understanding, stemming from the early 1900s, that "time is a conception that is itself continually constructed, relative, and local," as well as the present notion that "time is running out."[3] My claim in this book is that critical thinkers who lived through the early and mid-1900s were already aware of this notion of time and built their analytical systems accordingly. The rise of destructive, exclusionary politics during the 1930s and 1940s further radicalized this temporal sensitivity. Reflecting on her friend Walter Benjamin, Hannah Arendt wrote that he "knew that the break in tradition and the loss of authority which occurred in his lifetime were irreparable, and concluded that he had to discover new ways of dealing with the past."[4] Many German Jewish thinkers shared Arendt and Benjamin's conclusion.

These German Jews were not alone in noting fundamental historical changes, nor did they make this discovery at a single moment or in reaction to a single event. Rather, they came to this realization as the result of a long historical process. The nineteenth century thought about time as reasoning, or a movement of emancipation from pervious dogmas.[5] During the period identified as the fin de siècle, an explosion of time-related concepts in both the humanities and the social sciences resulted from the growing pressure of industrialization, secu-

---

(primarily in the West) also re-organise real time in terms of order, duration, frequency and tempo in order to create meaning. In this respect the history narrative is a story space (and what Dilthey called 'a nexus') in which all that constituted the past is made to connect by the historian." Alun Munslow, *Narrative and History* (New York: Palgrave Macmillan, 2007), 49. Here Munslow follows Paul Ricoeur's analysis.

3. Sarit Kattan Gribetz and Lynn Kaye, "The Temporal Turn in Ancient Judaism and Jewish Studies," *Currents for Biblical Research* 17, no. 3 (2019): 339, 366. For a succinct summary of the Jewish "spatial turns" that followed this more general trend, see Charlotte Elisheva Fonrobert, "The New Spatial Turn in Jewish Studies," *AJS Review* 33, no. 1 (2009): 155–64.

4. Hannah Arendt, "Walter Benjamin," in *Men in Dark Times* (New York: Harcourt Brace Jovanovich, 1983[1968]), 193.

5. "As a concept, emancipation conveys motion." François Hartog, *Chronos: The West Confronts Time*, trans. Samuel Ross Gilbert (New York: Columbia University Press, 2022), 200.

larization, urbanization, and the rise of the nation-state. Science and technology appropriated the discourse of temporality as well and found new ways to measure space and time, as well as their relation, more precisely. A temporal turn around 1900 was itself the culmination of a century-long development. One of the earliest and best-known considerations in this development is Immanuel Kant's argument, made from 1781 to 1787, that space and time are a priori forms of intuition and that they are empty "forms of representation."[6] According to Kant, time cannot be experienced directly and is to be deduced from changing phenomena in a unitary flow. In that respect, the cultural historian Stephen Kern writes, Kant's understanding of time belongs to the age of railways and trains.[7] As early as the late eighteenth century, Jewish thinkers such as Moses Mendelssohn and Salomon Maimon rebelled against the Enlightenment's mechanistic and universalist language, while adopting Kant's terminology. Intellectual historians such as Anson Rabinbach have argued that the second half of the nineteenth century and the early twentieth century brought about a "cultural modernity" that understood the world "in terms of the intimate connection between the rapid industrialization . . . and the corresponding disruption of traditional time-space perceptions in science, art, literature, and philosophy."[8] Peter Fritzsche has argued that even if the actual changes we identify with the Industrial Revolution were slower to arrive, the rhetoric "only under-

---

6. See the discussion in Gary Hatfield, "Kant on the Perception of Space (and Time)," in *The Cambridge Companion to Kant and Modern Philosophy*, ed. Paul Guyer (Cambridge: Cambridge University Press, 2007), 84–85.

7. For a succinct discussion of Kant's philosophy of time, I rely on Kant authorities such as Dina Emundts, "The Refutation of Idealism and the Distinction between Phenomena and Noumena," in *The Cambridge Companion to Kant's Critique of Pure Reason*, ed. Paul Guyer (Cambridge; Cambridge University Press, 2010), 168–89, esp. 172; and Sebastian Gardner, *Routledge Guidebook to Kant and the Critique of Pure Reason* (New York: Routledge, 1999), 173.

8. Anson Rabinbach, *The Human Motor: Energy, Fatigue, and the Origins of Modernity* (Berkeley: University of California Press, 1992), 84. See also Marshall Berman, *All That Is Solid Melts into Air: The Experience of Modernity* (New York: Simon and Schuster, 1982); Stephen Kern, *The Culture of Space and Time, 1880–1918* (Cambridge, MA: Harvard University Press, 1983); Andreas Killen, *Berlin Electropolis: Shock, Nerves, and German Modernity* (Berkeley: University of California Press, 2006).

scores how forceful the new categories of temporality were in creating a compelling view of the world in which the evidence of fragmentation and unsettlement stood out."[9] In industrial modernity, time thus became a concept that was no longer continuous but open to rupture, discontinuity, and fragmentation. This idea of time as rupture, writes Bruno Latour, is essential to "the adjective 'modern,' [which] designates a new regime, an acceleration, a rupture, a revolution in time. . . . 'Modern' is thus doubly asymmetrical: it designates a break in the regular passage of time, and it designates a combat in which there are victors and vanquished."[10]

The contributions of nineteenth-century German Jewish thinkers to this new modernity were unmistakable. From Leopold Zunz to Heinrich Heine, the exceptional group of historians belonging to the *Wissenschaft des Judentums* and beyond, many writers in Jewish periodicals started using compound nouns such as *Zeitlage* (condition of time), *Zeitfrage* (question of time), *Zeitbetrachtung* (observation of time), *Jetztzeit* (present time, now-time), and *Zeitschäden* (damage of time). All of these terms, as Nils Roemer has noted, "highlight the obsession with the present time. Moreover, time was increasingly accelerated and hence appeared as 'stormy movement.'"[11] With the failure of assimilation and the rise of racialized nationalism, German Jewish thinkers and historians did indeed enter modern history during a storm.

A growing frustration with inequality—historical, theological, and institutional—turned attention to the most basic fact of human existence: living time. Kant's aim at the end of the eighteenth century was to describe our sense of movement in terms of spatial and temporal categories; the following decades recognized time as the organizing principle of production, moneymaking, and imperial expansion. In the late 1850s Karl Marx explored the implications of

---

9. Peter Fritzsche, *Stranded in the Present: Modern Time and the Melancholy of History* (Cambridge, MA: Harvard University Press, 2004), 48.

10. Bruno Latour, *We Have Never Been Modern*, trans. Catherine Porter (Cambridge, MA: Harvard University Press, 1993), 10.

11. Nils Roemer, "Between Hope and Despair: Conceptions of Time and the German-Jewish Experience in the Nineteenth Century," *Jewish History* 14 (2000): 351.

industrialization on "labor-time" and "time-wages."[12] Half a century later, Georg Simmel's *Philosophy of Money* (1900) noted the way "money symbolizes acceleration in the pace of life" and how this acceleration fused together "the modern concept of time . . . with the growth of capitalism in Germany."[13] "Despite all the good scientific and military arguments for world time," writes Stephen Kern, "it was the railroad companies and not the governments that were the first to institute it."[14] In the late nineteenth and early twentieth centuries the concept of time achieved a central place not only in transportation and mass production but also in political praxis and philosophy. Life was redefined on the basis of its precariousness and finality (instead of eternal life) and through its freedom of movement (against boundaries), so that living time broke through the individual and private bubble to become a characteristic of modernity.

As a result, the early twentieth century placed time not only at the heart of change but also at the heart of a new, radical, revolutionary historical consciousness.[15] The temporal turn—a movement whose beginnings are usually identified with Wilhelm Dilthey, Friedrich Nietzsche, Edmund Husserl, and Henri Bergson—was a response to the recognition of the limitations of idealist space.[16] This philosophical and scientific turn was accompanied by an overall reconsideration of historical thinking and its principal categories: "Historicity . . . extending from Hegel to Ricoeur, via Dilthey and Heidegger . . . refers to how individuals or groups situate themselves and develop in time, that is, the forms taken by their historical condition."[17] In other

---

12. See chaps.19 and 20 of Karl Marx, *Capital: A Critique of Political Economy*, trans. Ben Fowkes (London: Penguin Classics, 1992), 675–91.

13. Georg Simmel, *The Philosophy of Money*, trans. Tom Bottomore and David Frisby (New York: Cambridge University Press, 2005), 511–12.

14. Kern, *Culture of Space and Time*, 12.

15. "While there was no doubt that events came one after the other, there was little sense that they followed an orderly, linear pattern, the dominant rendition of history [since] the eighteenth century." Fritzsche, *Stranded in the Present*, 32.

16. For more about the history and sources of life philosophy, see the introduction and first chapter of Nitzan Lebovic, *The Philosophy of Life and Death: Ludwig Klages and the Rise of a Nazi Biopolitics* (New York: Palgrave Macmillan, 2013), 1–52.

17. François Hartog, *Regimes of Historicity: Presentism and Experiences of Time*, trans. Saskia Brown (New York: Columbia University Press, 2015), xv.

words, the rise of history during the nineteenth century came as a response to the changing rhythm of time; but history itself became a tool of regulating, ordering, and grasping time's power and impact. The grip of history as an overall explanatory force broke in the early twentieth century, as history was replaced by, as Simmel put it in 1907, the "personal and differential elements which we distinguish from the conditions of their organic development."[18]

During the nineteenth century, political and economic institutions tightened their grip on the public sphere, using the clock to regulate work and the growth of capital. The intellectual historian Reinhart Koselleck notes, "The clock could measure acceleration but not symbolize it. This first became possible with the railroad and its metaphorics: Marx spoke of revolutions as the 'locomotives of history,' not the clocks of history."[19] As railways aided the expansion of imperial forces, production and synchronicity further promoted the causes of nationalism and corporations.[20] Accelerated processes of industrialization and urbanization changed the human understanding and experience not only of time and space but also of the individual body and the body politic. Anson Rabinbach has shown that over the nineteenth century the temporality of bodies, both individual and collective, came to be measured by their production and labor, and in ways that extended beyond Marx's materialism. "The sin of idleness shifted from a physical and spiritual *taedium*, or world weariness," writes Rabinbach, "to a disturbance of temporal regularity whose best therapy was work."[21]

---

18. Georg Simmel, *The Problems of the Philosophy of History: An Epistemological Essay*, trans. and ed. Guy Oakes (New York: Free Press, 1977), 79.

19. Reinhart Koselleck, "Does History Accelerate?," in *Sediments of Time: On Possible Histories*, trans. Sean Franzel and Stefan-Ludwig Hoffmann (Stanford, CA: Stanford University Press, 2018), 85.

20. See Frederick Jameson's separation between "real time," "the time of objects," "clock time," "the time of a machine," "a peculiar spatial machine," and "measurable time" versus "postmodern time" or the "total flow" of the late capitalistic simulacra world. Frederick Jameson, *Postmodernism, or the Cultural Logic of Late Capitalism* (Durham, NC: Duke University Press, 2003), 76. Michael Hardt and Antonio Negri use the building of railways to explain the expansion of "global information infrastructure" to "further the interests of imperialist economies." See Hardt and Negri, *Empire* (Cambridge, MA: Harvard University Press, 2000), 298.

21. Rabinbach, *The Human Motor*, 26.

While companies prescribed more work for the sake of economic growth, nationalist movements used the regulation of time to control the body politic through centralized institutions. Railways were said to "annihilate" time and space, but daily newspapers and telegraphs were also critical to modern nationalism.[22] In his *Imagined Communities*, Benedict Anderson follows the growing use of time, actual and symbolic, for the sake of sociopolitical centralization and homogenization. He gestures toward Walter Benjamin's identification of modern temporality with the rise of the corporatist state, technological reproduction, and the symbolic language of profit.[23] Benjamin's friend the German Jewish essayist Siegfried Kracauer observed in the 1920s that the rhythm of the assembly line was also the rhythm of the nationalist spectacle.[24] The sociologist Henri Lefebvre explained the emphasis on economic growth and nationalist centralization using the language of militarization. Capitalist economics and nationalist ideology, he argued, drove an expanding "military mode," with the capacity to create a "rhythm through all phases of our temporality."[25] In turn, the philosophers Paul Virilio and Michael Shapiro recognized how such rhythms were shaped by the confluence of mobilized nationalism and political-economic centralization and how this corporatization of the state changed our understanding of time and movement.[26] Turning back to the image of the train in the late nineteenth and early twentieth centuries, we see that railways not only opened new horizons but also fostered growth for the sake of progress as well as the survival of existing institutions

---

22. Priya Satia, *Time's Monster: How History Makes History* (Cambridge, MA: Harvard University Press, 2020), 142.

23. Benedict Anderson, *Imagined Communities: Reflections on the Origin and Spread of Nationalism* (London: Verso Books, 2006), 22–24. On the move into the "symbolic turn," see Warren Breckman, *Adventures of the Symbolic: Post-Marxism and Radical Democracy* (New York: Columbia University Press, 2013), 11.

24. Thomas Y. Levin, introduction to Siegfried Kracauer, *The Mass Ornament: Weimar Essays*, trans. Thomas Y. Levin (Cambridge, MA: Harvard University Press, 1995), 18. I thank Sophie Duvernoy for this reminder.

25. Henri Lefebvre, *Rhythmanalysis*, trans. Stuart Elden and Gerald Moore (London: Continuum, 2004), 39.

26. See Paul Virilio, *Speed and Politics*, trans. Mark Polizzotti (New York: Semiotext(e), 1986), 30. Quoted and analyzed in Michael Shapiro, *Politics and Time: Documenting the Event* (Malden, MA: Polity Books, 2016), 94.

and borders. The train became the principal transportation system of products and armies.

Time Out of Joint

In the second half of the nineteenth century the popular image of modernity was the speeding steam engine—think of Jules Verne's 1873 *Around the World in Eighty Days.* In the twentieth century the human understanding of the potential of movement was fundamentally altered via the transformation of the concept of time. The attempt to synchronize time for industrial coordination was accompanied by a growing awareness that time was potentially nonlinear, ungraspable, and indomitable. "It can hardly be pure coincidence," the physicist Carlo Rovelli writes, "that, before gaining a university position, the young Einstein worked in the Swiss patent office, dealing specifically with patents relating to the synchronization of clocks at railway stations. It was probably there that it dawned on him that the problem of synchronization was, ultimately, an insoluble one."[27]

Considering the issue from a cultural perspective, Kern shows that "in the fin de siècle, time's arrow did not always fly straight and true."[28] The new problem became apparent in the arts, popular culture, and everyday language as well. At the end of the nineteenth century, Henri Bergson, philosopher of living time or *élan vital* (vital force or vitalism), pointed out that in the modern era humanity tried its best to absorb individual forms of expression into a mechanistic language, but the attempt to eliminate our individualist forms in favor of "motor impulses" (*Bewegungsantriebe*) owes first and foremost to our notion of duration (*durée*) or "to the consciousness of this organization."[29]

Bergson's stress on vitalist individual experience of time was well-received in Germany, after none other than Georg Simmel recom-

---

27. Carlo Rovelli, *The Order of Time*, trans. Simon Carnell and Erica Segre (New York: Penguin, 2018), 61.
28. Kern, *Culture of Space and Time*, 29.
29. Henri Bergson, *Matter and Memory*, trans. Nancy Margaret Paul and W. Scott Palmer (New York: Zone Books, 1996), 94.

mended that Bergson's work be translated into German.³⁰ Both Bergson and Simmel emphasized the primacy of living time over any scientific measurement of it, including clock time. "If the clocks and watches in Berlin would suddenly go wrong in different ways, even if only by one hour," Simmel wrote in 1903, "all economic life and communication in the city would be disrupted for a long time."³¹ Although in the early twentieth century the use of clocks and clockwork increased, trust in their value decreased.³² The growing affinity of politics, science, and technology made clock time common, but clock time also benefited a sovereign and institutional relation to time. The individual body lost its sense of autonomy. Historians of the twentieth century use the language of disciplining and management of the body, as the individual body's movements were synchronized with the rest of the body politic. As Jeffrey Herf put it, "The era of total mobilization would bring about an 'unleashing' (*Entfesselung*) of a nevertheless disciplined life"; this required, in turn, a close supervision of time management.³³ Total mobilization promised to turn each body into a smooth, efficiently moving steam engine; but history delivered a messier outcome: "The war, with its 'rationalized slaughter,'" writes Andreas Killen, "came to be imagined as an immense runaway locomotive."³⁴

The metaphor of a runaway locomotive is a spatialized image of time out of joint. The nature of time itself came up for debate following Einstein's proposal of the theory of relativity in 1905. The intellectual historian Jimena Canales has noted that until the twentieth century, clockwork had remained "the perfect metaphor for a universe in which the future unfolded at a predictable and constant

---

30. For Simmel's recommendation to the conservative publisher Eugen Diederichs to translate Bergson, see Lebovic, *Philosophy of Life and Death*, 83.
31. Georg Simmel, "The Metropolis and Mental Life," in Simmel, *On Individuality and Social Forms: Selected Writings*, ed. Donald N. Levine (Chicago: University of Chicago Press, 1971), 329.
32. Jimena Canales, *The Physicist and the Philosopher: Einstein, Bergson, and the Debate That Changed Our Understanding of Time* (Princeton, NJ: Princeton University Press, 2015), 253.
33. Jeffrey Herf, *Reactionary Modernism: Technology, Culture, and Politics in Weimar and the Third Reich* (Cambridge: Cambridge University Press, 1984), 94.
34. Killen, *Berlin Electropolis*, 130.

velocity."[35] Yet Einstein's theory of relativity proposed that time did not, in fact, unfold in a regular fashion but instead could expand or contract depending on velocity. Time thus depended on one's frame of reference and was not an external constant. This theory led to the so-called clock paradox—the idea that time works differently by bodies that are moving at different speeds—which was debated by Einstein and Bergson on April 6, 1922. Bergson objected to Einstein's characterization of time as a measurable entity or simply a facet of psychic experience. Bergson believed instead that time was far more plural and manifold, marked by meaning and a sense of significance when experienced by humans. Canales writes, "The philosopher did not understand why one would opt to describe the timing of a significant event, such as the arrival of a train, in terms of how that event matched against a watch. . . . Bergson searched for a more basic definition of simultaneity, one that would not stop at the watch but that would explain why clocks were used in the first place."[36] As historians of time demonstrate, clocks measuring time were measuring, not the universe itself, but the experience of those using them: "Clocks were not equal in every way because one of them had gone through something that the other one had not."[37] This rift between one experience and another introduced the idea of multiple presents or nows.

Seven years later, in the spring of 1929, another major debate in Davos, Switzerland, raised similar concerns about the nature of experience, multiple presents, and the relationship between politics and time. The debate involved the neo-Kantian Ernst Cassirer, who had researched Einstein's theory of relativity, and the philosopher Martin Heidegger. In the Davos debate Cassirer and Heidegger put forward fundamentally opposing views of the task of philosophy. Cassirer believed that human reason is a creative, spontaneous force that allows for world making, whereas Heidegger emphasized ontology above epistemology and the question of being above the possibilities of world making through thought. For Cassirer, the category

---

35. Canales, *Physicist and the Philosopher*, 253.
36. Canales, *Physicist and the Philosopher*, 42.
37. Canales, *Physicist and the Philosopher*, 65.

of time occupied a role both as a scientific category—a Kantian a priori—and as a structuring condition of experience; it was a concept that was permeable to historical change and experienced by humans as an evolving category that allowed for varied perceptual and epistemological possibilities in each time period. Heidegger, in contrast, viewed the Kantian a priori time as a condition that existed beyond the realm of the human mind—time meant finitude, the inevitability of death, even if Western culture denied it.[38] The two philosophical positions cannot be easily translated into political terms, but Cassirer's stress on neo-Kantian ideals positioned him in the liberal camp, whereas Heidegger's darker understanding of finitude as the fundamental basis of experience, action, and thought would later express itself through an affinity with nationalist ideas of a primeval Germanic past.

The two debates have rarely been considered together: the first seems to concern the scientific explanation of time, the latter a philosophical question. Yet the two are linked by a fundamental interest in time and by German Jewish thinkers' explanations of the relevance of time in wider cultural terms. Both debates, about the mechanics of time and about the language of time, were considered to have been won by the philosophies of ontology—represented by Einstein and Heidegger—over metaphysics and humanism, the positions of Bergson and Cassirer. Both debates saw time as the key to history and politics, science, metaphysics, literature, and reality.

Heidegger rejected Cassirer's philosophical positions in favor of the immanent and self-referential finality of *Dasein*, the existential being-there. For him, temporality was intrinsic to *Existenz* and "the

---

38. For a close reading of the debate, see Peter E. Gordon, *Continental Divide: Heidegger, Cassirer, Davos* (Cambridge, MA: Harvard University Press, 2010), 47. Gordon ties the political views of the two thinkers to their understandings of the history of philosophy. For example, "On Cassirer's view the Enlightenment in general was animated by a basic commitment to self-determination and progressive development. It was united in its conviction that reason can 'determine for itself the direction of its journey,' but that reason's essence therefore cannot be known wholly a priori as an essence or substance but can be recognized only through its self-realization, its activity and 'function'" (294).

existential structure of being-toward-the-end."[39] Dasein, like the ripening fruit, "is always already its not-yet as it is."[40] Heidegger's ideas of "not-yet" and "still to come" were meant to attack the canonical course that led from Aristotle, via Augustine, to modern metaphysics, ending with Husserl, Simmel, Bergson and Cassirer's stress on the value of life and what Heidegger perceived as Husserl's universalism.

In *Lectures on the Structure of Internal Time*, delivered as a series of lectures in 1910, Edmund Husserl identified "the transformation of the now into the *no-longer*—and in the other direction, of the *not-yet* into the now."[41] For him, the transformation reveals "something like a common form of the now, a universal and perfect likeness in the mode of flowing."[42] Heidegger, who became Husserl's assistant in Freiburg in 1919, concluded the opposite. In *Being and Time* (1927) and postwar essays such as "What Is Called Thinking?" (1951–52), Heidegger stressed the sequential nature of time for Husserl, Simmel, and Cassirer "out of the not-yet 'now' into the no-longer 'now'" (*Aus dem 'noch nicht jetzt' in das 'nicht mehr jetzt'*).[43] For Heidegger, the shared stress on duration implied a universal metaphysics and therefore an incorrect lineage that led from ancient Greece, via modern neo-Kantianism, to Bergson and to his teacher, the phenomenologist. Heidegger rejected Husserl's understanding of the present, and his given preference for scientific awareness, in favor of an inherent understanding of life on a temporal, existential, and ontological basis.[44] The philosophical disagreement

---

39. Martin Heidegger, *Being and Time*, trans. Joan Stambaugh (Albany: SUNY Press, 2010), 248.
40. Heidegger, *Being and Time*, 235.
41. Edmund Husserl, *On the Phenomenology of Consciousness of Internal Time*, trans. John Barnett Brough (Dordrecht: Springer, 1991), 81, my emphases. For a discussion of the close relation between Husserl's double phenomenological transformation and the modern eschatological one, see Neal Deroo and John Panteleimon Manoussakis, eds., introduction to *Phenomenology and Eschatology: Not Yet in the Now* (Burlington, VT: Ashgate, 2009), 1–12.
42. Husserl, *On the Phenomenology*, 77.
43. Martin Heidegger, *What Is Called Thinking?*, trans. J. Glenn Gray (New York: Harper and Row, 1968), 99; Heidegger, *Was heisst Denken? Vorlesungen Wintersemester 1951/2* (Stuttgart: Reclam, 1992), 62.
44. Georg Imdahl, *Das Lebens-Verstehen: Heideggers formal anzeigende Hermeneutik in den frühen Freiburger Vorlesungen* (Würzburg: Königshausen und

had real repercussions in the world: in April 1933, now a rector of Freiburg University under the Nazi state, Heidegger collaborated with the termination of Husserl's position, and removed the dedication to Husserl from his Sein und Zeit. In other words, for Heidegger the scientific or universal understanding of time fails to acknowledge the internal nature of human experience of finality, a quality he identified with authentic Germanness. As we shall see in later chapters, Martin Buber, Walter Benjamin, Hannah Arendt, and Paul Celan all attempted to retrieve the moment that lies between a not-yet and no-longer without falling back into either old-fashioned universalisms, or the more recent forms of nationalism. Half a century later, one finds similar idioms of temporality at the center of Jacques Derrida's deconstruction and Giorgio Agamben's biopolitical critique.

In spite of political and philosophical differences, Bergson, Simmel, Husserl, and Heidegger did, however, agree on the notion of "uncertainty," which was introduced as a principle in Nietzsche's philosophy and in modern physics, before it was popularized around and after World War I. In Aldous Huxley's *Brave New World* (1931), for example, linear progress and static rest were abandoned for a more complex understanding of time and politics. In its new sense, time became one with the paradox of existence, or the moment that shaped "a time without time, time without *chronos*, a momentary segment."[45] In contrast to Nietzsche and Heidegger, who clamored for the destruction of metaphysics, Benjamin advocated for an innovative analysis that concentrated on the temporal relation between events and that identified mankind as a demonic agent of change without control over time's direction and movement.[46] Benjamin imagined progress in terms similar to the "immense runaway

---

Neumann, 1997), 21. Imdahl characterizes the "early" and the "late" Heidegger slightly differently than most scholars do. In his account, the key change occurs between Heidegger's editorial work in Dilthey's texts and his investment in *Lebensphilosophie*, and the period that begins with *Sein und Zeit* in 1927.

45. Heidrun Friese, ed., *The Moment: Time and Rupture in Modern Thought* (Liverpool: Liverpool University Press, 2001), 8.

46. In a recent history of time, Rüdiger Safranski explains that in the new world, "time is not only a medium in which man moves, but also one that man coproduces." Rüdiger Safranski, *Zeit: Was sie mit uns macht und was wir aus ihr machen* (Munich: Carl Hanser, 2015), 39, my translation.

locomotive" Killen described.⁴⁷ "The concept of progress," Walter Benjamin wrote in 1939, "must be grounded in the idea of catastrophe. That things are 'status quo' *is* the catastrophe."⁴⁸ Without refuting uncertainty, as I show in chapter 3, the alternative to unmitigated progress was what Benjamin titled—against idealist stress on reason, duration, and progress, and against Heidegger's stress on finality—"the womb of time."⁴⁹

Jewish Time in Europe

Against this backdrop, European Jewish thinkers concerned with questions of identity came to develop progressive political frameworks. In this book I focus on close readings of a small number of German Jewish thinkers, yet I also consider a wider context of Jewish history, German politics, and Jewish-Christian relations. Since 70 CE, after all, European Jews had been forced into a dialectical relationship to Christian and empirical forms. After the destruction of the Second Temple, the rabbinic understanding of time became embedded in a dualistic order—with a liturgical calendar following the cycles of the moon, and a public, sun-based calendar.⁵⁰ This relational understanding of collective identity was supported by multiple temporalities. In historian Sylvie Anne Goldberg's words, "In contrast to the West, which, deeming heathen times obsolete, takes as its bench-

---

47. Killen, *Berlin Electropolis*, 130.
48. The uncertainty principle was introduced by Heisenberg in 1927. The physicist Lee Smolin explained it recently as "a very general principle, as it says that we cannot know exactly both where a particle is and with what momentum it is moving." Lee Smolin, *Einstein's Unfinished Revolution: The Search for What Lies Beyond the Quantum* (New York: Penguin Press, 2019); Walter Benjamin, "Central Park," in *Selected Writings*, vol. 4, *1938–1940*, trans. Edmund Jephcott et al. (Cambridge, MA: Harvard University Press, 2003), 184.
49. I follow here Susan E. Shapiro's Benjaminian advice to "shore up a philosophical argument . . . [that can] be found precisely in the seemingly peripheral metaphors, figures, and tropes of philosophical texts." See Shapiro, "A Matter of Discipline: Reading for Gender in Jewish Philosophy," in *Judaism since Gender*, ed. Miriam Peskowitz and Laura Lewitt (New York: Routledge, 1997), 166.
50. Sylvie Anne Goldberg, *Clepsydra: Essay on the Plurality of Time in Judaism*, trans. Benjamin Ivry (Stanford, CA: Stanford University Press, 2016), 110.

mark the birth year of the Christian savior, the *annus domini*, Jews take as theirs the origin of time itself: the creation of the world, based on biblical chronology."[51] Unlike rabbinic Judaism, which viewed itself in light of biblical creation, medieval Jewish sources, both mystical and poetic, were suffused with rich Christian allusions to infinity, messianism, and eschatology. Historians of Kabbalah have shown that the precise understanding of infinity (*ein-sof*) was determined on the basis of Jewish and Christian cultures, which synthesized the power of creation as a cosmological event and a divine understanding of an unchangeable order for humankind, grounded in a substantial list of laws. According to Tamar Rudavsky, "Jewish philosophers, both medieval and modern, have had to wrestle with the project of reconciling these 'outside' sources and influences with their understanding of scriptural dicta."[52] The medieval works of Maimonides and Ibn Ezra show how Jewish calendars represented the movement of time through the lens of neo-Aristotelian scientific principles, Arabic science and philosophy, and Christian politics and theology.[53] As material representations of temporality, these calendars provide written and visual records of how Jews "incorporate[d] into Jewish culture . . . new wisdom, new structures, and new arguments from the science of non-Jews."[54] Jewish calendars evolved into tools of political and religious ideology and economic or social coordination, and Jews learned to integrate by adopting the symbols and public holidays that were often forced upon them.[55]

The dialectic of inside and outside enabled the freedom of movement and thought from the position of minority. This back-and-

---

51. Goldberg, *Clepsydra*, 4.
52. Tamar Rudavsky, *Time Matters: Time, Creation, and Cosmology in Medieval Jewish Philosophy* (Albany: SUNY Press, 2000), xii.
53. Elisheva Carlebach, *Palaces of Time: Jewish Calendar and Culture in Early Modern Europe* (Cambridge, MA: Harvard University Press, 2011), 15.
54. Carlebach, *Palaces of Time*, 21.
55. Carlebach, *Palaces of Time*, 51. This is what James Robinson calls "indirect transmission." See James T. Robinson, "Al-Farabi, Avicenna, and Averroes in Hebrew: Remarks on the Indirect Transmission of Arabic-Islamic Philosophy in Medieval Judaism," in *Judeo-Christian-Islamic Heritage: Philosophical and Theological Perspectives*, ed. Richard C. Taylor and Irfan A. Omar (Milwaukee, WI: Marquette University Press, 2011), 59–87.

forth between external Christian sovereignty and internal Jewish rhythm structured the social temporality of Jews in Europe. With the rise of modern European states and modern social thought, the scope of emancipation narrowed at the same time as it became more acute, as the language of toleration and human equality often stood in tension with the actions of European governments and societies.[56] Such was the case in Germany as well, perhaps even more so because of its particular Protestant cast. As has been the case since the late eighteenth and early nineteenth centuries, writes David Sorkin, "the religionist defines the 'Jew' as opposed to the 'Christian.' Assimilation means Christianization: the Jews attempted to enter German society either by denying their own religion, readily transforming it to conform to Christian standards, or by renouncing it altogether."[57] This denial or transformation was not shared by everyone, but accompanied a growing stress on emancipation through assimilation through economy and secular politics.[58] Those societal constructs, in turn, were defined on the basis of Protestant ideals of work and assimilation or integration from above. The major push for emancipation and assimilation resulted from economic and political pressure to "break down state barriers" thanks to economic and industrial mechanisms.[59] German Jewish assimilation was both a symptom and a result of the modern, industrialized nation-state.

---

56. "A dialectic between, on the one hand, the idea of one Jewish people and of a unified Jewish culture, and, on the other, the history of multiple communities and cultures." David Biale, ed., *Cultures of the Jews: A New History* (New York: Schocken Books, 2002), xxiv. For a discussion about the intricacies of Jewish identity in the subfield of American Jewish history, see Lila Corwin Berman's excellent article "Jewish History beyond the Jewish People," *AJS Review* (2018): 1–24.

57. David Sorkin, *The Transformation of German Jewry, 1780–1840* (Detroit: Wayne State University Press, 1999), 4.

58. Scott Spector identifies Buber, Benjamin, Bloch, and Arendt as standing on the side of "the German-Jewish radical resacralization [of the political]." Spector, *Modernism without Jews? German-Jewish Subjects and Histories* (Bloomington: University of Indiana Press), 48.

59. Robert Liberles specifically mentions the railway as one mechanism of German unification. See Liberles, "Was There a Jewish Movement for Emancipation in Germany?," *Leo Baeck Institute Year Book* 31, no. 1 (1986): 35–49.

German Jewish Time

Modernity called to "render history radically open."[60] Breaking away from linear forms of history-making were seen in the pressure to adapt language, clothing, and gestures to the changing times. (It is not by coincidence that Georg Simmel and Walter Benjamin were among the first to point to fashion and bodily gestures as part of the social norms that separated men from women and foreigners from natives.)

German Jewish thinkers stood at the forefront of a new Nietzschean avant-garde that withdrew from the transcendental self, or theological structures of legitimacy, in favor of an autonomous language. Andrew Bowie writes, "In one of his most influential moves ... Nietzsche tries to undermine the modern conception of the autonomous subject by insisting upon its dependence on the language it speaks."[61] After Schopenhauer and Feuerbach's understanding of language as *logos*—the manifestation of the order of God's universe—Nietzsche and his followers not only removed God from the equation, but called for a new temporal order and the immanence of life. German Jewish thinkers trapped between the Christian state and the requirement to secularize used the new philosophy of life to open new horizons. Martin Buber, Gustav Landauer, Gershom Scholem, and Franz Rosenzweig reflected on this new discourse in their works.

---

60. For a broad overview about the work and impact of the Wissenschaft des Judentums, see *Jewish Historiography Between Past and Future*, eds. Paul Mendes-Flohr, Rachel Livneh-Freudenthal, and Guy Miron (Berlin: DeGruytre, 2019); for a plea to "render history radically open," see Martin Kavka, who refers to the lineage extending from Maimonides, Rosenzweig, Cohen, Levinas, and Derrida to the "Jewish neontological tradition," in which "a tradition of Jewish thinkers ... uses either the explicit concept of *nonbeing* or implicit adjunct concepts as prisms for viewing the Jewish tradition." These concepts, he notes, "are thematically associated with 'privation, lack, not-yet,'" and with "rendering history radically open, unfulfilled, and ungraspable." See Kavka, *Jewish Messianism and the History of Philosophy* (Cambridge: Cambridge University Press, 2004), 6, emphasis in original.

61. Andrew Bowie, "Critiques of Culture," in *The Cambridge Companion to Modern German Culture*, ed. Eva Kolinsky and Wolfried van der Will (Cambridge: Cambridge University Press, 1998), 142.

In the dissertation he wrote under Heidegger's supervision, dedicated to Nietzsche's concept of the eternal recurrence of the same, Karl Löwith explained the logic of Nietzsche's Zarathustra: As he comes down from his solitude on the mountain and returns to the company of humans, Zarathustra concludes that the only way to overcome human imperfection, or the human's inability to grasp animal "wholeness," is to develop an alternative sense of time, which he frames as an "eternal recurrence."[62] Löwith explains that this alternative temporality allows Zarathustra to transgress the limits of idealist temporality that progressively leads from promise to realization, or from wish to fulfillment.

As I describe in chapter 2, Martin Buber attempted to translate *Thus Spoke Zarathustra* at the age of seventeen, and his friendship with Gustav Landauer began in 1895 with a conversation about the use of Nietzsche's philosophy for socialist reform. In 1915 Gershom Scholem spoke about the need for ecstasy (*Rausch*) and a "Jewish Zarathustra" (*Judenzarathustra*).[63] Nietzsche's vitalist plea for a "new man" and ecstatic lived experience (*Erlebnis*) spread among the Jewish youth and became a discourse among both supporters of assimilation and cultural Zionists.[64]

In his essay on lament, conceived during the early twentieth century, Scholem—who considered himself a cultural Zionist who rejected both assimilation and political Zionism—described the essence of Jewish language as one of temporal deferral. The essay was written in the context of an intensive dialogue with Buber and Benjamin about the nature of Jewish language. Scholem spoke of "the infinite character of language," with its "positive expression of being. . . . Infinity resides in the two bordering lands of the revealed and the

---

62. Karl Löwith, *Nietzsche's Philosophy of the Eternal Recurrence of the Same*, trans. J. Harvey Lomax (Berkeley: University of California Press, 1997 [1935]), 73.

63. Quoted and analyzed in David Biale, *Gershom Scholem: Master of the Kabbalah* (New Haven, CT: Yale University Press, 2018), 15. For a broad discussion of Jewish Nietzscheans, see Jacob Golomb, *Nietzsche and Zion* (Ithaca, NY: Cornell University Press), 2004.

64. For the impact of this language on the young Jewish circles in Europe and Palestine, see Ofer Nur, *Eros and Tragedy: Jewish Male Fantasies and the Masculine Revolution of Zionism* (Boston: Academic Studies Press, 2014).

silenced."⁶⁵ According to Scholem, this nonspatial border between the revealed and the silenced is the *differentia specifica* of Jewish language. Vivian Liska has pointed out that the basis of Scholem's lament, his understanding of Jewish language, rests on a new temporality of deferral; that is, "deferral in the word, the linguistic principle of lament."⁶⁶ A deferral implies the suspense of decisionist language, the suspense of sovereign norms, and an attempt to cut into the progressive idealist course that leads from an idea to realization. Scholem's understanding of the inherent deferral of Hebrew, Liska explains, is a sibling to Benjamin's "dialectics at a standstill" and Kafka's "immobile assault" (*stehender Sturmlauf*), an "intense movement that does not progress, stays itself and leaves everything unchanged."⁶⁷

Recent analyses of German Jewish culture identify Franz Rosenzweig's understanding of Hebrew as paradigmatic for German Jewish intellectuals of his period. Rosenzweig understood the Hebrew language as "always in time flow" (*Zeitfluss*) between the "already" (*schon*), "still" (*noch*), and "no longer" (*nicht mehr*) "as the great unrests in the 'clock of world history.'"⁶⁸ Here, Rosenzweig argued, "the language of the prophets is 'still in the making'" and "does not let the past rest either by merely saying that 'it was.'"⁶⁹ Here, the purpose of "betweenness" was not only to keep an interpretive, live

---

65. Gershom Scholem, "On Lament and Lamentation," trans. Lina Barouch and Paula Schwebel, *Jewish Studies Quarterly* 21, no. 1 (2014): 6.

66. Scholem, "On Lament and Lamentation," 6. Scholem pointed out, in this context, that the symbolic is placed between the revealed and the silenced, which opens a door to analyze the symbolic and aesthetic language of Jewish mystical texts. See also Vivian Liska, *German-Jewish Thought and Its Afterlife: A Tenuous Legacy* (Bloomington: Indiana University Press, 2016), 77.

67. Scholem, "On Lament and Lamentation," 6.

68. Lina Barouch, *Between German and Hebrew: The Counterlanguages of Gershom Scholem, Werner Kraft, and Ludwig Strauss* (Berlin: De Gruyter Oldenbourg, 2016), 166. Barouch translates here from Franz Rosenzweig, "Vom Geist der Hebräischen Sprache," in *Gesammelte Schriften*, vol. 3 (The Hague: Martinus Nijhoff, 1984), 720–21.

69. Rosenzweig brought together Jewish scripture and Nietzschean hermeneutics: "Revelation taught us to recognize in these [pagan] gods the hidden God, the hidden one who is nothing other than *the not yet* manifest one." Franz Rosenzweig, *Star of Redemption*, trans. Barbara E. Galli (Madison: University of Wisconsin Press, 2005), 411, my emphasis.

connection open to Jewish scripture, but also to propose a political alternative to the Christian imperialistic narrative.[70] Although scholars debate to what degree Christian terminology informed Rosenzweig's discussion of creation, revelation, and redemption, they agree that a melding of Jewish and Christian notions of life—via Hegel and Nietzsche—inspired Rosenzweig to see human life as the "not-yet-infinite," for what matters is the meeting of different time frames and where their world "becomes fully alive."[71]

As I will elaborate in the next chapters, the temporal shape of German Jewish betweenness originated both with and against the Christian witness doctrine and the destructive, self-referential Heideggerian notion of Dasein. While accepting that the Jew is an exception to the norm, betweenness rejected triumphalist Christian, Idealist, or nationalist, logic. In temporal terms, German Jewish thinkers who were writing of deferral, suspense, and becoming were also driven by a particular sense of survival felt by Jewish minorities in Europe.[72] Rosenzweig's experience as a soldier, during World War I, brought him in contact with Polish Jewry for the first time, and, as one historians depicts it, "the image of the 'integral' *Ostjude* remained with him, as with Buber (and Franz Kafka), as a kind of yardstick for measuring the 'fragmentary' existence of the Western Jew."[73] Negative theology and Scholem's understanding of history

---

70. Miguel Vatter considers a "Jewish political theology" along those lines. Rosenzweig's notion of betweenness, in Vatter's eyes, starts with a rejection of Paulinian antinomianism, Hegelian progress, and a Schmittian stress on sovereignty and instead builds on Maimonides's view of political messianism and Nietzsche's doctrine of eternal recurrence. See Vatter, *Living Law: Jewish Political Theology from Hermann Cohen to Hannah Arendt* (Oxford: Oxford University Press, 2021), 84, 130.

71. Rosenzweig, *Star of Redemption*, 240. For a critical analysis of Rosenzweig's Christian framing of the finite–infinite relation, see Adam Stern, *Survival: A Theological-Political Genealogy* (Philadelphia: University of Pennsylvania Press, 2021), 100–101.

72. See Saba Mahmood, *Religious Difference in a Secular Age: A Minority Report* (Princeton, NJ: Princeton University Press, 2016), 65. Mahmood argues that although "the Jewish experience in Europe has come to be treated as the paradigm through which the minority problem is elaborated," each minority experiences its own, particular struggle that cannot be generalized.

73. Howard M. Sachar, *A History of the Jews in the Modern World* (New York: Vintage Books, 2006), 467, emphasis in the original.

were the opposite of triumphalist eschatology and the vulgar social-Darwinist "struggle for life" in the *Lebensraum*. Instead, German Jewish thinkers committed to "a constant failure," such as Scholem's lament or "Benjamin's view of history as 'one single catastrophe.'"[74]

The catastrophe that starts every "already not" of Jewish exile did not translate to a destructive message.[75] Instead, a close examination of their understanding of politics and time shows that most of these German Jewish thinkers, especially the non-Zionists, became suspicious of any fusion of triumphalist philosophy and affirmative identity. The thinkers I am interested in rejected both Max Nordau's chauvinistic response to antisemitism and Heidegger's philosophical destructivism, even as they accepted the political lessons of cultural Zionism or Heidegger's stress on becoming.

For Buber, Benjamin, Arendt, and Celan, decadence and degeneration were signs of the culmination of the nineteenth-century belief in linear progress, whether in support of the Zionist or the German cause. Nordau turned against modern degeneration in favor of an early Zionist nationalism;[76] Heidegger undertook an antimodern turn that led him from his attempt to counter Kantian and Husserlian metaphysics and into the camp of reactionary politicians.[77] This turn toward violence led his German Jewish students to characterize Heidegger's position as "inner nihilism of this naked resoluteness in

---

74. Moshe Idel, *Old Worlds, New Mirrors: On Jewish Mysticism and Twentieth-Century Thought* (Philadelphia: University of Pennsylvania Press, 2010), 105. See also Vivian Liska, *German-Jewish Thought*, 117.

75. Moving from Heidegger's "obsession with the imperatives of 'destroying' and 'destruction'" to his German Jewish intellectual "children," as Richard Wolin has done in his contested *Heidegger's Children* (2003), limits the contribution of German Jewish thinkers to confirming or negating Heidegger's system. See Richard Wolin, Heidegger in Ruins: Between Philosophy and Ideology (New Haven: Yale University Press, 2023), 211.

76. "The *fin-de-siècle* generation differed significantly from that of its fathers. The process of secularization was accelerating throughout Jewish society, accompanied by the growing influence of socialism." Anita Shapira, *Land and Power: The Zionist Resort to Force, 1881–1948*, trans. William Templer (Stanford, CA: Stanford University Press, 1992), 36.

77. Heidegger, *Being and Time*, 270. Heidegger criticizes here the legacy leading from Kant to modern supporters of "the idea of a court of justice" and "metaphysics of morals."

the face of Nothing."[78] The German Jewish response to Heidegger comes close to Reinhart Koselleck's comment that "the non-Aryan is merely the negation of one's own position."[79] German Jews had to take this negation into account if they wanted to imagine a future beyond it.

Koselleck has observed that the more we experience the modern, "the more ... demands made of the future increase." A recent history of time, grounded in German Jewish critique, reverses the process: "We now know that it has ever also been the increase in the demands that the future made of us."[80] One form of the latter demand, the one the future made of German Jews, was the realization that spatial categories need to be measured vis-à-vis "proximity and distance ... [they] may only be experienced through time."[81] German Jewish thinkers and authors figured as much, thanks to their understanding of catastrophes in their historical context and against eschatological end-time. They imagined a future not only beyond a particular negation of identity, but also beyond the very idea of identity itself.

All of this sounds rather pessimistic. Yet in this book I do not wish to repeat the cultural pessimist's view of twentieth-century thought. Neither do I wish to give proof to Nils Roemer's claim that "German Jewish notions of time followed a distinct rhythm, shaped by their political, social, and cultural conditions."[82] Instead, I want to identify possible opportunities for radical change in Buber, Benjamin, Arendt, Celan, and others. For them, critique also implied thinking beyond easy solutions and smooth operations. Walter Benjamin, recalling a statement by Marx, compared the badly needed socialist revolution to the emergency brake on a speeding train—the

---

78. Karl Löwith, *Martin Heidegger and European Nihilism*, trans. Gary Stiner (New York: Columbia University Press, 1992), 214.

79. Reinhart Koselleck, *Futures Past: On the Semantics of Historical Time*, trans. Keith Tribe (New York: Columbia University Press, 2004), 190.

80. Koselleck, *Futures Past*, 3. For the more recent reversed view, see Thomas Moynihan, "The End of Us," *Aeon*, August 7, 2019, https://aeon.co/essays/to-imagine-our-own-extinction-is-to-be-able-to-answer-for-it.

81. Notably, this realization lies at the heart of Koselleck's characterization of modern space. See Koselleck, *Sediments of Time*, 34.

82. Roemer, "Between Hope and Despair," 356.

modern industrialized human.⁸³ The image of the emergency brake, close to the suspense, deferral, or in-betweenness explained above, recalls another emergency brake: The emergency clause known as Article 48 of the Weimar Republic's constitution, which allowed the president to assume full sovereignty in a state of exception, and which played an important role in the thought of Heidegger and legal theorist Carl Schmitt. However, in his *Theses on the Philosophy of History* (1940), a series of fragments he left with his friend Hannah Arendt, Benjamin contrasted the "sovereign state of emergency" with the "*real* state of emergency."⁸⁴ By "real" he did not mean "worse" or more severe, as many interpreters seem to think, but the state of emergency that reflects the time and politics of the people and not of the sovereign.

Each of the German Jewish intellectuals considered here developed a specific disciplinary system. What they shared, beyond the disciplinary difference, was an ontology of time I characterize as "temporal egalitarianism." Temporal egalitarianism refers to the fundamental temporal framework of life: all forms of life are born (Arendt says "inserted") into the world, live in it, and die in it. German Jewish thinkers realized that all life, regardless of political affiliation, identity, or territory, owes its existence to that temporal order.

The fusion of temporal principles and political philosophy was part of a German Jewish countermovement to reconstitute an alternative temporality within given spatial boundaries. Martin Buber reshaped religious studies on the basis of immediate (*Unmittelbar*) dialogue between self and other. Walter Benjamin developed a critical theory

---

83. "Marx says that revolutions are the locomotives of world history. But perhaps it is quite otherwise. Perhaps revolutions are an attempt by the passengers on this train—namely, the human race—to activate the emergency brake." Walter Benjamin, Thesis XVII, "Paralipomena to 'On the Concept of History,'" in *Selected Writings*, vol. 4, *1938–1940*, ed. Howard Eiland and Michael Jennings (Cambridge, MA: Belknap Press of Harvard University Press, 2006), 402. See also Michael Löwy, "The Revolution Is the Emergency Brake: Walter Benjamin's Political-Ecological Currency," in *On Changing the World: Essays in Political Philosophy, from Karl Marx to Walter Benjamin* (Chicago: Haymarket Books, 2013), 186–89.

84. Walter Benjamin, Thesis VIII, "On the Concept of History," in *Selected Writings*, 4:392.

through his understanding of now-time as a shared flash of "recognizability." Hannah Arendt reshaped modern political thought on the basis of a revolutionary change at the heart of democracy. Paul Celan recharged the word (*logos*) with the power of a fundamental "breath-turn," a comma or a temporal break, an interval or caesura between the German and the Jewish, the Christian and the Jew, memory and nothingness. A German Jewish *differentia specifica* is indeed a specific form of temporal in-betweenness that revises the Christian *parousia*, Hegel's historicism, Kantian a priori, Nietzsche's last man, or Heidegger's being-toward-death in favor of a general plea for equality. German Jews understood their temporal order flickering between the "no longer" of Jewish exile, and the "not-yet" of full emancipation.

Time and Rupture after the Holocaust

When World War II broke out, German Jews were again pushed from their dual identity into the role of social and cultural nemesis. The figure of the German Jew, to paraphrase Buber and his friend and colleague Hugo Bergmann, was trapped between cultures, times, and nations. But it is precisely this trap that enabled the German Jew to realize, as Bergmann wrote, that it was "no longer possible to live in the past or in some undefined future but only in the present of warfare."[85] Buber and Rosenzweig's project of translating the Hebrew Bible into German anchors the present in the living language of Jewish and Christian political-theological relations in modern Europe, rather than in an idealized past or universalist utopia.[86]

---

85. "Buber says that the war will create a new dictionary and new concepts," Bergmann writes. "It is *finis populorum* but not *finis religiosum*." Hugo Shmuel Bergmann, diary entry from December 2, 1939, in Bergmann, *Tagebücher und Briefe*, vol. 1, ed. Miriam Sambursky (Königstein: Jüdischer Verlag bei Athenäum, 1985), 509, my translation.

86. For more on this, see Nitzan Lebovic, "The Jerusalem School: The Theopolitical Hour," *New German Critique* 35, no. 3 (2008): 97–120. For recent analyses of Buber's engagement with secularization, see Samuel Hayim Brody, *Martin Buber's Theopolitics* (Bloomington: Indiana University Press, 2018); Daniel M. Herskowitz, *Heidegger and His Jewish Reception* (Cambridge: Cambridge University Press,

The rise of the Nazi Party from within the constitutional democratic structure determined not only the past but also the future of the hyphenated identity. After the war came a deep sense of "rupture with civilization" (*Zivilisationsbruch*), in the wake of which a large group of German Jewish thinkers tried to conceive of new ways to understand society and social relations.[87] In the spirit of post-Holocaust trauma studies—discussed in chapter 5—moving from Heidegger's Dasein (being there) to "being back there" reflects a traumatic experience and a different temporal order: the trauma of the Holocaust forced survivors to consider a ruptured chronological order, trapped between the no-longer of nineteenth century German, and the not-yet of a new one. Benjamin called to "expound the nineteenth century."[88] Celan's poetics of intervals builds on Heidegger's reading in Hölderlin and Rilke, or "thrownness" (*Geworfenheit*) into nothingness (*Nichts*).

But German Jewish thinkers moved beyond Heidegger's ontological nothingness and spoke of a non-anthropocentric, yet humanist, temporality.[89] Rosenzweig, Arendt, and Celan, among others, realized that life is in transition, that it does not need to be "expropriated, 'taken back' or 'shattered' in its fragile resoluteness, as in Heidegger's account."[90] After the Holocaust both the nihilistic resistance to politics and the Enlightenment understanding of historical time as "tied to social and political units of action, . . . each of which has its own

---

2021), 118–74; Asher Wycoff, "Between Prophecy and Apocalypse: Buber, Benjamin, and Socialist Eschatology," *Political Theory* 49, no. 3 (2020): 356.

87. Dan Diner, *Zivilisationsbruch: Denken nach Auschwitz* (Frankfurt: Fischer, 1988). See also Anson Rabinbach, *In the Shadow of Catastrophe: German Intellectuals between Apocalypse and Enlightenment* (Berkeley: University of California Press, 1997), 10.

88. Benjamin, Conv. K1, 4, in *The Arcades Project*, trans. Howard Eiland and Kevin McLaughlin (Cambridge, MA: Belknap Press of Harvard University Press, 2002), 389.

89. This is how Dominick LaCapra describes the temporality of a haunted Dasein after Auschwitz. See LaCapra, *Writing History, Writing Trauma* (Baltimore: Johns Hopkins University Press, 2014), 89.

90. Agata Bielik-Robson, *Another Finitude: Messianic Vitalism and Philosophy* (New York: Bloomsbury, 2019), 77.

temporal rhythm," seemed insufficient.⁹¹ Instead, social and political thought needed to consider a new order that was life-oriented rather than based on institutions.⁹² Reevaluating the concept of time also involved a reconsideration of an ahistorical and untimely notion of identity, this time dictated by forces of liberal economy.

To conclude, German Jewish thinkers proposed radical changes to existing disciplines and forms of thinking. They changed the way we have understood religion, politics, and culture since the 1920s, but especially after 1945. The generation of German Jewish thinkers taught us, the children of the late twentieth century, about the surprising transition of oppression and power relations between contrasting ideological frameworks. They taught us the importance of in-betweenness as a temporal dynamic, as well as a spatial settlement. Characterizing Jews from the perspective of in-betweenness, sociologist Franz Oppenheimer explained—against his own Zionist conclusion—that Jewish in-betweenness "remain[s] between past and presence, activity and passivity, with class and racial influence becoming interrelated and even blurred."⁹³ This message stood in sharp contrast to territorial or nationalist framing of time, whether German or Zionist. Furthermore, it stood apart from theological and philosophical pleas—such as Heidegger's self-referential philosophy of time—to release the European from the chains of (Jewish and Christian) metaphysics.⁹⁴

---

91. Reinhart Koselleck, "Time and History," in *The Practice of Conceptual History: Timing History, Spacing Concepts*, trans. Todd Samuel Presener et al. (Stanford, CA: Stanford University Press, 2002), 110.

92. In that respect I agree with Shahzad Bashir in his critique of the Western understanding of time. See Bashir, "On Islamic Time: Rethinking Chronology in the Historiography of Muslim Societies," *History and Theory* 53, no. 4 (2014): 519–44.

93. As paraphrased in Dekel Peretz, *Zionism and Cosmopolitanism: Franz Oppenheimer and the Dream of a Jewish Future in Germany and Palestine* (Munich: De Gruyter Oldenbourg, 2022), 66.

94. For an analysis of Heidegger's "Lutheran" take on a *theologia crucis* vis-à-vis the Greco-Roman and scholastic *theologia gloriae*, see Marc C. Taylor, *Abiding Grace: Time, Modernity, Death* (Chicago: University of Chicago Press, 2018). Taylor follows Heidegger's view, expressed in an unpublished lecture presented in Rudolf Bultmann's seminar in 1923–24, in which "Heidegger argues that the appropriation of Platonism in patristic theology and Aristotelianism in medieval scholasticism corrupted 'primal Christianity.'" (Bultmann was the Marburg profes-

I opened this introduction by quoting A. J. Heschel's statement that "Judaism is a religion of time."[95] Heschel, who emigrated to the United States and became an acclaimed critic of racial segregation, noted that "we cannot conquer time through space. We can only master time in time."[96] In the opening to this chapter, I mention that German Jewish thinkers strived to master the time that opens between the Augustinian no-longer and the failure of emancipation or a modern not-yet. A German Jewish time builds on this essentialist observation with a twist: the German Jewish gift to our post-postmodern age is the possibility of thinking in non-anthropocentric terms that remain humanist. Thinking from within their own temporal turn, German Jewish thinkers imagined a new world based on temporal equality. As Hannah Arendt wrote about Franz Kafka, a relevant political philosophy for the age of catastrophe must be written "as though ... from the vantage point of a distant future, as though he were or could have been at home only in a world which is 'not yet.'"[97]

---

sor of theology and had an obvious impact on Heidegger and Jonas.) In this sense, "Luther's interpretation of Paul's dismantling of Greek metaphysics provides the prototype for Heidegger's 'destruction' of ontotheology, and by extension, Derrida's deconstruction." Taylor, *Abiding Grace*, 89.

95. A. J. Heschel, *The Sabbath: Its Meaning for Modern Man* (New York: Farrar, Straus and Giroux, 1951), 8.

96. Heschel, *The Sabbath*, 99.

97. Hannah Arendt, "No Longer and Not Yet," in *Reflections on Literature and Culture* (Stanford, CA: Stanford University Press, 2007), 158. "Er ist, als schriebe er schon von einem Standpunkt aus, der in ferner Zukunft angesiedelt ist, so als ob er nur in einer Welt hätte beheimatet sein können, die 'noch nicht' existiert." Arendt, *Hannah Arendt / Hermann Broch Briefwechsel, 1946–1951*, ed. Paul Michael Lützeler (Frankfurt: Jüdischer Verlag, 1996), 169.

2

MARTIN BUBER

A Time for Theopolitics

Martin Buber is the thinker most identified with the "Jewish renaissance" of modern Jewish culture, beginning around 1900.[1] For Buber, this revival reconnected the ancient Jewish past with the immediate present and the anticipated future of Jewish culture and politics. Throughout his career Buber continuously issued exegetic texts, political statements, and prophetic declarations. These texts,

---

1. Martin Buber's "Jewish Renaissance"—an essay published in the first issue of the journal *Ost und West* (1 [1901]: 7–10)—is the starting point for various historical accounts of twentieth-century Jewish culture. See Michael Brenner, *The Renaissance of Jewish Culture in Weimar Germany* (New Haven, CT: Yale University Press, 1996). As Paul Mendes-Flohr has noted, in 1960 the Israeli Academy of Sciences and Humanities named Martin Buber its first president in recognition of his singular contribution to the renaissance of Jewish studies. See Paul Mendes-Flohr, "Buber's Rhetoric," in *Martin Buber: A Contemporary Perspective*, ed. Paul Mendes-Flohr (Syracuse, NY: Syracuse University Press, 2002), 1. See also Mendes-Flohr, *Martin Buber: A Life of Faith and Dissent* (New Haven, CT: Yale University Press, 2019), 312.

indebted equally to Jewish tradition, political analysis, and the thought of Friedrich Nietzsche and the Jewish prophets, featured key words such as "lived experience" (*Erlebnis*), "immediacy" (*Unmittelbarkeit*), and "ecstatic" or "ecstasy" (*Ekstatisch, Rausch*), a "presentist" lexicon that captured the minds of a whole generation of young Jews during the early 1900s.[2] Some, like Franz Kafka, Walter Benjamin, Gershom Scholem, and Hannah Arendt, responded with a degree of skepticism. Others, like the philosophers Franz Rosenzweig and Hugo Bergmann, the Protestant theologian Paul Tillich, and the essayist Margarete Susman, responded warmly. The latter group, members of Buber's closest circle, remained devoted to him for the rest of their lives. Both admirers and critics treated Buber's understanding of time as the essence of his prophetic and political thought, what Buber himself would come to identify as the core of "theopolitics."

Buber dedicated most of his career to prophetic thinking and thematized his engagement with prophecy in general terms. His engagement with prophecy included the tradition of Isaiah and Jeremiah but also went beyond the confines of Jewish identity to embrace other sources of inspiration, including the life philosophy (*Lebensphilosophie*) and prophetic rhetoric of Nietzsche. In his eulogy of the philosopher in 1900, the same year of his plea for a Jewish renaissance, Buber wrote that Nietzsche "belonged to those 'apostles of life' whose greatness was as undefinable as life itself. He was a visionary who could intuit future human forms in ways that went beyond everyday language and longings. He was the prophet of immanence and creative renewal."[3] Indeed, Buber relied on the thought of this "prophet" at every key moment of his early work. Later, when Buber became increasingly invested in theorizing his "hour of need," his thoughts remained shaped by residues of Nietzschean rhetoric.

---

2. I am thinking here of François Hartog's critique of modern forms of presentism. See Hartog, *Regimes of Historicity: Presentism and Experience of Time*, trans. Saskia Brown (New York: Columbia University Press, 2015).

3. Quoted in Steven E. Aschheim, *The Nietzsche Legacy in Germany: 1890–1990* (Berkeley: University of California Press, 1992), 106. See also the discussion in Jacob Golomb, *Nietzsche and Zion* (Ithaca, NY: Cornell University Press, 2004), 159–88.

Early on, Buber took his cue from *Thus Spoke Zarathustra* (1883–85) and called for a heroic Jewish spiritual thinker, a modern fusion of the biblical prophet and Nietzsche's Zarathustra. To describe the advent of such a figure of renewal he needed temporal images, language reverberating with echoes of collective hope and apocalyptic destruction. *Zarathustra*'s hyperbolic rhetoric informed Buber's conception of a Jewish soul threatened by antisemitism, industrial progress, and the rise of nationalism. Those concrete political and social circumstances preoccupied Buber more than they had Nietzsche, who never offered the sorts of practical proposals for change found in Buber's articles and public addresses.[4] For example, during a lecture given in Prague not long before the outbreak of World War I, Buber offered, as described in Maurice Friedman's biography of him, "speculations, some of which strike us today as prophetic, [on] the unique role that the Jew might play as mediator between East and West."[5] This mediator might combine, as had Zarathustra, the status of a spiritual leader and that of a mediator between world powers, but his actions depended on temporal, not spatial, terms: immediacy and the vibrancy of life echoed Zarathustra's plea for a superman, not a pragmatic political leader. Buber's lectures and writings thus galvanized many German Jewish intellectuals.[6]

Prophetic rhetoric and Jewish revivalism would remain Buber's trademarks over the years. In the speech he gave at the Hebrew University in Jerusalem in 1938 when he joined its faculty, nearly four decades after his Zarathustrian plea for a Jewish renaissance, Buber said: "The prophetic spirit receives . . . a mission for each situation. . . . It does not present a general image of the future,

---

4. Martin Buber, "Zarathustra," in *Werkausgabe*, vol. 1, *Frühe kulturkritische und philosophische Schriften*, ed. Martin Treml (Gütersloh: Gütersloher Verlagshaus, 2001), 103–17.

5. Maurice Friedman, *Martin Buber's Life and Work: The Early Years: 1878–1923*, vol. 1 (Detroit: Wayne State University Press, 1988), 143. Jacob Golomb mentions that Nietzsche liked to call himself a prophet. Others, such as Buber and Stefan Zweig, followed suit. See Golomb, *Nietzsche and Zion*, 162.

6. Buber's lectures in Prague (1911–13) "inspired a generation of central European Jewish youth." Even critics such as Gershom Scholem testified to the impact of the lectures. See Mendes-Flohr, *Faith and Dissent*, 83.

whether perpetual bliss [*Pantopia*] or utopia."[7] Neither messianic nor utopian, the prophetic spirit nonetheless strives for immediate critical impact. Indeed, from his earliest attempts to shape an alternative to political Zionism, to his (admittedly wrongheaded) support of the German cause in 1914 and his work with pacifist organizations in the early 1920s, as well his administrative work at the university, Buber always viewed his mission in concrete terms, seeking political reforms and the creation of a binational state. In *The Prophetic Faith* (*Torat ha-Nevi'im*, 1942) he explained that prophets were often critics of sovereignty, which enabled them to develop both a "universal pathos of expression" and a concrete understanding of "the reality of the hour."[8] Buber's uniqueness as a thinker, I shall demonstrate, was his ability to bring together different, even contrary, political and cultural forces, such as Germans and Jews, ancient and modern, East and West. In philosophical terms, his thinking integrated political theology with Nietzschean Lebensphilosophie. This fusion, he realized, had to be dynamic, not static; dialogical, not monological; and temporal, not spatial. By emphasizing concepts such as immediacy, dialogism, and theopolitics, Buber wove together past and future, the human and the divine, thought and action.[9]

---

7. Martin Buber, "Die Forderung des Geistes und die geschichtliche Wirklichkeit," in *Werkausgabe*, vol. 11, part 2, *Schriften zur politischen Philosophie und zur Sozialphilosophie*, ed. Francesco Ferrari, Stefano Franchini, and Massimiliano De Villa (Gütersloh: Gütersloher Verlagshaus, 2019), 20.

8. Martin Buber, *Torat Ha-nevi'im* [*The Prophetic Faith*] (Tel-Aviv: Dvir, 1942), 117–42. This characterization follows Buber's debate with the neo-Kantian Hermann Cohen. In a well-known exchange between the two they seemed to agree about the universal message of prophetic critique but parted ways on its legacy; Cohen looked to an assimilatory German-Jewish fusion, whereas Buber thought that the critique supported Zionist revivalism. For an excellent analysis of the debate between Buber and Cohen, see Robert Erlewine, *Judaism and the West: From Hermann Cohen to Joseph Soloveitchik* (Bloomington: Indiana University Press, 2016), 100–106; Willi Goetschel, *The Discipline of Philosophy and the Invention of Modern Jewish Thought* (New York: Fordham University Press, 2013), 58–82.

9. For some Buber interpreters, there is a fundamental difference between Buber's earlier dedication to mystical *Erlebnis* and his later dialogical—and rational—hermeneutics. Dan Avnon writes, "The decade between 1914 and 1923 marks Buber's rejection of *Erlebnis* (lived or inner experience) philosophy and mystical ecstasies and his ... philosophy of dialogue." See Dan Avnon, *Martin Buber: The Hidden Dialogue* (Lanham, MD: Rowan and Littlefield, 1998), 34. According to Jacob Golomb,

No philosophical life or political career is devoid of continuity or change. Scholars know Buber for his work in existentialism and comparative religious studies.[10] But Buber's role as a public figure was much wider. He routinely exhibited a familiarity with German discourses of secular Lebensphilosophie and the Judeo-Christian vocabulary of revival. The temporal concepts of immediacy and political action lay at the heart of his handling of these discourses.[11] Buber and Ahad Ha'am (literally, "one of the people," the pen name of Asher Ginsberg, 1856–1927) founded a movement devoted to cultural Zionism to resist Theodor Herzl's better-known political Zionism; they advocated instead for a "'cultural amelioration' of the Jewish people through a spiritually invigorating 'national education.'"[12] During the early 1900s this position translated into a popular call for individual and collective action. In 1914 Buber's effort to integrate the Jewish renaissance with Germany's nationalistic enthusiasm was stymied by the opposition of fellow intellectuals and the senseless bloodshed in the trenches. After 1916 Buber shifted from speaking of a shared "community of blood" (*Blutgemeinschaft*) to an openly dialogical philosophy based on what he called the "interhuman."[13] Merging Nietzsche's superman with Kant and Simmel's concept of

---

the change grew from Buber's attempt to distance himself from Nietzsche, an attempt whose outcome Golomb found rather limited: "The impact of Nietzsche's 'invasion' of Buber's life and thought became more subtle.... A complete liberation? Hardly. Nietzsche was quite alive in Buber's universe till the last moments of this first and foremost Hebrew humanist philosopher." See Golomb, *Nietzsche and Zion*, 188.

10. Leora Batnitzky, "Revelation and *Neues Denken*: Rethinking Buber and Rosenzweig on the Law," in *New Perspectives on Martin Buber*, ed. Michael Zank (Tübingen: Mohr Siebeck, 2006), 149.

11. In his chapter about Buber's revival, Asher Biemann explains that Buber stressed a "non-gradual" revival. See Biemann, "Revival as Imperative: Reflections on the Normativity of Jewish Renaissance," in *Jewish Revival Inside Out: Remaking Jewishness in a Transnational Age*, ed. Daniel Monterescu and Rachel Werczberger (Detroit: Wayne State University Press, 2022), 23–42.

12. It is telling, perhaps, that Herzl supported this movement in spite of its reservations about his path. Paul Mendes-Flohr, *Faith and Dissent*, 33.

13. "By the sphere of the interhuman I mean solely actual happenings between men, whether wholly mutual or tending to grow into mutual relations." Martin Buber, "Elements of the Interhuman," in *Martin Buber on Psychology and Psychotherapy: Essays, Letters, and Dialogue*, ed. Judith Buber Agassi (Syracuse, NY: Syracuse University Press, 1999), 75.

the "intersubjective" sent Buber—now an acclaimed speaker and influential thinker—on a quest for a new form of communication that would reconcile the prophetic and the practical.

Whether prophetic or practical, revivalist or critical, German or Zionist, every layer of Buber's rhetoric was an attempt to fashion a uniquely German Jewish temporal order. During the early 1900s his concept of a new, separate temporal order offered an alternative to German assimilation, Jewish exilic separation, and German and Zionist chauvinism alike. Anchored in a particular place and time, it offered a philosophical solution to ahistorical concepts of identity. A mediator between earthly and transcendental forces might fuse the ancient power of prophets with modern German Jewish life. Inspired by both Nietzsche and the Jewish prophets, Buber aspired to act as a modern prophet to both Jews and gentiles.

To combine three typically separate fields—theology, politics, and practical experience—Buber created various intellectual communities. In 1909 he helped to organize a group of Jewish intellectuals in Prague dedicated to the revival of Jewish culture. During the 1910s he and a group of liberal Protestant theologians formed the Forte circle, which went on to become the basis of the journal *Die Kreatur*. He also conscripted German Jewish intellectuals to contribute to the pioneering journal he established and edited, *Der Jude* (1916–28). With Franz Rosenzweig, Buber established the Jewish Lehrhaus in Frankfurt (1921), which became a center for Jewish thinking all over Europe. Together with Bergmann and Gershom Scholem, he helped found the Hebrew University in Jerusalem in 1925 and became a member of its faculty in 1938.

His efforts were not limited to intellectual life, however. With other German Jews (for the most part), he dreamed up the first pacifist organizations in Palestine, Brith Shalom (Covenant of Peace) and, later, Ichud (Union), which supported the notion of a binational state against an ethnic vision of political Zionism. He did all in his power to make the young generation of socialist Zionists feel at home in organizations such as Hapoel Hatzair (The Young Worker) and the kibbutz movement. Finally, he joined Bergmann, his colleague and friend since the early days in Prague, in assisting publishing houses and serving on advisory boards. The administrative roles

Buber played have never been subject to in-depth study, yet they were central parts of his activity and philosophy. The academic protocols he wrote repeatedly stressed prophetic terms and brought together political-theological and living experiences.[14]

In this chapter I argue that Buber's philosophy, both early and late, owes much to his innovative understanding of temporality; in religious, political, and institutional discourses, as in living experience itself, temporal terms crucially shape his message. For example, he dwelt on the dialogical encounter (*Mifgash* in Hebrew; *Begegnung* in German) between I and Thou, man and world, Jew and gentile. The heart of every encounter was its betweenness, itself a negation of spatiality, and instead shaped in temporal terms. When the self met the other, Buber explained, the divine spoke, but this speech act emerged from a non-space or non-place (u-topia). Inspired by the mystical thought of Rebbe Nachman of Breslov, as well as by his teacher Georg Simmel, Buber wrote, "The narrow bridge, where I and Thou meet; [that is] the realm of 'between.'"[15] When we are in between, we are neither here nor there—a bridge is an event rather than a place. While the metaphor is spatial, Buber dwelt not on where but when: "The relation to the You is unmediated. . . . The present—the actual and fulfilled present—exists only insofar as presentness, encounter, and relation exist. Only as the You becomes present does presence

---

14. Martin Buber faculty file, Hebrew University Archives, Jerusalem, folders 3–4. For an analysis of Buber's speeches at the founding of Hebrew University and other critical moments, see Uri Cohen, *Ha'har ve'ha'giva: Ha'universita ha'ivrit bi'tekufat terom ha'atzma'ut* [The mountain and the hill: The Hebrew University of Jerusalem during the pre-independence period] (Tel-Aviv: Am Oved, 2006).

15. Martin Buber, "Das Problem des Menschen," in *Werke*, vol. 1, *Schriften zur Philosophie* (Munich: Kösel, 1962), 405; translated in Martin Buber, *Between Man and Man*, trans. Ronald Gregor Smith (New York: Macmillan, 1965), 203. Buber's "narrow bridge" echoes a famous proverb by Rebbe Nachman that was later turned into a popular Hasidic song: "All the world is a very narrow bridge, and the most important thing is not to be overwhelmed by fear." It also echoes Georg Simmel's essay "Brücke und Tür" (Bridge and door) of 1909, which contrasts the connecting nature of bridges in the public sphere with the separating function of doors in the private sphere. See Simmel, "Brücke und Tür," in *Das Individuum und die Freiheit: Essais* (Frankfurt: Suhrkamp, 1993), 7–11.

come into being."¹⁶ In speeches, pamphlets, and essays he linked the mission of the "community"—which he often envisioned as a clandestine spiritual collective—to the ongoing Jewish present: "'If not now, when?' The realization of the 'then' [*Dann*] is the realization of the now [*Jetzt*], with secret dedication."¹⁷ Buber's bridge—a recurrent motif in his later writings and those of his fellow Brith Shalom members—connected different temporal orders, not two points in space; it relied on a vocabulary of time in order to deconstruct and undermine spatiality and territoriality.

In keeping with Buber's own stress on dialogue, I will proceed by depicting a few of his personal and intellectual relationships that illustrate the entanglement of past promise and present or future realization in the "hour of need"—the hour of emergency, war, violence, and decision-making. All of these relationships reveal a consistent interest in engaging critically with a prophetic rhetoric, spiritual communities, and political theory of sovereignty—whether Zionism, German nationalism, or Israeli nationalism. Like other German Jewish thinkers discussed in this book, Buber consistently expressed a clear preference for a temporal understanding of politics. I have chosen to scrutinize his thinking on time and action through a chronological examination of his engagement with several key intellectual associates: socialist and anarchist Gustav Landauer (1870–1919), German Jewish philosophers Franz Rosenzweig (1886–1929) and Hugo Bergmann (1883–1975), and authors Stefan Zweig (1881–1942), Franz Werfel (1890–1945), and Franz Kafka (1883–1924).¹⁸ I shall have

---

16. "Die Beziehung zum Du ist unmittelbar. . . . Die wirkliche und erfüllte, gibt es nur insofern, as es Gegenwärtigkeit, Begegnung, Beziehung gibt. Nur Dadurch, dass das Du gegenwärtig wird, entsteht Gegenwart." Martin Buber, *I and Thou*, trans. Walter Kaufmann (New York: Touchstone, 1996), 62–63; the German passage is from Martin Buber, *Ich und Du* (Gütersloh: Gütersloher Verlagshaus, 2010), 18–19.

17. Martin Buber, "Wann Denn," in *Werkausgabe*, vol. 21, *Schriften zur zionistischen Politik und zur jüdisch-arabischen Frage*, ed. Samuel Hayim Brody and Paul Mendes-Flohr (Gütersloh: Gütersloher Verlagshaus, 2019), 141, my translation.

18. As Yemima Hadad has recently shown, women were central to Buber's thinking and worldview. Yet none of his closest collaborators were women, and Buber's dialogue with women was partial at best. See Yemima Hadad, "Feminism, Nashim ve'Nashiut: Nochechutan ve'Trumatan la'Hagut Ha'Buberianit" [Femi-

occasion to note, in counterpoint to these friendly encounters, Buber's more complicated relationships with female intellectuals, Protestant and Catholic theologians, and a number of German philosophical rivals.

Lebensphilosophie and Lived Immediacy

Buber and Gustav Landauer shared what Michael Löwy calls "a romantic utopian vision"—both adopted a Nietzschean prophetic rhetoric and a socialist worldview.[19] They had come to know each other in 1899 through a reading group in Berlin that was devoted to mysticism and hermetic philosophy. Buber was twenty-two years old; the thirty-year-old Landauer was already fairly well-known as an intellectual, socialist, and anarchist.[20] According to Buber's biographer, "Landauer undoubtedly encouraged the switch in Buber's university studies" from science and art history to Christian mysticism.[21] While Landauer worked on the philosophy of Meister Eckhart, Buber prepared a dissertation on the mysticism of Jakob Böhme and Nicolas of Cusa. During the early 1900s Landauer translated and adapted Eckhart into modern German and became one of the best-known socialist thinkers of his generation, while Buber revived the Jewish mystical Hasidic tradition and embraced Zionism.

The two friends were brought together by a deep admiration for Nietzsche's rhetoric. In 1895, writing in the journal *Sozialist* about the individual anarchist as an agent of social change, Landauer invoked Nietzsche as a philosophical and political authority.[22] In Berlin

---

nism, women, and femininity: Their presence and contribution to Buberian thought], *Alpaim ve'Od*, no. 3 (2021): 151–64.

19. Michael Löwy, "Romantic Prophets of Utopia: Gustav Landauer and Martin Buber," in *Gustav Landauer: Anarchist and Jew*, ed. Paul Mendes-Flohr and Anya Mali (Berlin: De Gruyter Oldenbourg, 2015), 64.

20. Samuel Brody has discussed the men's shared interest in the "anarchist canon." See Samuel Hayim Brody, *Martin Buber's Theopolitics* (Bloomington: Indiana University Press, 2018), 21.

21. Friedman, *Buber's Life and Work*, 1:77.

22. Yossef Schwartz, "The Politicization of the Mystical in Buber and His Contemporaries," in Zank, *New Perspectives*, 210.

he joined a group of Nietzschean anarchists—a self-described "new community of knowledge and life"—led by the brothers Heinrich and Julius Hart.[23] Buber joined shortly thereafter. He had set out to translate *Thus Spoke Zarathustra* at the age of seventeen and explained that Nietzsche "contrasted the ideal of a comfortable and painless life with a stormy and dangerous life, whose powerful beauty is enhanced by the pain.... The creation of great people and great ideas [is] the purpose of humanity."[24] Nietzsche proposed a rich, defiant, anti-institutional language that contrasted with a statist and authoritative language.

Between 1900 and 1916 Buber and Landauer met and corresponded regularly. They often exchanged ideas about socialism, which they viewed, in Friedman's words, "not as political action but as immediate beginning, as an elemental commitment to living and realizing."[25] Buber, who studied under Wilhelm Dilthey and Georg Simmel, submitted his dissertation in 1904. Between 1906 and 1912 he edited *Die Gesellschaft*, a series of sociological monographs commissioned from thirty-seven European intellectuals. Paul Mendes-Flohr describes Buber's series as revealing his interest in Nietzsche's philosophy of life in addition to "the unmistakable imprint of his esteemed teacher [Georg Simmel], as well as traces of Dilthey's hermeneutics of lived experience, *Erlebnis*."[26] As Mendes-Flohr shows, traces of life philosophy mark Buber's pre-dialogical period, even when he approached key matters in Jewish tradition and cultural Zionism.[27] During this period he fused the impact of life philosophy with his exploration of Hasidic tales. From 1909 to 1911 he delivered the first in a series of three lectures on cultural Zionism in Prague to the circle around Franz Kafka and Hugo Bergmann.

---

23. The group established a journal titled *Das Reich der Erfüllung* [The kingdom of fulfillment]. See Brody, *Martin Buber's Theopolitics*, 28–29.

24. Quoted in Gilya Gerda Schmidt, *Martin Buber's Formative Years: From German Culture to Jewish Renewal, 1897–1909* (Tuscaloosa: University of Alabama Press, 1995), 25.

25. Friedman, *Buber's Life and Work*, 1:235.

26. Mendes-Flohr, *Faith and Dissent*, 50.

27. Paul Mendes-Flohr, *From Mysticism to Dialogue: Martin Buber's Transformation of German Social Thought* (Detroit: Wayne State University Press, 1989), 15.

Landauer, too, was cultivating a philosophical career. In addition to a new translation of Meister Eckhart, he produced a work titled *Skepticism and Mysticism* (*Skepsis und Mystik*, 1903). In his exchanges with Buber, Landauer sounds more Nietzschean than Marxist, more interested in prophecy and revolutionary temporality than class struggle.[28] In *The Revolution* (1907), Landauer's contribution to *Die Gesellschaft*, he wrote about revolutionary existence "in between time" (*Zwischenzeit*).[29] Landauer was, one commentator wrote, "straddling the revolutions of the past and the utopian revolution of the future."[30] Discussing this in-betweenness in terms such as "the not-yet" (*noch nicht*) and "immediacy and becoming," Landauer thus reconsidered the relationship between individual, community, and state. Recalling that work in 1947, Buber quoted his friend: "Landauer writes, 'the end which revolution actually attains is not so very different from what went before.' . . . 'Everything comes in time,' says Landauer, 'and every time after the revolution is a time before the revolution for all those whose lives have not got bogged in some great moment of the past.'"[31] In other words, here was a vocabulary of time and life, with its stress on the not-yet of betweenness, on the one hand, and immediate realization, presented as a revolutionary hope, on the other. Politically, terminology reframed the relationship between the people and the state: "It is a connection between people which is actually there; only it has not yet become bond and binding, is not yet a higher organism."[32] As we shall see in this chapter and in later chapters, stressing the time between the not-yet and the no-longer (*Schon Nicht*) will become the mark of a whole generation of German Jewish thinkers.

---

28. Corinna R. Kaiser, *Gustav Landauer als Schriftsteller: Sprache, Schweigen, Musik* (Berlin: De Gruyter Oldenbourg, 2014), 27.
29. Gustav Landauer, *Die Revolution*, in *Gesellschaft*, vol. 13 (Frankfurt: Rütten und Leoning, 1907), 107.
30. Ulrich Linse, "'Poetic Anarchism' versus 'Party Anarchism': Gustav Landauer and the Anarchist Movement in Wilhelmian Germany," in Paul Mendes-Flohr and Anya Mali, *Gustav Landauer*, 58.
31. Martin Buber, *Paths in Utopia*, trans. R. F. C. Hull (Boston: Beacon Press, 1949), 51–52.
32. Buber, *Paths in Utopia*, 46. See also Martin Buber, *Pfade in Utopia: Über Gemeinschaft und deren Verwirklichung* (Heidelberg: L. Schneider, 1985), 91.

The terminology connected the two friends, though it served them in opposite ways. For Landauer, the Nietzschean emphasis on life, immediacy, and a "higher organism" led to an absolute rejection of state structure, militarism, and hierarchy. As a proper anarchist, he embraced all-encompassing equality. For the young Buber, a vocabulary of life and immediacy supported a cultural and spiritual approach to Zionism that was inimical to political Zionism but not to the idea of sovereignty. He expressed these views in the first book he published with the Jüdischer Verlag, the press he had established to spread the thought of Ahad Ha'am. Buber saw no contradiction between cultural Zionism and an organic view of Judaism. As he explained in the *Jüdischer Almanach* (1902), which appeared after the fifth Zionist congress in Basel, "In its everyday life, a people relies on the shared forces of blood, fate, and cultural creativity—in other words, on the purely physiological."[33] The language of life and blood, of spirituality and prophecy, distinguished his understanding of the prophetic mission from the pragmatic realpolitik of Theodor (Binyamin Ze'ev) Herzl, the father of political Zionism. Buber's early emphasis on a "community of blood" also separated his mission from Landauer's.

In the early 1900s Buber explained that language had a physical aspect, shaping the nation's body as well as its temporal and spatial character. This idea was exemplified in the collections of Hasidic tales he edited (*The Tales of Rabbi Nachman* [1906], *The Legend of the Baal-Shem* [1908]) and in *Ecstatic Confessions* (1909), an anthology of mystical experiences from a variety of cultures. In the latter work, he defined ecstasy—an immediate relation between mind and body—as the experience of oneness that transcends everyday life.[34] "Is not

---

33. Martin Buber, "Die Schaffenden, das Volk und die Bewegung," *Jüdischer Almanach* (1902): 24–30, my translation. For an excellent critical reading of the messianic motifs in this essay, see Elke Dubbels, *Figuren des Messianischen in Schriften deutsch-jüdischer Intellektueller, 1900–1933* (Berlin: De Gruyter, 2011), 222–24. Dominique Bourel ascribed the language in this article to a "Nietzschean vocabulary" that was popular in Central Europe during that period. See Bourel, *Martin Buber: Was es heisst, ein Mensch zu sein* (Gütersloh: Gütersloher Verlagshaus, 2017), 100.

34. Martin Buber, *Ecstasy and Confession: The Heart of Mysticism*, trans. Esther Cameron (Syracuse, NY: Syracuse University Press, 1996), 2.

the experience of ecstasy," Buber asked in his introduction, "a symbol of the primal experience of the universal mind? Are not both a living, inner experience?" This sort of questioning, full of Nietzschean terms ("living experience," "ecstasy," "primal") indicates a rich understanding of Lebensphilosophie fused with Hassidic enthusiasm. Buber's editor at the time stated that he was preoccupied by "presence, presentness, immediacy, ineffability."[35] Buber routinely used such terms as "organic," "life-form," and "immediacy" in key texts, such as his "Zionism as a Life Phenomenon and as a Life-Form," a lecture Buber delivered in 1914.[36] Landauer celebrated his friend's accomplishments, noting that whereas Nietzsche was "an apostle of life," Buber was "the Jewish apostle to humanity."[37]

A number of scholars have discussed Buber's fascination with Nietzsche and Lebensphilosophie, as well as Hassidism, but few have connected Buber's early terminology with his later political analysis or his commitment to Lebensphilosophie with his Zionism. None have dwelt on the temporal stress that weaves so much of his life's work together. Biographers such as Maurice Friedman, Paul Mendes-Flohr, and Dominique Bourel, and historians of Nietzscheanism such as Steven Aschheim and Jacob Golomb have all noted Buber's use of a post-Nietzschean vocabulary. The relation between Buber's "mystical" (pre-1914) and "dialogical" (post-1916) periods is much debated. Bourel, Friedman, and others opt for thematic continuity, whereas Mendes-Flohr (among others) argues for a deeper, fundamental change. A post-Nietzschean stress on *Erlebnis* is essential for both continuity and change, Jewish and gentile, East and West. But where does it come from?

Lebensphilosophie came to Buber via Landauer and the New Community (*Neue Gemeinschaft*) group he met in Berlin during his studies, when a new jargon of life grew up around Nietzsche's phi-

---

35. Paul Mendes-Flohr, introduction to Martin Buber, *Ecstatic Confessions: The Heart of Mysticism*, trans. Esther Cameron (Syracuse, NY: Syracuse University Press, 1996), xix.

36. Martin Buber, *Werkausgabe*, vol. 3, *Frühe jüdische Schriften, 1900–1922*, ed. Barbara Schäfer (Gütersloher: Gütersloher Verlaghaus, 2007), 134–42.

37. Gustav Landauer, "Martin Buber," in *Der werdende Mensch: Aufsätze über Leben und Schrifttum* (Potsdam: Kiepenheuer, 1921), 244–46, my translation.

losophy. Take, for example, the modernist poetry of Stefan George and his circle, which was deeply invested in Nietzsche's Lebensphilosophie; its devotees in Berlin included Georg Simmel, Buber's mentor. Buber, much like Walter Benjamin and Gershom Scholem, was an avid reader and admirer of Nietzsche, as were many in the rapidly growing youth movements. Buber developed his response to this stream of thought in concert with other friends and colleagues. One was Fritz Mauthner, a close friend of Landauer's and a member of the Prague circle; his thinking has been seen as foreshadowing linguistic philosophy and the "linguistic turn."[38] All three—Mauthner, Landauer, and Buber—shared Nietzsche's fascination with ecstasy (*Rausch*) and its linguistic expression, as well as the spontaneity of life and its abstract expression so evident in prophetic rhetoric.

Buber never fully deserted either the vocabulary of his youth or an attendant Nietzschean antihistoricism.[39] Dominique Bourel, the French historian and Buber's biographer, emphasized Buber's Nietzschean "hymns to life" that dwell on "a new language that foregrounds action, reality, and life."[40] Buber's Nietzschean life philosophy was at odds with the nineteenth century's scientific approach to history, a movement whose epigones propped up German nationalism and Jewish emancipation.[41] As Yossef Schwartz has shown, Landauer and Buber combined a rebellious post-Nietzschean vocabulary with an interest in "the mystical phenomenon" and philosophical ideas that, if put into practice, could lead to revolutionary action and anarchic communities.[42] The key was a "radical critique of language" that would render religion and politics "not so much the binding power of society as its utopian vision and destruction."[43] A

---

38. Phil Huston, *Martin Buber's Journey to Presence* (New York: Fordham University Press, 2007), 33–35.
39. For more about antihistoricism among German Jewish intellectuals, see David N. Myers, *Resisting History: Historicism and Its Discontents in German-Jewish Thought* (Princeton, NJ: Princeton University Press, 2003).
40. Bourel, *Martin Buber*, 71.
41. On the German Jewish science of history, see Myers, *Resisting History*; David N. Myers and David B. Ruderman, eds., *The Jewish Past Revisited: Reflections on Modern Jewish Historians* (New Haven, CT: Yale University Press, 1998).
42. Schwartz, "Politicization of the Mystical," 210.
43. Schwartz, "Politicization of the Mystical," 210–11.

deep interest in anarchism and revolutionary change, sparked by his friendship with Landauer, continued to define much of Buber's later writing.⁴⁴

The Language of Life

The years prior to World War I were the salad days of Nietzschean Lebensphilosophie.⁴⁵ This new vocabulary, thanks to Nietzsche's growing acclaim, opened revolutionary thought to all forms of ideology. In contrast to the antisemitic versions produced by Elisabeth Foerster-Nietzsche and later the Nazi philosopher Alfred Baeumler, *The Will to Power* employed the language of blood and physiology while denouncing German nationalism, Christianity, and antisemitism. Both critics and supporters of German nationalism welcomed Nietzschean life philosophy, if somewhat selectively, and the critical potential on both sides is detectable in "apostles" of Nietzsche to this day.⁴⁶ As apostles, Buber and Landauer advocated revolution through immediate action (*Tat*), an idea borrowed from Nietzsche that permitted them to develop, with a little help from Eckhart, the ideas of a "master of living" (*Lebensmeister*) and "lived religion."⁴⁷

Their attraction to Lebensphilosophie seems to have had less of a connection to ideology than to terminology, and particularly the function of revolutionary terms in aesthetic and temporal contexts. In *Daniel: Dialogues on Realization* (*Daniel: Gespräche von der Verwirklichung*, 1913), Buber offered a Jewish philosophy of lived experience and realization, based on the idea of a "time of movement."⁴⁸

---

44. Brody, *Martin Buber's Theopolitics*, 270.
45. Aschheim, *The Nietzsche Legacy*, 36.
46. Peter Sloterdijk, *Nietzsche Apostle*, trans. Steven Corcoran (Madison: University of Wisconsin, 2013).
47. Martin Buber, *Der heilige Weg: Ein Wort an die Juden und an die Völker* (Frankfurt: Rütten und Loening, 1920), 76; Schwartz, "Politicization of the Mystical," 215, 219.
48. As Avraham Shapira—who edited works by Buber, Scholem, and Bergmann—wrote, "Upon the matrix of these early groupings Buber went on to develop dual structures. . . . The most important duality is embodied in his *Daniel* (1913), in the structure of realization [*Verwirklichung*]-orientation [*Orientierung*].

In his mind, the fundamental link connecting singular and plural, humanity, world, and divinity is the shift from potential to realization, creative promise and fulfillment in the world. Shortly after finishing *Daniel*, Buber explained in an article that kinesis, or movement, denoted the shift "from the potential to realization."[49] Kinesis was the power that overcame political stasis—the outcome was exstasis. "Kinesis, in and of itself," he wrote, "has no object, an object being defined solely by direction or by 'consciousness.' Accordingly, the significance of kinesis does not lie in a specific referent such as fatherland or a nation.... [Instead] it pushes men to unconditional action."[50] "Become real, lived life. And that is life of immediacy and of human fellowship; for in genuine community ... is immediacy which alone makes it possible to live the realizing as real."[51]

Buber's *Daniel* project was crucially indebted to his intellectual relationship with Landauer. In a letter from September 1912 Buber wrote to him, "Among my friends you are the only one for whom *Daniel* was always there. It is thus more than an expression of a feeling when I dedicate the first announcement of its birth to you."[52] The book is organized as a series of dialogues between the prophet Daniel and five interlocutors addressing ecstatic experience, the power of eros, the choice of the Other, and the immediacy of life and death. In the fifth dialogue the Zarathustrian imagery Buber had shared with Landauer is prominent: "[God] sent me to dwell alone [in the] secluded mountains."[53] In political terms, Landauer supported Buber in a public debate with Hermann Cohen in 1916. While Cohen supported a cultural German Jewish symbiosis and rejected with scorn

---

From these leads a developmental line, to which he himself points, toward the I-Thou, I-it structure." Avraham Shapira, *Hope for Our Time: Key Trends in the Thought of Martin Buber*, trans. Jeffrey M. Green (Albany: SUNY Press, 1999), 4.

49. Martin Buber, "Bewegung: Aus einem Brief an einen Holländer," *Der Neue Merkur* 1, no. 10 (1915): 490.

50. Buber, "Bewegung," 490.

51. Martin Buber, *Daniel: Dialogues on Realization*, trans. Maurice Friedman (New York: Holt, Rinehart and Winston, 1964), 78.

52. Martin Buber to Gustav Landauer, September 1912, quoted in Paul Mendes-Flohr, *Divided Passions: Jewish Intellectuals and the Experience of Modernity* (Detroit: Wayne State University Press, 1991), 74.

53. Mendes-Flohr, *Divided Passions*, 75.

"the Palestinian Party" (Zionists), Buber stressed a cultural difference and autonomous Zionist politics, which Landauer supported on socialist grounds.[54]

Buber's support for the German war effort in 1914, however, led to a gradual rift between the two friends. In 1914 Buber used Nietzschean terms such as "immediacy," "kinesis," "lived experience," "ecstasy," "organic," "action," "and "realization" when promoting the war. For him, Jews in German military uniforms would bring about the full and final integration of the Jewish community into the state; they would seize their own time of unconditional action. This belief proved both naive and shortsighted. Buber's friends and admirers criticized him harshly for this translation of ecstasy and realization into warmongering. When Buber devoted an editorial to the German cause in the first issue of *Der Jude* (April 3, 1916), he appealed to Jews to join the military effort in the name of Jewish *Erlebnis*.[55] Landauer responded with a furious letter: "I say that you have no right to go about issuing statements on the present political events known as the world war, nor have you any right to insert this confusion into your beautiful and sapient generalizations."[56] For Landauer, Buber was out of his depth when he turned to the concrete world of politics, armies, and battles. Landauer felt personally betrayed and accused his friend of rhetorical manipulation, or

---

54. For an overview, see Myers, *Resisting History*, 54–55. For a brief but succinct framing of Cohen's perspective, see Dana Hollander, "Buber, Rosenzweig, and the Politics of Cultural Affirmation," *Jewish Studies Quarterly* 13, no. 1 (2006): 87–103; and Andrea Poma, "Hermann Cohen: Judaism and Critical Idealism," in *The Cambridge Companion to Modern Jewish Philosophy*, ed. Michael L. Morgan and Peter Eli Gordon (Cambridge: Cambridge University Press, 2007), 87.

55. Mendes-Flohr, *From Mysticism to Dialogue*, 98. The purpose of the journal was "to create a bridge among the cultural Zionists," who struggled with the more militant voice of political Zionists. The journal opened with a series of articles by and about Ahad Ha'am. See Eleonore Lappin, *Der Jude, 1916–1928: Jüdische Moderne zwischen Universalismus und Partikularismus* (Tübingen: Mohr Siebeck, 2000), 5.

56. Cited and translated in Mendes-Flohr, *From Mysticism to Dialogue*, 100. For the original, see Gustav Landauer to Martin Buber, May 12, 1916, in Martin Buber, *Briefwechsel aus sieben Jahrzehnten*, 2 vols. (Heidelberg: L. Schneider, 1972), 1:435. Translated in Mendes-Flohr, *From Mysticism to Dialogue*, 100.

"attempting to force" his worldview "into [his] schemata."[57] By the end of 1916 Landauer had broken off all contact with Buber.

For some time Buber characterized the war as a lived experience, an action, and "something livable" (*Lebbares*).[58] But his language shifted after 1916. Was it just the argument with Landauer? Perhaps. But Buber had also been lambasted by Kafka, Benjamin, Scholem, Bergmann, Hans Kohn, and others whose views he valued.[59] However one weighs the impact of these varied blows, Mendes-Flohr is right to trace a discursive change to the spring of 1916. From that time onward, Buber adopted an antiheroic rhetoric. For example, in December 1916 he wrote that a true hero is opposed to "the principle of force" and prefers "the principle of the spirit."[60] He shifted from a folkish and mystical concept of *Erlebnis* to a philosophy of dialogue.[61] Whether we choose to view Buber's Jewish renaissance as an anarchic movement, as Samuel Brody has recently argued; as "direct theocracy," to use Asher Wycoff's label; or as "a hidden dialogue," the poetic term Dan Avnon uses as a title, Buber never deserted his great cause, but he certainly changed his philosophical grounding to a more nuanced discourse.[62]

---

57. Translated in Mendes-Flohr, *From Mysticism to Dialogue*, 100. It is not surprising to find that when Buber was preparing his correspondence with Landauer for publication, he chose to omit this letter.

58. Buber, "Bewegung," 489–92. Translated in Paul Mendes-Flohr, *From Mysticism to Dialogue*, 96.

59. See Franz Kafka to Felice Bauer, January 19, 1913, in Franz Kafka, *Letters to Felice*, trans. James Stern and Elisabeth Duckworth (New York: Schocken, 1973), 161. Scholem elaborates on the complicated relationship with Buber. Benjamin expressed his deep disappointment with Buber's support of the war in a letter written in July 1916. Gershom Scholem, *Walter Benjamin: The Story of a Friendship*, trans. Harry Zohn (New York: New York Review of Books, 2003), 37. See also Walter Benjamin, *Briefe*, vol. 1, ed. Gershom Scholem and Theodor W. Adorno (Frankfurt: Suhrkamp, 1966), 125–28.

60. Martin Buber, "Ein Heidenbuch," in *Die Jüdische Bewegung: Gesammelte Aufsätze und Ansprachen*, vol. 2 (Berlin: Jüdischer Verlag, 1920), 80. Translated in Mendes-Flohr, *From Mysticism to Dialogue*, 103.

61. Mendes-Flohr, *From Mysticism to Dialogue*, 102.

62. Brody, *Martin Buber's Theopolitics*; Avnon, *Hidden Dialogue*; Asher Wycoff, "Between Prophecy and Apocalypse: Buber, Benjamin, and Socialist Eschatology," *Political Theory* 49, no. 3 (2020): 356.

Gustav Landauer was killed on May 2, 1919. Not long after assuming the role of minister of education in the Communist Council Republic that was proclaimed in Munich on April 7, 1919, Landauer was shot dead by the reactionary militia of the Freikorps, cooperating with the Social Democratic government in Berlin. Buber honored the memory of his friend by editing his writings and letters; he spoke about him for the rest of his life. But the war had driven a wedge between Buber and Landauer, and soon Hugo Bergmann and Franz Rosenzweig stepped in as Buber's closest collaborators.

The Advent of Dialogism and the Politics of the Encounter

The friendship between Buber and Hugo Bergmann took off as Buber's relationship with Landauer faded. This second friendship had its ups and downs—the gentle Bergmann occasionally confided to his diary that he was allergic to Buber's "pathos, which I cannot endure"—but the relationship provided each of them the most stable intellectual and personal friendship of their rather long lives.[63] Buber's influence on Bergmann and other cultural Zionists from Prague set the tone for a whole generation; years later Scholem would refer to followers of Buber simply as "Prague."[64] Buber's friendship with Landauer had been grounded in their mutual attraction to both Nietzsche and anarchist politics; the friendship with the neo-Kantian Bergmann was a more mature and stable lifelong cooperation. Buber's close collaboration with Bergmann has not received the same scrutiny given to his friendships with Landauer or Rosenzweig, even though it was the longest and most fruitful of his intellectual associations. In order to understand its importance, we need to return briefly to the early 1900s, before picking up the story again in 1919.

---

63. Hugo Bergmann, journal entry, May 12, 1949, in Bergmann, *Tagebücher und Briefe*, vol. 2, *1948–1975*, ed. Miriam Sambursky (Königstein: Jüdischer Verlag bei Athenäum, 1985), 18.

64. David Biale, "Experience vs. Tradition: Reflections on the Origins of the Buber-Scholem Controversy," *Simon Dubnov Institute Yearbook* 15 (2016): 37.

Bergmann was born in Prague in 1883. At the age of eighteen he was elected head of the Zionist group Bar Kochba, supporters of cultural Zionism who constituted the most important group of German-speaking Jewish intellectuals in Prague. The group considered Buber, next to Ahad Ha'am, a major force. It sponsored the invitation that culminated in Buber's 1909 lecture series on Judaism. The audience for this lecture series included many future luminaries, such as Max Brod and Franz Kafka, the historian of nationalism Hans Kohn, the editor Robert Weltsch, the critic and editor Felix Weltsch (cousin to Robert), and many other well-known intellectuals and literary figures. Bergmann served as the group's spiritual guide, asserting a cultural and anti-territorial approach to identity, stressing the Hebrew language as the "bearer of a new, burgeoning life," and promoting a general "Judaism of life and of the future."[65] Several members of this informal association belonged to the later Prague circle, as Brod called it, a group of Czech German nationals and cultural German Jews.[66]

The two intellectuals met in 1903, when Buber was twenty-five and Bergmann, five years his junior, was a student at Charles University in Prague. A decade later Bergmann played the leading role in publishing Buber's acclaimed three lectures on Judaism (*Drei Reden*

---

65. Dimitry Shumsky, *Ben Prague Li-Yerusalaim* (Jerusalem: Leo Baeck Institute and Zalman Shazar Center, 2010), 97; Scott Spector, *Prague Territories: National Conflict and Cultural Innovation in Franz Kafka's Fin de Siècle* (Berkeley: University of California Press, 2000), 83, 138. Spector quotes from Hugo Bergmann, "Über die Bedeutung des Hebräischen für die jüdischen Studenten," *Unsere Hoffnung* 1, no. 3 (1904): 86. For a precise history of the formation of this group of intellectuals, see Dimitry Shumsky, *Zweisprachigkeit und binationale Idee: Der Prager Zionismus, 1900–1930*, trans. Dafna Mach (Göttingen: Vandenhoeck und Ruprecht, 2013), 122ff.

66. Binationalism and bilingualism stand at the center of historical investigations that emphasize plural identities and take German Jewish thinkers to be ultimate representatives of this plurality. See Steven E. Aschheim, *Beyond the Border: The German-Jewish Legacy Abroad* (Princeton, NJ: Princeton University Press, 2007); Hillel J. Kieval, *Languages of Community: The Jewish Experience in the Czech Lands* (Berkeley: University of California Press, 2000); Hagit Lavsky, *Before Catastrophe: The Distinctive Path of German Zionism* (Detroit: Wayne State University Press, 1996); Shumsky, *Ben Prague Li-Yerusalaim*.

über das Judentum, 1909–11).⁶⁷ Buber had premiered the lectures before a study group devoted to the thought of Ahad Ha'am, whom Buber lauded as "the deepest thinker of Jewish renewal."⁶⁸ The invitation to give the lectures came from Leo Herrmann (1888–1951), but Bergmann was the one to initiate the contact. After the lectures in Prague, the two became close colleagues and friends. Buber continued to give different parts of the lectures to audiences over the next decade.

It is fitting that Buber's pathbreaking lectures, which catalyzed the friendship, were to shape much of his dialogical approach. But that would come later. During the early part of the 1900s Buber was still captivated by what scholars called a Nietzschean "neo-Romantic tradition."⁶⁹ As recent scholarship has demonstrated, the young men and women who attended the lectures were "captivated by the subversive allure of [Buber's] blood rhetoric. Blood was subversive because it countered liberal integrationist aspirations and rational individuals."⁷⁰ (Bergmann had been less moved by talk of blood and Jewish origins than by Landauer's stress, in his contribution to the volume, on "heretical thoughts" and an appeal to "multifarious

---

67. The lectures were translated and published, with other lectures Buber gave about the topic in Buber, *On Judaism*, ed. Nahum N. Glatzer (New York: Schocken, 1967).

68. Martin Buber, "Ein geistiges Zentrum," *Ost und West* 2, no. 10 (1902): cols. 663–72. Translated in Martin Buber, *The First Buber: Youthful Zionist Writings of Martin Buber*, trans. Gilya G. Schmidt (Syracuse, NY: Syracuse University Press, 1999), 119.

69. Scott Spector, *Modernism without Jews? German-Jewish Subjects and Histories* (Bloomington: Indiana University Press, 2017), 13. Spector argues that "the central figure in the lectures is not blood or even Jewish essence; it is the idea of choice." If that is the case, then members of the Bar Kochba circle, as explained above, seem to have departed unconvinced; Steven E. Aschheim, *In Times of Crisis: Essays on European Culture, Germans, and Jews* (Madison: University of Wisconsin Press, 2001), 70.

70. Adi Gordon, *Toward Nationalism's End: An Intellectual Biography of Hans Kohn* (Waltham, MA: Brandeis University Press, 2017), 39. Daniel Herskowitz has shown how both Jews and Nazis recognized the subversive quality of Buber's blood metaphors. See Daniel M. Herskowitz, "Between Exclusion and Intersection: Heidegger's Philosophy and Jewish Volkism," *Leo Baeck Institute Yearbook* 65, no. 1 (2020): 135–36.

unity.")[71] In his introduction to *Vom Judentum* (*On Judaism*), the 1913 essay collection in which the lectures were published, Hans Kohn explained that they "wanted to find a path for people, a path to the realities of new Jewish life."[72] The three lectures focused on a distinctly Jewish temporality that combines a state of expectation with the hope for revival, based on *Erlebnis* and the "natural rhythm of life."[73] The first lecture, interestingly enough, concluded with an old Jewish tale that sounds very similar to Kafka's "Before the Law": "Before the gates of Rome a strange-looking beggar sits and waits. It is the messiah. Once I visited the old man and asked, 'What are you waiting for?' The old man offered an answer I did not understand at the time and would only understand much later. He said, 'For you.'"[74] In contrast, however, to Kafka's more famous parable, Buber's "For you" instead signified the hope for a leader and the realization of communal revival.

Buber's third Prague lecture discussed the renewal of Judaism and echoed the "yearning for a new, heroic life" enunciated by Nietzsche. The same vocabulary—*Erlebnis*, "rhythm," "immediacy," "renewal," "life"—that enhanced Buber and Landauer's revolutionary Lebensphilosophie enabled Buber to envision the rise of a new Jewish politics anchored in practical life: unity, action, and futurity were not

---

71. Gustav Landauer, "Sind das Ketzergedanken?," in *Vom Judentum: Ein Sammelbuch*, ed. Hans Kohn (Leipzig: Kurt Wolff, 1913), 256–57. The English translation is found in Gustav Landauer, "Jewishness Is an Inalienable Spiritual Sensibility," in *The Jew in the Modern World: A Documentary History*, 2nd ed., ed. Paul R. Mendes-Flohr and Jehuda Reinharz (New York: Oxford University Press, 1995), 276–77. See also the discussion in Gordon, *Toward Nationalism's End*, 49.

72. "wir wollten Menschen . . . einen Weg suchen, *eine Weg zu den Wirklichkeiten neuen jüdischen Lebens*." Hans Kohn, introduction to *Vom Judentum*, v.

73. Marc Volovici connected the terminology of folk, blood, and life found in these lectures to Buber's essentialist notion of Hebrew as the mark of a "life community." See Marc Volovici, *German as a Jewish Problem: The Language Politics of Jewish Nationalism* (Stanford, CA: Stanford University Press, 2020), 142.

74. Martin Buber, "The Renewal of Judaism," in Buber, *On Judaism*, ed. Nahum N. Glatzer (New York: Schocken, 1967), 21. The original German folktale is found in Buber, *Drei Reden über das Judentum* (Frankfurt: Rütten und Loening, 1920), 31. Buber introduces here his free interpretation of the Talmudic *Tractate Sanhedrin* 98a. Franz Kafka, "Before the Law," in *Complete Stories*, ed. Nahum Glatzer (New York; Schocken Books, 1971), 3–4.

abstract concepts, but the conditions for "a genuine and total renewal."[75] After criticizing Nietzsche for falling short in his attempt to "free himself from the dogma of evolution"—he still strove for a superman, after all—Buber declared that he intended to go beyond old-fashioned ideas of progress and instead gesture toward the unknown: "I am aware that when I speak of renewal [*Erneuerung*], I am leaving the domain of our time and entering that of a new time—a time to come."[76] Framing his principal message in terms of temporality, Buber explained that for him, renewal was not a gradual process of enlightenment or progress, but, instead, "something sudden and immense—by no means a continuation or an improvement, but a return [*Umkehr*], and a complete transformation." He continued:

> Indeed, just as I believe that in the life of individual man there may occur a moment of elemental reversal, a crisis and a shock, a becoming new that starts down at the roots and branches out into all existence, so do I believe that it is possible for such an upheaval to take place in the life of Judaism as well.[77]

In short, from early on Buber understood the transformative power of renewal to propel the past for the sake of present and future change. Unlike Nietzsche, he was willing to leave the secure space of philosophy and throw himself into the political whirlpool, an act accompanied by countless misunderstandings and mistakes.

When the lectures were published, in 1913, they became a must-read for liberal Central European Jews. Members of the Bar Kochba and Stefan George circles responded to *On Judaism* with articles inspired by Buber's work. Kafka bought a copy and discussed it with Bergmann, who had been instrumental in the book's publication.[78]

---

75. Buber, "The Renewal of Judaism," in Glatzer, *On Judaism*, 36; in the original German in Buber, *Drei Reden*, 62.

76. Buber, "The Renewal of Judaism," 36. Buber, *Drei Reden*, 61: "Ich bin mir also bewusst, dass ich, wenn ich von Erneuerung spreche, den Boden dieser Zeit verlasse und den einer neuen, kommenden Zeit betrete."

77. Buber, *Drei Reden*, 61.

78. Noah Isenberg, *Between Redemption and Doom: The Strains of German-Jewish Modernism* (Lincoln: University of Nebraska Press, 1999), 26; Gordon, *Toward Nationalism's End*, 27.

Buber's allusions to Hasidism in terms of immediacy and ecstasy appealed to readers of German Romanticism and adherents of life philosophy who focused on "primal human reality."[79]

In 1913 Buber returned to Prague for a second series of lectures. The first lecture series had grown out of the questions Bar Kochba members brought to Buber, but the second series brought his wide-ranging thought into meaningful synthesis. This series revolves around a distinction between the worldview of the Jew as a representative of the Orient, and of the Greek as a representative of the Occident. Buber declared, "For the Greek the world *exists*; for the Jew, it *becomes*.... The Greek apprehends it under the aspect of measure, the Jew as intent."[80] The dichotomy between the Eastern Jew and the Western Greek begins spatially but possesses a far more significant temporal quality, contrasting the dynamic sequence of *becoming*, which leads from intention to renewal and realization, with the cyclical, natural time of *being*.

Buber and Bergmann continued their intensive correspondence when Bergmann was drafted into the Austro-Hungarian army, where he served as an officer. He and Rosenzweig—who was stationed in the Balkans—continued to write to Buber and report from the front. A shared enterprise united them as they confronted the rise of antisemitism in German-speaking lands and the territorial ambitions of political Zionists. For Bergmann, Buber was himself part of the legacy of Ahad Ha'am, an opponent of territorial ambitions who described his spiritual position as the "way inward" and his work as the spiritual "present labor" (*Gegenwartsarbeit*)—a policy that focused on the varied circumstances of Jewry in the diaspora and that was rejected by the political Zionists.[81] Ahad Ha'am and his followers distanced themselves from statehood as an ultimate value and rejected Herzl's vision of an ethnic revival, which they viewed as beholden to Western liberalism and imperial powers.[82] Buber expressed

---

79. Buber, "Judaism and Mankind," in Glatzer, *On Judaism*, 23–25.
80. Martin Buber, "The Spirit of the Orient and Judaism," in Glatzer, *On Judaism*, 66, emphases in the original. See also the discussion in Mendes-Flohr, *From Mysticism to Dialogue*, 70.
81. Spector, *Prague Territories*, 140.
82. Aschheim, *Beyond the Border*, 16.

his resentment in a letter to Bergmann written in February 1918: "We should not be disappointed the majority of the Zionists turned into avid nationalists (on the European model), imperialists, and mercantilists pursuing profits. They speak about the revival, but they have only business in mind."[83]

After serving as a secretary of the Department of Culture of the Zionist Organization in London, Bergmann moved to Jerusalem in 1920, where he founded and directed the National Library and was one of the founders of the Hebrew University. He also opened a dialogue between Jewish and Palestinian intellectuals and political leaders. While in Jerusalem, Bergmann attempted to live his life according to the dialogical philosophy he adopted from Buber. Translating Buberian dialogical principles meant an openness to the Other, be it in terms of religion, ethnicity, gender, or culture. That openness served as a philosophical as well as personal motto. Bergmann's son, the psychoanalyst Martin Bergmann (1913–2014), shared with me during an interview that his father had himself taught his son Latin and had hired a teacher to teach him Arabic as well.[84] Bergmann sent Buber constant updates about life in Palestine and the cultural and academic plans he made with their mutual friends.

The heart of Buber and Bergmann's fifty-year-long friendship and cooperation was their shared understanding of dialogical philosophy, which they upheld against every form of discrimination and intolerance. At times their trust in dialogism sounded closer to faith than to a rational analysis, or political plan. Building on Platonist idealism, neo-Kantian principles, and Nietzschean critique, all mixed with prophetic rhetoric, the two integrated a long tradition of Western metaphysics with Ahad Ha'am's Jewish spiritualism.[85] But unlike Ahad Ha'am, they translated theoretical principles into an organized set of political and institutional practices.

---

83. Martin Buber to Hugo Bergmann, February 3–4, 1918, in Buber, *Briefwechsel*, 1:526, my translation.

84. My private interview with Martin Bergmann at his apartment and clinic on Fifth Avenue, New York City, October 22, 2005.

85. For more about Ahad Ha'am and his exchange about Nietzsche with Zionist leaders, see Steven J. Zipperstein, *Elusive Prophet: Ahad Ha'am and the Origins of Zionism* (Berkeley: University of California Press, 1993).

Buber acted as a major cultural force and edited the Zionist newspaper *Die Welt* (1901), established the Jüdischer Verlag publishing house (1902), and organized numerous meetings to introduce Jewish intellectuals to each other. Bergmann would later write that Buber "helped many young Zionists experience an inner liberation and a [renewed] Jewish orientation, and this spiritual impact decided the course of their lives in every possible way."[86] His friend's dialogical philosophy was notable for building bridges, for "uniting the poles," and for relying on both speech and action.[87] A new generation of secular Jews adopted a dialogical approach, embracing difference rather than assimilation, communication rather than *völkisch* unity. Buber had turned toward dialogism through his experience with German Jewish intellectuals, liberal Christian theologians, and existential philosophers, all foes of Europe's recent wave of nationalism.[88]

The foremost expression of the dialogical approach was Buber's *I and Thou* (*Ich und Du*, 1923). The book was an immediate hit among both Jewish and Christian thinkers because it argued for a close connection between the two worldviews, focusing on how both religions view the relationship between the human, the divine, and the world. Buber explained, "The attitude of man is twofold. . . . One basic word is the word pair I-You. The other basic word is the word pair I-It."[89] Unlike neo-Kantian or vitalist conceptions of the subject, Buber imagined the "I" as a relational entity, not defined in purely isolated terms but always in dialogue with another subject or object. Buber read into this framework the relationship between man, nature, and the divine, yet he was primarily fascinated by the interchange between human beings, which for him was the foundation for all other relationships. The ethical and existential dimensions of these relationships have captivated the readers of *I and*

---

86. Hugo Bergmann, "Ha'Hashiva Ha'Du-Sichit shel M.M. Buber," in *Anashim u'Drachim* [Men and ways] (Jerusalem: Mosad Bialik, 1967), 251, my translation.

87. Bergmann, *Anashim u'Drachim*, 252.

88. The theologians included Karl Barth, Emil Brunner, Friedrich Gogarten, Reinhold Niebuhr, and Paul Tillich. See Maurice S. Friedman, *Martin Buber: The Life of Dialogue* (New York: Harper, 1960), 270.

89. Buber, *I and Thou*, 53.

Thou ever since. Protestant theologian Paul Tillich, for instance, welcomed "a reaction against the tendency in the industrial society in which we are living to transform everything into an object, an 'It.'"[90] Thanks to dialogism—built on the inherent contrast between the immediacy of the I-Thou relation versus the mediated relation between I-It—German-speaking intellectuals began to appreciate the potential of merging political philosophy with the philosophy of religion and of the crucial role played by temporal concepts such as immediacy.

Attending to the recurrent stress Buber placed on temporal concepts sheds new light on the ethical and existential aspect of his thought. Responding to Augustinian Christianity, Buber declared, "[The divine/Thou] cannot be found by seeking." Instead, human relations were uniquely electrifying: "The relation to the You is unmediated. . . . Before the immediacy of the relationship everything mediate becomes negligible."[91] Similarly to Ahad Ha'am and, as we will later see, Martin Heidegger, Buber charged the present moment with spiritual meaning: "The present—not that which is like a point and merely designates whatever our thoughts may posit as the end of 'elapsed' time, the fiction of the fixed lapse, but the actual and fulfilled present—exists only insofar as presentness, encounter, and relation exist. Only as the You becomes present does presence come into being."[92]

Buber's focus on immediacy, presentness, and spiritual meaning was commensurate with the intellectual zeitgeist of the 1920s. *I and Thou* was published one year after Franz Rosenzweig's *Star of Redemption*, and four years before Heidegger's *Being and Time*. During those years, Paul Tillich was working on *The Religious Situation* (*Die religiöse Lage der Gegenwart*, 1925);[93] Walter Benjamin and Florens Christian Rang exchanged letters about time in Judaism

---

90. Paul Tillich, "Jewish Influences on Contemporary Christian Theology," *CrossCurrents* 2/3 (Spring 1952): 38.
91. Buber, *I and Thou*, 63.
92. Buber, *I and Thou*, 63.
93. Between 1942 and 1944, when Buber was engaging with the late Jewish prophets, Tillich was investigating the concept of time in theology. His work on *kairos* became a classic for postwar liberal theologians. For more on the topic, see Daniel

and Christianity; and a whole group of post-Nietzschean thinkers was adapting the thought of Dilthey, Nietzsche, and Simmel into the far-flung category of life philosophy.[94]

The project of becoming relies on the temporal gap that opens within an encounter between our past and our expectations of the future. In a recent book of essays, novelist Zadie Smith presented *I and Thou* in temporal terms: "When you meet someone you love, when you give birth, when you seem to encounter yourself in a moment of extreme physical peril—something funny happens to time on these occasions. You are uniquely attentive to the present moment. You are aware of living in it."[95] Buber himself explained this suspension of time as a state of ecstatic in-betweenness, as residing "no longer and not yet again." But the gap that forms our sense of becoming can be inhabited by the wrong kind of present-mindedness: one that reifies, rather than acknowledging the You. For Buber, this approach betrays the increasing materialism and lack of spirituality in the world: "It is the sublime melancholy of our lot that every You must become an It in our world."[96]

Indeed, for Bergmann, Kohn, and other members of Bar Kochba, the temporal order of the immediate relationship between man, nature, and the divine implied a new discourse. Bergmann explained, "We encounter in *I and Thou* new terms for the duality we discovered in *Daniel*. What was called realization in *Daniel* is now the 'relationship' between the I and Thou. What was 'orientation' in *Daniel* appears here as the 'relation' between I and It. When Buber speaks of the 'basic words,' ... [there] is a transition from one to the other."[97] The encounter of I and Thou,

---

Weidner, "Prophetic Criticism and the Rhetoric of Temporality: Paul Tillich's *Kairos* Texts and Weimar Intellectual Politics," *Political Theology* 21, no. 2 (2020): 71–88.

94. Heinrich Rickert—Benjamin and Heidegger's teacher—angrily decried Lebensphilosophie as "the most fashionable philosophy of the present." See Rickert, *Die Philosophie des Lebens: Darstellung und Kritik der philosophischen Modeströmung unserer Zeit* (Tübingen: J. C. B. Mohr, 1920).

95. Zadie Smith, "Meet Justin Bieber!," in *Feel Free* (New York: Penguin, 2018), 386.

96. Buber, *I and Thou*, 68.

97. Hugo Bergmann, *Dialogical Philosophy from Kierkegaard to Buber*, trans. Arnold A. Gerstein (Albany: SUNY Press, 1991), 226.

Bergmann explained, was not just an exchange of views and ideas, but an ontological fact, a new thing in the world. "In Buber's terminology," he wrote, "we ought to say: In the beginning is relationship, and man entered into it, and only inasmuch as man has the power to live in genuine relationship is he man, possessor of spirit and creator of culture."[98] In 1928, on the occasion of Buber's fiftieth birthday, Bergmann sent his friend a letter in which he wrote, "I read your words when I was just a high school student, and my cheeks burned.... Then came your three speeches, ... which completely changed our way of thinking as a group."[99] Bergmann moved, then, to adapt the I and Thou terminology to his everyday life and political engagement. Leading the pacifists of Brith Shalom with Buber and Scholem, he was full of hope and energy; the violent clashes between Arabs and Jews in 1929 were yet to come.

Brith Shalom collapsed in 1932–33, after a long internal debate about the right response to the rise of Arab nationalism, but its leaders continued to work for a viable spiritual and political compromise, applying the I-Thou language to ethnic conflict. In that capacity they found themselves in a paradoxical position. Though they were some of the leaders of cultural Zionism, they had little political impact outside the university and cultural centers. From 1935 to 1938 Bergmann served as the first rector of the Hebrew University in Jerusalem. In this capacity he was able to secure Buber, then living in Frankfurt, the academic position that convinced him to immigrate. After years of intense correspondence, from 1938 onward Bergmann and Buber could now meet daily to discuss their passions—reforming Jewish education in Palestine, promoting Jewish-Palestinian dialogue, and combating the foes of democracy and dialogue, first and foremost within the nationalist Zionist institutions they collaborated with and even helped run.

---

98. Bergmann, *Dialogical Philosophy*, 236.
99. Hugo Bergmann to Martin Buber, January 24, 1928, in Bergmann, *Tagebücher und Briefe*, vol. 1, *1901–1948*, ed. Miriam Sambursky (Königstein: Jüdischer Verlag bei Athenäum, 1985), 236.

The National Library in Jerusalem served the two not just as a workplace but also as an intellectual refuge. They met there often and collaborated to save Jewish collections, during and after the Holocaust. The two friends also established the translation committee at the Mosad Bialik publishing house. Joining high-level intellectuals and public figures who served as translators or edited translations, this committee united some of the best-known names of the time, including their other close collaborator, Gershom Scholem, and David Ben Gurion, the prime minister of the young Israeli state. (Ben Gurion resigned from the committee when Bergmann, Buber, and Sholem criticized his authoritarian conduct during the mid-1950s.) In their work for the committee, Buber and Bergmann secured a series of translations from German, English, and French, bringing the modern philosophical canon into modern Hebrew for the first time. In addition to holding the personal archives of the two philosophers, the National Library still houses documents attesting to this great philosophical endeavor. Their archives contain thousands of letters, the majority of which attest to the intensive exchange between the two men over six decades, from the Prague lectures to their deaths. Moving back and forth between German and Hebrew, they cover every personal trouble and philosophical contemplation, political analysis and institutional deliberation. In contrast to Buber's close cooperation with Franz Rosenzweig, dedicated to the theological aspects of the Jewish revival, the conversation with Bergmann was a deeply committed and intimate dialogue about institutional realization. I shall return to Bergmann and the question of realization at the end of this chapter. First, though, a short synopsis of Buber's close collaborations with Franz Rosenzweig, Franz Werfel, and Stefan Zweig is due.

The Imperative of Reconsidering Jewish-Christian Relations

Martin Buber and Franz Rosenzweig met briefly in 1914, when the former was a leading member of the Forte circle (1910–15) founded by Florens Christian Rang, a Catholic philosopher who expressed views critical of the Church. The circle also included the convert Eugen Rosenstock-Huessy, Rosenzweig's other lifelong friend.[100] In addition to his work as a social philosopher and theologian, Rosenstock-Huessy helped found the Patmos circle, a group that was associated with the Protestant publishing house Patmos Verlag and that based itself on the Forte circle. The Patmos group included the theologian Karl Barth, the philosopher Hans Ehrenberg (Rosenzweig's cousin), Viktor von Weizsäcker, Buber, and Rosenzweig. Discussion often centered on biblical eschatology and the war.[101]

Rosenstock-Huessy, Buber, and Rosenzweig would later work on *Die Kreatur* (1926–30), a journal edited by Buber, Weizsäcker, and the Catholic theologian Joseph Wittig. The title of the journal alluded to the idea that, as Rosenstock-Huessy said, the creaturely was not only the meeting place of the three confessions, but also the basis for the "rebirth of the German language."[102] *Die Kreatur* extended the work begun by another journal, *Der Jude* (1916–28)—which had created a space for "the Jew who experiences the fate of Europe"—by emphasizing "the shared messianic longing of . . . Jewish, Protestant, and Catholic constituents, longings grounded not only in the figure of exile but also in a solidarity with all creaturely life."[103] As we shall see below, both the temporality (kairology) of

---

100. The Forte circle included Erich Gutkind, Florens Christian Rang, Frederik Willem van Eeden, Walter Rathenau, and Theodor Däubler. Buber and Landauer joined early, only to withdraw later. See Gershom Scholem, *From Berlin to Jerusalem: Memories of My Youth*, trans. Harry Zohn (Philadelphia: Paul Dry, 2012), 81. Christine Holste tells us that Buber proposed inviting Margarete Susman to join. See Christine Holste, "'Menschen von Potsdam': Der Forte-Kreis (1910–1915)," in *Der Potsdamer Forte-Kreis: Eine utopische Intellektuellenassoziation zur europäischen Friedenssicherung*, ed. Richard Faber and Christine Holste (Würzburg: Königshausen und Neumann, 2001), 21.

101. Knut Martin Stünkel, "Eugen Rosenstock-Huessy's Early Symblysmatic Experiences: The Sociology of *Patmos* and *Die Kreatur*," *Culture, Theory and Critique* 56, no. 1 (2015): 15.

102. Eugen Rosenstock-Heussy, *Ja und Nein: Autobiographische Fragmente* (Heidelberg: L. Schneider, 1968), 268. Translated in Stünkel, "Symblysmatic Experiences," 20.

103. Martin Buber, "Die Losung," *Der Jude* (1916–17): 1–3. For translations from *Die Kreatur* 1, no. 2, see Eric L. Santner, *On Creaturely Life: Rilke, Benjamin,*

divine intervention and the rebirth of language were crucial for Buber's understanding of how dialogue served Jews as they came to grips with Christianity and what it meant to be a European.

I and Thou is a philosophical reflection about dialogue or communication in general, but it is equally a book about Jewish-Christian relations.[104] In September 1922, a short time before the book's publication, Buber exchanged a series of letters with Rang about the meaning of relation (*Beziehung*), an exchange Buber discussed with Rosenzweig.[105] Rang, who had also read the book's galleys, asked, "What makes you hit upon so pallid a word as 'relation'?" He then answered his own question by contrasting Buber's secular starting point with Augustine's committed religiosity:

> Answer: Because you proceed from the I-Thou (and I-It) as if these existed humanly, still without God—and were thus expressible along the line of general speech. . . . Augustine—in a situation similar to yours, he too addressing himself to the scientifically cultivated minds of his age—spoke in his *Confessions* in language full of intellectual juices because he did not say I-Thou but only Thou, only God—and *I* not as others but as God's reflection. I am speaking not of Augustine's theology but of the emotionality of his speech *in* God.[106]

Sebald (Chicago: University of Chicago Press, 2006), 38. A competing group of theologians, among them Karl Barth, Friedrich Gogarten, and Emil Brunner, worked in parallel terms, founded the journal *Zwischen den Zeiten* (1922), and laid out the origins of dialectical theology. As Peter Gordon has demonstrated, however, Gogarten turned increasingly to nationalist ideology and decisionist politics for inspiration, and the group broke up. See Peter E. Gordon, "Weimar Theology: From Historicism to Crisis," in *Weimar Thought: A Contested Legacy*, ed. Peter E. Gordon and John P. McCormick (Princeton, NJ: Princeton University Press, 2015), 160.

104. Rivka Horwitz has argued that a clear change became apparent in Buber's rhetoric between 1922 and 1923, following the start of his close cooperation with Rosenzweig at the Frankfurt Lehrhaus and before the writing of *I and Thou*. The change occurred in parallel to his dialogue with Tillich and Rang. See Horwitz, *Buber's Way to I and Thou: An Historical Analysis and the First Publication of Martin Buber's Lectures "Religion als Gegenwart"* (Heidelberg: Schneider, 1978), 184–85.

105. Rang, a close friend to Walter Benjamin and a theologian and member of the Forte circle, took Nietzsche's emphasis on *Erlebnis* and life to be the dynamo behind a new alliance of politics and theology. See Carrie L. Asman, "Theater and Agon / Agon and Theater: Walter Benjamin and Florens Christian Rang," *MLN* 107, no. 3 (1992): 610.

106. Florens Christian Rang to Martin Buber, September 19, 1922, in *The Letters of Martin Buber: A Life of Dialogue*, trans. Richard Winston, Clara

Rang recognized that *I and Thou*, like Augustine's *Confessions*, is written in the first person to a divine Thou, and that, like Augustine, Buber was concerned with the birth of new language to express the I-Thou relation. Unlike Augustine, the father of systematic theology, however, Buber's theology assumed a divine presence that functions as a metaphor or as a presence that is implied rather than literal.[107] Rang's critical comment was important enough to merit a response in the book's epigraph, as well as in its interpretation of "Thou." "So, waiting I have won from you the end: In all elements—God's present [*Gegenwart*]."[108] The book advances, contra Rang, a parallel, perhaps a counter, Augustinian relationship with both worldly and transcendent Thous on the basis of human time and experience. Although Augustine intends to mark only an intimate and immediate relation to the divine, Buber always begins in the presence of a human Thou.[109] Unlike Augustine, or his Protestant interpreters, Buber found in cultural Zionism a concrete answer that extended the I from the I-Thou of the man-God relation to the I-Thou of modern politics. Augustine was the father of Christian "self," and Buber became the originator of modern Jewish "dialogue."

Rosenzweig, like Rang, also objected to Buber's assertion that the origin of the dialogical relation was intrahuman. In a letter dated

---

Winston, and Harry Zohn (New York: Schocken, 1991), 28, letter no. 277, emphasis in original.

107. A few commentators have noted the close and explicit affinity between Rosenzweig's *Star of Redemption* and Augustine's *City of God*. Virginia Burrus pointed out, following Elliot Wolfson, that each positions his system as the beginning of a "new theology" or "new thinking," and the notion that the Jewish and Christian miracle "marks the openness of time's flow." See Burrus, "Augustine, Rosenzweig, and the Possibility of Experiencing Miracle," in *Material Spirit: Religion and Literature Intranscendent*, ed. Gregory C. Stallings, Manuel Asensi, and Carl Good (New York: Fordham University Press, 2013), 98.

108. Buber quoted Goethe in this epigraph: "So hab ich endlich von dir erharrt: In allen Elementen Gottes Gegenwart" (Goethe, "Der Schenke," in Goethe's poetry collection *West-Östlicher Divan*). My translation of the motto changes Buber's translator's (Walter Kaufmann) stress on "God's presence" to "God's present."

109. According to Walter Kaufmann, *I and Thou* responds to a motto from Augustine—*Mundus vult decipi, ergo decipiatur* (The world wants to be deceived, so let it be deceived). Kaufmann's ironic reference responded to Buber's own opening sentence—"Men's attitudes are manifold"—but also to his own present. Walter Kaufmann, "I and You: A Prologue," in Martin Buber, *I and Thou*, 9.

September 20, 1922, Rosenzweig instead argued that a dialogical relation originated between the individual and God. He emphasized how difficult it is to ground dialogue in an ontology of I and Thou: "These past few days I have been obsessed by the question of what it means in general that 'another' 'also' thinks. When we are up against alien thinking, really alien, such as Simmel's, say, this question doesn't even arise; such thinking simply does not concern us." The reason Rosenzweig considered the relation to the stranger or alien so different from Buber's ideal of pure communication was that with a stranger there is no "community of thought only now coming into being. It is not aimed toward any particular goal."[110] In other words, although Rosenzweig accepted Buber's emphasis on relation—loosely anchored in Jewish ethics—he thought that imposing a communal ideal on an urban, possibly alienated set of relationships was a mistake. Rosenzweig tried to convince Buber to cleave more closely to Jewish political theology.[111]

In his responses to both Rang and Rosenzweig, Buber emphasized the temporal ontology of all relations. Similarly to Walter Benjamin's analysis of the law in mythic and political terms (*Critique of Violence*, 1921), Buber understood the I-Thou relationship in temporal-political terms that implied an alternative understanding of the law, both divine and human. In a letter to Rosenzweig dated July 13, 1924, he wrote: "I do not consider God a lawgiver; only man can be a lawgiver. For that reason, for me the law is personal, not universal."[112] The meeting between I, Thou, and world was a temporal relation, stressing a personal quality of lived experience

---

110. Franz Rosenzweig to Martin Buber, September 20, 1922, in *Letters of Martin Buber*, 285.

111. As Steven Kepnes has shown, quoting from Rosenzweig's *Star of Redemption* and Augustine's *Confessions*, Rosenzweig's interpretation of Jewish holidays and practices stands close to Augustine's perception of time, especially in relation to creation and redemption. The performative aspect of Jewish liturgy is meant to celebrate remembrance of "the history . . . [that] is a fully compact present," and that is "'born anew' in each generation." Kepnes, "Rosenzweig's Liturgical Reasoning as Response to Augustine's Temporal Aporias," in *Liturgy, Time, and the Politics of Redemption*, ed. Randi Rashkover and C. C. Picknold (Cambridge: Eerdmans, 2006), 120.

112. Martin Buber to Franz Rosenzweig, July 13, 1924, in Buber, *Briefwechsel*, 2:200.

and the immediacy of Jewish life. Buber explained this idea in *I and Thou*: "The You appears in time, but in that of a process that is fulfilled in itself—a process lived through not as a piece that is a part of a constant and organized sequence but in a 'duration' whose purely intensive dimension can be determined only by starting from the You."[113] He juxtaposed this temporal understanding of the "living experience of relation" (*Beziehungserlebnis*) with the literal understanding of a divine lawgiver in the spatial world, and "the exclusive way" in which "the You appears in space."[114]

Though Buber and Rosenzweig disagreed about the basic relationship at the heart of I-Thou relations, they agreed that the temporal structure of this relationship was linked to German Jewish culture and thought. In the words of Sylvie Anne Goldberg, Rosenzweig, much like Buber, thought that Jewish thinking about time could be summarized quite neatly: "Ideas about creation, revelation, and redemption represent the past, embody the present, and foresee the future."[115] Both men understood their initiative as a simultaneous contribution to both German and Jewish culture, and both attempted to distance themselves from the "vulgar speech" of nationalists who hoped to revive an authentic sense of biblical "living there and then."[116] According to the two thinkers, the German Jewish mission was to forge a tight connection between the ancient past and the modern present, monotheistic ethics and modern universal politics. Neither Buber nor Rosenzweig, however, proved immune to the racial rhetoric that became popular in Germany after 1900. By the late

---

113. Buber, *I and Thou*, 81. As Walter Kaufmann, Buber's translator and editor, adds in his fn. 8, in 1937 Buber explained that "duration" was an explicit allusion to Henri Bergson's *durée*.

114. Buber, *I and Thou*, 81.

115. Sylvie Anne Goldberg, *Clepsydra: Essay on the Plurality of Time in Judaism*, trans. Benjamin Ivry (Stanford, CA: Stanford University Press, 2016), 54.

116. Marc Volovici, *German as a Jewish Problem*, 171–72. Volovici described Rosenzweig and Buber's approach as "rendering the German language 'more Jewish'" even as they aimed to make it less Zionist-Hebraist. But the partisans were good Nietzscheans, and they also aimed to make German more German. Not identity, but one's understanding of temporality or life, would affect one's approach to language. In other terms, translating the Bible was a political and philosophical initiative as well as an attempt to reshape Jewish identity.

1910s, David Biale argues, the antisemitic use of blood as a racial signifier forced Rosenzweig "to adopt the very accusation that anti-Semites made against Jews—that the Jews were a quintessentially racial community—and drew the opposite conclusion. . . . The Jewish blood community had no need for miscegenation or intermarriage, for it remained splendidly autochthonous."[117] The two collaborators entertained, then, a corresponding notion of the Jewish community but colored it differently.[118] After the end of World War I and the assassination of Landauer, Buber took a more coolheaded and careful approach as he shifted to a more institutional mode of operation. Their ideas of Jewish community thus implied an alternative idea of time, both political and theological. Buber's commitment to cultural Zionism conflicted with Rosenzweig's rejection of national realization, and Buber's practical institutional interests remained distinct from Rosenzweig's theological metaphors. Still, both thinkers saw consciousness as what must be in the present, located in "the hour of need" between past and future, set on the path that leads from one to the other. In short, a spiritual and ethical understanding of the encounter contains the highest form of abstraction: the inversion of time.[119]

---

117. David Biale, *Blood and Belief: The Circulation of a Symbol between Jews and Christians* (Berkeley: University of California Press, 2007), 204.

118. As Andrea Dara Cooper has noted, Rosenzweig took on Buber's earlier Prague lectures in his *Star of Redemption* a decade later, and continued to develop filial blood lineages, while integrating the symbol of maternal milk into the patriarchic line of succession. See Cooper, *Gendering Modern Jewish Thought* (Bloomington: Indiana University Press, 2021), 24–63, esp. 43–44. For more on the subject, see also Elliot R. Wolfson, "Light Does Not Talk but Shines: Apophasis and Visions in Rosenzweig's Theopoetic Temporality," in *New Directions in Jewish Philosophy*, ed. Elliot R. Wolfson and Aaron W. Hughes (Bloomington: Indiana University Press, 2010), 103–4; Zachary Braiterman, *The Shape of Revelation: Aesthetics and Modern Jewish History and Culture* (Stanford, CA: Stanford University Press, 2007), 235; Sam Shonkoff, "Gender in Martin Buber's Hasidic Tales," *Leo Baeck Institute Year Book* (2023): 1–17.

119. Cynthia D. Coe has shown how this notion of immediacy contributed to Emmanuel Levinas's perception of ethics after 1945. Grounded in Bergson, Husserl, Heidegger, and Rosenzweig, Levinas identified immediacy with "an urgency of responsibility." Coe explains: "In its immediacy, the face imposes the command 'Thou shalt not kill,' and that command forbids both physical violence and the violence that assimilates the other into a mere idea." Coe, *Levinas and the Trauma of Responsibility:*

From 1925 until Rosenzweig's death in 1929, the two men collaborated on translating the Hebrew Bible into German. After Rosenzweig's death Buber continued to work on the translation, which was published in increments and completed in 1961. This project was deeply informed by both men's desire to capture the immediacy of the Bible, to find a language that would make it fresh to present-day readers. Buber wrote, "The passage of time had largely turned the Bible into a palimpsest. The original traits of the Bible . . . had been overlaid by a familiar abstraction, in origin partly theological and partly literary."[120] The answer to this project of renewal lay in a novel use and understanding of language. The project was anchored in their mutual understanding, described by Rosenzweig in 1921, that "we are the inheritors and carriers of this [revived] language. We are those who grasp its power of 'not yet' [*noch nicht*] and bring it back to history."[121] What is the not-yet? Writing in 1930, a year after Rosenzweig's death, Buber explained that they had hoped to capture the immediacy of the book's language while recognizing its archaic form.[122] They meant to revive

---

The Ethical Significance of Time (Bloomington: Indiana University Press, 2018), x, 125. Adorno marks the opposite disposition, especially in his response to the student revolution and his warning that immediate or hasty political action amounts to a misguided action against "an index of what is right and better." Theodor W. Adorno, "Critique," in *Critical Models: Interventions and Catchwords*, trans. Henry W. Pickford (New York: Columbia University Press, 1998), 281–88. For a discussion of Adorno's text, see Martin Shuster, *How to Measure a World? A Philosophy of Judaism* (Bloomington: Indiana University Press, 2021), 79.

120. Martin Buber, "On Word Choice in Translating the Bible," in Martin Buber and Franz Rosenzweig, *Scripture and Translation*, trans. Lawrence Rosenwald and Everett Fox (Bloomington: Indiana University Press, 1994), 73. Quoted in Batnitzky, "Revelation and *Neues Denken*," 92.

121. "Und wir sind die Erben und Träger dieser Sprache. Wir sind die, die in Kraft dieser Sprache ihr 'Noch nicht' in die Geschichte hineinrufen." Franz Rosenzweig, "Vom Geist der hebräischen Sprache," in *Der Mensch und Sein Werk*, vol. 3, *Zweistromland: Kleinere Schriften zu Glauben und Denken* (The Hague: Nijhoff, 1984), 721, my translation.

122. Rosenzweig also makes this claim in "Das Formgeheimnis der biblischen Erzählung," in Martin Buber and Franz Rosenzweig, *Die Schrift und ihre Verdeutschung* (Berlin: Schocken, 1936), 239–61. I thank Sophie Duvernoy for this reference.

"the original character of the book as manifested in word choice, in syntax, and in rhythmical articulation."[123]

Curiously, this definition resembles Benjamin's notion of "translatability," formulated in "The Task of the Translator" (1921) as "a specific significance inherent in the original [that] manifests itself in its translatability, ... [just as] the manifestations of life are intimately connected with the phenomenon of life ... [and] its afterlife."[124] There are no indications that Buber and Rosenzweig had read Benjamin's essay, but all three wished to reconnect a German Jewish sense of time to ideas of the German avant-garde of the early 1920s.[125] All three men stressed, as did the followers of Stefan George, performative elements such as translatability, or vocal and rhythmic reading. Buber and Rosenzweig were convinced that the transition from reading out loud to silent reading meant that "the Hebrew sounds stopped having an immediate effect on the reader who is not a hearer."[126] In their translation, they wished to bring out this immediate effect for readers, so that they could "grasp again the uniting life of the Bible and the essence of our interlacing flow of time."[127]

One finds Buber and Rosenzweig's temporal concepts echoing in other close contexts. For example, Gershom Scholem—another avid reader of Buber, Rosenzweig, and Stefan George—emphasized "the silent rhythm" as the secret of Jewish scripture.[128] For Scholem, the verbal performance of the liturgical texts stressed its temporal

---

123. Quoted in Batnitzky, "Revelation and *Neues Denken*," 93.
124. Walter Benjamin, "The Task of the Translator," in *Selected Writings*, vol. 1, *1913–1926*, ed. Marcus Bullock and Michael W. Jennings (Cambridge, MA: Harvard University Press, 1996), 254.
125. Benjamin met and corresponded with Buber. He met Rosenzweig in 1922, but by then Rosenzweig was already paralyzed with the amyotrophic lateral sclerosis that would cause his death in 1929. Benjamin met Eugen Rosenstock-Huessy at Rosenzweig's bedside. See Howard Eiland and Michael W. Jennings, *Walter Benjamin: A Critical Life* (Cambridge, MA: Harvard University Press, 2014), 179.
126. Martin Buber, *Broschüre* (Berlin: Lambert Schneider, 1930), in Martin Buber, *Werke*, 14:68–85. See the discussion in Bourel, *Martin Buber*, 366.
127. Martin Buber, "Der Mensch von heute und die jüdische Bibel," in Buber and Rosenzweig, *Die Schrift*, 55.
128. Gershom Scholem, "On Lament and Lamentation," trans. Lina Barouch and Paula Schwebel, *Jewish Studies Quarterly* 21, no. 1 (2014): 6.

characteristics: repetition and difference recapitulate both an inherited traditional form and a revolutionary "Zarathustrian truth" about lived experience.[129]

The translation, published in installments, was not met with universal acclaim. The critic and writer Siegfried Kracauer declared that the tremendous sense of immediacy with which Martin Luther had endowed his German translation was lacking because of the archaizing influence of Stefan George's German on Buber and Rosenzweig's vocabulary. Kracauer instead found the translation overdetermined and accused the translators of "Wagnerizing" their material.[130] Buber and Rosenzweig replied by describing their effort as an attempt to reach "a thing of unanchored spirit ... [the] superstructure of life."[131] The beating heart of the text was revealed, in their opinion, through their choice of rhythmic language.[132]

Hannah Arendt reviewed the translation far more positively. In her view, Buber and Rosenzweig's translation reversed and overcame the achievement of Moses Mendelssohn one hundred and fifty years earlier. Mendelssohn had "enabled the youth of the ghetto to learn German [while] in our own day, Buber's marvelous undertaking is but a circuitous way of bringing the Jews back to Hebrew, the language of the Bible; a way of bringing them back to the Jewish past, its values and requirements."[133] She praised the translators' desire to emulate the Bible's oral poetry, the rhythm of what they described as

---

129. See the excellent summary in Ghilad H. Sehnhav, "Abyss and Messiah: Gershom Scholem and the Question of Language" (dissertation submitted to Tel-Aviv University, 2021), 73–76.

130. Siegfried Kracauer, "Die Bibel auf deutsch," in *Werke*, vol. 5, part 1, *Essays, Feuilletons, Rezensionen, 1906–1923*, ed. Inka Mülder-Bach (Frankfurt: Suhrkamp, 1990), 258.

131. Buber and Rosenzweig, *Die Schrift*, 15. See also Lawrence Rosenwald, "On the Reception of Buber and Rosenzweig's Bible," *Prooftexts* 14, no. 2 (1994): 147.

132. Rosenwald acknowledged the debt to George but argued that in contrast to the "rich but often bland ephony of George's pentametric melody," Buber and Rosenzweig's rhythm had "more in common with the rhythm of some of the best Gentile religious verse of its time: the Rilke of *Duino Elegies*, or even the Eliot of *The Wasteland*." See Rosenwald, "Buber and Rosenzweig's Bible," 155.

133. Hannah Arendt, "A Guide for Youth: Martin Buber," in Arendt, *The Jewish Writings*, ed. Jerome Kohn and Ron H. Feldman (New York: Schocken, 2007), 33.

its "breathing units," and the "signaling of underlying themes by the repetition of words."[134] The German, wrote Buber and Rosenzweig, was organized into "natural speech-units, dictated by the laws of breathing and delineated according to meaning."[135]

Buber and Rosenzweig's translation was a paradigmatic example of a German Jewish understanding of temporality that integrated ancient and modern language, Jewish and Christian theologies, secular and religious layers of meaning, and the individual body and collective connotation. But above all, their translation attempted to convey the presentness of the Hebrew language. The breathing unit—probably following the advice Stefan George famously gave to readers of poetry—put the stress on the equality of all living and breathing creatures, as they attempt to adapt their means of expression to the demands of the changing times.[136]

The Theopolitical Hour: Between Jeremiah and Paul

From the mid-1920s onward, Buber attempted to unite the "breathing unit" with both the theological and the political dimensions, revival and dialogue, in the form of a new theopolitics. In a key chapter in *The Prophetic Faith* entitled "The Theopolitical Hour" (*HaSha'a Ha'Theo-Politit*), Buber summed up one decade of thought on the matter.[137] The heart of his concept of theopolitics was the ability of humans—and prophets—to identify the "real decision."[138]

---

134. Buber and Rosenzweig, *Scripture and Translation*, 65. See also Leora Batnitzky, "Translation as Transcendence: A Glimpse into the Workshop of the Buber-Rosenzweig Bible Translation," *New German Critique* 70 (1997): 88.

135. Martin Buber and Franz Rosenzweig, *Scripture and Translation*, 179. See also Volovici, *German as a Jewish Problem*, 169.

136. Stefan George identified reading aloud "with a sonorous, retrained voice that reverberated like a bell" with true poetic sensibility. He often made his disciples read aloud naked. Robert E. Norton, *Secret Germany: Stefan George and His Circle* (Ithaca, NY: Cornell University Press, 2018), 397–98.

137. The book was first published in Hebrew in 1942. Buber, *Torat Hanevi'im* (Tel-Aviv: Dvir, 1942).

138. I am referring here to Giorgio Agamben's stress on the "real state of exception" after Walter Benjamin's *Theses on the Concept of History* (1940). See

The language of decision—distinct from Carl Schmitt and Martin Heidegger's use of the concept—alludes to the *actuality* of the hermeneutic effort. Translating the Bible sent a message to German Jews and Christians about its relevance for contemporaneous German Jewish relations.[139] This "real decision" at the "hour of need" would bring about a concrete and critical moment of unity with the Other and the Thou, and (in contrast to Schmitt's 1922 *Political Theology*) a rejection of hierarchy. Likewise, prophetic language was truly dialogical and egalitarian, a quality that Buber believed distinguished his thought from Heidegger's: "In Heidegger's world there is no such Thou, no true Thou spoken from being to being."[140]

Buber's stress on the "hour of need" was grounded in a broader view of individual and collective ethics, but also in a critical understanding of history. During the 1950s Buber argued against Heidegger's claim that history disclosed the ontological meaning of being and against Hegel's view that history is the arena in which the world spirit attains self-consciousness. "For Heidegger historical existence is the illumination of being itself; in neither [Hegel nor Heidegger] is there room for a suprahistorical reality that sees history and judges it."[141]

In political terms, understanding life and history as an active communication between equal human beings translates into what I call temporal egalitarianism: all life is equal, and every life defines itself in relation to another, a Thou. In that respect Buber united his understanding of immediacy and *Erlebnis* with the critical mission of

---

Giorgio Agamben, *Homo Sacer: Sovereign Power and Bare Life*, trans. Daniel Heller-Roazen (Stanford, CA: Stanford University Press, 1998), 55.

139. In his later writings Buber "intimates that reaching the heart of his philosophical differences with Heidegger would necessitate a 'religious dialogue.'" See Daniel M. Herskowitz, *Heidegger and His Jewish Reception* (Cambridge: Cambridge University Press, 2021), 130.

140. Martin Buber, "What Is Man?," in *Between Man and Man*, trans. Ronald Gregor-Smith (London: Routledge, 2002), 204. See also Herskowitz, *Heidegger*, 133.

141. Martin Buber, "The Validity and Limitations of Political Principle," in *Pointing the Way*, trans. Maurice Friedman (New York: Harper, 1957), 215. See also Paul Mendes-Flohr, "Martin Buber and Martin Heidegger in Dialogue," *Journal of Religion* 94, no. 1 (2014): 10.

the late Jewish prophets. He positioned a realist understanding of "usable past" with an ethical-political stance. Buber contrasted realism and ethics with Paul's complacency when he instructs, "Let every soul be subject unto the higher powers" (Letter to the Romans 13:1), and he denounced the exclusionary political theology of modern Paulinians such as Schmitt and the Lutheran theologian Friedrich Gogarten.[142] As we shall see below, Buber believed their positions would inherently incline toward hierarchy and violence.

Buber had already pursued the topic of prophetic rhetoric in the Prague lectures, but it became the heart of a new theopolitical theory in the *Kingship of God* (1932) and, eight years later, in *The Prophetic Faith*. Historical circumstances, "the hour of need," changed Buber's earlier aim: the "prophetic" idea of 1913—at the time committed to the future of German-speaking Jews and cultural Zionism—turned into a defense against fascism. Beginning in the early 1930s, Buber spoke about the "theopolitical realism" of the prophets, noting their willingness to stand up to secular potentates in concrete political terms. Sometimes they were called on to act outside of their religious vocation.[143] In both his political and his theological role, the prophet was oriented toward the future and committed to dissent. Still, hope and rebelliousness were channeled into the attempt to reform the state—not abolish it, as Landauer had wished to do. Buber wrote,

> The world of prophetic faith is in fact historical reality, seen in the bold and penetrating glance of the man who dares to believe. What here prevails is indeed a special kind of politics, theopolitics, which is concerned [with] establishing a certain people in a certain historical situation under

---

142. In the second preface to *Political Theology* (1934), Schmitt identifies Gogarten as a major inspiration for his theory of secularization. See Carl Schmitt, *Political Theology: Four Chapters on the Concept of Sovereignty*, trans. George Schwab (Chicago: University of Chicago Press, 1985), 2. For a splendid discussion of biblical hermeneutics as a usable past, see Claire E. Sufrin, "Buber, the Bible, and Hebrew Humanism: Finding a Usable Past," *Modern Judaism* 38, no. 1 (2018): 29–43.

143. "In order to show that at times they are expected to go beyond religious activities . . . sometimes it [i.e., the prophecy] turned into [a call] to rebel." Buber, *Torat Ha-nevi'im*, 141.

the divine sovereignty, so that this people is brought nearer the fulfillment of its task, to become the beginning of the kingdom of God.[144]

The theocratic and revolutionary optimism of this passage, the plan to fix both divine and human rule, attracted little attention. Nothing is more characteristic of Buber's theopolitics, however, than this stress on concrete action and fulfillment. It would not be far-fetched to assume that Buber identified this theopolitical realism with his own principle as a public intellectual. The relationships he developed with leading voices of that generation illustrate this point.

Nietzsche's *On the Use and Abuse of History for Life* demonstrates that reading historical or scriptural texts to suit current needs was standard practice in the late nineteenth and early twentieth centuries.[145] That practice can be found in the works of liberal theologians, such as Ernst Troeltsch's *On the Historical and Dogmatic Methods in Theology* (1898); Adolph von Harnack's revival of the Paulinian Gnostic interpretation in *Marcion: The Gospel of the Alien God* (1920); Julius Wellhausen's *Prolegomena to the History of Israel* (1878); Hermann Cohen's "The Style of the Prophets" (1901); and Leo Baeck's *Das Wesen des Judentums* (1905). Among those acclaimed innovators, many of them close readers and interpreters of the prophets, Buber was the first to cast the prophets as advocates of an egalitarian worldview. For him they represented foes of free-market capitalism who foreshadowed Nietzsche, offering human beings the opportunity to engage in an equal dialogue with both world and God. For Buber, a direct line led from antimonarchic judges such as Samuel to antimonarchic prophets, and from there to a post-Nietzschean Jewish revival; he stressed a consistent resistance to human hierarchy in Jewish scripture, next to a presentist stress on realization.

In early twentieth-century Germany, there was a great intellectual vogue for the concept of prophecy. Wolf Lepenies has shown that

---

144. Buber, *The Prophetic Faith* (Princeton: Princeton University Press, 2016), 167–68. The current translation is based on a 1949 translation by Carlyle Witton-Davies with a new introduction by Jon D. Levennson.

145. David Myers pointed to the crucial importance of this text to early 1900s German Jewish intellectuals. See Myers, *Resisting History*, 4.

prophetic epithets were attached to leading thinkers from Nietzsche to Heinrich Mann.[146] For his best seller about Rembrandt (1890), Julius Langbehn was labeled a prophet of modern aesthetics.[147] Modern philosophy adopted the figure of the poet—from Hölderlin, via Nietzsche and his followers, to George—as a new, modern version of the prophet.[148] Followers identified every philosopher-king with a poetic prophet.[149] A common thread was tracing the lineage that connected the Germans to the ancient Greeks while Christianizing the Jewish prophets. German Jewish authors viewed this revisionist work with suspicion and responded by reclaiming the figure of the *navi* (*navi la-goyim*, the prophet to the gentiles) as a unifying force between Orient and Occident, Jew and Christian, ancient and modern.[150] A secularized version of that view linked a modern version of an aesthetic or political seer with ancient ancestors. As mentioned above, Buber referred to Nietzsche as "an apostle to life"; Landauer, in turn, called Buber "the Jewish apostle to humanity."[151] Had not Jeremiah offered a "prophecy to the nations," and Paul a "prophecy to the gentiles"?[152] Both prophets became the center of speculation and writing for German Jewish thinkers during the 1910s.

---

146. Wolf Lepenies, *The Seduction of German Culture in German History* (Princeton, NJ: Princeton University Press, 2006), 26–29.

147. Julius Langbehn, *Rembrandt als Erzieher* (Leipzig: C. L. Hirschfeld, 1896).

148. Charles Bambach, *Heidegger's Roots: Nietzsche, National Socialism, and the Greeks* (Ithaca, NY: Cornell University Press, 2003), 245–80; Daniel Weidner, "Mächtige Worte: Zur Politik der Prophetie in der Weimarer Republik," in *Prophetie und Prognostik: Verfügungen über Zukunft in Wissenschaften, Religionen und Künsten*, ed. Daniel Weidner and Stefan Willer (Munich: W. Fink, 2013), 37–58.

149. For a Neoplatonist interpretation and reception of the "philosopher-king," see Dana Hollander, "'Plato Prophesied the Revelation': The Philosophico-Political Theology of Strauss's Philosophy and Law and the Guidance of Hermann Cohen," in *Judaism, Liberalism, and Political Theology*, ed. Randi Rashkover and Martin Kavka (Bloomington: Indiana University Press, 2014), 74.

150. For more about Protestant theology and "political-religious dialectics," see Daniel Weidner, "The Political Theology of Ethical Monotheism," in Rashkover and Kavka, *Judaism, Liberalism, and Political Theology*, 178–96.

151. Gustav Landauer, "Martin Buber," in *Der werdende Mensch: Aufsätze über Leben und Schrifttum* (Potsdam: Kiepenheuer, 1921), 244–46.

152. For a close reading of Jeremiah's "prophet unto the nations" (Jer. 1:5) next to Paul's "prophecy to the gentiles," see Femi Adeyemi, *Covenant Torah in Jeremiah and Paul: The Law of Christ in Paul* (New York: Peter Lang, 2006).

In this context, then, we can trace Buber's interest in the prophets, Jewish and Christian, an essential step in developing a thorough understanding of his theopolitics. In the fall of 1917 Bergmann and Buber corresponded about the relevance of Paul to Jewish and Christian eschatology, with Bergmann warning, "We should not narrow the abyss that has opened between Paul and later generations."[153] In his response, Buber took up the question of how the experience of time interacted with belief:

> Persistent experience with the unredeemed world ... forced the believers to divide Christ [as Paul does] into he who had come and he who would come. ... This meant the splitting of the temporal aspect of existence into something within and something without. Such splitting is at odds with the Jewish faith in the Messiah, which regards the messianic function of man to be, in addition to absolute fulfillment, an indissoluble blending of within and without, "rising of the sparks" and raising of humanity.[154]

Simply put, in his response Buber warned against the Paulinian separation between the prophetic (past, Jewish, inclusive) and the messianic (future, Christian, exclusive) as a means of excluding Jews. As I have shown, both Buber and Bergmann believed that modern Jewish prophecy would bridge the gap between within and without, Jew and Christian, modern and ancient, East and West. In 1919, five months after Landauer was murdered, Bergmann discussed the historical role of Judaism in different nations in Europe and different minorities in a multicultural entity, which later would develop into his description of Prague's German Jews as a "culture of bridges," between not only Jews and Christians but also Muslims and Buddhists. For Bergmann and Buber, Judaism had a cultural mission among the nations. It was an international network that crossed political boundaries, in which "all windows turning to the outside will stay open."[155] It would continue to

---

153. Hugo Bergmann to Martin Buber, October 4, 1917, Hugo Bergmann Literary Remains, National Library, Jerusalem, Sig. Arc 4o.
154. Martin Buber to Hugo Bergmann, December 4, 1917, in *Letters of Martin Buber*, 225.
155. Bergmann, "Proslov," in the Prague Zionist weekly *Zidovske Zpravy*, December 1919, 1–3. Quoted in Shumsky, *Ben Prague Li-Yerusalaim*, 188. In a

challenge those who used cultural differences as an excuse for ethnic and national separation.

This short analysis of Jewish temporality anticipated both Jacob Taubes's discussion of Jewish messianism three decades later and Giorgio Agamben's analysis of Jewish prophecy versus Christian eschatology in *The Time That Remains*.[156] Buber's concentration on time allowed him to view prophecy and messianism—and their reception by Christian and Jewish thinkers—in terms of the gap between potential and realization. In Jewish messianism (a strand within Judaism) the "space of experience" is constantly weighed against the expected arrival of the messiah, and leads forward from the present. In contrast, Christianity considers Christ, past and future, as a suspended space of experience, and his reappearance is anticipated. A Christian believer faces both backward and forward, but the most obvious distinction from Judaism is that for the Christian, the suspense and anticipation are weighed vis-à-vis the secular sovereign, and she is asked to "render therefore unto Caesar the things which are Caesar's" (Matthew 22:21, Mark 12:17, Luke 20:25).[157] During Paul's time it was Julius Caesar; in later times it would be the monarch or the secular government. Buber's distinction between the Jewish blending of within and without and

---

conclusive letter to Dr. Kurt Wehle, a short time before his death, Hugo Bergmann explained: "We have taken Prague into our hearts as the city of bridges, and learned from it how to overcome states of enmity. It is not a coincidence that Bohemian Jews represent the idea of the 'Covenant of Peace.' That is the lesson, I believe, we will pass down to the generations." Hugo Bergmann to Kurt Wehle, January 22, 1974, in Bergmann, *Tagebücher und Briefe*, 2:698.

156. See Giorgio Agamben, *The Time That Remains: A Commentary on the Letter to the Romans*, trans. Patricia Dailey (Stanford, CA: Stanford University Press, 2005). In *The Political Theology of Paul*, a work left incomplete at his death, Jacob Taubes quoted from Jeremiah 1:5 to prove that even before his birth Jeremiah's task was to be a *navi' la-goyim* (a prophet to the gentiles): "Before I created you in the womb, I appointed you a prophet concerning the nations." Taubes added a comment: "And this is how Paul sees himself called to be an apostle—one always has to add this, otherwise one misses what is essential—from the Jews to the Gentiles." Jacob Taubes, *The Political Theology of Paul*, trans. Dana Hollander (Stanford, CA: Stanford University Press, 2004), 14.

157. Jacob Taubes alludes to Buber's texts from the 1930s when he explains this passage as a Christian eschatology. See Taubes, *Occidental Eschatology*, trans. David Ratmoko (Stanford, CA: Stanford University Press, 2009), 21.

Christian splitting of past and future suggests that for him, Christianity is more spatial, hierarchical, and repetitive than the Jewish stress on a hope-filled present.

Buber's temporal analysis was pedagogical. It was meant to attach, affiliate, engage, and encounter, not differentiate. Yet, as Taubes—the scholar most often identified with Jewish political theology—pointed out, Buber divided Christian temporality into two periods, before and after the arrival of the Messiah, because he wanted to classify Jesus, rather than Paul, as the last Jewish prophet. Like his close colleagues among the religious socialists and reformers—he cooperated closely with Viktor von Weizsäcker and Catholic reformer Joseph Wittig, the coeditors of *Die Kreatur*, and later with Swiss Protestant socialist Leonhard Ragaz—Buber portrayed Jesus as a Jewish opponent of hierarchy, clericalism, and the political dictates that limit religious practice. He contrasted Jesus's present-oriented social activism with Paul's eschatological understanding of Christ as the one "who would come" (*parousia*).[158] Taubes, who corresponded with Buber and promoted his reception in the United States and Germany, rejected Buber's revival of an ideal prophetic past: "Now I have no patience, neither with respect to Heidegger nor with respect to Buber, for this apotheosis of the early [beginnings of Christendom]. Why the early should be better than the later I simply don't understand."[159]

The conversations about Paul and prophecy that Buber had with friends and colleagues left a deep mark. During the 1910s he

---

158. Taubes, *Political Theology of Paul*, 7.
159. Taubes, *Political Theology of Paul*, 7. Taubes, who paid close attention to Paul's temporality, was too impatient. In contrast to Taubes's argument, Buber had not denounced Paul as a lesser prophet. Instead he resisted Paul from a present perspective: he meant to prove that Paul's understanding of faith had a different temporal basis than the prophetic tradition, one predicated on inequality between Christians and Jews and not between sovereignty and the people. Paul would in time endorse a separation between two political traditions, one leading to antisemitism and the other leading to the "letting be" of sovereignty. Buber saw the first as the result of Paul's anti-Judaism, and the latter as an acceptance of the prophet–sovereign relation. Agamben's interpretation in *The Time That Remains* follows Taubes's understanding of prophecy and therefore misses Buber's point about Jewish temporality. Agamben also chose to view Paul's passive "let be" or "no longer be in the act" as a form of coded esoteric protest against sovereignty. See Agamben, *The Time That Remains*, 96.

was still testing out his ideas while developing his dialogical conception with Rosenzweig and Bergmann. After the rise of antisemitism and fascism, a critical image of prophecy and Paulinian anti-Judaism would become major topics of conversation in his wider circle. Buber's correspondence with Zweig gives further evidence of the prominence of this political-prophetic discourse. Buber and Zweig had known each other since the early 1900s, when Buber invited Zweig to contribute to *Die Welt* in 1901 and later to the Prague collection *Vom Judentum*. As Mark Gelber has argued, Buber's 1916 invitation to contribute a piece about prophecy to the newly established *Der Jude* led Zweig to conceive his play *Jeremias*.[160] Zweig's title character, beset by visions of destruction, takes solace in the idea of a Nietzschean "eternal return": "As the fathers wanted us to suffer ... oh, from the eternal return ... oh, you king of sorrow.... Begin your wonderful return through the world into eternity!"[161] In a letter to Buber, Zweig presented his play as "a large (and timeless) Jewish tragedy," which he connected to the war and the destruction of Jerusalem.[162] Buber argued in succeeding letters against Zweig's anti-Nietzschean and idealist-universalist attempt to reach a "spiritual Jerusalem" in exile.[163]

In 1918 Zweig sent his play to Buber, who sent it along to Franz Werfel. Werfel's reaction took some time. He had professed his belief in Jesus as a savior in 1916—even if he did not formally convert—so he received the play as a Christian drama. A decade later Werfel's *Paul among the Jews* was in some regards a theatrical rejoinder to Zweig. The growing interest in prophetic themes attracted the attention of Sigmund Freud, who saw the play and engaged Werfel in a private debate on the nature of religion and the psychology of its prophets. More specifically, Buber, Zweig, and Werfel obsessed

---

160. Mark H. Gelber, *Stefan Zweig, Judentum und Zionismus* (Vienna: Studien, 2014), 101.

161. Stefan Zweig, *Jeremias: Eine dramatische Dichtung in neun Bildern* (Leipzig: Insel, 1919), 208–13.

162. Stefan Zweig to Martin Buber, May 8, 1916, in Zweig, *Briefe zum Judentum*, ed. Stefan Litt (Frankfurt: Suhrkamp, 2020), 45.

163. For a different interpretation of the exchange, see chap. 6 of Gelber, *Stefan Zweig, Judentum und Zionismus*.

about the link that connected Jeremiah's and Paul's prophecies. In spite of their different views and interpretations, for all three these were sad stories that began with great hope and ended with despair, which they connected to the hope of European universalism and their despair at the rise of fascism, which Buber would come to identify with "the theopolitical hour."[164]

As they watched the gradual intertwining of secular sovereignty and ethnic identity and mourned the flagging energy of peace and universalism, Werfel, Zweig, and Buber became avid critics of the modern state in spite of the differences between their individual interpretations. They embraced the image of a new covenant between the last and first prophets, which they fashioned into a new means of fighting the absolute power of the state. The soldier at the gate, the doorman barring the way to the law, turns out to be one's own reluctance to press forward into the world. Max Brod pointed out, with hindsight, that for Buber "there are no political spheres outside of the theopolitical."[165] But Buber's turn toward the theopolitical as a hermeneutic system marked a significant change from his earlier stress on the individual encounter between self and the other within.

As we shall see, Buber developed the idea of prophecy and the stranger's gaze as an essential component of post-Holocaust Jewish humanism. He continued to develop the opposition between

---

164. Buber, *Torat Ha-nevi'im* [*The Prophetic Faith*], 117–42. For more about Werfel and Buber, see Peter Stephan Jungk, *Franz Werfel: A Life in Prague, Vienna, and Hollywood*, trans. Anselm Hollo (New York: Grove Weidenfeld, 1991). For Zweig and Buber's dialogue about Jeremias and the "spiritual barrenness that afflicts whole nations as a result of victory," see Zweig, *Jeremias*, 204. In that context, see also Robert Wistrich's stress on Zweig's "defeatism," in Robert S. Wistrich, "Stefan Zweig and the 'World of Yesterday,'" in *Stefan Zweig Reconsidered: New Perspectives on His Literary and Biographical Writings*, ed. Mark H. Gelber (Tübingen: Max Niemeyer, 2000), 68–70.

165. Max Brod, "Judaism and Christianity in Buber's Work," in *The Philosophy of Martin Buber*, ed. Paul Arthur Schilpp and Maurice Friedman (La Salle, IL: Open Court, 1967), 321. Max Brod dedicated important passages to the same Jeremiah and Paul connection in "Paganism, Christianity, Judaism: A Confession of Faith," a manuscript he sent to Kafka. Brod made an attempt to differentiate Judaism from Christianity and both from paganism. He considered Paul and Jeremiah's competing visions of the *neuer Bund* (new covenant). See Max Brod, *Heidentum, Christentum, Judentum: Ein Bekenntnisbuch* (Munich: Kurt Wolff, 1921), 74.

Jewish late prophecy and the Christian apostle Paul, between theopolitics and political theology in relation to the hour of need.

Two Types of Faith: Theopolitics vs. Sovereignty

By the 1940s Buber had turned his attention to reports about the destruction of European Jewry, developing his dialogical approach, now wedded to the prophecy of destruction, as an alternative to totalitarianism and sovereign decision. He contrasted the late Jewish prophets, whom he cast as proponents of a critical dialogue, with a Christian political theology. A figure he could not ignore in this context was the legal scholar Carl Schmitt, whose ideas about political theology and Paulinian sovereign decision paralleled his own.[166] Schmitt focused on three principal claims: "Sovereign is he who decides on the exception." "All significant concepts of the modern theory of the state are secularized theological concepts." "The specific political distinction to which political actions and motives can be reduced is that between friend and enemy."[167] Such ideas grew out of a fierce opposition to liberalism and democracy, seen as forms of "neutralization" and "depoliticization." Against them, borrowing from 2 Thessalonians 2:6–7, Schmitt proposed the power of "agonal friend/enemy binary" take by the sovereign decision and the katechon, which is a force that could hold back the apocalypse and prevent the destruction of the state.[168] According to Schmitt's theory,

---

166. Raphael Gross identified Schmitt's negative investment in Jews as the counterpart of every essential category, from political theology to the enemy, and to nomos (law). See Raphael Gross, *Carl Schmitt and the Jews: The "Jewish Question," the Holocaust, and German Legal Theory*, trans. Joel Golb (Madison: University of Wisconsin Press, 2000), 9–13. See also the short summary in Spector, *Modernism without Jews?*, 53–54.

167. Schmitt, *Political Theology*, 5, 36; see also Carl Schmitt, *The Concept of the Political*, trans. Georg Schwab (Chicago: University of Chicago Press, 1996), 26.

168. Benno Teschke, "Carl Schmitt's Concept of War: A Categorical Failure," in *The Oxford Handbook of Carl Schmitt*, eds. Jens Meierhenrich and Oliver Simons (New York: Oxford University Press, 2016), 377. Tracy Strong, foreword to Schmitt, *Political Theology*, xxxii. Schmitt wrote, "[Eusebius's] view on the Roman as the restrainer of the antichrist, the Kat-Echon (Katechin) in Paul's letter (2 Thessalonians 2:6), . . . [considers] the unbelief of the Jews, their continued refusal,

every age has its katechon, a *decider* who helps to avert chaos and creates an authoritative persona for the legal and political institution. For Schmitt, the katechon stands for theological political action, which is also the historical event, for it is the force that has to keep off the eschatological end of time.[169]

Buber first mentioned political theology in the introduction to the first edition of *Divine Kingdom* (1932), where he cast the prophet as the opponent of sovereignty. In his theory, the prophets, rather than the sovereign, stood for a historically oriented theopolitical event that united politics and religion.[170] In *The Question of the Single* (1936), a response to Kierkegaard's understanding of Christian time, Buber mentioned Schmitt by name and agreed with him that talking about the law implies talking about a utopian harmony, either secular or religious.[171] Contrary to Schmitt, however, Buber explained that there was no need for any "state of exception," or a sovereign decisionist moment—and furthermore that the moment of decision precedes and outlasts the sovereign. In contrast to Schmitt's absolute sovereign, Buber believed the sovereign should be limited to the role of executive authority, as the people's elected representative. Politically this implied a form of egalitarianism, and methodologically it implied a specific temporal hermeneutics: The prophet is elected not by the people but by God, and the prophet's role is not to execute

---

until the present day, to become Christians as the withholding of the end of the Christian aeon." See Carl Schmitt, *Political Theology II: The Myth of the Closure of Any Political Theology*, trans. Michael Hoelzl and Graham Ward (Cambridge, MA: Polity, 2014), 87.

169. For more about this aspect of Schmitt's katechon, see Matthias Lievens, "Carl Schmitt's Concept of History," in *The Oxford Handbook of Carl Schmitt*, 418.

170. Martin Buber, *Königtum Gottes* (Berlin: Schocken, 1936), xv. The introduction from 1932 was left unchanged in the 1936 edition.

171. Gillian Rose has shown that Buber warned against adopting Kierkegaard's universal time and identified its modern adapters with Stirner, Spengler, Schmitt, and Gogarten. "Buber returns to 'Attempts at Severance' and allows selected political thinkers to misdescribe modernity for him. . . . Stirner, Spengler, Schmitt, and Gogarten all reduce the relation between universal and particular to individual or collective arbitrary acts of power." Gillian Rose, "Reply from 'The Single One,'" in *Martin Buber: A Contemporary Perspective*, ed. Paul Mendes-Flohr (Syracuse, NY: Syracuse University Press, 2022), 161.

but to express and transmit. The prophet is there to mediate, not determine. This role, according to Buber's theopolitical realism, was the best way to keep a dialogical Jewish principle (faith, or *emunah*) intact.

In order to conceptualize the gap between past and present, Buber turned his attention to the ancient moment of change with Paul. In the first three lectures Buber delivered in Prague, he referred to Paul, in passing, as a Jew who "perceives himself as a battleground of prodigious contradictions."[172] He elaborated on Paul and Paulinian Christianity in the lectures he delivered on prophecy at the Jüdisches Lehrhaus in Frankfurt between 1929 and 1930, and Paul was central to his later understanding of prophets and theopolitics after 1930. After the rise of fascism, Buber came to express his understanding of prophecy and sovereignty as a countermodel to Paul.

In *The Question of the Individual* and *Between Man and Man*, Buber traced a continuity from Paul's rejection of Jewish life to Schmitt's "possibility of physical killing," going on to write that for Schmitt, "men can bring about a judgment of God."[173] Decisionist sovereigns, in contrast to prophets, do not care about dialogue; they only care about establishing authority and hierarchy and controlling life and death in a God-like manner. "That is," Buber argued, "what Schmitt, carrying it over to the relation of peoples to one another, calls the specifically political."[174] Here, the possibility of killing turns into "the intention of physical killing," for Schmitt projected onto public life a custom that belonged strictly to private life—the duel.[175]

While the prophets' "mission to the nations"—their critique of sovereignty—had been grounded in a critical approach to the past and a hope for a better future, Buber's return to ancient scripture

---

172. Buber, *On Judaism*, 65.
173. See the Buber–Taubes correspondence at the Martin Buber Archive, National Library in Jerusalem, Martin Buber Literary Remains, Sign 806a. My translation. In his capacity as a lector and editor in the 1950s, Jacob Taubes invited Buber to contribute essays in English and to translate his existing works. This unexplored aspect of Buber's reception is responsible, to a large degree, for Buber's fame in the English-speaking world.
174. Buber, "Validity and Limitation," 216.
175. Buber, "Validity and Limitation," 216.

had given him a starting point for his earlier attempts to revive Jewish culture, as it also did for his post-1930 consideration of theopolitics. Paul's reading of the message of Christ led him to a consideration of power relations in the eastern Mediterranean and to a reflection on end-times. In his introduction to the English translation of *I and Thou*, Walter Kaufmann points out that "the conception of return has been and is at the very heart of Judaism . . . but the theology of Paul in the New Testament is founded on the implicit denial of this doctrine, and so are the Roman Catholic and the Greek Orthodox churches, Lutheranism and Calvinism."[176] As Samuel Brody has shown, Buber's prophet "is not one who 'predicts,'" but one who wishes "to set the audience, to whom the words are addressed, before the choice and decision, directly or indirectly."[177] Although the prophet served as a spiritual guide who used moments of catastrophe as occasions to act against discrimination and inequality, the apostle instead attempted to convert those around him by wielding the threat of a coming catastrophe.[178]

The figure of the prophet matters to our discussion because it establishes a shared space of the political and the theological, coercion and dissent, God and humanity. The prophet speaks the language of time, the language of long-term consideration, and contrasts it with short-term sovereign control. By warning of impending disasters, the prophet asks us to consider the long-term consequences of our actions, even though we might not often make the big decisions. When Buber and Schmitt debated the relevance of theopolitics versus political theology, they did so in the name of two collective systems. They agreed that every political discussion originated in a discourse that encountered the political and the theological, but Buber positioned ethics in the midst of the discourse and appealed for responsibility. In contrast, Schmitt, relying on a Paulinian terminology,

---

176. Walter Kaufmann, introduction to Buber, *I and Thou*, 37.
177. Brody, *Martin Buber's Theopolitics*, 179.
178. Giorgio Agamben extended this tradition by opposing the prophet, "defined by his relation to the future," to the apostle, who "speaks forth from the arrival of the Messiah." Prophecy falls silent on the arrival of the messiah; this is the principle of "[Paul's] *ho nyn kairos*, 'the time of the now.' This is why Paul is an apostle and not a prophet." See Giorgio Agamben, *The Time That Remains*, 61.

assumed that the catastrophe has already happened, that we are at the "beginning of the end," and that a *parousia* (second coming) awaits.[179]

Buber's commitment to religious socialism—a commitment to a utopian form of socialism enacted through "voluntary association and nondomination"—expressed, and even extended, the work of critical Jewish prophets at an apocalyptic time.[180] In modern time, he hoped, religion and socialism would work in unison in order to preserve their critical spirit.[181] In other words, if theopolitics was Buber's alternative to decisionism, the prophets replaced the katechon, and socialism substituted for authoritarianism. Buber shared this vision with Paul Tillich, on the one hand, and with Hugo Bergmann, on the other hand.[182]

In that context, theopolitics called for resistance and reform guided by prophetic justice—and it had little good to say about sovereignty, messianism, or anarchism. However, the theocratic world in which theopolitics was born was vanishing. In *Paths in Utopia* (1946), which he wrote at the time of the fall of fascism and with a new Europe in mind, Buber took another step toward translating theopolitics into an explicit political creed, dividing socialist movements into two types of eschatology: utopian, open-ended socialism, which was prophetic by nature, and Marxist socialism, which was apocalyptic in its belief in grand, predetermined historical revolutions.[183] But he described them as having little actual power to change things. In the modern world, theopolitics is revealed via divine presence or the realization of momentary potential. In his book on Moses (1946), Buber stressed the temporality of becoming as the core of Jewish being. When Moses inquires about God's identity, he

---

179. For an attempt to characterize the role of the prophet from this perspective, see Nitzan Lebovic and Daniel Weidner, introduction to *Prophetic Politics*, special issue, *Political Theology* 21, no. 2 (2020): 1–8.
180. Wycoff, "Between Prophecy and Apocalypse," 354.
181. Buber, "Three Theses of Religious Socialism," in *Pointing the Way*, 112.
182. See also Marc A. Krell, "Fashioning a Neutral Zone: Jewish and Protestant Socialists Challenge Religionswissenschaft in Weimar Germany," in *Modern Judaism and Historical Consciousness: Identities, Encounters, Perspectives*, eds. Andreas Gotzmann and Christian Wiese (Leiden: Brill, 2007), 193–223.
183. Wycoff, "Between Prophecy and Apocalypse," 354.

is told, "I am who I am" (*eheye asher eheye*). Buber explained that this utterance referred, not to the essence of the divine, but to its presence.[184] Putting the stress on the divine's presence demonstrates a temporal rather than a spatial understanding of the divine. For that reason, Buber and Rosenzweig translated Exodus 3:14 as "Ich werde dasein, als der ich dasein werde" or "I shall be-there as the one I shall always be-there."[185] This is the opposite of the modern Schmittian understanding of the state as the continuation of monarchy by other means. Like Schmitt, Buber advocated recycling theological vocabulary previously associated with the sacred sovereign for modern sovereignty, yet he resisted Schmitt's perpetual appeal to the principle of enmity. Instead of violence and oppression, for Buber the basis of his politics was "defending the weak from the power of the strong ... applied by the legislator himself," and the ontology of presence shared by human beings, the world, and the divine.[186] Buber called for a new kind of politics—embedded in the past, giving a meaning to the experience of the present, and opening up a horizon of equality and shared dialogue. The danger of wrong sovereignty, a wrong sense of presence in the world, was not an abstract threat for him, and he was open and courageous enough to see its relevance for every form of nationalism, in Germany or elsewhere.[187]

In 1947, as the world awaited Israel's declaration of independence, Buber believed that Jews should draw upon Jewish prophetic hope, prophetic realism, and the theopolitical in crafting their state. Instead

---

184. Martin Buber, *Moses: The Revelation and the Covenant* (New York; Harper Books, 1958). Hermann Cohen observes: "Moses is to name the name of God by this verb form of the first person in answering the question of the Israelites about the name of their God. In such a definite way *being* is named as that element in the name that designates the *person* of God. If this is not yet philosophy, it is certainly reason in the original sense of the word." Cohen, *Religion of Reason out of the Sources of Judaism*, trans. Simon Kaplan (New York: Ungar, 1972), 43.

185. The German translation of the Buber-Rosenzweig Bible translation (1929) can be found online at https://bibel.github.io/BuberRosenzweig/index.html. For the English translation, see Buber and Rosenzweig, *Scripture and Translation*, 195.

186. Buber, Moses, 26. On Buber's reaction to Schmitt's political theology, see Nitzan Lebovic, "The Jerusalem School: The Theo-Political Hour," *New German Critique* 103 (2008): 97–120.

187. For Buber's response to Schmitt's *Leviathan*, see Buber, *Paths in Utopia*, 40.

of an atemporal state of exception, Jewish theopolitics and political equality required historical understanding. He warned Jews against adopting the Paulinian exception and Schmitt's political theology:

> All relative valuation of the state rests for the most part just on the fact of plurality.... The accumulated power of the master thrived on drawing profit from—so to speak—*latent exceptional conditions*.... Thus in times like ours the cold war tends to become *the normal historical condition*. Already at the beginning of our historical period we saw teachers of the law appear who, obedient to this trait of the times, defined the concept of the political so that everything disposed itself within it according to the criterion "friend-enemy," in which the concept of the enemy includes "the possibility of physical killing." The practice of states has conveniently followed their advice. Many states decree the division of mankind into friends who deserve to live and enemies who deserve to die, and the political principle sees to it that what is decreed penetrates the hearts and reins of men.[188]

In March 1949 Buber and Bergmann took part in a small gathering at the home of David Ben-Gurion, the first prime minister of Israel. Buber and Ben-Gurion clashed a few times, disagreeing about the mission of Zionism. When the politician spoke of "normalization" and "étatism" (*mamlachtiut*) in terms that sounded too close to those of the katechon, Buber quoted Plato, Kant, and the Jewish prophets. His vision of the state stressed critique, transparency, and dialogue, rather than hierarchy and opacity. He was not afraid to link all three aspects in drawing parallels between the Jewish experience of being driven out and that of Arab refugees.[189] During that gathering, Bergmann echoed Buber's parallels and warned of "horrible danger, among us, our second generation, which is the danger of dehumanization and the loss of human values among the youth."[190] Buber and Bergmann understood the state as a counterforce to imperialism and nationalism. Like Benjamin, Arendt, and Celan, they hoped to render transparent the language of the workings of power.

---

188. Martin Buber, "Validity and Limitation," 216. The essay was written in 1947. Emphases in original.

189. First Protocol, in *Mifgash Divrei Sofrim*, a meeting called by the prime minister on March 27, 1949 (Tel Aviv: Ha'madpis ha'memshalti, June 1949), 6.

190. *Mifgash Divrei Sofrim*, 9.

Buber continued to reflect on theopolitics and the state of exception after the establishment of the Israeli state. In *Good and Evil* and *The Eclipse of God* (1952), he distinguished between two types of politics and alluded explicitly to Nietzsche and his nationalist reception in Schmitt and Heidegger, which he contrasted with a prophetic form of theopolitics. At the center of the distinction stood the hour of need, not the state of exception. "The hour" reflected a dark moment, after the Holocaust and the disappearance of the divine from the human world. But all was not lost, Buber claimed. If the hour selected a prophet rather than a sovereign, the prophet would express the people's suffering instead of trying to mobilize them. The prophet instead needs to make a decision to choose good and further the deep connection offered by a dialogical relation to both the other and the divine. This account is far from Schmitt's sovereign decision and Heidegger's stress on "a time of need, because it stands ... in the no-longer of the gods who have fled and in the not-yet of the god who is coming."[191] For Buber, in-betweenness was not a process of secularization that could fill the gap between the death of God and a modern human sovereign, but an internalization of the power of creation. Here, a human creator resists the temptation of false idols: "*No longer* 'all the imagery,'" but rather a commitment to "master the vortex of possibility and realize the human figure purposed in the creation, as it could *not yet* do prior to the knowledge of good and evil."[192]

Kafka's Metaphysics of the Door

As we have seen, it is impossible to understand Buber's friendships, politics, and theology without a firm grasp of his thinking on temporality in general and immediacy in particular. A simple chronology reveals the continuity and change in his thought. During the early

---

191. Martin Heidegger, *Elucidations of Hölderlin's Poetry*, trans. Keith Hoeller (Amherst, NY: Humanity Books, 2000), 64.
192. Martin Buber, *Good and Evil: Two Interpretations*, trans. Ronald Gregor Smith (Upper Saddle River, NJ: Prentice Hall, 1997), 93, my emphases.

1900s he responded to the rise of German and Zionist nationalism by advocating a revival of Nietzschean-Jewish *Erlebnis* and "blood community," and in the 1920s he deployed dialogism and the immediate presence of both an Other (*Du*) and a God instead of the language of blood. The 1930s saw him advance the notion of theopolitics with a heavy stress on the Jewish prophets. During the 1940s he contrasted prophecy and apocalypse through Jewish dialogism, which he opposed to German eschatology, decisionism, and monologism. From the late 1920s to the start of the 1950s, Buber developed a critique of Paulinian eschatology and an embrace of Jewish "betweenness" vis-à-vis both German and Israeli chauvinism. During the early 1950s he contrasted the biblical prophets—who opposed the sovereign—with the ominous threat of passive cooperation, represented by Paul and his modern followers: A Christian Paulinian temporality, recent interpreters pointed out, assumed that "time contracted itself ... for passing away is the figure of this world."[193] According to Paul's logic, then, one acts "as not" (*Hōs mē*), or a "revocation of every vocation." Buber's stress on prophetic action and present realization was its opposite.

As Buber took a theopolitical stand against fascism, he marshaled the insights gained from a series of dialogues with both Jewish and Christian thinkers. He turned to the theology in Jeremiah and Josiah, contrasted with Paul and Augustine and their modern interpreters. In Franz Kafka he found a modern response to much of this theopolitical discussion, specifically in two of Kafka's works—*The Trial* and *The Castle*.[194] He interpreted the former as a tale about the inaccessibility of modern law, and the latter as one about the bureaucratic "maze of intermediate beings" found in the Pauline world.[195]

Two Types of Faith and *Good and Evil*, published in the decade after World War II, marked the end of Buber's encounters with Rosenzweig, Landauer, and Bergmann. These men received no more

---

193. Giorgio Agamben, *The Time That Remains*, 23.
194. Martin Buber, *Two Types of Faith*, trans. Norman P. Goldhawk (Syracuse, NY: Syracuse University Press, 2003), 163. See also Daniel Weidner, "Political Theology of Ethical Monotheism," 178–96.
195. Buber declares that *The Trial* is a story about time while *The Castle* is about space, but he treats both as temporal forms. Buber, *Two Types of Faith*, 166.

than a passing mention in either work. Buber had moved on—and back. As we saw, Bergmann identified Judaism with the idea that "all windows turning to the outside will stay open," yet in his writing about Kafka, Buber expanded the architectural metaphor to Kafka's "metaphysics of the door."[196] A dialectical opening and closing of the door represented a critical and a transparent gaze, something that was badly needed after the Holocaust in order to confront the "eclipse of God" or the "hidden face of God."[197] Buber disclosed here that he had not completely abandoned the hope of his earlier period and that he prized the idea that "every person has his own door and it is open to him.... The parable itself is not Pauline, but its elaborations are, only ... with salvation removed."[198]

What elaborations were those? In tackling Schmitt, Heidegger, and Paul, Buber rejected approaches that foregrounded the temporality of sovereign exception and Schmitt's "possibility of physical killing."[199] Instead Buber elevated praxis, experience, and openness in the present and living moment. Kafka's stress on the open door stood in sharp contrast to the Pauline view of Judaism as a closed and punitive custom. Here, Buber opposed not the ancient theology but "the strength of Pauline tendencies in present-day Christian theology."[200] In other words, Christians and Germans were acting on the basis of a hidden, exclusionary agenda they borrowed from the scripture and used for their own political purposes. A Paulinian notion of faith, grounded in the Greek *pistis* (faith) rather than the Jewish *emunah* (faith, return), was a form of Christian experience

---

196. Buber, *Two Types of Faith*, 165.
197. Buber, *The Eclipse of God* (Princeton, NJ: Princeton University Press, 2016). In 1928 Benjamin contemplated this image as a dialectics of transparency and called it "a revolutionary virtue par excellence. It is also intoxication [*Rausch*], a moral exhibitionism, that we badly need." Walter Benjamin, "Surrealism," in *Selected Writings*, vol. 2, part 1, *1927–1930*, ed. Michael Jennings, Howard Eiland, and Gary Smith (Cambridge, MA: Harvard University Press, 2005), 209.
198. Buber, *Two Types of Faith*, 165.
199. Scott Spector and Daniel Weidner point out another aspect of this resistance to identity by explaining, "The German-Jewish radical impulse to harness the secularization narrative and perform a kind of political resacralization ... identified with the resistance to political theology." Spector, *Modernism without Jews?*, 48.
200. Buber, *Two Types of Faith*, 166–67.

that resisted the dynamics of historical change.[201] In contrast, *teshuva*, the Jewish commitment to return, required concrete realization and dialogue and a historical understanding of change. The Jewish *teshuva* and *emunah* were grounded, Buber argued, in "factual event, lived life in dialogue."[202] With this hermeneutic move, Buber turned the Paulinian criticism of the Jews—that they were exclusionary and enigmatic—on its head. Jewish *Erlebnis* called for an immediate and communal realization, an ethical emphasis on presence and equality, and a progressive political vision.

Hugo Bergmann's diaries mention Kafka, a friend from his youth, usually in the context of conversations with his close German Jewish compatriots in Jerusalem during the 1920s and 1930s. In a diary entry from April 1928, he reported an exchange with Buber and Max Brod about Kafka's story "Before the Law," in which they argue "that meaning [in the text] isn't ours to give, and therefore returns to us."[203] For Buber, that is also an important aspect of Jewish return, or *teshuva*. Buber took a central part in such conversations, and it is clear that he and Bergmann shared a similar view of Kafka as a modern prophet-philosopher. Kafka inspired Buber to do what the prophets did millennia before him. By refusing literal language, not walking into the open space, and also not following the law (the door is kept ajar), Kafka's parables amounted to modern versions of prophetic principles and philosophical queries. The parables always contain threats of destruction, but as with the stories of the biblical prophets, there is no eschatological telos, only questions and reflections. Rather than a direct encounter between I and Thou, this ambiguity amounted to a struggle for meaning in "the crisis of our

---

201. Buber, *Two Types of Faith*, 173–77.
202. Martin Buber, *Believing Humanism: My Testament, 1902–1965*, trans. Maurice Friedman (New York: Simon and Schuster, 1967), 133. For an analysis of the contrast between pistis and emunah, see Laurence J. Silberstein, *Martin Buber's Social and Religious Thought: Alienation and the Quest for Meaning* (New York: NYU Press, 1990), 216–17. More recently, see Shaul Magid, "Defining Christianity and Judaism from the Perspective of Religious Anarchy: Martin Buber on Jesus and the Ba'al Shem Tov," in *Martin Buber: His Intellectual and Scholarly Legacy*, ed. Sam Berrin Shonkoff (Leiden: Brill, 2018), 45–52.
203. Hugo Bergmann, journal entry, April 17, 1928, in Bergmann, *Tagebücher und Briefe*, 1:241.

time."[204] In the post-Holocaust era, theology had to assume that "God is hiding Himself from the time in which he lives."[205]

Where does all of this place Buber, in political terms? As we saw, a stress on an internal, hidden essence positioned Buber as a revolutionary from within, a subversive force perhaps, but he never advocated the toppling of the state or rejected the state as a political engine. He may have agreed with Kafka's dialectical metaphysics of the door—half open and half shut—but unlike Kafka, he believed in the work of communal institutions, such as universities and publishing houses. His general approach to prophecy as a rhetoric of mediation and reform, expressing his view of experience as action, extended the idealist drive to realization. Unlike Kafka, Buber survived the rise and fall of fascism. This concrete "need of the hour" shaped his opposition to the thinking of Heidegger and Schmitt, as well as to Landauer's anarchism and—as we shall see in chapter 3—Benjamin's critique of realization.[206]

It is impossible to dissociate Buber's philosophy from his politics, and both are deeply beholden to a hermeneutics of temporality. Theocrat, religious socialist, existentialist—I see no reason to push him into one camp to the exclusion of the others. He and Bergmann, for instance, remained very open-minded regarding the strengths and weaknesses of democracy and fascism, stressing the primacy of equality and life above every political form. Both men considered the dialogical encounter as a question of living time, as Bergmann wrote in his conclusion to *Dialogical Philosophy from Kierkegaard to Buber*. Diachronically it led from the Bible, via Augustine and Paul, to Nietzsche, Landauer, and Kafka; synchronically it ran from Protestant theology to a reconsideration of values. Buber was courageous enough

---

204. Buber, *Two Types of Faith*, 170.
205. Buber, *Two Types of Faith*, 168. The "eclipse of God" or "hidden face of God" echoes certain Gnostic themes and discussions. For more about this aspect in Buber's work, see Daniel Herskowitz, *Heidegger*, 128–74.
206. The "need of the hour" can be found in Heidegger, *Gesamtausgabe*, vol. 75, *Unveröffentlichte Abhandlungen: Zu Hölderlin/ Griechenlandreisen* (Frankfurt: Vittorio Klostermann, 2000), 260. See Benjamin's dismissal of Buber's "religiosity," in Walter Benjamin, "World and Time," in *Selected Writings*, 1:226. Quoted and translated in Herskowitz, *Heidegger*, 144. For more about Benjamin's critique of Buber, see chapter 3 of this book.

to investigate and critique the theological roots of his own utopia, the utopia of I and Thou: "I confirm him as creature and as creation, I confirm him who is opposed to me as him who is over against me."[207] In other words, opening a conversation with the Other implies opening a door to the unknown and to change. Accordingly, during the 1950s Buber turned his attention to betweenness as a form of spoken word or an "actual occurrence of language."[208]

Such themes echo in other exchanges that have received no scholarly attention thus far. In an unpublished letter from Taubes to Buber in June 1953, Taubes discussed topics dear to his correspondent: a theopolitical resistance to imperialism, which he identified with globalization, and opposition to nationalism, in regard to which he spoke of the "physical element" of both Israeli and German nationalism.[209] Buber's response was telling: "Precisely at this point [after the Holocaust], at the turning, as you say, . . . [we] use the word of the prophets; the prophetic element is the spiritual economy of Israel."[210] Buber suggested adopting the critical stance of the prophets as an ethical system that overcomes any and every form of injustice.

Reading between the lines of Buber's writings of the 1950s, both private and public, we find that he saw himself as a modern prophet, an opener of doors. His rhetoric reflected a presentist preference with a strong claim over both past and future. Still, his enduring relevance did not rely on a stable identity as much as on the development of a dynamic hermeneutical force. He hoped to open the door that separates theology and politics, the absolute time of the divine and the living temporality of human communication. His dialogical legacy shaped much of the postwar discussion of democracy, left a

---

207. Martin Buber, *Knowledge of Man: Selected Essays*, ed. by Maurice Friedman (Amherst, MA: Humanity Books, 1988), 79.

208. Herskowitz, *Heidegger*, 164. Herskowitz insisted that this was a counter-Heideggerian "theory of language," but this theory of language owes more to Nietzsche and to Stefan George's notion of *Rhythmus* than to Heidegger's poetics.

209. Jacob Taubes to Martin Buber, June 7, 1953, Martin Buber Archive 806a, letter no. 7, National Library in Jerusalem, Martin Buber Literary Remains. Both sides of the correspondence are kept at the Buber archive.

210. In his response Buber is cautious to warn that a prophet can also become a lawgiver in certain conditions, especially if "unity breaks." Martin Buber Archive 806a, letter no. 7.

deep mark on German Jewish critique, and recast how Jewish–Christian relations were pursued.[211] This legacy was one of the most significant German Jewish contributions to the temporal turn whose consequences were felt over the second half of the twentieth century.

---

211. As Robert Erlewine has demonstrated, A. J. Heschel developed a parallel language of encounter; like Buber and Rosenzweig, "he uses the language of actuality to describe the interaction between God and the prophet." Erlewine, *Judaism and the West: From Hermann Cohen to Joseph Soloveitchik* (Bloomington: Indiana University Press, 2016), 123.

3

Walter Benjamin

The Rhythm of Time

Throughout his career Walter Benjamin positioned time at the center of his investigations as he sought to upend conventional temporalities and progress narratives in developing a novel approach to the topics of history, narrative, and allegory.[1] His first major essay asked, "When we stand there quivering, one question remains: Are we time?"[2] This placed Benjamin neatly within the temporal

---

1. When referring to writings by Walter Benjamin, I have relied on the following English translations: Walter Benjamin, *Early Writings: 1910–1917*, trans. Howard Eiland et al., ed. Howard Eiland (Cambridge, MA: Harvard University Press, 2011); Benjamin, *Selected Writings*, vols. 1–5, ed. Howard Eiland et al. (Cambridge, MA: Harvard University Press, 2004–6); Benjamin, *The Arcades Project*, trans. Howard Eiland and Kevin McLaughlin (Cambridge, MA: Belknap Press of Harvard University Press, 2002). I also reference the German edition of collected writings: Benjamin, *Gesammelte Schriften*, 7 vols., ed. Rolf Tiedemann and Harald Schweppenhäuser (Frankfurt: Suhrkamp, 1991–2012).

2. Walter Benjamin, "The Metaphysics of Youth," in *Early Writings*, 153.

turn of the early twentieth century, from which this book takes its timeline.

During this time period there was a growing anxiety about time. Had something so seemingly transparent been utterly misunderstood? As Benjamin and others broke with convention, daring to define time as "heterogeneous, fluid, and reversible," they opened the horizons of both time and space.³ The next one hundred years, which witnessed unprecedented technological advances, as well as two world wars, genocides, and global environmental degradation, made the twentieth century a fertile ground for catastrophic imagination and existential anxiety. Acknowledgment of the cost of progress spread, especially among those communities that suffered most from the repercussions of industrialization.

Accordingly, Benjamin's critique of progress has continued to resonate in our time in subaltern and critical race studies, as well as in environmental criticism. Adapting Benjamin's stress on the present as a time of catastrophe, theoreticians Saidiya Hartman, Joseph Winters, and Alexander Weheliye have shown how Western progress lies at the heart of modern racial biopolitics.⁴ Hartman drew inspiration from Benjamin's "reading against the grain" in order to find "a combination of foraging and disfiguration—raiding for fragments upon which other narratives can be spun."⁵ For Hartman, Benjamin's hermeneutics of time offer a different path to read "scenes of subjection." Dipesh Chakrabarty and François Hartog, historians of the Anthropocene, consider Benjamin's call to adapt historical thinking to our post-European and postindustrial age. In *Regimes of Historicity*, François Hartog recently pointed out, gesturing to his colleague, that "Chakrabarty turned to Walter Benjamin to evoke the

---

3. Stephen Kern, *The Culture of Time and Space, 1880–1918* (Cambridge, MA: Harvard University Press, 1983), 34.

4. Alexander Weheliye, *Habeus Viscus: Racializing Assemblages, Biopolitics, and Black Feminist Theories of the Human* (Durham, NC: Duke University Press, 2014); Joseph R. Winters, *Hope Draped in Black: Race, Melancholy, and the Agony of Progress* (Durham, NC: Duke University Press, 2016).

5. Saidiya Hartman, *Scenes of Subjection: Terror, Slavery, and Self-Making in Nineteenth-Century America* (New York: Oxford University Press, 1997), 12.

emergence of a potentially new universal history."[6] All five thinkers—Hartman, Winters, Weheliye, Hartog, and Chakrabarty—debate the heavy cost of Western telos. Chakrabarty observes, "Our usual historical practices for visualizing time, past and future times, [are] inaccessible to us personally . . . [and] are thrown into a deep contradiction and confusion."[7] This confusion results not only in suppression along class, race, and peripheral lines, but also in environmental suppression: "The geological now of the Anthropocene has become entangled with the now of human history."[8]

Chakrabarty, Hartog, Hartman, Winters, and Weheliye have turned back to Benjamin and the temporal turn of the early 1900s in order to ground their sense of radical change. With the exponential rise of new technologies, trans- or post-humanism—the idea that humanity is in urgent need of technological enhancement, of adopting a new mode of existence—now joins the temporal turn to a new history and theory of the Anthropocene.[9] "The Moderns," a group that, for the environmental philosopher Clive Hamilton, includes those living in the twentieth century and the twenty-first century, "are like Walter Benjamin's Angel of History, flying into the future but facing backwards, fleeing from a horrible past of suffering and oppression but unable to see the destruction that lies ahead."[10] Indeed, in this new world, Hamilton argues, "everything

---

6. François Hartog, "Chronos, Kairos, Krisis: The Genesis of Western Time," trans. Samuel Gilbert, *History and Theory* 60, no. 3 (2021): 425–39.

7. Dipesh Chakrabarty, "The Climate of History: Four Theses," *Critical Inquiry* 35, no. 2 (2009): 198.

8. Chakrabarty, "Climate of History," 211.

9. "Trans/posthumanism promotes the idea that the convergence of advanced technologies . . . will bring about a new phase in the evolution of the human species. At first enhanced humans (or transhumans) will transcend, in which humans will be eventually replaced by super-intelligent machines (posthumanism). . . . [Both] endorse a 'post-natural' vision of human flourishing, dismissing 'nature' as that which humans must subdue and master in order to overcome." Hava Tirosh-Samuelson, "Human Flourishing and History: A Religious Imaginary for the Anthropocene," *Journal of the Philosophy of History* 14, no. 3 (2020): 394, 396.

10. Clive Hamilton, "Human Destiny in the Anthropocene," in *The Anthropocene and the Global Environmental Crisis: Rethinking Modernity in a New*

is [now] in play. Every cubic meter of air and water, and every hectare of land."[11]

In this chapter I contend that Benjamin's oeuvre engaged not only with time as political hermeneutics, but also with the time that precedes and outlasts humankind. For Benjamin, temporality was a condition for human language and not its result. Creation and destruction frame our modes of thinking and expression. Primal sources of creation, within femininity and matriarchy for example, figure large in his philosophy. Whether it is his early focus on "pre-Adamite" language (1916), his midcareer references to standstill (1924), his metaphors of womb, swamp, and whirlpool (1934), or the angel of history (1940)—all of which I shall explore—concepts of time open up a wide landscape in which humankind stands quivering before creation. To the question of whether human beings were time, Benjamin answered in the affirmative, but then he warned his reader, "Pride tempts us to answer yes—and then the landscape would disappear."[12] If we are time, we become the creators of all, but also the destroyers of all.

As I demonstrate below, such questions long troubled Benjamin, framing his investigations of self (early writing), world (middle period), and catastrophe (late writing). Yet in spite of a multiplicity of themes, and the shifts that allow us to distinguish among these periods, his investigation into the nature of time unites his work, gesturing finally toward a view of humanity, tradition, and history that defies progress, anthropocentrism, and logocentrism. An absolute commitment to critique prevented Benjamin from imagining a world and time with no humans in it. As we shall see toward the end of this chapter, the creation of the world or its end, with the Nietzschean "eternal return" and the "last man" (who is "the good European"), marked both the process of time and its limitations.

In hindsight, Benjamin's interest in time seems so evident that it is surprising that it has not received more consistent attention. To take

---

Epoch, ed. Clive Hamilton, Christophe Bonneuil, and François Gemenne (London: Routledge, 2015), 43.
11. Hamilton, "Human Destiny in the Anthropocene," 36.
12. Benjamin, "Metaphysics of Youth," in *Early Writings*, 153.

just one example, the now-standard, comprehensive two-volume collection of essays titled *Benjamins Begriffe* (Benjamin's concepts), edited by Michael Opitz and Erdmut Wizisla (2000), includes essays on aura, experience, eros, memory, revolution, fate, and theology, but no entries on time or temporality. When the subject does come up, temporality is always a secondary hermeneutic device that helps explain the ideological, historical, and cultural themes that receive greater attention. Still, not one of the aforementioned concepts can be understood without an appreciation of Benjamin's unique understanding of temporality. Even though that understanding overlaps in a number of ways such recent concerns as biopolitics and the dawn of the Anthropocene, the principal reference point for those concerns is twentieth-century modernization (itself the product of the age of idealism), industrialization, fascism, and mass killing.

Much like Benjamin, we ought to recognize our own moment and hubris, our own quivering landscape, our own now of human history, which are no longer those of Benjamin and his followers. Benjamin's followers, whom he taught to scoff at the nineteenth century's naive belief in progress, developed in the wake of World War II, in their own "moment of recognizability": the ascendance of critical theory, which embraced new ways of thinking about art, history, and capitalism.[13] The sustained efforts of Gershom Scholem, Hannah Arendt, and Theodor Adorno to canonize Benjamin ushered in a wave of scholarship that produced many shelves of books dedicated to Benjamin's messianism (written mostly by religious studies scholars), dialectics at a standstill (by neo-Marxist scholars), the dialectical image and the aura (art history and media studies), now-time

---

13. See Howard Eiland and Michael W. Jennings, *Walter Benjamin: A Critical Life* (Cambridge, MA: Harvard University Press, 2014), 511. In a letter to Gretel Karplus written October 9, 1935, Benjamin spoke of his recent insights into the links between contemporary art and the art of the previous century, then announced, "I have realized my epistemological theory—which is crystallized around the very esoteric concept of the 'now of recognizability' (a concept that, very probably, I haven't shared even with you)—in a decisive example. I have found that aspect of nineteenth-century art which only 'now' is recognizable, as it never was before and never will be afterward." In the German, Benjamin referred in this letter to the "Jetzt der Erkennbarkeit"; see Walter Benjamin, *Gesammelte Briefe*, vol. 5, *1935–1937*, ed. Christoph Gödde and Henri Lonitz (Frankfurt: Suhrkamp, 1999), 171.

and the afterlife (cultural studies), antihistoricism (critical historians, myself included), and critiques of progress (almost everyone). Yet little has been written about his treatment of temporality as an overall framework of his work. Temporality, I contend, supplies us with a comprehensive framework for the oeuvre as a whole, and enables us, as readers in the early twenty-first century, to recognize the potential and limitations of Benjamin's critique for his time and our own.

Benjamin's time-related concepts do not conform to familiar disciplinary categories, yet they have proved remarkably effective in reshaping our understanding of identity, philosophy, and disciplinary habits. Consider how temporal concepts open the possibility of fluidity, heterogeneity, and reversibility that spatial categories curb and separate, and how these concepts blur binary oppositions such as high and low, private and public, political and aesthetic, linear and fragmentary. Time is not only the main thread that runs through Benjamin's critical theory; it is the dynamic force that activates his reading of critique, justice, learning, and—most importantly—politics. From this perspective, human history cannot have a telos; instead it exists as an interim, as what Werner Hamacher called "the time of the unfinished ... the time of that which is *not yet* and perhaps never *will be*."[14] More specifically, much of Benjamin's understanding of his time and the human condition was the result of turning the tables on Kant and Hegel and on the German Jewish bourgeoisie. Nothing for him was less interesting than doctrines that blindly supported progress. Drawing on concepts from *Lebensphilosophie* and German Jewish critique enabled him to rebel against simplistic idealism and collective reductionism. An unconventional use of philosophical terminology allowed him to counter assimilatory conventions and a reductive understanding of identity.

Before we can translate Benjamin's ideas into our situation, we must understand his original context and terminology. In the

---

14. Werner Hamacher explained that such an approach contrasts with the notion of "an already constituted subject"; the approach favored "the possibilities ... not only *in* its but *as* its time." See Hamacher, "'Now': Walter Benjamin on Historical Time," in *The Moment: Time and Rupture in Modern Thought*, ed. Heidrun Friese (Liverpool: Liverpool University Press, 2001), 164, my emphases.

following eight sections of this chapter I unpack Benjamin's use of temporal concepts from an unconventional perspective: by highlighting concepts that were ignored before and by discussing works that escaped the attention of important interpreters, I propose to work *with* Benjamin instead of merely following, hagiographically, his observations. Much has been written of such crucial themes as shock and rupture, messianism and the Nietzschean leap (*Sprung*), dialectics at a standstill, the "one-timeness" of artistic response to the reproduction, and the decline of the aura. But close reading reveals a long-term emphasis on rhythm, sources of primal origin, and a series of related metaphors—the womb, the swamp, the whirlpool, the never-ending storm—which allowed him to deconstruct the historical nineteenth century.[15] Jacques Derrida, an avid reader and interpreter of Benjamin, would later explain: "Rhythm has always haunted our tradition, without ever reaching the center of its concerns."[16] Following rhythmic forms, rather than linear progress, allowed Derrida to apply Benjamin's hermeneutics of time in a plural, anti-institutional setting that invigorated a "reading against the grain." Half a century before Derrida, Benjamin had written, "Every age must strive anew to wrest tradition away from the conformism that is working to overpower it."[17] As Derrida, Hartman, and Chakrabarty noted, learning from Benjamin in his, or our, time means more than reproducing his critique of nineteenth-century forms.

---

15. By working with Benjamin in this context, I suggest something along the lines of Miriam Peskowitz and Laura Lewitt's humorous and succinct suggestion to "upset the myth of detached scholars" by working with and on "embodied intellectuals who draft articles about patriarchy and Jewish studies with live guitar music in the background, who think about Walter Benjamin's 'Theses on History' while fetching a child from its great-grandmother, and who write about colonialism while caring for infants." Miriam Peskowitz and Laura Lewitt, eds., *Judaism since Gender* (New York: Routledge, 1997), 2.

16. Jacques Derrida, introduction to Philippe Lacoue-Labarthe, *Typography: Mimesis, Philosophy, Politics*, trans. C. Fynsk (Cambridge, MA: Harvard University Press, 1989), 33.

17. Walter Benjamin, "On the Concept of History," in *Selected Writings*, 4:391.

The Early Years: Infinity and Fulfillment

Ceaselessly attacking progress, linearity, and idealism, Benjamin preached a revolution in time. From his early rebellion against the idealist obsession with the individual and collective self, he figured human existence as turbulent and discontinuous, yet set in "the womb of time" (*Schosse der Zeit*), an image that framed his first texts as well as his last, valedictory *Arcades Project*.[18] The image of the womb is crucial for Benjamin, yet it has never received much attention. Appearing in the first essays and the last, it holds the key to his notion of life. In "The Metaphysics of Youth" (1913–14), he composed a series of reflections on the writing of a diary, declaring, "If the 'I' is sent out as time, within it things storm on, countering it in their distancing, humble bearing, on course toward the center of the interval, toward the womb of time, whence the self radiates outward."[19] That movement of life is the "new storm" of "an agitated self" he would later come to identify with the "the last day of humankind" ("Karl Kraus," 1931),[20] or "the last man" (Arcades), who is also "the good European," who—once again—lives within "the womb of time."[21]

Benjamin borrowed the phrase "womb of time" from Hegel's *Lectures on the Philosophy of History* (1837). For Hegel, the concept of the womb helped to frame world history when activated by great politicians who were "thinking men, who had an insight into the requirements of the time—*what was ripe for development*. This was the very Truth for their age, for their world; the species next in order, so to speak, and which was already formed in the womb of

---

18. Walter Benjamin, Conv. F: "Iron Construction," fragment F1, 1, in *The Arcades Project*, 150.
19. Benjamin, "Metaphysics of Youth," 156.
20. Walter Benjamin, "Karl Kraus," in *Selected Writings*, 2:444. Benjamin referred to Kraus's position as "the last judgment," underlining the secular reading of that phrase, for "this is the last official act of this zealot: to place the legal system itself under accusation."
21. Benjamin, Conv. J: "Baudelaire," in *The Arcades Project*, 315. In this passage Benjamin connected Baudelaire's notion that "this world is coming to an end" with Nietzsche's "last man."

time."[22] Benjamin used the phrase, in 1913 and again in 1940, to sketch out a Nietzschean alternative to Eurocentric idealism and essentialism. Hannah Arendt would allude to the concept in her final piece, *The Life of the Mind* (1975), when discussing Hegel's concept of world history and the task that Hegel, as a representative of historical thinking, had allocated to philosophy: "Now one could indeed consider every moment in the world's historical sequence as an 'it was to be' and assign to philosophy the task of 'comprehending this plan' from its beginning, its 'concealed fount' or 'nascent principle' . . . in the 'womb of time,' up to its 'phenomenal, present existence.'"[23] According to Arendt, this course assumed the telos of thinking, will, and contemplation (dwelling).

As Grace Jantzen has shown, in the Western tradition the womb stands for a metaphorical abyss, the source of both creation and its end.[24] Ilana Pardes has noted the heavy presence of natal images in the Exodus story, depicting God as the "opener of the womb" (*peter rechem* in Hebrew) and the result: "From now on, time will be perceived differently. Everything will be measured in relation to the moment in which God delivered Israel from Egypt."[25] After Buber smuggled Nietzschean vocabulary into Jewish traditions, the circle around Bergmann and Kafka turned it into a new source of interpretation, both Jewish and German. Benjamin expanded the critical potential: what echoes a post-Nietzschean critique of religious and philosophical tradition in Benjamin's early texts, then disrupted and fragmented during the late 1920s and early 1930s, and transient

---

22. G. W. F. Hegel, *The Philosophy of History*, trans. J. Sibree (New York: Colonial Press, 1956), 30; emphases and capitalized letters in the original translation. I quote from the same translation Arendt used in 1975.

23. Hannah Arendt, *Life of the Mind*, Part 2: Willing (Boston: Houghton Mifflin Harcourt, 1981), 47.

24. Grace Jantzen, "Eros and the Abyss: Reading Medieval Mystics in Postmodernity," *Literature and Theology* 17, no. 3 (2003): 255. In a recent dissertation Ghilad Shenhav mentions this analysis within a short discussion of "the tomb-womb structure" in the Talmud. Shenhav points to Gershom Scholem's resistance to the "female otherness" of womb symbolism. See Ghilad H. Shenhav, "Abyss and Messiah: Gershom Scholem and the Question of Language" (diss., Tel-Aviv University, 2021), 223.

25. Ilana Pardes, *The Biography of Ancient Israel: National Narratives in the Bible* (Berkeley: University of California Press, 2000), 26.

and apocalyptic in 1940, becomes a consistent, long-term rejection of both religious and secular conventions, Enlightenment, and counter-Enlightenment formulations. It refers to a new birth, not of an individual, a nation, reason, or religious community, but instead of temporal consciousness. Traces of aesthetic traditions were the last to dissolve: Benjamin's rejection of nineteenth-century linear historicism is quite noticeable when one reads the writings from the early 1910s, which focus on Romantic terms such as "the genius" and "self." Later these terms disappear when he begins to engage more critically with Nietzsche and his followers.[26] I shall return to the interval, the eternal return, and the last man later in this chapter, but let us begin chronologically with the post-Nietzschean moment of the 1910s.

The period around the First World War was a crucial time for young Benjamin's intellectual development.[27] He completed his studies at the universities of Freiburg and Berlin, met with Gershom Scholem and other notable intellectuals of his generation, and shaped the principles of his philosophy. In Freiburg he studied religion in late antiquity, medieval German literature, history, and philosophy, became acquainted with Edmund Husserl's phenomenology, and, in a seminar led by the neo-Kantian Heinrich Rickert, met an older student named Martin Heidegger. The two would also attend a seminar by Rickert on Henri Bergson's vitalism.[28]

The time in Freiburg marked the start of Benjamin's political involvement. He joined a student group inspired by Gustav Wyneken's call for educational reforms; Wyneken, who became a mentor, was inspired by the *Lebensphilosophie* of Friedrich Nietzsche.[29] In Berlin

---

26. In an unpublished, undelivered speech to fellow students, Benjamin used this terminology critically. He thought that "false romanticism" encouraged "unpolitical youth, eternally limited to art, and literature, and experience of loving." Yet he attempted to build an alternative from within: "What is never outmoded is the romantic *will* to beauty." See Benjamin, "Romanticism: An Undelivered Address to Students," in *Early Writings*, 103, 105.

27. My biographical comments here follow Eiland and Jennings, *Walter Benjamin*, 32–74; Eiland, introduction to Benjamin, *Early Writings*, 1–13.

28. For a consistent, positive analysis of this philosophical relationship, see Peter Fenves, *The Messianic Reduction: Walter Benjamin and the Shape of Time* (Stanford, CA: Stanford University Press, 2011), 70–73, 118–21.

29. Eiland and Jennings, *Walter Benjamin*, 39.

Benjamin audited lectures by the founder of sociology, Georg Simmel, another follower of Nietzschean Lebensphilosophie and the post-Nietzschean poet Stefan George. Simmel was a member of George's poetic circle and the driving force behind translating Henri Bergson's works into German. Benjamin admired George and his circle of post-Nietzschean followers and told friends about traveling to Heidelberg, in 1914, and waiting for hours to see the poet walking by. That year, Benjamin met his lifelong friend Gershom Scholem and assumed the presidency of the Berlin University chapter of the Freie Studentenschaft (Free Students Association). During this period, the young philosopher began to develop a critique of social norms, evidenced in his sharp critique of the war and expressed in several of his essays from that period.[30]

As Steven Aschheim has shown, in the early 1900s "Nietzsche and the Nietzscheans were both makers and beneficiaries of a broader iconoclastic process that cut across and obscured such predictable left and right, progressive and reactionary distinctions. They also challenged simple dichotomies between modern and premodern, rational and irrational.... The Nietzscheans combined archaic with futuristic elements."[31] Martin Buber responded to the work of Nietzsche and Ahad-Ha'Am by positing the creation of a Jewish homeland as "not simply a political movement but a '*Lebensphilosophie.*'"[32] As I explained at length in chapter 2, *Vom Judentum* (*On Judaism*), the acclaimed series of speeches Buber delivered in Prague between 1909 and 1918, called for a "decisive transformation" and a "transvaluation of values" to unite radical Germans and Zionists.[33]

---

30. For a detailed history of the relationship between Stefan George, his circle, and Benjamin, see Robert Norton, *Secret Germany: Stefan George and His Circle* (Ithaca, NY: Cornell University Press, 2002), 475, 672–74.

31. Steven E. Aschheim, *The Nietzsche Legacy in Germany, 1890–1990* (Berkeley: University of California Press, 1992), 7.

32. Anson Rabinbach has argued that much of the German Jewish encounter with Nietzschean ideas was mediated after 1911 by the impact of Martin Buber's "Drei Reden," a lecture series on Judaism; see Rabinbach, *In the Shadow of Catastrophe: German Intellectuals between Apocalypse and Enlightenment* (Berkeley: University of California Press, 1997), 35.

33. Martin Buber, *Vom Judentum*, quoted and translated in Rabinbach, *In the Shadow of Catastrophe*, 35.

Benjamin was not impressed. He wrote dismissively of Buber's intense interest in realization and of the German Jewish Zionists who "make propaganda for Palestine and then get drunk like Germans."[34] It is true, as James McFarland has recently argued, that Buber's "theological Nietzscheanism" helped shape Benjamin's thinking about Nietzsche.[35] Yet ultimately the two thinkers applied the concepts of *Beyond Good and Evil* and other works in quite different ways.[36] Buber affirmatively adapted the vocabulary of Lebensphilosophie and in 1914 enthusiastically applauded the German war effort, whereas Benjamin and Scholem remained skeptical about the collective value of "lived experience" (*Erlebnis*). Their mistrust of Buber's nationalism and spiritual inclinations only increased with time.

For them, engaging with Nietzsche meant not only channeling a general critique of values toward unity and harmony, but adapting Nietzsche's critique of progressive linearity to a new modern world flooded with crises and revolutionary change. As Benjamin explained in the opening to "The Life of Students," published in September 1915, "The elements of the ultimate condition do not manifest themselves as formless progressive tendencies but are deeply embedded in every present in the form of the most endangered, excoriated, and ridiculed creations and ideas."[37] This engagement reveals, according to McFarland, a "tragic temporality [that] is always the juncture of a 'no longer' and a 'not yet,' a birth that appears simultaneously with its death, as the potential for its rebirth."[38] Such an interim or circular logic of in-betweenness reminds us again of the womb of time, where there is creation but without a clear end goal

---

34. Walter Benjamin to Ludwig Strauss, October 10, 1912, in Walter Benjamin, *Gesammelte Briefe*, vol. 1, *1910–1918*, ed. Christoph Gödde and Henri Lonitz (Frankfurt: Suhrkamp, 1999), 72, my translation.

35. James McFarland, *Constellation: Friedrich Nietzsche and Walter Benjamin in the Now-Time of History* (New York: Fordham University Press, 2012), 39.

36. As Jennings and Eiland tell us, the Benjamin of the early 1910s sounded much like Nietzsche in his critique of nineteenth-century historicism. Eiland and Jennings, *Walter Benjamin*, 98–102.

37. Benjamin, "The Life of Students," in *Early Writings*, 197.

38. McFarland, *Constellation*, 145.

or purpose other than itself. As we shall see below, such ideas stood in contrast to Buber's notion of a renaissance of Jewish culture.[39] The no-longer and not-yet of Benjamin's "hour of Zarathustra" were "a unique hiatus of nonidentity at the juncture of past and future" and a direct attack on every form of theological-political realization.[40]

Reading Nietzsche's philosophy was not enough. In 1914, shortly after his election to the leadership of his chapter of the Free Students Association, Benjamin invited Buber and Ludwig Klages, both advocates of Nietzschean Lebensphilosophie, to address his group. How might these supporters of the German national cause explicate the crisis that occurred in that fateful year and the opportunities embedded in the present? As a fierce champion of an essentialist Germanic identity and a former member of the Stefan George circle, Klages crafted a popular life philosophy that harked back to quasi-mythical notions of blood and soil.[41] In the 1920s he turned reactionary, then pro-Nazi. During the mid-1910s Benjamin followed the publications of both thinkers and exchanged a number of letters with both, but soon he began to develop an alternative system that distanced him from both men and their Nietzschean ideas. His cause was not one of realizing Nietzschean critique but of utilizing it for the sake of an alternative temporal order.

---

39. For a broad history of this renaissance, see Michael Brenner, *The Renaissance of Jewish Culture in Weimar Germany* (New Haven, CT: Yale University Press, 1996).

40. McFarland, *Constellation*, 171.

41. Benjamin's relationship with post-Nietzscheans such as Klages helps answer that question. Ancillary to his work on Lebensphilosophie, Klages had a keen interest in dream imagery, graphological analysis, and what could be called psycho-diagnostic systems. He believed that Nietzsche viewed "every rhythmic condition, in which every single movement reflects the entire personality," as the basis for describing a holistic psychology. From 1923 Klages edited and supervised the journal *Rhythmus*, which considered life, at its root, as movement, integrating both birth and death into its inherent flow. For more about Klages and his Nietzschean psychology, see Nitzan Lebovic, *The Philosophy of Life and Death: Ludwig Klages and the Rise of a Nazi Biopolitics* (New York: Palgrave MacMillan, 2013), 89, 193.

Benjamin vs. the Nietzscheans

Focusing on temporal rather than ideological terms enabled Benjamin to concentrate on the mechanism of Nietzschean philosophy rather than its ideological translations. Exploring with subversive discursive tools expanded his ideological horizons: a glance through his biography reveals a "strange attraction" to reactionary movements, as Scholem noted.[42] Although Benjamin followed George and Klages during the early 1900s, after his move to Paris in the 1920s he explored Marxist thought as he signed up with Action Française and even attended a meeting of the Strasser group, the socialist-nationalist side of the Nazi party.[43]

Klages and other conservative advocates of Lebensphilosophie provided Benjamin with an absolute focus on living temporality that avoided the usual liberal clichés. The result was a form of anti-liberal radicalism that could skew either right or left. In this new and unstable era, Benjamin found himself wondering: When Lebensphilosophie preached a nationalist understanding of *Lebensraum* (the idea that the German people defined their territory on the basis of race), and cultural Zionism advocated a cultural and political appropriation of Palestine, weren't their leaders missing Nietzsche's warning against the use and abuse of history? The twenty-two-year-old was fascinated, instead, with the "rhythm of one's own words in the empty space."[44] In a realm where politics was rendered nugatory, Benjamin dwelt on the experience of the individual rhythm, represented by the images of the storm and interval.

In order to illuminate Benjamin's view of history as a storm, let's return to a passage quoted earlier: "The new storm rages in the agitated self. If the 'I' is sent out as time, within it things storm on,

---

42. Gershom Scholem, "Walter Benjamin," *Neue Rundschau* 76, no. 1 (1965): 19.
43. Eiland and Jennings, *Walter Benjamin*, 347.
44. Benjamin, "Metaphysics of Youth," 146. Benjamin gave a speech in Weimar about "the future of our educational institutions"; see Walter Benjamin to Herbert Belmore, April 15, 1914, in Scholem and Adorno, *Correspondence of Walter Benjamin*, 66.

countering it in their distancing, humble bearing, on course toward the center of the interval, toward the womb of time, whence the self radiates outward."[45] Here, Benjamin used temporal terms to unpack Nietzsche's rejection of the nineteenth century's idealist self or "transcendental ego," which he anchored in a series of intervals and disruptions.[46] But the use of temporal concepts is even more suggestive than a mere Nietzschean mark of disruption. In fact, such concepts suggest a link between Hegel's *Lectures on History*, Zarathustra's stress on life, and an ancient Jewish understanding of creation. That is, if Hegel conceives of the self, after medieval scholastics, as "coextensive with substance," Zarathustra pleads for a storm that will shake off the many that "hang on their branches far too long."[47] The young German Jewish philosopher already saw the realization of both Hegel's idealism and Nietzsche's anti-idealist dream in the rise of blind, fanatical nationalism. Aschheim has shown that the pages of Nietzsche's followers are flooded with Nietzsche's imagery of the storm and the interval; for example, Klages and Buber question the previous century's historicism and its values even when their aim was a renewed harmony of self and world via life or lived experience.[48] In a public speech Klages sent to a gathering of youth movements at the Hohe Meissner, which Benjamin read in 1913, Klages vehemently

---

45. Benjamin, "Metaphysics of Youth," 156.
46. Nietzsche, and Benjamin, following him, build on Hegel's dialectics of internal and external, self and world, the "self-relating" and "projecting outward." See Robert B. Pippin, *Hegel on Self-Consciousness: Desire and Death in the Phenomenology of Spirit* (Princeton, NJ: Princeton University Press, 2011), 37.
47. For a careful analysis of Hegel's notion of self, see Karen Ng, *Hegel's Concept of Life: Self-Consciousness, Freedom, Logic* (New York: Oxford University Press, 2020), 151; Friedrich Nietzsche, *Thus Spoke Zarathustra: A Book for Everyone and Nobody*, trans. Graham Parkes (New York: Oxford University Press, 2005), 63.
48. "Buber's use of Nietzsche, like other nationalist appropriations, had to somehow reconcile the emphasis on activist transvaluation, on intensely lived *Erlebnis*, with the belief in the eternal organic properties of the nation." Aschheim, *The Nietzsche Legacy*, 42. Eugene Sheppard, David N. Myers, and Jacob Golomb have pointed out the central role of Nietzsche for German Jewish thinkers critical of historicism; see Eugene R. Sheppard, *Leo Strauss and the Politics of Exile: The Making of a Political Philosopher* (Waltham, MA: Brandeis University Press, 2006); David N. Myers, *Resisting History: Historicism and Its Discontents in German-Jewish Thought* (Princeton, NJ: Princeton University Press, 2003); Jacob Golomb, *Nietzsche and Zion* (Ithaca, NY: Cornell University Press, 2004).

rejected high-flown idealist claims for human will. The "absolute ego" of Johann Gottlieb Fichte "is infinite and independent while the ego or ordinary experience is finite and dependent. Nevertheless... they ought to be one and the same ego."[49] Life philosophers after Nietzsche expressed their disdain for an abstract idealist self, which they considered disconnected from nature and lived experience. Nietzsche's stress on ecstasy and immediacy, storms and intervals, stood in sharp contrast to both the stable sense of self in Fichte and Hegel and the Kantian notion of "long experience" (*Erfahrung*).[50]

Yet Benjamin rejected the political claims made by other Nietzscheans and began to view their language with suspicion. For example, Buber's cultural Zionism reconciled lived experience with the belief in collective revival and Jewish renaissance. Buber contended that "only a dynamic movement such as Zionism would be able to tap the unbroken but historically repressed 'life-feeling of the Jews.'"[51] Scholem, himself a proponent of cultural Zionism, recalled in 1980 the revulsion such nationalist language had inspired in Benjamin—who called Buber "a man who lived in a permanent trance."[52] The mystical elevation of lived experience for nationalist causes, à la Buber and Klages, Benjamin argued, amounted to the "degeneration" of language, the reduction of philosophy to "an impoverished, weak act."[53]

---

49. See the translation and discussion in Frederick C. Beiser, *German Idealism: The Struggle against Subjectivism, 1781–1801* (Cambridge, MA: Harvard University Press, 2009), 307–19.

50. Much like his political rivals on the left, Klages considered the idea of the ego coterminous with a bourgeois, hierarchical, linear world. Seeing life from an idealist perspective assumed a Kantian and Fichtean understanding of life as a process of growth and maturation—the opposite of death. Instead, the Lebensphilosopher stressed the importance of ur-images (*Urbilder*) and the immediacy of the "reality of images" in lived experience. See Lebovic, *Philosophy of Life and Death*; John McCole, *Walter Benjamin and the Antinomies of Tradition* (Ithaca, NY: Cornell University Press, 1993), 238–43.

51. Aschheim, *The Nietzsche Legacy*, 107. For the German, see Martin Buber, "Jüdische Renaissance," in *Die Jüdische Bewegung: Gesammelte Aufsätze und Ansprachen* (Berlin: Jüdischer Verlag, 1920), 1–13.

52. Gershom Scholem, *Walter Benjamin: The Story of a Friendship*, trans. Harry Zohn (New York: New York Review Books, 2001), 37.

53. Scholem, *Walter Benjamin*, 37.

Benjamin instead chose a radically different approach to Nietzschean lived experience and ecstasy (*Rausch*), turning it against every convention—of authority, norm, and form. Politically speaking, this approach translated into a comprehensive rejection of Hegelian historicism, be it German or Zionist.[54]

Buber and Klages might well have agreed with Benjamin that Nietzsche was "the only person who had seen historical experience in the nineteenth century."[55] For both German conservative and German Jewish critics, Nietzsche's concept of life proposed a break with old-fashioned hierarchies of state and class. Likewise, Benjamin saw himself as a critic of the historicist tradition. Much like his counterscientific understanding of messianism, his fondness for the counterfactuals of human experience, chaos, and destruction attested to a commitment to a nonlinear understanding of history, a deep resistance to teleology. From "The Life of Students" (1915) to "The Destructive Character" (1931), Benjamin hoped "to liberate the future from its deformation in the present" for the sake of "destructive dwelling—a mode of dwelling that undoubtedly prevents the development of any habits."[56] It was a subversive political project, to try to cultivate an alternative rhythm of history and of acting in the world. In response

---

54. In that regard, as Sigrid Weigel has shown, Benjamin is close to Foucault's understanding of Nietzsche. See Weigel, *Body and Image-Space*, trans. Georgina Paul et al. (New York: Routledge, 2003), 39. For further scholarship on Benjamin's complex relationship to Nietzsche, see McCole, *Antinomies of Tradition*, 174; McFarland, *Constellation*, 8; Peter Osborne, *The Politics of Time: Modernity and Avant-Garde* (London: Verso Books, 1995), 137; Samuel Weber, *Benjamin's -abilities* (Cambridge, MA: Harvard University Press, 2008), 263.

55. Benjamin is quoted in Scholem, *Walter Benjamin*, 60. This comment has been linked to Benjamin's interest in Klages's circle; see Eiland and Jennings, *Walter Benjamin*, 102.

56. Benjamin, "The Life of Students," 198; Benjamin, "May–June 1931," in *Selected Writings*, 2:480. A common mistake of Benjamin interpreters is to view his reflective reading of the destructive character as fully nihilist. Benjamin undoubtedly set out to defamiliarize common social norms, but this description of the destructive character identifies a more nihilist version of destruction than his own. For how Benjamin's temporality differs from the temporality of nihilism and absolute stasis or destruction, see Nitzan Lebovic, "Benjamin's Nihilism: Rhythm and Political Stasis," in *Benjamin-Studien 2*, ed. Daniel Weidner and Sigrid Weigel (Munich: Fink, 2011), 145–58.

to Buber's invitation to contribute to the journal *Der Jude*, Benjamin claimed—in July 1916—to be too busy with other matters; he said he believed good political writing would "awaken interest in what was denied to the word."[57] Whatever "the word" may have been, it was not the kind of word—or the kind of politics—idealists, liberals, and men such as Buber advocated for.

In 1916 Benjamin began working on the *Trauerspiel*—the Baroque German drama—a project that involved him for the first time in an extended investigation of history, experience and temporality.[58] In this work he contrasted the temporal scheme of the mourning play, which has no clear endpoint or resolution, with the temporality of the more familiar tragedy and its concluding effect of catharsis.[59] The *Trauerspiel* lacked the mythic unity, determinism, and sense of "fulfilled time" of a tragedy, possessing instead a spectral, disjointed indeterminacy. Its strength lay in its creaturely, nonhumanist, prescientific openness; only such a drama could convey a true feeling of history. "The determining force of historical time," he wrote, "cannot be grasped by . . . any empirical process. Rather, a process that is perfect in historical terms is quite indeterminate empirically."[60] Instead of the idealist desire for "fulfilled time," the protagonists of *Trauerspiel* "bore witness to the shattered dreams of the past" and mourned

---

57. Walter Benjamin to Martin Buber, unspecified day, July 1916, in Gershom Scholem and Theodor W. Adorno, eds., *The Correspondence of Walter Benjamin, 1910–1940*, trans. Manfred R. Jacobson and Evelyn M. Jacobson (Chicago: University of Chicago Press, 1994), 80.

58. The principal idea of the German mourning play, Samuel Weber explains, is to distinguish the Baroque mourning play from the Greek tragedy. Unlike tragedy, which relates to the mythic order and its notion of being, the mourning play, and its allegory, refers to a "guilt-ridden nature [*phusys*]." Samuel Weber, *Benjamin-abilities*, 152. For that reason, Benjamin explained, the mourning play "knows neither heroes nor selves, but only constellations." Walter Benjamin, *Origins of the German Drama*, trans. John Osborn (London: Verso, 1998), 132.

59. Walter Benjamin, "*Trauerspiel* and Tragedy," in *Selected Writings*, 1:55–57. The brief summary of the principal argument of the book *Trauerspiel* (*Origins of the German Drama*) was written in 1916 but not published during Benjamin's life. It is worth noting that in his opening paragraph Benjamin returned to Bergson's distinction between historical and mechanical time without rejecting it. Rather, he declared that his own focus was on historical time. Neither Bergson nor Heidegger is mentioned here, but the allusion is clear.

60. Benjamin, "*Trauerspiel* and Tragedy," 55.

for what was lost.⁶¹ Here was a language of allegories and metaphors of lost time, rather than of facts, norms, heroes, and utopias.

In the summer and fall of 1916, Benjamin completed his first major work, "On Language as Such and on the Language of Man." This and other early texts initiated his search for a "new beginning" outside of history, mostly within a search for "pure language."⁶² While deeply engrossed in the essay on language, Benjamin wrote Scholem about reading Martin Heidegger, who in the previous year had submitted a *habilitation* (a second dissertation) on the medieval scholastic theologian Duns Scotus. In Benjamin's view, Heidegger had blundered by following the Bergsonian distinction between historical time, full of duration and relation, and mechanical time—a "mere empty form measured by movements in space," as Benjamin depicted it, adding: "Precisely how this subject should *not* be treated. An awful piece of work."⁶³ His own essay would redress this distinction. The analysis of language, Benjamin's biographers wrote, was "inseparable from the problematic of time," because without the appropriate attention to the temporal *rhythm* of language, beyond its historicity or mechanics, one could not grasp either linguistic or philosophical structures properly.⁶⁴ Benjamin spoke of the loss of "a blissful Adamite language" through telos and

---

61. Martin Jay, *Songs of Experience: Modern American and European Variations on a Universal Theme* (Berkeley: University of California Press, 2005), 337. "Fulfilled" or "realized" time is a key term in Martin Buber's *Daniel*, the work Benjamin read in 1913 before inviting Buber to meet his student organization. See Martin Buber, *Daniel: Gespräche von der Verwirklichung* (Wiesbaden: Insel Verlag, 1913).

62. Vivian Liska, "Denkfiguren des Neuanfangs im 20. Jahrhundert (Heidegger, Benjamin, Arendt, Agamben—und Kafka)," in *Renaissances: Über ein Muster der Aneignung von Tradition*, ed. Jürgen Fohrmann (Göttingen: Wallstein, 2022), 120.

63. Walter Benjamin to Gershom Scholem, November 11, 1916. Quoted in Eiland and Jennings, *Walter Benjamin*, 91. See also McCole, *Antinomies of Tradition*, 65; For a careful reading of Benjamin's objection to Heidegger, coming from within phenomenology, see Ronald Mendoza-de Jesús, "Index and Image: Benjamin, Héring, Heidegger, and the Phenomenology of History," *Qui Parle* 30, no. 2 (2021): 293–335.

64. Eiland and Jennings, *Walter Benjamin*, 91. "Dwelling" appears in the English edition of Benjamin's *Arcades Project* as the translation of *Lebensraum* (literally, "living space"). The term *Lebensraum* was identified with Nazi rhetoric; Benjamin used it in the opposite way to mark the private space most appropriate for reflection, not militant action.

linearity, in which language had been left in the lurch, expressing nothing but its commitment to progress.[65] Once again, extinguishing all belief in progress and stressing a nonlinear rhythm helped to focus attention on the means rather than the ends of linguistic activity.

As the young Benjamin and Scholem considered the origins of language within a political theological setting—paradise and destruction are constant references in their works—they frequently engaged with the idea of deferral and infinity. Openly rejecting Buber's plea for realization, they developed a philosophy of suspense they identified with the messianic possibility, itself a moment of suspension between divine justice and human realization or execution. In 1919 Scholem stressed the notion that a divine not-yet opens up a new temporal condition, which he contrasted with the Greco-Roman pagan drive to execute a sentence immediately.[66] Similarly, Benjamin's dissertation about "the concept of criticism in German Romanticism," submitted in April 1919, addressed the theme of suspension via an account of critique in art. In this short study Benjamin explained that the true nature of Romanticism was the "temporal infinity" of its poetic form and its stress on "an infinite process of fulfillment, not just of becoming."[67] By resisting both idealist utopian emphasis on realization and Romantic depoliticization, he meant to leave behind teleological approaches to language, the arts, and the work of critical thinking. Analyzing temporal concepts

---

65. A certain "mental being communicates itself in language and not through language. Languages, therefore, have no speaker.... Language therefore communicates the particular linguistic being of things. The clearest manifestation of this being, however, is language itself." See Walter Benjamin, "On Language as Such and on the Language of Man," in *Selected Writings*, 1:63, 71.

66. In his interpretation of the prophet Jonah, Scholem observes that in the conclusion to the eponymous book in the Bible, God "had passed a sentence in order to carry it out, and he did not (yet) do it, . . . [which] is a classic statement of the idea of justice. Where the court pronounces a verdict, justice raises a question." Gershom Scholem, "On Jonah and the Concept of Justice," trans. Eric J. Schwab, *Critical Inquiry* 25, no. 2 (1999): 357. See also Shenhav, "Abyss and Messiah," 119.

67. Walter Benjamin to Ernst Schoen, April 7, 1919, in Scholem and Adorno, *Correspondence of Walter Benjamin*, 139–40. See also Walter Benjamin, *Gesammelte Briefe*, vol. 2, *1919–192*, ed. Christoph Gödde and Henri Lonitz (Frankfurt: Suhrkamp, 1996), 23.

allowed him to form a critical view of such utopian dreams while keeping his distance from messianic realization.

"World and Time" (1919–1920)

An overlooked gem by Benjamin is the posthumously published "World and Time." This pithy work, if mentioned at all, is viewed as a rehearsal of arguments for the better-known "Critique of Violence" (1921).[68] The text responds to the atmosphere of crisis that prevailed in Germany during the late 1910s and early 1920s; it should be read as an intricate critique of idealism, post-Nietzscheanism, and early phenomenology. In "World and Time" Benjamin incorporated earlier concerns such as time, language, and self into new political and metaphysical themes, such as power and violence, the sacred and the profane, law and freedom. An increasingly complex path would lead him beyond any essentialist understanding of life as he attempted to liberate representation from bourgeois conventions.

In the fall of 1917 Benjamin and his wife, Dora Kellner Pollak, left Berlin so that he might study at the University of Bern.[69] In Switzerland Benjamin first encountered the post-Nietzschean Carl Albrecht Bernoulli and became friendly with the German-Jewish Marxist philosopher Ernst Bloch, and one can see the impact of his renewed interest in Lebensphilosophie and political messianism shortly thereafter. In a two-page fragment that became "World and Time," written soon after his stay in Switzerland, Benjamin explored the world undergoing metaphysical decline.[70] Hegel had transformed the "theater of the world" into the "theater of history," but

---

68. Brendan Moran, "Nature, Decision, and Muteness," in *Towards the Critique of Violence: Walter Benjamin and Giorgio Agamben*, ed. Brendan Moran and Carlo Salzani (London: Bloomsbury Academic, 2015), 79.
69. Eiland and Jennings, *Walter Benjamin*, 98–101.
70. Walter Benjamin, "World and Time," in *Selected Writings*, 1:226. In another unpublished fragment from that same period, Benjamin equated "the theater of history" with nature, beyond humanity; see Walter Benjamin, "Categories of Aesthetics," in *Selected Writings*, 1:221.

Benjamin examined both world and history within a process that started with creation, passed through a human play (*Schauplatz*), and ended with destruction, but not necessarily in this order.[71] In the first paragraph of the essay, he addressed the metaphysical understanding of reality: "In the revelation of the divine, the world—the theater of history—is subjected to a great process of decomposition, while time—the life of him who represents it—is subjected to a great process of fulfillment. The end of the world: the destruction and liberation of a (dramatic) representation. Redemption of history from the one who represents it. But perhaps in this sense the profoundest antithesis to 'world' is not 'time' but 'the world to come.'"[72]

Benjamin's "revelation" is not theological; instead it is linguistic and cognitive—a revelation that happens in medias res. What is revealed is not a divine entity, but the precondition of human time, the creator and destroyer of things. World and time move in opposite directions in this passage. The world is the locus of the natural, biological time of birth, growth, and decline, whereas time is carried forward by "the life of him who represents it" (*das Leben des Darstellers*)—namely, the "life of the actor."[73] The process of fulfillment has less to do with time itself and more with its manifestation in human language. If the world is measured against its own prospect of decline, then time, as the dynamo of life, becomes visible in the agency of a will to act and a phenomenological will to represent.

In short, what brings world and time together is life, itself marking the temporal existence between birth and death: an organic life in the *world*, and a specifically human life in the case of *time*. If the "profoundest antithesis to 'world' is not 'time' but 'the world to come,'" then the antithesis is not between two forms of life in the world, but between the living forms inside it and those we imagine outside it. This is a world beyond life, preceding it or surpassing it. While human life and time are subject to our (pagan) sense of fulfillment, it is "the world to come"—the future we can only strive

---

71. The theater of history is a concept most commonly identified with Hegel; see Donald Phillip Verene, *The History of Philosophy: A Reader's Guide* (Evanston, IL: Northwestern University Press, 2008), 121.
72. Benjamin, "World and Time," 226–27.
73. Benjamin, "World and Time," 226.

for—that overcomes earthly biological processes. If all this sounds messianic (as Benjamin has often been interpreted), consider the world to come, *HaOlam Haba*, as the world that lies beyond us humans. If it is messianic, it is messianism without redemption or God. It is an ecstatic, possibly delusional, hope that expresses the futility of human thought, language, and action.

In other words, if metaphysics and human representation (of the divine, the world, and history) control our language, then the fundamental contrast is not between two different directions (decline and fulfillment) but instead between a fundamental world, with its time of living, and that of an afterlife: the world of revelation, the creaturely post-human, and messianic forms. Here the beginning and the end of the world frame the very substance of human life and its essence as temporal living, but they do not give it a direction, a telos.

Such ideas were unconventional at the time, but not at odds with those of other radical German Jewish thinkers. Margarete Susman, another post-Nietzschean disciple of Simmel's close to Bloch and Buber (and later Paul Celan), reported in her memoirs on a similar experiment. The eschatological Marxist thinker Ernst Bloch, she wrote, "self-consciously tried to break through the conventional life forms [*Lebensformen*], and expected the same from every human being whom he recognized as kindred."[74] The temporal terms in "World and Time" reflect similar radical tendencies. Benjamin wrote in a separate fragment that breaking through norms required a critical view of (phenomenological) intention: "The knowledge of truth: this does not exist. For truth is the death of intention."[75]

"World and Time" undermines the essentialist opposition between fact and representation, as well as political-ideological

---

74. Quoted in Rabinbach, *Shadow of Catastrophe*, 47. As Susanne Hillman put it, "Like so many of her contemporaries, Susman at some point fell under the spell of Nietzsche. . . . She had been gripped by the 'overwhelming beauty' of *Also Sprach Zarathustra*, a work that seemed to illuminate all life like a 'golden dusk.'" See Hillman, "'A Germ So Tiny': Margarete Susman's Messianism of Small Steps," *Soundings: An Interdisciplinary Journal* 96, no. 1 (2013): 44.

75. Ursula Marx et al., eds., *Walter Benjamin's Archive: Images, Texts, Signs*, trans. Esther Leslie (London: Verso, 2007), manuscript fig. 2.1. The fragment is from 1921.

oppositions such as religious and secular, Judaism and Christianity, law and anarchy. Instead, we are encouraged to see politics as "the fulfillment of an unimproved humanity" and anarchy as "freedom in the philosophy of history."[76] Deconstructing oppositions was Benjamin's opening move in critiquing linear forms, starting with the highest authority itself. "What is at issue here," he wrote, "is not the 'realization' of divine power." Instead, "the question of 'manifestation' is central." This question was not an issue of religious authority but of how mankind used that authority for its own purposes. Benjamin focused, not on religiosity—a notion he identified with Buber and declared "nonsense" in "World and Time"—but on a temporal and phenomenal process that questioned the role mankind ascribed to itself: "In the present state, the social is a manifestation of spectral and demonic powers ... [and] their efforts to transcend themselves."[77]

Peter Fenves, one of the few Benjamin scholars to address "World and Time" at any length, shows how Benjamin employed temporality as a tool to examine secular idealism and the end of metaphysics. Fenves argues that Benjamin was not interested in Kant and Hegel's universal self, just as he rejected Nietzsche and Buber's emphasis on the immediacy of lived experience. "So little does Benjamin want the concept of experience to be associated with 'lived experience,'" writes Fenves, "that he avoids all mention of the term."[78] But Fenves is too quick to dismiss the role of experience in Benjamin's thought.[79] Benjamin's interest in *Erlebnis* was critical but consistent with his long-lasting critique of Kantian

---

76. Benjamin, "World and Time," 227.
77. Benjamin, "World and Time," 227.
78. But as Fenves points out, "He borrows, as it were, the pathos of contemporaneous *Erlebnis*-discourse." See Fenves, *Messianic Reduction*, 156.
79. As Fenves put it, "The term time ... refers neither to the time of 'inner time consciousness' (Husserl) nor to time as the 'possible horizon for any understanding of being' (Heidegger), but, rather, to a 'plastic' time, which is shaped in such a way that its course is wholly without direction, hence without past, present, or future, as they are generally understood." But in spite of the previous distinction, there was an echo of Heidegger's destructive mission in Benjamin, whom Fenves described as "emphatic about the destructive character of pure *Gewalt* [power—N.L.]." Fenves, *Messianic Reduction*, 16, 221.

Erfahrung (long, individual experience). Otherwise, why do forms of life (*Lebensformen*) surface in every essay throughout his career?

The intellectual tendency that Benjamin detested most was the reduction of time, world, and life to the simplest of linear models. Progress was the execrated myth. Benjamin's plasticity of time assumed that creation and destruction are immanent to our notion of life, and he therefore concluded his discussion of world and time not with destruction but with transience, which opened, as Benjamin explained "in every direction."[80] "World and Time" therefore sheds a new light on the drive behind "The Critique of Violence": when Benjamin drove wedges between means and ends, positive law and natural law, and the justified and unjustified use of violence, he was moving toward a new hermeneutics of time that left linearity behind.

Rhythm as Transience

Benjamin's theory positions time not as a development but as a storm, a swamp, and a whirlpool. The temporal rhythm of our environment changes our view and understanding of the world.[81] Benjamin's view of temporality as the basis of his critical mission led him to assail every form of linearity (mythical, historical, psychological, nationalist), realization (idealist, utopian), and messianic consummation (economic, political, religious). An important aspect of that thought about time is rhythm.

---

80. Benjamin, "*Trauerspiel* and Tragedy," 55.
81. This is what Hans Ulrich Gumbrecht has called "rhythmic language," which results from the meeting between the "physicality" of language, and its "light touch of sound on our skin." A physical effect is created thanks to "a rhythm that we can feel and identify independently of the meaning language 'carries,'" and that stands "against its status of being a time object in the sense proper (*ein Zeitobjekt im eigentlichen Sinn*), according to Husserl's terminology." See Hans Ulrich Gumbrecht, *Our Broad Present: Time and Contemporary Culture* (New York: Columbia University Press, 2014), 4. Curiously, in spite of this fundamental stress on temporality, Gumbrecht chooses to build his argument on the basis of Heidegger's metaphor of "language as the house of Being," an essentially "spatial denotation." Gumbrecht, *Our Broad Present*, 8.

Peter Osborne has argued that Benjamin identified modernity with the rhythmic uniformity of technology, industrial labor, the movement of urban crowds, fashion, inflation, and gambling.[82] If "each beats out a similar rhythm," then the modern identification with "the new" results in "the new itself as the ever-always-the-same."[83] In contrast to a view common among those who identify radical critique with a nihilistic sentiment, an emphasis on rhythm enabled Benjamin to sketch out an alternative to the values-based politics of nineteenth-century idealism.[84]

A number of scholars have already demonstrated the importance of rhythm to Nietzsche, calling it in one case "the guideline . . . for [his] examination of mankind as temporary entities in and outside the flow of time."[85] One finds a similar use of rhythm in Benjamin's early essays "Experience" (1913), "Two Poems by Friedrich Hölderlin" (1914), "The Metaphysics of Youth" (1914), "The Life of Students" (1915), and "On Language as Such and on the Language of Man" (1916). All of them discuss rhythm as conveying the human awareness of time. For Benjamin's initial question "Are we time?," rhythm serves as the way to answer it. In "The Metaphysics of Youth," he writes: "When our time expelled us from our isolation into the landscape and our beloved strode toward us, . . . we could feel how time, which sent us forth, flooded back toward us. This rhythm of time, which returns home to us from all corners of the earth, lulls us to sleep."[86] The rhythm of time thrusts us forward, and then rocks us back to the land of dreams. When it is disrupted, it

---

82. Osborne, *The Politics of Time*, 136–37.

83. Osborne, *The Politics of Time*, 136–37.

84. This understanding of nihilism as a temporal phenomenon is very different from that evoked in a number of acclaimed interpretations, such as those by Irving Wohlfarth, Ansgar Hillach, Richard Wolin, Michael Jennings, Uwe Steiner, and Werner Hamacher. For more about Benjamin's stasis, rather than nihilism, see Osborne, *The Politics of Time*, 56.

85. Friederike Felicitas Günther, *Rhythmus beim frühen Nietzsche* (Berlin: De Gruyter, 2008), 1. For Nietzsche's stress on rhythm in his analysis of tragedy, see Babette Babich, "Who Is Nietzsche's Archilochus? Rhythm and the Problem of the Subject," in *Philosophers and Their Poets*, ed. Charles Bambach and Theodore George (Albany: SUNY Press, 2019), 85–109.

86. Benjamin, "Metaphysics of Youth," 13.

awakens us. Johannes Steizinger has pointed out, "Seeing history as a disruptive rhythm does not allow a linear view, grounded in continuity and causality, or delivered in a homogeneous way."[87] This idea of rhythm Benjamin would later develop into the "flash" that is the dialectical interpretation of dreams and images or sudden wakefulness. As a disruption it would become the "dialectics at a standstill" and the *apocatastasis* (restoration, return) of a moment that "blasts out of the continuum of history."[88]

Benjamin had earlier attempted to define the rhythm of creation, or what "expels us from our isolation," in "On Language as Such," where he explained that the rhythm of time defines the very essence of creation, in which nature and mankind are unified. Commenting on the book of Genesis, Benjamin wrote, "The manifold rhythm of the act of creation in the first chapter establishes a kind of basic form from which the act that creates man diverges significantly.... In the creation of man the threefold rhythm of the creation of nature has given way to an entirely different order."[89] Rhythm thus points to an ontology of time beyond language and mankind, even when language helps us shape our connection and relation to time.

Rhythm occurs at the center of major texts Benjamin wrote in the 1920s. In "Theological-Political Fragment" (ca. 1920) Benjamin describes secularization as a reframing of ongoing rhythm and its transience, a principle of "eternal and total passing away," while in "Goethe's *Elective Affinities*" (1919–22) the concept occurs as "the rhythmic sequence of the representations" and the "communal rhythms" of architecture.[90] In "The Right to Use Force" (1920),

---

87. Johannes Steizinger, *Revolte, Eros und Sprache: Walter Benjamins "Metaphysik der Jugend"* (Berlin: Kulturverlag Kadmos Berlin, 2013), 56.
88. Benjamin, Conv. N 10, 3, in *The Arcades Project*, 475. For a comprehensive interpretation of apocatastasis, see Michael Jennings, "The Will to *apocatastasis*: Media, Experience, and Eschatology in Walter Benjamin's Late Theological Politics," in *Walter Benjamin and Theology*, ed. Colby Dickinson and Stéphane Symons (New York: Fordham University Press, 2016), 179–214.
89. Benjamin, "On Language as Such," 68.
90. Benjamin, "Theological-Political Fragment," in *Selected Writings*, 3:306; Benjamin, "Goethe's *Elective Affinities*," in *Selected Writings*, 1:416. At the close of the "Theological-Political Fragment," Benjamin shifts gears, offering a theory of secularization and equating a messianic form with "eternal and total passing away"

written between "World and Time" and "The Critique of Violence," he explains, "What is at issue is the violent rhythm of impatience in which the law exists and has its temporal order, as opposed to the good rhythm of expectation in which messianic events unfold."[91] In "Naples" (1925) Benjamin uses rhythm to explain the fundamental movement of collective activity and the porousness of space, in a passage reverberating with Nietzschean and Kafkaesque terms: "As porous as this stone is the architecture. Building and action interpenetrate in the courtyards, arcades, and stairways. In everything, they preserve the scope to become a theater of new, unforeseen constellations. The stamp of the definite is avoided. No situation appears intended for ever, no future asserts it 'thus and not otherwise.' This is how architecture, the most binding part of the communal rhythm, comes into being here."[92] A temporal architecture is also at the heart of "One-Way Street" (1923–26), where the "vital rhythms" of night are distinguished from those of day, and those of the age of the pen from the period of the typewriter, or what was "constructed metrically."[93]

Rhythm as Origin

Benjamin was interested in nineteenth-century sciences, such as morphology and physiognomy, as a storage of rhythmic and phenomenological metaphors. He deployed morphology toward a different form of representation, where rhythm is immanent to every subject and movement, though lacking a telos. Hence, it expresses both singularity and the repetition basic to movement. As the historian Janina

---

or "the rhythm of this eternally transient worldly existence, transient in its totality. . . . The rhythm of messianic nature is happiness"; see *Selected Writings*, 3:307.

91. Benjamin, "The Right to Use Force," in *Selected Writings*, 1:231. Rhythm serves here as an indicator of means. A passage from "The Critique of Violence" notes, "Violence can first be sought only in the realm of means, not in the realm of ends." As the means to an end, the role of violence is to expedite the realization and fulfillment of absolute power and the establishment of "new law." Benjamin, *Selected Writings*, 1:242.

92. Benjamin, "Naples," in *Selected Writings*, 1:416.

93. Benjamin, "One-Way Street," in *Selected Writings*, 1:445, 457.

Wellmann has shown, during the early modern period the concept of rhythm was often linked to an immanent life force (*Lebenskraft*) that united the individual body with a general understanding of nature: "The rhythm in which the transformations of the life force reorganize a living being from the inside, over and over again, is the rhythm that characterizes nature as a whole."[94] The cultural historian Stephen Kern has located in the early years of the twentieth century a growing realization that "time was closely connected with social organization" because, as Emil Durkheim claimed, "the foundation of the category of time is the rhythm of social life." Durkheim was moved to separate "private time" and "time in general."[95] By the time Benjamin began work on his habilitation, *The Origins of the German Tragic Drama* (1916–25), he had internalized this idea.

Benjamin's writing exhibits a deep, consistent interest in the concept of rhythm as an internal quality of every life-form as well as in its sociopolitical use. Because rhythm undermined the notion of a set beginning and ending, it opened up new paths for critical thought. Both Kantian and Nietzschean critiques, despite their many differences, assume a moment of creation and a moment of death, which Benjamin transformed into a dynamic process of becoming and disappearance. In the introduction to the *Trauerspiel* book (*Origins of the German Drama*) Benjamin developed the ideas he first tried nine years earlier in the short essay "*Trauerspiel* and Tragedy." In the book he unpacks the relation between origin and phenomenon, noting, "The term origin . . . describe[s] that which emerges from the process of becoming and disappearance. . . . Its rhythm is apparent only to a dual insight."[96] The "dual insight"—the commitment to

---

94. Here Wellmann specifically discusses the natural philosophy of Johann Christian Reil (1759–1813), who was mentioned a few times in Benjamin's writings. See Janina Wellmann, *The Form of Becoming: Embryology and the Epistemology of Rhythm, 1760–1830*, trans. Kate Sturge (New York: Zone, 2017), 139. For another excellent analysis along these lines, see Peter Hans Reill, *Vitalizing Nature in the Enlightenment* (Berkeley: University of California Press, 2005), 212–13.

95. Stephen Kern, *The Culture of Time and Space: 1880–1918* (Cambridge, MA: Harvard University Press, 1983), 19. Quotation is from Émile Durkheim, *Elementary Forms of Religious Life* (Oxford: Oxford University Press, 2008 [1912]), 20.

96. Walter Benjamin, *The Origins of German Tragic Drama*, trans. John Osborne (London: Verso, 1998), 45. Beatrice Hanssen has also argued as follows: "That

seeing every life-form from the simultaneous perspective of beginning and end—contrasts with a straightforward, hereditary drive toward an end point and stresses instead what is "imperfect and incomplete"—that is, unrealizable.[97]

Rhythm, natural and human, became the key to a new theory of ideas in the *Trauerspiel*. From a critique of teleology—"ideas are timeless constellations"—he proceeded to a revolutionary conclusion in which rhythm played a crucial role in giving timeless ideas their powerful impact.[98] Positing the dialectical origin of ideas, open to the present and the future—and shaped retroactively by them ("the rhythm of becoming and disappearance")—he determined that political outcomes were based on the rhythmic maelstrom-like movement of social ideas.[99] If origin is an idea, it emerges in retrospect, from the becoming and disappearance of phenomena. The rhythmic movement of the whirlpool exposes the fundamental changes, singular or repeating, in the world. It is part of a process that is ongoing without being sequential and has no beginning or end point. In short, rhythm forms the ontological principle of all temporal systems, the heartbeat of every cyclical order.

Benjamin's understanding of graphology as a form of living expression provides an example of how every phenomenon is the sum of its immanent diverse rhythms. In a discussion of handwriting in an August 1928 review of Anja and Georg Mendelssohn's *Der Mensch in der Handschrift* (Man through his handwriting), Benjamin

---

the new term 'origin' was meant to revoke the fallacies not only of neo-Kantianism and historicism but also Nietzsche's eternal return is clear if one reads the prologue in conjunction with the earlier draft." See Hanssen, *Walter Benjamin's Other History: Of Stones, Animals, Human Beings, and Angels* (Berkeley: University of California Press, 1998), 42.

97. Benjamin, *German Tragic Drama*, 45.

98. Benjamin, *German Tragic Drama*, 34, and 36: "It is the task of the philosopher to restore, by representation, the primacy of the symbolic character of the word."

99. Benjamin, *German Tragic Drama*, 45. "Im Ursprung wird kein Werden des Entsprungenen, vielmehr dem Werden und Vergehen Entspringendes gemeint. Der Ursprung steht im Fluss des Werdens *als Strudel* und reisst in seine Rhythmik das Entstehungsmaterial hinein." See Benjamin, introduction to the *Urspring des Deutschen Trauerspiel*, in *Gesammelte Schriften*, 1:226, my emphasis.

analyzed the phenomenon in terms of rhythm.[100] The couple, who followed Klages's graphological system, depicted graphology as "a surface phenomenon"—the withdrawal of the pen and the breaks between letters were "a free ticket to the great world theater (*Welttheater*). [Writing] reveals the pantomime of the whole essence of mankind and human life in one hundred thousand tiny pieces."[101] If writing was a "material" expression, or surface phenomenon, it also expressed an internal flow of life or a "plastic depth behind the writing" that can be articulated through the tracing of interruptions or intervals.[102] This graphological trace of the breaks and continuities in writing would produce a kind of rhythmical index of the writer's human essence.

Why did a post-Nietzschean understanding of rhythm come to play a role in studies of such varied subjects as drama, violence, architecture, and handwriting? Benjamin moved from his earlier reactions against neo-Kantianism, post-Nietzscheanism, and Bergsonian vitalism to a rhythmic conception of living as a critical system. Bergson had written, in *Matter and Memory*, that the rhythm of duration and sense perception "lived by our consciousness is a duration with its own determined rhythm, a duration very different from the time of the physicist," which Bergson identified with intervals of empty time.[103] In response, Benjamin developed a notion of rhythm as a central mode for social and political involvement that followed, not the senses, but the movement of time itself, beyond the human understanding of origin and history, biology and psychology. The

---

100. Walter Benjamin, "Review of the Mendelssohns' *Der Mensch in der Handschrift*," in *Selected Writings*, 2:132.

101. Benjamin, "Mendelssohns' *Der Mensch*," 134. I have modified the translation of the second passage, which reads in German: "Ihm zeigt er die Pantomime des ganzen Menschenwesens und Menschenlebens in hunderttausendfacher Verkleinerung." The English translation misses the stress on the human—*Menschen*—using instead the words "nature" and "existence," respectively.

102. Benjamin, "Mendelssohns' *Der Mensch*," 134. The English translation used "sculptural depth" for the Nietzschean "plastische Tiefe."

103. Henri Bergson, *Matter and Memory*, trans. N. M. Paul and W. S. Palmer (New York: Zone Books, 1996), 205. The book appeared in German in 1908, translated by the neo-Kantian Wilhelm Windelband as *Materie und Gedächtnis*. The translation was commissioned by the conservative publisher Eugen Diederichs on the urging of Georg Simmel.

category, when used properly, could thus shed critical light on human teleology.

Rhythm united different classes, nationalities, and intellectual worlds against dogmatic ideology. In the final sentence of "Introductory Remarks on a Series for *L'Humanité*" (1927), Benjamin wrote: "Above all, I have tried to reproduce the physiognomy of . . . [the] workday and the new rhythm that permeates the life of worker and intellectual alike."[104] The worker and the intellectual share some rhythms, such as the work–leisure rhythm of industrial modernity, while experiencing its impact in different, often opposing, ways. Rhythm functions in such fragments as an analytical category that expresses a commitment to the egalitarian force of life-forms before they separate into different, contrasting social forms. In the diary he kept during a visit to Moscow, also in 1927, Benjamin wrote, "Here the newcomer learns perhaps most quickly of all to adapt himself to the curious tempo of this city and to the rhythm of its peasant population."[105] Rhythm was an attribute that cut through socially defined categories; a capitalist tempo and the rhythm of peasant life might be shared processes felt by the human aligning his own, natural, base rhythm with that of the world around him.

It is impossible to understand Benjamin's consistent attention to rhythm without appreciating the importance of the concept in his post-Nietzschean methodology. The beating heart of Benjamin's temporal politics arose from his methodological analysis, a process that favored the event (what Arendt would later call "natality"): "The origin of great works has often been conceptualized in terms of the image of birth. . . . In the act of completion, the created thing gives birth once more to its creator."[106] In other words, origin and creation are as much the outcome of a process as their initiation. As will be demonstrated below, the metaphor of rhythmic breath, before and while giving birth to its creator, was semantically consistent with Benjamin's understanding of a pre-language in "the womb of

---

104. Walter Benjamin, "Introductory Remarks on a Series for *L'Humanité*," in *Selected Writings*, 2.1:21.
105. Benjamin, "Moscow," in *Selected Writings*, 2.1:32.
106. Benjamin, "Little Tricks of the Trade," in *Selected Writings*, 2.2:730.

time."[107] The insistent reappearance of this trope, from "The Metaphysics of Youth" to *The Arcades Project*, attests to a reading of rhythm as the apparatus that upends norms, conventions, and political expectations.[108] As such, rhythm was meant to unite the singularity of the event and its repetitive potential, or the contingent and the structural.[109] Though this may sound all too Nietzschean, the singularity and repetition of time lie at the heart of Jewish temporality. The historian Sylvie Anne Goldberg put it, "The rhythm of Jewish temporality ... forms both a circle and a line, for the goal toward which it tends is nothing less than the suspension of time."[110]

Benjamin, Bachofen, and Kafka

I opened this chapter by quoting an enigmatic question and answer from Walter Benjamin: "Are we time?"[111] But what did Benjamin mean by "time," and who is his "we"? From his discussions of lived experience, unfulfilled time, transience, and rhythm—all of which he wrote about before the better-known "now-time" and "dialectics at a standstill"—he clearly was referring to an anthropocentric time: the time of the human, where "we" (humans) stand in opposition to the landscape. Stressing (the wrong) rhythm instead of direction—

---

107. Carolin Duttlinger pointed out that here "breathing" represents the rhythm that connects the body and the intellect. See Duttlinger, "Studium, Aufmerksamkeit, Gebet: Walter Benjamin und die Kontemplation," in *Profanes Leben: Walter Benjamins Dialektik der Säkularisierung*, ed. Daniel Weidner (Berlin: Suhrkamp, 2010), 102.

108. For Richard Wolin, Benjamin's commitment to temporal terms shows his "decisive break from the Enlightenment (and social-democratic) notion of historical progress." See Wolin, *Walter Benjamin: An Aesthetic of Redemption* (Berkeley: University of California Press, 1994), 49. Wolin was not wrong, but the emphasis he places on Benjamin's resistance to social democratic politics—which would lead Benjamin to issue a general condemnation of those he called the "Jewish children of Heidegger"—ignores Benjamin's use of temporal concepts for the sake of stressing radical democratic ideas.

109. Hanssen, *Walter Benjamin's Other History*, 42, 44.

110. Sylvie Anne Goldberg, "Categories of Time: Scales and Values in Ashkenazi Culture," *Jewish Studies* 39 (2000): 91.

111. Benjamin, "The Metaphysics of Youth," 153.

man's advance into and over nature—also demonstrates an awareness that the man–nature division itself is wrong and in need of correction. In contrast to the legacy that led from early Romanticism to Nietzsche, Benjamin did not attempt to overcome the division for the sake of a Romantic, organic collective.[112] Rather, Benjamin endeavored to discuss the repetitive, present, aimless rhythm of life, or human transience, as an inherent quality of human time itself. This acknowledgment was, I argue in this chapter, Benjamin's greatest contribution to the vocabulary of a temporal turn.

From the late 1920s on, Benjamin worked with temporal concepts as hermeneutic tools in his study of literary and philosophical texts and in his attempts to circumscribe an ontological condition. The rise of fascism forced Benjamin, as it had forced Buber, to reconsider the specific political relevance of his general understanding of time. During the 1930s Benjamin continued to engage with life philosophy, now clearly identified with fascist politics and radical German Jewish critique. The essays Benjamin wrote on Franz Kafka and the idiosyncratic thinker Johann Jakob Bachofen explored life philosophy and its temporality as a matriarchal form, shifting his approach toward a notion of pre-human and post-human time, while rejecting the industrial and patriarchal status quo.[113] When transience characterizes human temporality, it also reveals how limited and conditioned our language and our tools of measurement are in their attempts to reach the outside world. Bachofen exposed this limitation as a top-down structure: Patriarchal, power-driven, and coercive language used a set of symbols that obliterated all traces of pre-Roman matriarchal culture. Kafka exposed the internalization of normative and institutional language, driven by the modern obsession with the absence of telos. Written in 1934, Benjamin's essays on Kafka and Bachofen use the concept of rhythm to counter nineteenth-century conventions of patriarchy, sovereignty, and logic.

---

112. See Ian Balfour, *The Rhetoric of Romantic Prophecy* (Stanford, CA: Stanford University Press, 2002), 189.

113. Feminist interpretations of Benjamin have not recognized the centrality of either matriarchic or rhythmic motifs to his oeuvre. For an overview of various feminist interpretations of Benjamin, see Eva Geulen, "Toward a Genealogy of Gender in Walter Benjamin's Writing," *German Quarterly* 69, no. 2 (1996): 161–80.

While Kafka is well-known, Bachofen has remained a more niche figure within German intellectual history. Johann Jakob Bachofen (1815–87) was a student of the historian of law Friedrich Karl von Savigny and a public critic of the father of modern historicism, Theodor Mommsen. As a professor of law at the University of Basel, Bachofen developed a critique of Western logocentrism and patriarchy, two phenomena he identified with the Prussian state. Instead of the systematic use of legal and historical precedent, he proposed the idea of a matriarchy (*Mutterrecht*), the fruits of his ethnographic studies. Only the feminine, Bachofen argued, united the sensuous and the otherworldly, Orient and Occident.[114] He hoped to revive a long-lost mythic world of immanent life, femininity, and sisterhood that predated Hellenism.[115] Nietzsche, who taught in Basel from 1869 to 1878, came to appreciate Bachofen as a major intellectual force.[116] During the early 1900s a revival of Bachofen's ideas was led by Karl Wolfskehl, a German Jewish poet devoted to the teachings of Stefan George. Another member of the George circle, Ludwig Klages, introduced masses of German readers to Bachofen through the edited and republished volumes of Bachofen's oeuvre he produced. By tracking down Bachofen's widow, he obtained previously unpublished manuscripts, fostering a Bachofen renaissance in the 1920s.[117]

Benjamin took part in this renaissance, joining a lively debate over the correct interpretation of Bachofen and Nietzsche. Bernoulli was much influenced by Klages and Nietzsche, and his essays seem to

---

114. Damien Valdez, "Bachofen's Rome and the Fate of the Feminine Orient," *Journal of the History of Ideas* 70, no. 3 (2009): 422.

115. Lionel Gossman, *Orpheus Philologus: Bachofen versus Mommsen on the Study of Antiquity* (Philadelphia: American Philosophical Society, 1983); Andreas Cesana, *Johann Jakob Bachofens Geschichtsdeutung: Eine Untersuchung ihrer geschichtsphilosophischen Voraussetzungen* (Basel: Birkhäuser, 1983), 87.

116. The Nietzsche biographer Julian Young argues that during his decade as a professor at the University of Basel, the philosopher was most intellectually indebted to Bachofen, Jacob Burkhardt, and Wilhelm Vischer-Bilfinger. See Julian Young, *Friedrich Nietzsche: A Philosophical Biography* (Cambridge: Cambridge University Press, 2010), 103.

117. Lebovic, *Philosophy of Life and Death*, 79–110; Ernst Karl Winter, "Bachofen-Renaissance," *Zeitschrift für die gesamte Staatswissenschaft* 85, no. 2 (1928): 316–42.

have introduced Benjamin to the archaic elements in Nietzsche and Bachofen. Benjamin reviewed Bernoulli's book about Bachofen in 1926, and drew inspiration from Bachofen, Klages, and George even as he denounced their politics. Eight years later, in a study of Bachofen originally written in French for the *Nouvelle revue française*, Benjamin described Bachofen's matriarchal community moving to a "rhythm of creation and destruction"—a lost world of swamps and promiscuous Amazons.[118] The Amazon—rather than the male heroes in Homer—is the real agent of change in a borderless oriental world. If for Bachofen the Amazon and the swamp offered an autochthonic image of primordial myth as part of "the most ancient human community," Benjamin further radicalized their critical potential by stressing that in matriarchal society, "death in no way suggests a violent destruction."[119] Seen from a matriarchal viewpoint, destruction is an integral part of life, but unlike nihilistic interpretations, it does not stand above or beyond it.

Benjamin continued to refer to Bachofen's ideas, often mediated via Klages's reception, in different texts, most importantly in his paper "Franz Kafka."[120] The occasion for writing was an invitation from Robert Weltsch, chief editor of the *Jüdische Rundschau* and a close friend to Martin Buber and Hugo Bergmann. Benjamin accepted the invitation but warned Weltsch that his reading would not conform to the "straightforward theological explication of Kafka" (the form of interpretation Buber and Scholem offered) or agree with Max Brod's (and later, Buber's) labeling of Kafka as a prophet.[121] In

---

118. Walter Benjamin, "Johann Jakob Bachofen," in *Selected Writings*, 3:18; Benjamin, "Carl Albrecht Bernoulli, Johann Jakob Bachofen, und das Natursymbol: Ein Würdigungsversuch," in *Gesammelte Schriften*, 3:43–44. The essay remained unpublished during his lifetime (it was rejected by the magazine). Rodolphe Gasché thinks that Benjamin received such ideas from Ernst Bloch. The evidence I found for Benjamin's long relationship with Klages demonstrates the opposite. See Rodolphe Gasché, *The Stelliferous Fold: Toward a Virtual Law of Literature's Self-Formation* (New York: Fordham University Press, 2011), 283.
119. Benjamin, "Johan Jakob Bachofen," 14.
120. Liska, *German-Jewish Thought*, 57. Vivian Liska recently identified its message with "the Jewish juridical tradition," while demonstrating where Benjamin rejected Scholem's mystical key.
121. Walter Benjamin to Robert Weltsch, May 9, 1934, in Scholem and Adorno, *Correspondence of Walter Benjamin*, 442; Gershom Scholem to Walter Benjamin,

contrast to Scholem's emphasis on Kafka's Jewishness, Benjamin was fascinated to discover in *The Castle* and the short stories on animals a vision of time connected to Bachofen's swamp world.[122] He and Scholem had battled this out in countless letters written between 1925 and 1934; the article Benjamin wrote may be seen as an extension of the debate.

In the essay he problematized both the notion of origin and that of an ending, working from the assumption of an alternative nonlinear rhythm of existence. Three years before embarking on the article, he had remarked, "[Bachofen's] world is located ... in the study of the *hetaeric*. Kafka's novels are placed in [this] swamp world."[123] (For Bachofen, the Greek word *hetaeric* refers to an oriental nomadic phase in the evolution of human society, before the establishment of social hierarchy and family structures. It is characterized by

---

September 20, 1934, in *The Correspondence of Walter Benjamin and Gershom Scholem, 1932–1940*, ed. Gershom Scholem, trans. Gary Smith and Andre Lefevere (New York: Schocken, 1989), 72. For close readings of the double critique, see Liska, *German-Jewish Thought*, 57; Uwe Steiner, *Walter Benjamin: An Introduction to His Work and Thought*, trans. Michael Winkler (Chicago: University of Chicago Press, 2010), 134.

122. "Die Welt befindet sich, nach ihrer Naturseite, bei ihm in dem Stadium, das Bachofen das hetärische genannt hat. Kafkas Romane spielen in einer Sumpfwelt." See Walter Benjamin, "Franz Kafka," in *Gesammelte Schriften*, 2:1:236. "Kafka did not consider the age in which he lived as an advance over the beginnings of time. His novels are set in a swamp world. In his works, the creature appears at the stage which Bachofen has termed the hetaeric stage." Benjamin, in *Selected Writings*, 2.2:808–9. Vivian Liska has mentioned that in his 1931 outline for the essay, Benjamin contrasted Bachofen's "swamp world" with Jewish law, whose "purity and dietary laws display the defense mechanism against this world.... In other words, only the Halakha [Jewish law] still contains traces of this mode of existence of mankind that is long past." For Liska the opposition demonstrated a positive view of Judaism: "The lawless world of prehistory depicted by Kafka is, for Benjamin, also the measure of his own present. Writing as a Jew in the 1930s, Benjamin describes the legal system of his own times through a characterization of Kafka's swamp world in which the laws have become identical with the ultimate lawlessness reigning in an oppressive state of exception." See Liska, *German-Jewish Thought*, 58.

123. Walter Benjamin, "Aufzeichnungen zu einem ungeschriebenen Essay und zum Vortrag von 1931," in *Benjamin über Kafka: Texte, Briefzeugnisse, Aufzeichnungen*, ed. Hermann Schweppenhäuser (Frankfurt: Suhrkamp, 1981), 116, my translation.

sexual freedom and a struggle for survival.)[124] Why a swamp? Because the swamp, in Bachofen's theory, was where the prelinguistic rhythm of life took shape. Originating in the swamp and shaped by matriarchal society, the temporality of life led directly into linguistic and bodily expression and to their eventual decline and death through the death of the body that formed them. In contrast to the Western culture that emerged from Roman law, in this pre-civilized world life came before logic or conscious representation.

For Bachofen, the swamp was a long-lost paradise of vast potential, the "ever-becoming" of an alternate organic world; women were pre-symbolic, pre-rational creatures who represented an alternative form of sociality and government in a world dominated by a surplus of instrumental reason. Bachofen's world, the Romanist Lionel Gossman noted, was "situate[d] between the swamps and darkness of the original 'tellurian' unity of all nature and the blinding 'solar' light of nature, an Edenic moment on the threshold of history, a moment of peace and harmony before the long voyage through the wilderness which will be man's lot, and in the course of which he will have to earn his right to be reborn to a *vita nuova* of the spirit."[125] The harmony and unity of an Edenic moment offered a viable, attractive alternative to Enlightenment science, technological progress, and an assumed superiority of man over nature. Early in its story, humankind did not distinguish between beginning, middle, and end; creation, life, and death; the human, the creaturely, and the animal. An organic rhythm of life flowed among those states, regulating and reflecting their shifts. Life and death, creation and destruction, movement and stasis, outside and inside were immanent potentials within this world. Bachofen's Romantic politics idolized and elevated matriarchy and the feminine into concepts that could provide a countermodel to alienated instrumental rationality.

Benjamin followed Kafka along lines suggested by Bachofen, supplementing with his own "anti-lines," as it were—a distrust of

---

124. For more about the different stages, see Peter Davies, "Myth and Maternalism in the Work of Johann Jakob Bachofen," *German Studies Review* 28, no. 3 (2005): 501–18.

125. Gossman, *Orpheus Philologus*, 32.

progress and the dichotomies between human and nature, male and female, human and creaturely. "Kafka did not consider the age in which he lived as an advance over the beginnings of time, he wrote. "His novels are set in a swamp world. In his works, the creature appears at the stage which Bachofen has termed the *hetaeric age*."[126] Passages like this had political implications. As I discussed in chapter 2, in the 1920s there was intense interest in the creaturely (*Kreatürlichkeit*), exciting the likes of Buber, Viktor von Weizsäcker, and Eugen Rosenstock-Huessy. By the 1930s such counter-Enlightenment language became bound up with distinctly racist and colonialist impulses that had little to do with Bachofen's and Nietzsche's politics.

Instead of stressing a militant, Aryan *Lebensraum*, Benjamin read the swamp as an environment rich in egalitarianism that fostered political dissent and the critique of norms.[127] Viewing the swamp from that perspective explains how a site of disappearance, where everything is literally being swallowed, negates any gradual and linear advancement. In the swamp, time could flow backward. The swamp was a place where beings disappeared or appeared out of nowhere, where being and nonbeing met and fused. This paradigm ran counter to the hope for regulated and measured progress toward perfection. "Laws and definite norms remain unwritten in the prehistoric world," Benjamin remarked, noting that Kafka used ur-images (primordial images) drawn from that world to express a deep connection to living time.[128] The retroactive attempt to order this world could not help but fail, or at least leave unfulfilled gaps. Failing to acknowledge a moment of nonbeing in human experience

---

126. Benjamin, "Franz Kafka," in *Selected Writings*, 2:808–9.

127. One finds images straight out of Bachofen in later texts such as Benjamin's *The Arcades Project*. At one point Benjamin writes of "female giants," at another of the dialectical image born from the "womb of time," itself the result of an explosive clash and fusion of civilizations: "Another art ... will struggle from the womb of time to be born." See Benjamin, Conv. F: "Iron Construction," fragment F1, 1, in *The Arcades Project*, 150.

128. Benjamin, "Franz Kafka," 797. See also Nitzan Lebovic, "The Beauty and Terror of *Lebensphilosophie*: Ludwig Klages, Walter Benjamin, and Alfred Baeumler," *South Central Review* 23, no. 1 (2006): 23–39.

"does not mean that it does not extend into the present. On the contrary: it is present by virtue of its oblivion."[129]

The metaphor of the womb, like that of the swamp, links time to a lost creation, an alternative becoming, and an unknown future. Benjamin illustrates this by turning to Kafka's female protagonists:

> The ambiguous Frieda reminisces about her earlier life: "You never asked me about my past" [*The Castle*]. This past takes us back to the dark, deep womb, the scene of the mating "whose untrammeled voluptuousness," to quote Bachofen, "is hateful to the pure forces of heavenly light and which justifies the term used by Arnobius, *luteae voluptates* [dirty voluptuousness]." Only from this vantage point can the technique of Kafka the storyteller be comprehended. Whenever figures in the novels have anything to say to K., no matter how important or surprising it may be, they do so casually and with the implication that he must really have known it all along.[130]

Frieda is not the only female protagonist who evokes a primordial past in Kafka's stories. Josephine, the singing mouse, recalls her "brief childhood" and "something of lost happiness which can never be found again, but also something of active present-day life."[131] The story entitled "The Silence of the Sirens," along with Leni in *The Castle*, reminds us of the swamp world in which childhood and motherhood predate patriarchy: "It is from the swampy soil of such experiences that Kafka's female characters rise. They are swamp creatures."[132]

Indeed, Benjamin explained, Kafka's stories "[did] not belong entirely in the tradition of Western prose forms; they have, rather, a relationship to religious teaching" such as Jewish allegory or ancient myths, before a clear line separated literal and metaphorical, man and animal, male and female, before (childhood) and after (old age)."[133] And if this sounds like an invitation to reduce Kafka's storytelling to a psychological or theological form, Benjamin warned

---

129. Benjamin, "Franz Kafka," 808–9.
130. Benjamin, "Franz Kafka," 809.
131. Benjamin, "Franz Kafka," 799.
132. Benjamin, "Franz Kafka," 809.
133. Benjamin, "Franz Kafka," 803.

us: "There are two ways to miss the point of Kafka's works. One is to interpret them naturally; the other is to interpret them from a supernatural perspective. Both the psychoanalytical and the theological interpretations miss the essential points."[134] His essential point, he explained in a different allusion to Bachofen, was to warn us of conventional language and its hidden ideological agenda: "The history of authority, to the extent that it comprises the increasing integration of social compulsion through the inner life of the individual, essentially coincides with that of the patricentric family."[135]

The Womb of the Earth

The metaphor of the womb recurs in different works during the 1930s, always in relation to an alternative temporal-political order. In "The Storyteller" (1936), Benjamin's study of Nikolai Leskov, a nonlinear apprehension of life, history, identity, law, and politics begins from the womb, positioned outside time, from the points of view of the woman, the fetus, the dwarf, and the Jew, all of whom refuse the patriarchal, the material world, the apparatus. A passage from one of Leskov's stories must have resonated, as Benjamin quoted it at length. It evoked "that old time when the stones in the womb of the earth and the planets at celestial heights were still concerned with the fate of men—unlike today, when both in the heavens and beneath the earth everything has grown indifferent."[136] The "womb of the earth and the planets" connects humankind with both earth and heaven. Once the normal coordination between the living time of symbols, tradition, and long individual experience (*Erfahrung*)

---

134. Benjamin, "Franz Kafka," 806.
135. Benjamin, "The Storyteller," in *Selected Writings*, 3:153. Benjamin wrote in 1938, "Fromm's ... analysis of the family leads him back to Bachofen, ... which Engels and Lafargue regarded as one of the greatest historical discoveries of their century. The history of authority, to the extent that it comprises the increasing integration of social compulsion through the inner life of the individual, essentially coincides with that of the patricentric family." See Benjamin, "A German Institute for Independent Research," in *Selected Writings*, 3:310–11.
136. Benjamin, "The Storyteller," 3:153.

has been lost (Benjamin tempered Nietzsche's rather brutal label, the death of God), humanity was left with an anxious and obsessive bourgeois "self" and an abstract and internalized sense of authority—the great *ersatz* father. "The Storyteller" follows the history of a lost world of stones and stars that was once "the womb of the epic" or an alternative theory of recollection and experience, which, two years later, would accompany his own autobiographical journey in "Berlin Childhood around 1900" (1938).[137]

The symbol of the womb, sphere-shaped and nonlinear, reminds us of the swamp: both stand for fertility, but no fertilizer can be found. If there is a "seed" in this process, it is autogenerative, sent or created by and within the womb and the swamp. For Benjamin, there is no linear process leading from promise (impregnation) to realization (birth); rather, the process occasions the reverse, as the created conditions its creators. The created (the child, the creature) conditions its naming (the parent, God).[138] In "Berlin Childhood," Benjamin reminisces about his fascination with watercolor spots and soap bubbles, iridescent marvels that would "open their womb to me."[139] This spontaneous manifestation of iridescence recalls his short essay about "Painting, or Signs and Marks" (1917), in which an account of color blossoming prior to subjective perception already reveals Benjamin's fascination with ideas of generative creation independent of human creators.[140]

Another diary entry from that time was devoted to the books he had read as a boy: "In these books there were stormy goings-on. To

---

137. Benjamin, "The Storyteller," 3:154.
138. "Adam's naming of the creatures in Genesis is intended as a repudiation of the mythical view that names are riddles that have to be guessed.... The Jewish name (in Hebrew) is a mystery." Benjamin, "Riddle and Mystery," in *Selected Writings*, 1:268. As Benjamin explains in various essays since his 1916 essay on language, this temporality defines the language of humanity, and language, in turn, defines our understanding of the world.
139. My translation. The German reads "mir ihren Schoss auftaten." The translators who produced the English edition chose a slightly different translation—"when things would take me to their bosom"—acknowledging in a note that they had prioritized idiomatic language over accuracy. See Benjamin, "Berlin Childhood," in *Selected Writings*, 380n46.
140. Benjamin, "Painting and the Graphic Arts," in *Selected Writings*, 1:82.

open one would have landed me in the lap of the storm, in the very womb, where a brooding and changeable text—a text pregnant with colors—formed a cloud ... [that] always shaded into a violet that seemed to come from the entrails of a slaughtered animal."[141] The womb, the swamp, and the storm signaled a time of sudden change, which is a change in every direction. For Benjamin they offered a reminder, an opening into what has been lost.[142]

Indeed, such metaphors were not dissociated from the historical and political situation of the time. In diary entries from 1938 Benjamin reported a series of conversations with Bertolt Brecht; both men were refugees in Denmark at the time. Brecht had declared that fascists "don't think small. They plan thirty thousand years ahead.... They distort the child in the womb."[143] Indeed, in "On the Concept of History" (1940), Benjamin altered this observation ever so slightly to suit a more general dictum, quoted half a century later by Saidiya Hartman: "Even the dead will not be safe from the enemy if he is victorious."[144]

In *The Arcades Project*, his unfinished magnum opus, one finds repeated mentions of the same symbols in different fragments. Take, for example, the following: "The difficulty in reflecting on dwelling: on the one hand, there is something age-old—perhaps eternal—to be recognized here, the image of that abode of the human being in the maternal womb; on the other hand, this motif of primal history notwithstanding, we must understand dwelling in its most extreme form as a condition of nineteenth-century existence.... Today this world has disappeared entirely, and dwelling has diminished: for the living, through hotel rooms; for the dead, through crematoriums."[145] A short time after writing these lines,

---

141. Benjamin, "Diary Entries, 1938," in *Selected Writings*, 3:356.
142. In a study linking three domains central to Walter Benjamin's thought, Andrew Benjamin talked about "Fore-History" and "After-History," which are germane to this temporal theory; see Andrew Benjamin, *Present Hope: Philosophy, Architecture, Judaism* (London: Routledge, 1997), 40.
143. Benjamin, "Diary Entries, 1938," in *Selected Writings*, 3:340.
144. Benjamin, "On the Concept of History," Thesis V, in *Selected Writings*, 4:391. Hartman, *Scenes of Subjection*, 14.
145. Benjamin, Conv. P3, in *The Arcades Project*, 865.

the living would also be diminished through crematoriums and the condition of dwelling and "the image of that abode of the human being in the maternal womb" would have to go through another, aching, reevaluation.

On the Concept of History

In *The Arcades Project* and "On the Concept of History" (1940), Benjamin developed the principle of "now-time" (*Jeztzeit*) to turn his critical analysis of time into a coherent argument concerning the unity of critical thought.[146] Now-time is formed in a flash, a "now of recognizability," when an individual's various life courses meet; as the course of the future shifts, the past is imbued with retroactive meaning.[147] Reconfiguring the relation between past and present is accomplished by an interruption, a flash, or a standstill. If we recall the image offered in chapter 1 of this book, the attempt by a train's passengers to activate the emergency brake, we begin to understand Benjamin's distinctive thinking on history, which he viewed as a series of interruptions and deferrals.[148] Indeed, it is the moment of caesura that enables us to consider the rhythm of continuity. Benjamin's innovation was in pointing out that the dialectics of continuity and change always referred to a past story and a future hope. In his fourteenth historical thesis, he offered a general dictum: "History is the subject of a construction whose site is not homogeneous, empty time, but time filled full by now-time."[149] Although Benjamin otherwise rejects any form of fulfillment or realization, there is one place

---

146. Kia Lindroos has observed that Benjamin's earlier work is engaged with "the moment of Now, in which the acknowledgment between the singular moment of the present (Now) and past (Then) occurs. This moment is later marked as *Jetztzeit* in the Theses ["On the Concept of History"]. In this moment, the recognizing subject is characterized as a temporal mode of being, as Jetztzein." See Kia Lindroos, *Now-Time Image-Space: Temporalization of Politics in Walter Benjamin's Philosophy of History and Art* (Jyväskylä: University of Jyväskylä, 1998), 61.

147. Benjamin, "Paralipomena to 'On the Concept of History,'" in *Selected Writings*, 4:405.

148. Benjamin, "Paralipomena," 405.

149. Benjamin, "On the Concept of History," in *Selected Writings*, 4:395.

in which he considers it essential: in the modern, victorious, empty time of progress. History is regressive, even digressive: it is time in distress. In the eighteenth thesis, he elaborates: "Now-time, which, as a model of messianic time, comprises the entire history of mankind in a tremendous abbreviation, coincides exactly with the figure which the history of mankind describes in the universe."[150] In other words, the present is always a flash of now-time as a conclusive—even if changing—summary of experience and expectation, or what Reinhart Koselleck would identify, decades later, as the different "modes of temporal experience."[151]

Viewing now-time as an interval, a break in the flow of time, assumes a totality projecting backward and forward. Now-time held the key to correctly framing the past and bringing fulfillment in the future. But this totality was different from the messianic realization of hope. The totality of now-time was defined by interruption, not messianic fulfillment. Now-time, or the flash of recognition, was a political moment—and politics, as Benjamin commented in "World and Time," was "the fulfillment of an unimproved humanity." This is a theology of weak messianism, emptied of its transcendental value.[152]

"On the Concept of History" made it clear that history, rhythm, and interrupted movement were the agents of now-time, not of messianic and collective expectation. Consider the linear "method which historical materialism has broken with" (VII); how a collective faith in the power of duration led to "states of emergency" that have become the rule (VIII); or how the "new conception of labor" that "increase[s] efficiency" not only exploits nature, but "would help her give birth to the creations that now lie dormant in her womb" (XI). Thesis fifteen expands the above-mentioned themes by contrasting the ordained rhythm of clocks with the revolutionary decision to reorganize time: the revolutionary could break the rhythm of the clock by "firing on clock faces to make the day stand still."[153]

---

150. Benjamin, "On the Concept of History," 396.
151. Reinhart Koselleck, *Futures Past: On the Semantics of Historical Time*, trans. Keith Tribe (Cambridge: MIT Press, 2004), 94.
152. Benjamin, "Theological-Political Fragment," in *Selected Writings*, 3:305–6.
153. Benjamin, "On the Concept of History," 395.

This projects a different light on one of Benjamin's best-known ideas, that of a "weak messianic force."[154] Messianism cannot be understood here according to its usual meaning—namely, the realization of a transcendental understanding of history—because, as Werner Hamacher wrote, now-time brought things to a persistent standstill, "otherwise it would be [a] transition into timelessness, into the everlasting or ever-same, into a *sempiternitas* or *aesternitas*, that covers up finitude."[155]

The Arcades

The hermeneutics of time depicted in this chapter enabled Benjamin to shape a counter-idealist vocabulary and politics, as well as a demand that the early 1900s should, "in its wake," move to "expound the nineteenth century as its dream vision."[156] At the moment of awakening, this Arcades fragment explains, the task of the "female messiah" was to be a revolutionary,[157] an "intellectual sharpshooter" who took "the role of the intellectual pacesetter."[158] Awakening itself is described in the Arcades as "a not-yet-conscious knowledge of what has been," which Benjamin equates with "the dissolution of 'mythology' into the space of history."[159] The dense fragments he produced late in his career not only call for a reevaluation of past traditions, but do so while acknowledging the integral role of the observer, the

---

154. An exception to this critique is an enlightening chapter about Benjamin and Paul Celan in Michael G. Levine, *A Weak Messianic Power: Figures of a Time to Come in Benjamin, Derrida, and Celan* (New York: Fordham University Press, 2014), 14–36.
155. Hamacher, "'Now,'" 178.
156. Benjamin, Conv. K1, 4, in *The Arcades Project*, 389; Benjamin, in *Gesammelte Schriften*, 5:492: "um das XIX Jahrhundert ... als die Folge seiner Traumgeschichte zu deuten."
157. Benjamin, Conv. U 14a, 4, in *The Arcades Project*, 597.
158. Eiland and Jennings, *Walter Benjamin*, 272–73.
159. Benjamin, N1, in *The Arcades Project*, 9. For a close reading of this passage in the context of the competing interpretations of Leibniz's *Monadology* in Benjamin, Husserl, and Heidegger, see Paula Schwebel, "Monad and Time: Reading Leibniz with Heidegger and Benjamin," in *Sparks Will Fly: Benjamin and Heidegger*, ed. Andrew Benjamin and Dimitris Vardoulakis (Albany: SUNY Press, 2016), 137.

storyteller, and the future-oriented effect she could have.[160] The role of an "intellectual pacemaker" is similar to the "life of the actor" in the "world theater" of German Jewish letters. It is the life of the one who experiences the deepest and most troubling shock of all—a temporal turn—and instead of searching for justifications, or hiding place, embraces it with open arms.

Benjamin's texts belong to a period that was deeply engaged, both politically and philosophically, with the repercussions of the nineteenth century. Peter Osborne observed, "What Benjamin is seeking is a fissure in this temporal structure through which to break it open onto a new form of historical experience."[161] In *The Arcades Project* and "On the Concept of History," Benjamin made a courageous attempt to write from within the crisis and in a way that would reflect his key interest in rhythm, intervals, repetitions, and explosions of energy. But time ran out for him before the project could be completed. *The Arcades Project*—a work that began at the end of the 1920s and continued until Benjamin's suicide in 1940—demonstrated a full break with the modern Eurocentrism targeted by Nietzsche. In a letter he wrote to Stephan Lackner in May 1940, Benjamin recognized the danger of an "ingenious synthesis of two Nietzschean concepts, namely the 'good Europeans' and the 'last man.' This synthesis would result in the last European—something we are all striving not to become."[162] What was so dreadful about this imaginary last European? Nietzsche's engagement with temporality had led him to formulate an image of a mythical, cyclical ur-history (*Urgeschichte*) that contrasted with the nineteenth-century Western ideal of progress, but it was not sufficient to deter those fascists who utilized Nietzsche in order to distort, not just progress, but also "the child in

---

160. Daniel Weidner, "Fort-, Über-, Nachleben: Zu einer Denkfigur bei Benjamin," in *Benjamin-Studien 2*, ed. Daniel Weidner and Sigrid Weigel (Munich: W. Fink, 2011), 161–78.

161. Osborne, *The Politics of Time*, 143.

162. Walter Benjamin to Stephan Lackner, May 5, 1940, in Walter Benjamin, *Gesammelte Briefe*, vol. 6, *1938–1940*, ed. Christoph Gödde and Henri Lonitz (Frankfurt: Suhrkamp, 2000), 441. "On se demande si l'histoire n'est pas en train de forger une synthèse ingénieuse de deux conceptions nietzschéenes, à savoir des guten Europäers et des letzten Menschen. Cela pourrait donner den letzten Europäer. Nous tous nous luttons pour ne pas le devenir"; my translation.

the womb." Benjamin identified his attempt to overcome this heritage with his own life and thought. Hannah Arendt, a close friend, reflected in 1968 about his legacy and his reluctance to visit America, "where as he used to say, people would probably find no other use for him than to cart him up and down the country to exhibit him as the 'last European.'"[163]

Benjamin's now-time—or the "now of recognizability"—was committed to revolutionary praxis with an alternate temporality at its core. Benjamin's choice of reading reflects his political views and his interest in the revolution of time. One important example of this move was a fascination with a book by Louis Auguste Blanqui, written while Blanqui was imprisoned and could not participate in the Paris Commune. Benjamin read the book in 1937, shortly before reading Karl Löwith on Nietzsche's eternal recurrence; he would draw up his own interpretation of Nietzsche's theme.[164] As he explained in *The Arcades Project*, Blanqui's theory showed "a *répétition du mythe*—a fundamental example of the primal history (*Urgeschichte*) of the nineteenth century."[165] If repetition was the negative mirror-image of the nineteenth-century notion of progress, Nietzsche drew it to the fore: "The idea of eternal return in *Zarathustra* is, according to its true nature, a stylization of the worldview that in Blanqui still displays its infernal traits. It is a stylization of existence down to the tiniest fractions of its temporal process."[166] Once again, the temporal process sets the stakes of politics, style and story-telling, history and life.

Convolutes D and J in *The Arcades Project* revolve around those themes, linking the forgotten legacy of the last man (which Gilles Deleuze would later identify with "passive nihilism") to eternal recurrence and contrasting it with a happy "yet once again" of lesbian love. Benjamin, like his hero Baudelaire, was fascinated by Gustave

---

163. Hannah Arendt, "Walter Benjamin, 1892–1940," in *Men in Dark Times* (San Diego: Harcourt Brace Jovanovich, 1983[1968]), 170.
164. McFarland, *Constellation*, 234–35.
165. Benjamin, Conv. D10, 2, in *The Arcades Project*, 118.
166. Benjamin, Conv. S8, 3, in *The Arcades Project*, 557. Nevertheless, he continued, "*Zarathustra*'s style disavows itself in the doctrine that is expounded through it."

Courbet's *The Sleepers*—a painting of a lesbian couple resting after lovemaking; for him it was a great example of nonrepetition.[167] "Lesbian love," Benjamin wrote, "carries spiritualization forward into the very womb of the woman. There it raises its lily-banner of 'pure love,' which knows no pregnancy and no family."[168] In contrast to the bourgeois "phantasmagoria of happiness," which Benjamin identified with eternal recurrence, the pure love of lesbians and revolutionary politics indicted conventional family structures, social and political institutions, norms and habits as tools of oppression.[169] In contrast, the idea of a womb—Julia Kristeva identified it with a rhythm that precedes language—implied a "struggle from the womb of time to be born."[170] The maternal womb, as mentioned above, is the site of dwelling and of the formation of time: "existence not in the house but in the shell."[171]

In grappling with Benjamin's thought, Paul Celan adopted the metaphor of the shell in his discussions of time. Arendt positioned Benjamin alongside Kafka as modern political critics. Buber, Bergmann, and Scholem had read Benjamin's essay on Kafka in 1934, and kept him in mind as a great thinker. Celebrating his sixtieth birthday, in 1957, Gershom Scholem told those in the room—probably alluding to Heidegger's "what is called thinking?" (1954)—that Benjamin "taught me what is called thinking."[172] What is thinking according to Benjamin and his German Jewish compatriots? Arendt identified it with the struggle to break loose from the "linguistic impossibility" of the previous generation of bourgeois paternalism. The struggle forced this generation into complicity with bourgeois norms and required that critical minds take a stand. "[Benjamin's] outlook"

---

167. Benjamin, J7, 8, in *The Arcades Project*, 240.
168. Benjamin, S8a, 3, in *The Arcades Project*, 558.
169. Benjamin, S8a, 3, 558. For Benjamin's refutation of "phantasmagoria of happiness" see Benjamin, D9, 2, *The Arcades Project*, 117.
170. Benjamin, F1, 1, 150. For a focused discussion of the womb in Kristeva's theory, see Noëlle McAfee, *Julia Kristeva* (New York: Routledge, 2004), 18.
171. Benjamin, P, 3, in *The Arcades Project*, 865.
172. Hugo Bergmann, journal entry, December 5, 1957, in Bergmann, *Tagebücher und Briefe, vol. 2, 1948–1975*, ed. Miriam Sambursky (Königstein: Jüdischer Verlag bei Athenäum, 1985), 265. "Von Walter Benjamin habe er [Scholem—N.L.] gelernt, was es heist zu denken."

wrote Arendt, "was typical of an entire generation of German-Jewish intellectuals," a generation that had turned against its fathers.[173] Benjamin and Kafka confronted the Jewish question, which their fathers had tried to ignore, by creating an alternative mode of thought based on critique. In different ways, both rejected the nineteenth century's language of norms, laws, and linear temporality to make a place for themselves in the twentieth.

In that respect, Benjamin's revolutionary thought expounded the critique, rather than the erasure, of tradition. It deployed Nietzsche's critical reading of repetition. He attacked historicism but historicized his attack. In other words, Benjamin's consistent interest in time demonstrated his attentiveness to radical and subversive forms and answered an existing world of letters and ideas.

What would a relevant use of Benjamin look like in the first quarter of the twenty-first century? Two decades into a century shaped by very different concerns—as we confront the dangers posed not by enormously destructive weapons but by the very engines that we assumed were driving progress but instead are accelerating the damage to our planet—the time has come to break away from the twentieth century and its willful abandonment of all sense of history. Benjamin's temporal politics could provide some remarkable tools for evaluating our place in an era defined by the domination that human activity has come to exert on all aspects of the natural world. Hamacher has explained that Benjamin's understanding of time was not based on a "straightforwardly Judeo-Christian theology, but rather [on] a theology of the missed, or the deserted."[174] Perhaps, then, our now-time, the now-time of the 2020s, with its almost godlike ability to transform future bodies and past traditions, could transcend the limitations of *kairos* to take its place as a "proper time" or "full time."[175] Jérôme Baschet has pointed out, invoking both Benjamin and Hartog, that a new opening to the future means

---

173. Arendt, "Walter Benjamin," 179.
174. Hamacher, "'Now,'" 164.
175. I have followed here François Hartog's analysis of Christian eschatology as a "*Kairos* of now"—an understanding that the "*Kairos* is fulfilled." See Hartog, *Regimes of Historicity: Presentism and Experiences of Time*, trans. Saskia Brown (New York: Columbia University Press, 2015), 10.

a multidirectional model of history and time: "History cannot be thought of as made in the image of time itself, as a single flow, but must rather appear as an entanglement of multiple currents, sometimes turbulent, deliberately contradictory and made of up of different, occasionally out-of-sync rhythms."[176] Working with Benjamin's now-time means understanding the historical rhythm of the nineteenth and twentieth centuries, but not necessarily their particular future—the threat of the Anthropocene—which transcends the limitations of human time.

Benjamin's understanding of time was an attempt to separate all of the classic temporal dyads—origin and end, means and ends, rhythm and immobility—as well as, by implication, the relation between the plurality of potentials and the singularity of realization. Those who have recently turned their thinking to the Anthropocene, such as Hartog, Chakrabarty, and Hamilton, have combined plurality and singularity without relying on idealist language. In 2014 Hans Ulrich Gumbrecht wrote, "We are inclined to turn our backs on the future" because "we no longer know in what direction we should progress."[177] In the world of the Anthropocene, we need to expound the self-referential index not only of the nineteenth but of the twentieth century as well. It is impossible to understand Benjamin's thought without realizing that he wrote within both an intellectual context of post-Nietzschean Lebensphilosophie and a social context Arendt described as "the hell of German Jewish letters."[178] Like Arendt, our task, as translators of now-time, is to reevaluate its relevance and use for our time.

---

176. Jérôme Baschet, *Défaire la tyrannie du présent: Temporalités èmergentes et futurs inédits* (Paris: La Découverte, 2018), 230. Translated in Marek Tamm, "How to Reinvent the Future?," *History and Theory* 59, no. 3 (2020): 456.
177. Gumbrecht, *Our Broad Present*, 32.
178. Hannah Arendt, "Walter Benjamin," 187.

4

AGAINST SELF-REFERENTIALITY

Hannah Arendt Reads Augustine

In his preface to Hannah Arendt's Jewish writings, Jerome Kohn relates a telling anecdote about Arendt's Jewishness. Encountering a student who did not look Jewish but had a decidedly Jewish surname, Arendt inquired about his background. Assuming he knew what she was getting at, he responded by describing himself as half Jewish. Arendt, Kohn tells us, "looked at her student for what seemed to him an interminable time—though it probably lasted less than twenty seconds . . . before abruptly changing the subject. About six months later, when Rosh Hashanah came around . . . she asked him if he were going to celebrate the holiday, and when he said that he had no plans to do so, she said 'Well, anyway, I want to wish you a happy new year . . . to the Jewish half of you.'"[1] Though she was a radical secularist who often attacked her fellow Jews and refused to

---

1. Jerome Kohn, preface to *The Jewish Writings* by Hannah Arendt (New York: Schocken, 2007), xiv.

let her identity determine her sense of reality, she cared enough to greet him on the eve of Rosh Hashanah. Kohn reads the incident as addressing "the question of what being a Jew means to Arendt." Such celebratory moments still resonated with Arendt, evoking "her experience as a Jew" or what I identify in this chapter as her understanding of Judaism, identity, and politics, via her understanding of time.[2]

Like other German Jewish thinkers of her generation, Arendt was centrally concerned with temporality. Like Georg Simmel, Martin Buber, Walter Benjamin, and Gershom Scholem, as well as Karl Löwith and Hans Jonas, she considered time an answer to the question of identity.[3] Similarly to her Jewish compatriots, she noted the centrality of birth, the insertion of man [human] into time, the seasons of life, finality and death, to modern thinking. In spite of focusing on political forms and organizations, Arendt was unique in her ability to grasp wide historical currents that pushed such concepts to the fore. In her examinations of other German Jewish thinkers, she usually focused on their notions of time, history, and memory, tradition, and canonical texts. Committed to a critical reception of Jewish and Christian thinkers, as well as progressives and conservatives, in 1935 she diagnosed with a mixture of irony and admiration Martin Buber's theopolitical approach as planting "the seeds of the future in the past."[4] In her introduction to a collection of Benjamin's essays, she explained that "he was greatly attracted not by religion but by theology and the theological type of interpretation for which the text itself is sacred."[5] Her own contribution focused on the point

---

2. Kohn, preface, xxii.
3. Antonio Calcagno's otherwise excellent article about Arendt's philosophy of time misses that point and therefore does not achieve a coherent picture of the three axes he identifies in her work—the "time-experienced," time as spontaneity and natality, and "the philosophical position on the very nature of time itself"—and the engagement with her German Jewish identity vis-à-vis Heidegger and Christianity. Instead Calcagno focuses on her understanding of time-experienced and on forgetting. See Antonio Calcagno, "The Role of Forgetting in Our Experience of Time: Augustine of Hippo and Hannah Arendt," *Parrhesia* 13 (2011): 14–27.
4. Arendt, "The Jewish Question," in *The Jewish Writings*, 43.
5. Hannah Arendt, Introduction to Walter Benjamin, *Illuminations: Essays and Reflections*, trans. Harry Zohn (New York: Schocken Books, 2007), 4.

"between past and future," the title of her most paradigmatic collection of essays. As I will show in this chapter, time was the most important hermeneutic principle underlying Arendt's political and social thought. For Arendt, an ontology of time, and an epistemology of the present, were the condition of belonging in the world. The advent of a new year was therefore key to her own experience and understanding of the world.

Hannah Arendt was born in 1906 in Hanover to a German Jewish family with roots, on both sides, in Königsberg, the city of Immanuel Kant.[6] Her father died when she was eight years old, and in the years spanning World War I she lived with her mother in Berlin; after her mother's remarriage, the family returned to Königsberg. Arendt began taking courses in philosophy and theology even before her matriculation exams. Her college education was at the University of Berlin, where she studied with Romano Guardini, an acclaimed Catholic philosopher of religion. In the fall of 1924 she began her graduate studies at the University of Marburg, the home of the neo-Kantian Hermann Cohen, who had taught there only a few years before, and where she met the rising philosopher Martin Heidegger.[7] Arendt was eighteen to Heidegger's thirty-five, but her intellectual capacity and scope were already impressive. According to biographies, she was well-versed in Kantian philosophy and avidly read Kierkegaard, among others. In Heidegger's seminar Arendt met fellow students Karl Löwith, Leo Strauss, Hans Jonas, and others. As another student, the philosopher Hans-Georg Gadamer described it, "Heidegger's creative energies in the early 1920s seemed to sweep along the generation of students returning from World War I or just beginning its studies, so that a complete break with traditional academic philosophy seemed to take place with Heidegger's

---

6. This short biographical sketch relies primarily on Elisabeth Young-Bruehl, *Hannah Arendt: For Love of the World* (New Haven, CT: Yale University Press, 1982).

7. Cohen taught in Marburg between 1875 and 1912. Largely due to his efforts, Marburg became one important home for neo-Kantians. See Frederick Beiser, *Hermann Cohen: An Intellectual Biography* (Oxford: Oxford University Press, 2018), 75–93.

appearance—long before it was expressed in his own thought."[8] Hans Jonas explained that "even before *Being and Time* (1927) Heidegger had acquired a sort of crypto-fame."[9] Jonas himself met Arendt in 1924 and was immediately attracted to the "defiant Jew." "Of course I noticed her at once—who wouldn't have? ... What brought us together was that we were the only Jews in Rudolf Bultmann's seminar."[10] Later Jonas and Arendt would be two of Heidegger's most promising Jewish students. The topics and conversations that germinated in this context continued to engage Arendt for the rest of her life. Her lifelong friendship with Jonas revolved around their shared interest in Augustine and Paul, as a result of the seminars and conversations the two had with Bultmann and Heidegger in 1924.

In 1927 Heidegger published *Being and Time*. As I mentioned in chapter 1, Heidegger adapted Husserl's "transformation of the now into the no-longer—and in the other direction, of the not-yet into the now" to his own fundamental ontology.[11] Heidegger had stressed the not-yet as a working-toward-death and thinking-in-time that defines human *Dasein* (being-there). "In Dasein," he wrote, "there is undeniably a constant 'lack of totality' which finds an end with death. This 'not-yet' 'belongs' to Dasein as long as it is."[12] Karl Löwith, another one of Heidegger's leading students and later one of his loudest critics, explained the importance of the work in civilizatory

---

8. Hans-Georg Gadamer, "Heidegger and the Language of Metaphysics," in *Philosophical Hermeneutics*, trans. David E. Linge (Berkeley: University of California Press, 1976), 229.

9. Hans Jonas, *Memoirs*, trans. Krishna Winston (Waltham, MA: Brandeis University Press, 2008), 42.

10. Jonas, *Memoirs*, 61. See also Christian Wiese, *The Life and Thought of Hans Jonas: Jewish Dimensions*, trans. Jeffrey Grossman and Christian Wiese (Waltham, MA: Brandeis University Press, 2007), 67–86.

11. Edmund Husserl, *On the Phenomenology of Consciousness of Internal Time*, trans. John Barnett Brough (Dordrecht: Springer, 1991), 81.

12. Martin Heidegger, *Being and Time*, trans. John Macquarrie and Edward Robinson (New York: Harper and Row, 1962), 286. This passage stands at the center of a recent book about Emmanuel Levinas's response to Heidegger. See Ethan Kleinberg, *Emmanuel Levinas's Talmudic Turn: Philosophy and Jewish Thought* (Stanford, CA: Stanford University Press, 2021), 41.

and essentialist terms: "The unremitting persistence with which Heidegger has pursued Being from *Being and Time* until today is unequivocal. Indeed, according to him the destiny of the West and with it the whole 'earth' depends on the question of Being and on the translation of the Greek word for 'to be.'"[13] As Löwith and other interpreters demonstrated, Heidegger's most consistent stress was on the temporariness of being vis-à-vis the end of life. Löwith explained that in being-toward-death, or "Being-towards-the-end," Heidegger sublated the historicity of existence to "the anticipation of death, [where] Dasein acquires a 'prehistorical stability.'"[14] Löwith's discussion of Heidegger's philosophy was meant to demonstrate the absolute stress on temporality but also its solipsistic function. After the war, Arendt, Jonas, and Heschel, among others, joined Löwith in criticizing Heidegger's circularity.[15]

In her own work Arendt would formulate a counterposition to Heidegger's being-toward-death—namely, the concept of natality, which holds that the fact of being born implies that humans have the capacity to continually begin anew. Arendt's emphasis on new beginnings in the present became a central component of her political philosophy. Arendt responded to Heidegger's ideas of temporality and action by retrieving and reconsidering the ancient sources he read, in particular the writings of Augustine.

Heidegger and Arendt chose two contrasting philosophical methods to approach the legacy of Western philosophy. Heidegger unpacked the political-theological legacy of Western metaphysics, whereas Arendt focused on the history of political forms and organization. For him, the point was a deconstruction of Western

---

13. Karl Löwith, "Heidegger: Thinker in a Destitute Time," in *Martin Heidegger and European Nihilism*, trans. Gary Steiner (New York: Columbia University Press, 1995), 47.

14. Löwith, "Heidegger," 92.

15. As the historian Daniel Herskowitz put it, Heschel criticized Heidegger for "ignoring the existential ground that God is," and therefore "substantiating a dangerous circularity by which the groundless Dasein, granted quasi divine attributes, grounds its own being." If we replace God with metaphysics, Heschel's critique stood close to Löwith's critique of Heidegger's nihilism and Arendt's critique of his self-referentiality. Daniel Herskowitz, *Heidegger and His Jewish Reception* (Cambridge: Cambridge University Press, 2020), 225.

philosophy. For her, it was a matter of establishing a legacy of pluralism and tolerance for the sake of republican democracy. This chapter will show how the two methods charged the concept of life with different histories, meaning, and future implications.

Theodore Kisiel has shown that Heidegger had lectured about Augustine and Paul as early as the 1920s, while he was editing Wilhelm Dilthey's writings on life philosophy. He eventually came to identify Augustine's *inquietum cor nestrum*, the great "never-ending restlessness of life," with a "program for the comprehensive 'destruction' of the entire history of philosophy," using the "'deconstructive regress' which would 'loosen up' prevalent traditional, habitual, and 'self-evident' interpretations of life."[16] In contrast to the Augustinian regressive approach to life, Heidegger identified Paul with the dynamic force of change and becoming, as well as an anti-Judaic "enactment of life" vis-à-vis the apocalyptic Antichrist or end of days. (In *Being and Time*, Heidegger would turn the explicit Christian reference into the more secular notion of worldlessness as a core existential experience.)

Arendt rejected the political-theological method in favor of a historical-political interpretation. Her critique was thoroughgoing, even if not delivered explicitly.[17] A year after *Being and Time* was published, she formulated an initial critique in her dissertation, "The Concept of Love in St. Augustine." Heidegger's interest in Paul was based not only on Christian eschatology, but also on Jews' rejection of Paul and Paul's "situation of struggle" with Jews and with the early Jewish-Christian community.[18] This struggle framed a sense of

---

16. Theodore Kisiel, "Situating Augustine in Salvation History, Philosophy's History, and Heidegger's History," in *The Influence of Augustine on Heidegger: The Emergence of an Augustinian Phenomenology*, ed. Craig J. N. de Paulo (Lewiston, NY: Edwin Mellen Press, 2006), 68.

17. The stark contrasts between Arendt's commitment to democracy and transparency vis-à-vis Heidegger's commitment to *Heimat* (homeland) and authenticity is evident when one notes a series of parallel discussions of terms—for example, in Todd Samuel Presner, "'The Fabrication of Corpses': Heidegger, Arendt, and the Modernity of Mass Death," *Telos* 135 (2006): 84–108.

18. Martin Heidegger, *The Phenomenology of Religious Life*, trans. Matthias Fritsch and Jennifer Anna Gosetti-Ferencei (Bloomington: Indiana University Press, 2010), 48, 61.

self that was deeply invested in destruction of past philosophical traditions (as I discuss later in this chapter). In her investigation of love in Augustine, Arendt implicitly provided a counterconcept to Heidegger's Paulinian tinged philosophy: "Love as *appetitus* is anticipatory, future-oriented; love as a relation with God the Creator is oriented to the ultimate past, the Creation. Neighborly love, love in the present tense, involves both."[19] *Appetitus*, Arendt shows, "concerns desiring an object thought to bring happiness."[20] In contrast to Heidegger, who sees love and desire as inherent forms of "love of oneself" and fear of world, God, or death, Arendt describes desire and love as striving for "life without fear."[21] Fascism forced Arendt to turn this ethical code into a future-oriented vision for political action.

While working on her dissertation, Arendt was more invested in the philosophical and personal, rather than the political, aspects of the work. Yet while Arendt came to rely more on Augustine—especially his emphasis on the continuity between Judaism and Christianity—Heidegger turned more and more to Paulinian concepts "as drawing attention to the very 'center of Christian life: the eschatological problem.'"[22] Heidegger wished to use Paulinian concepts to break from the long Jewish and Christian tradition; Arendt took the opposite course in her work: she regarded Augustine's Christianity within a wider context of historical dialogue and political collaboration.

In her early work, following Heidegger's own advice, Arendt pinpointed the human effort to "bring happiness" and preserve life

---

19. Young-Bruehl, *Hannah Arendt*, 76. See also Antonia Grunenberg, *Hannah Arendt and Martin Heidegger: History of Love*, trans. Peg Birmingham, Kristina Lebedeva, and Elizabeth von Witzke Birmingham (Bloomington: Indiana University Press, 2017), 76.

20. Hannah Arendt, *Love and Saint Augustine* (Chicago: Chicago University Press, 1996), 9.

21. Young-Bruehl, *Hannah Arendt*, 491. See also Karin Fry, "Natality," in *Hannah Arendt: Key Concepts*, ed. Patrick Hayden (London: Routledge, 2014), 25. For Heidegger's approach to love in this context, see Heidegger, *Phenomenology of Religious Life*, 173–75, 210–26.

22. Quoted in Ryan Coyne, *Heidegger's Confessions: The Remains of Saint Augustine in* Being and Time *and Beyond* (Chicago: University of Chicago Press, 2015), 30.

within the German Jewish legacy of Rahel Varnhagen.[23] After the Holocaust, Arendt's work denounced totalitarian worldlessness, and during the 1960s she focused on the opposition between right and wrong revolutionary and historical dynamics as well as on distinguishing between political missions that served equality and those that represented solipsist evasion.[24] Along these lines Arendt's critique of Heidegger became more explicit in her later years. "The most essential characteristic of this [Heideggerian] Self," she wrote in 1946, "is its absolute egoism, its radical separation from all its fellows."[25] Throughout her career she identified this narcissist egocentrism as the delusion of "self-referentiality" and a misunderstanding of politics, or as she expressed it in a letter from July 1963 to Jaspers: "[Heidegger] cites himself and interprets himself, as though he had written a Biblical text."[26]

Arendt was especially suspicious of Heidegger's use of the notion of "care" (*Sorge, Cura*), a concept he adopts from Augustine and interprets as central to the understanding of the self.[27] For him, *Sorge*

---

23. Rahel Varnhagen, born Levin in 1771, was brought up by a bourgeois Jewish family in Berlin. During the 1790s her salon attracted many of the acclaimed authors and public figures of the time. Popular topics of conversations in the salon were the French Revolution, Enlightenment philosophy, and Romantic literature.

24. Arendt, *The Human Condition* (Chicago: University of Chicago Press, 1969), 144.

25. Arendt, "What Is Existential Philosophy?," *Partisan Review* 13 (1946): 50. Dana Villa explains it in the following terms: "Her argument is that Heidegger's characterization of *existenz* as Being-in-the-world did not prevent him from promoting an idea of the self that measured authenticity in terms of a withdrawal from social relations. . . . Heidegger's 'Self,' according to Arendt, absorbs the figure of 'Man,' which had previously usurped the place of God." See Villa, *Arendt and Heidegger: The Fate of the Political* (Princeton, NJ: Princeton University Press, 1996), 232.

26. Arendt to Karl Jaspers, July 20, 1963, quoted and translated in Young-Bruehl, *Hannah Arendt*, 304–5. The Heidegger expert Richard Polt explains that "'care,' like the German *Sorge* and Latin *cura*, usually refers either to managing and looking after things, or to troubles and worries. But since 'Being-in-the-world is essentially care,' care is manifested even in moments that we would ordinarily describe as 'carefree' or 'careless.'" See Polt, *Heidegger: An Introduction* (London: Routledge, 1999), 79.

27. Arendt marks passages that propose a critical reading of Heidegger's Dasein as self-involved. See, for example, passages such as the following, marked with underlining and exclamation marks: "In taking care of the things which one has taken hold of, for, and against others, *there is constant care as to the way one*

(care, anxiety) is the Dasein of betweenness (*Sorge ist das Dasein des 'Zwischen'*).[28] For Arendt, Dasein's self-involvement and antagonism toward others went hand in hand; betweenness, in contrast, was embedded in natality, because life is all about re-creation. In a short text published in 1930 in the *Frankfurter Zeitung*, Arendt explained that Augustine "does not look back on his life to glorify himself, but for the glory of God."[29] Her statement was an indirect attack on what she perceived as the self-referentiality of Heidegger's philosophy. In contrast, Arendt anchored Augustine's value in his ability to advocate for the "love of the neighbor as oneself,"[30] which she linked to political action and memory. As Roy Tsao explains, "Memory opens up this life for us; only in memory does the past take an everlasting meaning; only in memory is the past both canceled out and preserved for all time."[31] Memory, in other words, is the individual quality that connects us with a community and with our present, past, and future. Memory is the pinnacle of betweenness and its "multi-directionality."[32]

In contrast to the circular, solipsistic "care" of Dasein, Arendt's interpretation of time offers a civic understanding of action,

---

differs from them." Heidegger, *Being and Time*, 118; my emphasis indicates Arendt's marginalia. For Arendt's marginalia, see her copy of Martin Heidegger, *Sein und Zeit* (Tübingen: Neomarius Verlag, 1949), 126, in the Hannah Arendt Collection, Digital Marginalia: https://blogs.Bard.edu/aerndtcollection/marginalia/. Although the copy of the book in Arendt's library is dated to the postwar years, there is no doubt she read *Sein und Zeit* as soon as it was published.

28. Martin Heidegger, *Sein und Zeit*, in *Gesamtausgabe*, vol. 2 (Tübingen: Max Niemeyer, 1976), 495.

29. Arendt, "Augustine and Protestantism," in *Essays in Understanding, 1930–1954* (New York: Harcourt Brace, 1994), 25.

30. "The interesting question, for Arendt," writes Roy Tsao, "concerns how he [Augustine] understood the last phrase in the latter commandment: to love the neighbour 'as oneself.'" Roy T. Tsao, "Arendt's Augustine," in *Politics in Dark Times: Encounters with Hannah Arendt*, ed. Seyla Benhabib (Cambridge: Cambridge University Press, 2010), 42.

31. Tsao, "Arendt's Augustine," 27.

32. I am thinking here of Michael Rothberg's interpretation of Arendt as an exemplary work of "multi-directionality," and her ability to "transform the supposed absence of certain forms of life (European culture) into lack of all culture, all as a means of identifying what is lost under totalitarian conditions." Michael Rothberg, *Multidirectional Memory* (Stanford: Stanford University Press, 2009), 61.

democracy, and agency in the public sphere. In depicting natality as "the insertion of man into time," Arendt implies that humanity has a responsibility toward action and renewing the world.[33]

As some close readers of Arendt's being-toward-birth have noticed, birth is not as radical a break as death is, for "in Arendt the caesura [in time] appears more dialectical: it is after all still a life."[34] Each term important to Arendt's work—birth, life, love, memory, action—is grounded in immanent presentness and the potential for solidarity and communication. In the following pages I offer a picture of Arendt's commitment to temporality—that is, her politics. I follow her analysis of time in history, politics, and sense of self, and I argue that this analysis is the core of her development as a thinker—from her 1928 dissertation to her final work, *The Life of the Mind*, left incomplete at her death on December 4, 1975.

Augustine and the Witness Doctrine

Arendt's lifelong interest in Augustine is linked to her philosophy of time in general and the notion of revolutionary beginnings—the fresh starts of every calendar, of personal love, and of communal politics—in particular. Accordingly, her work can be understood in three registers: as a grand narrative of Western politics; as a philosophical anthropology; and as a history and philosophy of concepts. Each of these registers is framed by a large temporal argument, and within this frame holds a smaller, Augustinian, German Jewish, and dialogical claim.[35]

---

33. For "the insertion of man into time," see Arendt, *The Life of the Mind*, vol. 2, *Willing* (New York: Harcourt Brace Jovanovich, 1978), 3. For the stress on action, see Anne O'Byrne, *Natality and Finitude* (Indianapolis: Indiana University Press, 2010), 8. O'Byrne characterizes Arendt's natality as an ethical "responsibility to action."

34. Agata Bielik-Robson, *Another Finitude: Messianic Vitalism and Philosophy* (New York: Bloomsbury, 2009), 88.

35. For the "three registers" that characterize Arendt's interest in philosophy and theology, political theory, and history, see Richard King, *Arendt and America* (Chicago: University of Chicago Press, 2015), 19.

I will explore such concepts at length below, but before I do, it is important to note that Arendt was not the only one to recognize Augustine's stress on time as a human condition. In his chapter about the semantics of historical time, Reinhart Koselleck identifies Augustine's consistent presence in the Western tradition with his understanding of the law, and with his analysis of modern historical time; Augustine's *ordo temporum* is inherently tied to the "'not yet' and the 'no longer,' the 'earlier' or 'later than,'" or the "doctrine of the three phases before, during, and after the Law (*Gesetz*)."[36]

The historian François Hartog explains that "the Christian order of time" is grounded in Augustine's question "What is time?" and his response that "'I am scattered [*dissilui*] in times whose order I do not understand,'" which Hartog understands as "Man's lot is dispersion."[37] Human time is change and movement and dispersion. If Christians staked their imperial claims in Rome "on a self-conscious appropriation of Jewish space and knowledge," as one expert claimed, they "scattered" and forced their order of time back on minorities living in their midst.[38]

Arendt's personal notes evince her lifelong interest in ancient writings, especially Augustine's, on time and on politics. So consistent is the focus on Augustine and time at the heart of her political theory, that the title to her personal notes about Augustine, added in handwriting above the typed notes, simply says: "Time."[39] In these notes Arendt collected key quotes from Augustine's *Confessions*, *De Libero Arbitrio* (The free choice of the will), and *De Trinitate* (On

---

36. Koselleck identifies it also with "the doctrine of *aetatis*." See Reinhart Koselleck, "History, Histories, and Formal Structures of Time," in *Futures Past: On the Semantics of Historical Time*, trans. Keith Tribe (Cambridge: MIT Press, 2005), 94, 100. In that respect, binding Jewish–Christian "love of the neighbor" to a political mission rather than "a commandment of self-denial" directs us to a path of "social *caritas*" and stresses that "human beings belong together due to their common historic descent from Adam." Arendt, *Love and Saint Augustine*, 95.

37. François Hartog, *Regimes of Historicity: Presentism and Experiences of Time*, trans. Saskia Brown (New York: Columbia University Press, 2015), 59. Hartog is quoting here from Augustine's Confessions XI, 39, dedicated to the *condition humaine*.

38. Andrew S. Jacobs, *Remains of the Jews: The Holy Land and Christian Empire in Late Antiquity* (Stanford, CA: Stanford University Press, 2004), 14.

39. Hannah Arendt Papers, Library of Congress, notes 024938–47.

the Trinity). In particular, Arendt marked passages such as this sentence from chapter 14 of book 11 of the *Confessions*: "There are three times, the present of things past, the present of things present, and the present of things future. These three are in the soul, but elsewhere I do not see them."[40] Under the quotes, Arendt wrote her own comments, contrasting Augustine's passage with Hegel's misdirected views of time and history. The major contrast concerns Augustine's realization that time offers a personal narrative of birth and rebirth, as well as a fundamental stress on equality under God. Hegel, in contrast, reframed the concept of history for the sake of a world history that would elevate the German nation above other communities. We shall return to this distinction below.

Though key interpreters of Arendt have identified her as "resolutely nontheological throughout,"[41] her continuous interest in Augustine's conception of time suggests a more complex relation to theology and to the opposition between religion and secularism. The last chapter of *The Life of the Mind*, part 2, *Willing*, is titled, "The Abyss of Freedom and the *novus ordo saeclorum*." The stress on Augustine's "new order of the ages," or *initium*, connects her whole oeuvre and shapes the essential principle of her politics. Natality, action, speaking, and plurality all depend on the activity of starting anew: "Because they are *initium*, newcomers and beginners by virtue of birth, men take initiative, are prompted into action. '[Initium] ergo ut esset, creates est homo, ante quem nullus fuit (that there be a beginning, man was created before whom there was nobody),' said Augustine in his political philosophy."[42] One way to go about handling the religious and secular, Arendt shows, is to focus on the appearance of temporality in both, and notice that the very source of theology is committed to *initium*, or the appearance of time itself.[43]

---

40. Hannah Arendt Papers, Library of Congress, notes 024938–47.
41. Martine Leibovici, "Hannah Arendt (1906–1975): Being in the Present," in *Makers of Jewish Modernity: Thinkers, Artists, Leaders, and the World They Made*, ed. Jacques Picard et al. (Princeton, NJ: Princeton University Press, 2016), 438.
42. Arendt, *The Human Condition*, 177.
43. Miguel Vatter recently debated Samuel Moyn's interpretation of Arendt's political theology. Whereas Moyn believes that Arendt fails to recognize her own political-theological sources, Vatter distances her republican notion of authority

Temporality explains not only her understanding of the modern Christian state, or Jewish life within it, but the organizing frameworks for collective and individual identities.

For Augustine, love necessarily meant the love of God and the love of self, which should lead, via charity and the love of the neighbor, back to a love of God.[44] Likewise, the city of God led to the earthly city, which, in glorifying God, led back to the city of God. Augustine integrated a circular temporality of self and divine with the promise of redemption, and Arendt followed suit by secularizing and politicizing both self and the divine. In her dissertation Arendt explains that Augustine's love functions as "the will to *be*" and that it is "under all circumstances ... characteristic of the human condition as such. Augustine's reflections on human existence in this Creator-creature context arise directly from Jewish-Christian teaching."[45] In another place she ties the Jewish-Christian teaching to "the voice of the law," which "summons [man] against what 'habit entangled him in.'"[46]

Augustine's theology and philosophy are of special importance to Jewish-Christian relations. Historians of the Middle Ages stressed

---

from a literal understanding of religious law. Vatter's argument is particularly interesting for us, because he recognizes Arendt's principal source of inspiration as Buber's rejection of human sovereignty. For Vatter, this position signals an anarchist understanding of law and politics. Focusing on Arendt's hermeneutics of time, however, shows a broader understanding of politics and equality. Here, Jewish and Christian time are measured against the most fundamental aspect of humanity, which is life itself. Being born and the looming threat of death are the ultimate equalizer. The metaphysical or political engagement comes only later, not before. See Samuel Moyn, "Hannah Arendt on the Secular," *Critical Inquiry* 105 (2008): 71–96; Vatter, *Living Law: Jewish Political Theology from Hermann Cohen to Hannah Arendt* (New York: Oxford University Press, 2021), 238–39, 260–61.

44. Jennifer A. Herdt, *Putting on Virtue: The Legacy of the Splendid Vices* (Chicago: Chicago University Press, 2012), 54–56.

45. Arendt, *Love and Saint Augustine*, 52, emphasis in original. The passage, in fact, belongs to the revision of the dissertation for the English translation Arendt made in the late 1950s and early 1960s. The two scans of the same pages, before and after the revision, show this sentence added. See Hannah Arendt Papers, Library of Congress, Speeches and Writings file, 1923–1975: https://www.loc.gov/resource/mss11056dig.050590/?sp=58&st=pdf&r=-0.232%2C-0.073%2C1.465%2C1.465%2C0&pdfPage=58. I thank Patchen Markell for this tip.

46. Arendt directs our attention to Augustine's view of law and testimony in the third part of the *Confessions*. See Arendt, *Love and Saint Augustine*, 84nn35–37.

the importance of the Augustinian "witness doctrine" as a concrete guideline for how to relate to a Jewish neighbor. David Nirenberg explained Augustine's witness doctrine as another expression of Christian anti-Judaism: "Within Augustine's historical approach, those who lived as Jews in a Christian age played an important role as 'witness.' Like fossils for the naturalist, their survival provided the best evidence for the transformation of God's promise in the distant past.... [The Jews] were milestones, mirrors, vessels, desks for the Christians."[47] In *Augustine and the Jews* Paula Fredriksen, an historian of ancient Judaism and Christianity, explains that, whereas a traditional view of Paul stood at the heart of a long anti-Jewish tradition, Augustine had contributed to the witness doctrine that, since his time, had protected the Jews and that was a key piece of his larger theology.[48] In his recent *What Are Jews For?* the historian of early-modern Judaism Adam Sutcliffe explains the imperative weight that the witness doctrine has received since Augustine and how it was expanded by his scholastic followers, secularized by seventeenth-century political thinkers, and integrated into a modern understanding of the state within Hegelian world history. The modern transformation of the witness doctrine in the era of emancipation and assimilation gave it, initially, a positive Jewish reception that then turned into grave disillusionment with the rise of antisemitism.[49]

As her unpublished notes show, Arendt did not refer specifically to Augustine's interpretation of Jews, but she identified Augustine's

---

47. David Nirenberg, *Anti-Judaism: The Western Tradition* (New York: W. W. Norton, 2013), 254–55. See also the excellent article by Jeremy Cohen, "Revisiting Augustine's Doctrine of Jewish Witness," *Journal of Religion* 89, no. 4 (2009): 564–78. In these two works Cohen and Nirenberg, both medievalists, debate the chronology and positivity of Augustine's doctrine but not its centrality or importance.

48. The witness doctrine accepted the presence of Jews within Christian communities as a "testimony" to the Christian narrative of transfiguration from the Old to the New Testament and from the Old Israel of the flesh to the new "Israel of the spirit." Fredriksen explains that for Augustine, Jews and Christians fought against a common pagan world, and that, in this context, Augustine "reimagined the relationship of God and Israel, and thus he reimagined as well the relationship of his church, past and present, to the Jews." Paula Fredriksen, *Augustine and the Jews: A Christian Defense of Jews and Judaism* (New York: Doubleday, 2008), 211.

49. Adam Sutcliffe, *What Are Jews For? History, Peoplehood, and Purpose* (Princeton, NJ: Princeton University Press, 2020), 17–19, 33, 74–75, 113.

emphasis on "the interval" in time with a fundamental understanding of pluralism and tolerance. Plural times mark the possibility of multiple interpretations of reality: "[In] the interval from some beginning up to some kind of end, . . . we measure times, not those which as yet are not, nor those which [are] no longer."[50] Arendt reread temporality, action, politics, plurality, and love as intervals or "insertions" between not-yet and no-longer—*with* Augustine. Here, reality preceded eschatology, and the interval between birth and death overcame suspense and *parousia* (the second coming).

So far Arendt scholars have not paid serious attention to the central role played by Augustine, a pioneer of in-betweenness, throughout Arendt's oeuvre. For that reason they have neglected the ontology of time that Arendt developed from Virgil and especially from Augustine, via the Greek *politeia*, Roman law, and Catholic scholasticism, as well as the modern German Jewish discussion of temporality as a critique of power.

The 1921–1924 Discussions with Heidegger

Heidegger began his exploration of the origins of metaphysics and existential temporality with a close reading of Paul and Augustine. In his lectures Heidegger presented Paul as the more significant of the two thinkers. Kisiel clarifies, in that context, that "*becoming* a Christian, never arriving at the *stasis* of fulfillment, is the very essence of being a Christian. Becoming itself is Being, in the context of being absolutely dependent upon the Divine."[51] During the winter of 1920–21 Heidegger came to see struggle as Paul's crucial characteristic. Struggle could be expressed as inner struggle, a struggle with the law, or, at the very least, with "the law as that which makes the Jew a Jew," following Paul's rejection of Jewish law as necessary for faith.[52]

---

50. Arendt's translation from Augustine's *Confessions*, bk. XI, 27. Hannah Arendt Papers, Library of Congress, "Excerpts and Notes," box 81, file 024938. Arendt divided her notes into themes. This major section of the notes is titled "Time." As Patchen Markell pointed out in his review of this manuscript, the note looks as if it was taken during the preparation for writing *The Life of the Mind* later in life.

51. Kisiel, "Situating Augustine," 75.

52. Heidegger, *Phenomenology of Religious Life*, 50–51.

In the summer of 1921 Heidegger examined the topic of Augustine and Neoplatonism.[53] Judith Wolfe showed that beginning in 1919 Heidegger considered Augustine "a major interlocutor," praising Augustine as "elementally encompassing" the insight of primitive Christianity. In his reading of Augustine's *Confessions*, book 10, in the 1921 lecture series, explains Wolfe, Heidegger framed Augustine's understanding of memory—as what develops "the self's non-coincidence with itself"—as the root of Augustine's insight into human history and sense of the world.[54] In contrast to his more principled discussion of Paul, in Augustine Heidegger identified the question of the self as *homo interior*, "dwelling in memory," presence of self as "not nothing," "dispersion of life," or adversary and care. Augustine, posits Heidegger, enables a close examination of the self as a dynamic dive into one's existence or "life-question":[55] "*Vita-questio* [Life—a question].... My 'being' is determined, somehow, by the sense of circumvention and the coping. Sum = I-am-existence: existence is pulled into a being and a change of being, so that precisely with this difference [*Unter-Schied*], it could modify itself and yet does not have to."[56]

Although both Augustine and Paul attempt to explain the Christian's life in time, Augustine stresses the disruption of human existence by sin and death into the self, whereas Paul's Christian eschatology requires a reverse movement, outward from the self.[57] Augustine stresses "a certain How of the being of life," or an expectation to grasp "life, my life," whereas Paul's eschatology "is radically different from all expectation.... The 'When' is already not originally grasped."[58] Heidegger approaches Augustine's metaphysics in order to

---

53. Heidegger, *Phenomenology of Religious Life*, 117–18. The text starts with a debate against Ernst Troeltsch's historicity, Adolph von Harnack's theological stress on Augustine as the reformer of Christian piety, and Wilhelm Dilthey's understanding of Augustine as "the origin of historical consciousness," preceding Schleiermacher and Kant.
54. Judith Wolfe, *Heidegger and Theology* (London: Bloomsbury, 2014), 51.
55. Heidegger, *Phenomenology of Religious Life*. The concepts listed are on the following pages, respectively: 131, 133, 137, 151, 152.
56. Heidegger, *Phenomenology of Religious Life*, 157.
57. Heidegger, *Phenomenology of Religious Life*, 72. See also Wolfe, *Heidegger and Theology*, 63.
58. Heidegger, *Phenomenology of Religious Life*, 72, 181.

revise "the care [*curare*] of a self" and to explain "[being's] own factically concrete horizon of awaiting,"[59] or what Koselleck would call, after World War II, the "horizon of expectation."[60]

Recent books in the history and philosophy of religion have noted the intimate relationship between Heidegger and his ancient friends.[61] Daniel Herskowitz identifies Heidegger's interest in canonical Christian texts as "core building blocks in the development of his thought toward *Sein und Zeit*."[62] For Herskowitz the point is Heidegger's *a-theistic* approach, as early as the 1920s, and building a contrast between faith and philosophy.[63] Ryan Coyne hews closer to the intricate differences Heidegger drew between one canonical thinker and another. He points out that in contrast to Augustine's commitment to metaphysical and transcendental concepts such as care, grace, and the divine, Heidegger's engagement with Paul is due mostly to Paul's theory of the *katechon*, "a worldly or decidedly secular power invested in staving off the chaos of the end of time."[64] According to Coyne, "the route Heidegger takes to isolate the function of the *katechon* is a circuitous one" and depends on "the ability of the Christian to recognize the Antichrist" and the ability to "await the *parousia* [the second coming]." In their treatment of Schmitt and Heidegger, William Cavanaugh and Giorgio Agamben contrast Paul's philosophy of deferral and the not-yet of

---

59. Heidegger, *Phenomenology of Religious Life*, 153.
60. Koselleck, "'Space of Experience,' and 'Horizon of Expectation': Two Historical Categories," in *Future Past*, 255–76.
61. See, for example, Ward Blanton, "Paul's Secretary: Heidegger's Apostolic Light," in *Displacing Christian Origins: Philosophy, Secularity, and the New Testament* (Chicago: University of Chicago Press, 2006), 126.
62. Daniel Herskowitz, *Heidegger and His Jewish Reception*, 8.
63. Daniel Herskowitz, *Heidegger and His Jewish Reception*, 10.
64. Coyne, *Heidegger's Confessions*, 41. Coyne begins his chapter about testimony in *Being and Time* by contrasting Heidegger's and Arendt's readings of Augustine and the notion of unity: "The philosophical question that emerges from this investigation is thus whether or not unity is a predicate of existence, or if every being is one. In *Love and Saint Augustine*, Hannah Arendt argues that according to Augustine's *Confessions*, 'man can ever have himself as a whole [*totum*].' . . . Written in 1929, [Arendt's] remark could easily be interpreted as leveling an implicit criticism against Heidegger's *Being and Time*, published two years earlier" (125).

resurrection with Augustine's redemption in history.[65] Coyne explains that for Heidegger, the theopolitical structure is temporalizing both the metaphysics of the self and eschatology. The separation between Augustine and Paul allows Heidegger to note how temporal concepts function differently within Christianity, or what he identifies as the history of the West. Time, not a divine voice or sacred word, determines the structures of their competing systems. For Heidegger, "eschatological time illuminates the essence of history ... the critical time or *kairos* has grown short for Paul."[66]

Just as temporal concepts determine the heart of Christian metaphysics, they also determine the relation to the Christian other. Historians have argued that Augustine's doctrine of the Jewish witness also served anti-Judaic polemics when it "[built] on the teachings of Paul [which] enshrined the place of the Jews as quintessential 'other.'"[67] Heidegger thus reversed the Augustinian witness doctrine into a Pauline self-referential Dasein. The thinker Ryan Coyne explains: "To reach [the goal of existential analysis], Heidegger must explain how Dasein attests or gives testimony to its own Being as a unified structural totality—how, that is, it shows itself to itself, essentially dictating to itself how it ought to be interpreted."[68]

---

65. For an excellent framing of the topic, see Vassilios Paipais, "'Already/Not Yet': St. Paul's Eschatology and the Modern Critique of Historicism," *Philosophy and Social Criticism* 44, no. 9 (2018): 1015–38.

66. Coyne, *Heidegger's Confessions*, 42. Eric Schumacher explored the closer relationship between Heidegger's analysis of *kairos* and *sterēsis* (privation, withdrawal, qualified nonbeing). "Withdraw[al] into non-being only to return 'back' into presence," writes Schumacher, "is the formal movement of Heidegger's notion of time." In the concluding paragraphs of his essay, Schumacher explains that "*kairos* jointly indicates the Not-yet and the already. This not yet and already characteristic of Dasein describes the double movement of the 'no.'" Schumacher, "Heidegger on the Relationship between Sterēsis and Kairos," *International Journal of Philosophy and Theology* 3, no. 1 (2015): 79, 84.

67. Cohen, "Revisiting Augustine's Doctrine," 577.

68. Coyne, *Heidegger's Confessions*, 124–25. Heidegger did not invent this strategy; Christian theologians used the witness doctrine to argue, as Peter the Venerable did in the twelfth century, that "there is a faith worse than death for the Jews." See Jeremy Cohen, *Living Letters of the Law: Ideas of the Jew in Medieval Christianity* (Berkeley: University of California Press, 1999), 247ff.; David Nirenberg, "Slay Them Not," *New Republic* 240, no. 4 (2009): 46.

Theologically, Heidegger favored Paulinian eschatology to Augustinian moderation. Philosophically, he favored the pre-Socratics to the metaphysics of Aristotle and Plato. Historically, he preferred a pre-Greek and an anti-Enlightened West to the Greco-Judeo-Christian tradition that had lasted for twenty-five centuries. As Theodore Kisiel has shown, Heidegger rejected the classic explanations of Aristotelian *ousia*, or particular being, that emphasize what one has: property (*oikos*) and time (*kairos*). According to Heidegger, Aristotle was really referring to, but did not properly explore, being. On similar grounds, another scholar shows, Heidegger rejected Augustine's understanding of being or *esse/essentia* the notion that being itself is inseparable from his discussion of God.[69]

Yet Augustine also supplied Heidegger with some of the most important terms of his philosophy (such as care, as mentioned above), and Heidegger derived from Augustine the one principle Arendt rejected more than anything else: self-referentiality. Augustine, in book 10 of the *Confessions*, depicts a self in front of and in dialogue with the divine, but Heidegger reinterpreted this self as immanent, committed to its own process of becoming. His understanding of being provided no space for Dilthey's humanism, Georg Simmel's "other" or "stranger," or a post-Nietzschean interpretation of life as will.[70]

---

69. Lewis Ayres, "Being (esse/essentia)," in *Augustine through the Ages: An Encyclopedia*, ed. Allan D. Fitzgerald (Cambridge: Eerdmans, 1999), 96–97.

70. Heidegger's *The Concept of Time* (1924) came out of a review he wrote about the exchange between two life philosophers, Wilhelm Dilthey and Count Yorck von Wartenburg. As Georg Imdahl and David Farrell Krell have demonstrated, Heidegger, as one of the editors of Dilthey's literary estate, engaged with German life philosophy during the early 1920s and developed his own "fundamental ontology" as a response to the "fashionable philosophy of our time," as Heinrich Rickert depicted it. In Heidegger's case, engaging with Lebensphilosophie involved two tactical moves: first, a return to the core concepts of life, time, existence, and—according to Imdahl—the "factual experience of life" (*faktische Lebenserfahrung*) in the sphere of one's house (*oikos*) and the time of his life. Georg Imdahl, *Das Leben verstehen: Heideggers formal anzeigende Hermeneutik in den frühen Vorlesungen (1919–1923)* (Würzburg: Königshausen und Neumann, 1997), 23. See also David Farrell Krell, *Daimon Life: Heidegger and Life-Philosophy* (Bloomington: Indiana University Press, 1992); Nitzan Lebovic, *The Philosophy of Life and Death: Ludwig Klages and the Rise of a Nazi Biopolitics* (New York: Palgrave Macmillan, 2013), chap. 5.

Care was directed, not toward another being, whether god or mortal, and certainly not toward a refugee or foreigner; it involved a purely personal struggle. In other words, Heidegger instrumentalized rival interpretations and turned the theological tradition against itself. As Edward Baring put it, "Heidegger's ontology required first the destruction of the ontological tradition."[71] Baring sees Heidegger's foregrounding of temporality as demonstrating how the potentiality of the Dasein or its existence as "*not yet be* something" foregrounds its existential structure.[72]

Heidegger's approach, marked by a language of friend and enemy, subordination and victory, unity and division, was framed by what Ryan Coyne has called "Heidegger's detheologization" of his religious sources, as Heidegger interpreted them, not in the light of the Kingdom of God to come, but instead as pointing to a self-referential horizon of existential expectation.[73] Judith Wolfe has argued that Heidegger's system was ultimately an "eschatology without eschaton" in rejecting the Christian vision of the divine kingdom and reframing the eschatological experience as being-unto-death.[74]

In the summer of 1924 Heidegger planned a seminar on Augustine in Marburg. Though the seminar was canceled, Heidegger's correspondence with Karl Löwith mentions a plan to hold it as a "*privatissimum* [very private seminar] every two weeks."[75] According to Theodore Kisiel, in the fall of 1924 Heidegger prepared to have his students read Aristotle, Augustine, and Kant. His inclusion of Augustine was due to his ambition to overturn the course of modern

---

71. In a recent book, Edward Baring has shown how phenomenology united Heidegger's interest in Catholic, post-Augustinian, and Protestant theology, on the way to destroying the history of ontology. See Baring, *Converts to the Real: Catholicism and the Making of Continental Philosophy* (Cambridge, MA: Harvard University Press, 2019), 113.
72. Baring, *Converts to the Real*, 112.
73. Coyne, *Heidegger's Confessions*, 113–15.
74. Judith Wolfe, *Heidegger's Eschatology: Theological Horizons in Martin Heidegger's Early Work* (Oxford: Oxford University Press, 2013), 84.
75. The correspondence is included in Martin Heidegger, *Becoming Heidegger: On the Trail of His Early Occasional Writings, 1910–1927*, ed. Theodore Kisiel and Thomas Sheehan (Evanston, IL: Northwestern University Press, 2007), 454n27.

philosophy. His main opponents at the time were the neo-Kantians Hermann Cohen, Paul Natorp, Heinrich Rickert, Wilhelm Windelband, and, most importantly, Ernst Cassirer. In his debate with Cassirer in 1929, he attacked Cassirer as a representative of neo-Kantianism, its "totality of knowledge," and the division of "the totality of being."[76] For Heidegger, stressing epistemology over ontology called for a "subordination of the theoretical to the practical," a failing he identified with a tradition that extended from Augustine to the neo-Kantians and pheomeologists' focus on individual values and to humanists such as Cassirer and Husserl.[77]

Hannah Arendt interpreted Heidegger's recursive, bleak system as a circular method that suggested a radical, violent form of nihilistic action. If there can be no open dialogue with friends and enemies nor hope of a divine kingdom to come, one is left with only the reaffirmation of one's own being and becoming. Accordingly, Arendt contrasted Augustine's *Confessions* with Paul's emphasis on resurrection. Both Heidegger and Arendt relied on Augustine in order to ground a "fear of death [that] serves as a constant reminder to the human psyche of its radical dependence on divine grace for whatever virtue it achieves and sin it avoids."[78] Heidegger judged the sense of contingency insufficient, but Arendt took contingencies to offer a new and radical opening toward both past and future.

Kisiel demonstrates that in the *Confessions* Augustine created much of the basis of future Western metaphysics, a system that came to rely on a deeper sense of the event and its kairological

---

76. Martin Heidegger, appendices to *Kant and the Problem of Metaphysics*, trans. Richard Taft (Bloomington: Indiana University Press, 1997), 193.

77. Heidegger, *Kant and the Problem of Metaphysics*, 193. For the Augustine quote, see Theodore Kisiel, "Situating Augustine," 60. Jeffrey Andrew Barash has shown that Heidegger's early motivation was a critique of Husserl's phenomenology and of the neo-Kantians from Marburg, especially Cassirer. Heidegger formed a philosophical-theological coalition with Bultmann and Gogarten on these grounds. See Barash, "Heidegger's Ontological 'Destruction' of Western Intellectual Traditions," in *Reading Heidegger from the Start*, ed. Theodore Kisiel and John van Buren (Albany: SUNY Press, 1994), 111–21. For an extensive interpretation of the confrontation between Heidegger and Cassirer, see Peter Gordon, *Continental Divide: Heidegger, Cassirer, Davos* (Cambridge, MA: Harvard University Press, 2012).

78. Robert Dodaro, "Fear of Death in the Thought of Augustine of Hippo," in De Paulo, *Influence of Augustine on Heidegger*, 51.

time and its accompanying, opposing chiliastic time.[79] The Augustinian-Paulinian road could be seen as a path that led Heidegger from metaphysics to his fundamental phenomenology and from there to the anti-humanism of the 1930s and 1940s. Hans Jonas, a careful reader of Augustine and Paul, cast Heidegger's philosophical speculation, and its Pauline thread, as "completely apolitical."[80]

To my mind, Arendt's critique of the self-referentiality of Heidegger's philosophy offers a more accurate explanation than the apolitical reading of Dasein that Jonas and Kisiel offer. Heidegger could not accept Augustine, who, because of his orientation toward the divine, situated human subjectivity within two "vulgar" orders of time, the chronological and the transcendental, both of them meeting in the *now* of the subject. Heidegger wrote in *Sein und Zeit*: "The vulgar understanding of time sees the fundamental phenomenon of time in the *now*," an aspect of which he identified with Aristotle and Augustine.[81] Heidegger's ontology locked the *now* within the closed system of becoming and being. Kisiel described Heidegger's Augustine as a "goal-oriented schematism" that defused "the note in *cura* of *quaero*, seeking, and its concomitant tribulation and anxiety."[82] Augustine's definition of *curare* (to worry, to care, to be troubled) led Heidegger back to Augustine's "'Quaestio mihi factus sum,' I am [have] become a question to myself"—and beyond it to Paul, who offers *parousia*—the second coming—as the messianic answer, justifying the sovereign act."[83] If Augustine's question leaves the Jew outside, as a passive source of inspiration, and a witness watching helplessly the self-evolving Christian, Paul sees the Jew as an internal critical voice, or a "cultural critic," that a good Christian must tame;[84] indeed, Heidegger had to overcome the presence

---

79. Kisiel, "Situating Augustine," 84.
80. Jonas, *Memoirs*, 59.
81. Heidegger, *Being and Time*, 391, emphasis in the original.
82. Kisiel, "Situating Augustine," 86–87.
83. Kisiel, "Situating Augustine," 86–87. Kisiel quotes the well-known sentence from Augustine's *Confessions*, bk. X, chap. 33. See also Arendt, *Love and Saint Augustine*, 7.
84. For "Paul as a Jewish cultural critic" see Daniel Boyarin, *A Radical Jew: Paul and the Politics of Identity* (Berkeley: University of California Press, 1994), 52.

of the Greco-Judeo-Christian metaphysician and her humanism in his journey to the new, pure, sovereign Dasein.

Arendt's Response

Hannah Arendt often alluded to the fact that Jews were forced into a position of mediation due to their historical condition as a political minority—for example, in her work on the early nineteenth-century Rahel Varnhagen: "The most notable aspect of Rahel's assimilation, its test case, so to speak, was that she was among the very first truly to understand Goethe, . . . the 'mediator' to whom she could attach herself and whom she could imitate."[85] For Arendt, the witness or outsider, often identified with the German Jew, was in fact ideally suited to the task of mediation: "That the outsider can understand history and the world without benefit of tradition, and without the natural self-assurance of social status, is more than merely a triumph for him. It is the only possible way he can bind himself to the world."[86] At the same time she noted that, unlike forced assimilation, mediation, communication, and dialogue in the public sphere implied an explicit political position in the world. Paul and Heidegger assumed a form of beginning that was grounded in destruction and "a stumbling block to Jews and folly to Gentiles" (1 Corinthians 1:23); for Arendt, the proper response involved embracing homo temporalis rather than moving in self-referential circles.[87]

In what follows, I will show how Arendt developed a temporal response to the condition of mediation, in-betweenness, and the collapse of the democratic public sphere. Trying to explain the rise of totalitarianism and modern genocidal antisemitism meant, in her system, a reconsideration of Augustine's ontology of new beginnings and a rejection of Heidegger's Paulinian emphasis on destruction and resurrection.

---

85. Hannah Arendt, "Original Assimilation: An Epilogue to the One Hundredth Anniversary of Rahel Varnhagen's Death," in *The Jewish Writings*, 26.
86. Hannah Arendt, *Rahel Varnhagen: The Life of a Jewess* (Baltimore: Johns Hopkins University Press, 1997), 183.
87. Arendt, *The Life of the Mind*, 2:3.

Love and Saint Augustine, 1928

Early in Arendt's intellectual life, she became absorbed in a deep analysis of homo temporalis, an idea introduced by Augustine. The idea would continue to shape her political interpretation all her life. It is the basis of her understanding of Augustine in her dissertation, her interpretation of Varnhagen in her habilitation, and shapes her immediate understanding of politics from the late 1940s to her death in 1975. The basis for this time philosophy is the existence of time, as given, and humanity's "insertion into time," which makes the human being the homo temporalis—the creature whose humanity is defined by time. In the preface to *Between Past and Future* (1961) she explained: "Man is inserted into time. . . . It is this *insertion*—the beginning of a beginning, to put it into Augustinian terms—which splits up the time continuum into forces which then [are] acting upon man in the way [that] . . . breaks up the unidirectional flow of time."[88] And later in this last, incomplete work, she wrote: "According to [Augustine], as we know, God created man as a temporal creature, *homo temporalis*; time and man were created together."[89] Homo temporalis—a human conditioned by time, living in time—uses that temporal condition as a way to make meaning and build worlds. This condition stands in opposition to Heidegger's idea about "thrownness" into existence: "Thrownness means that Da-sein has *not* brought himself into his being; he can only find himself already here. He can never go back behind the fact of thrownness . . . [and] is thus revealed as *impotent* to be the ground of himself."[90] In other words, Arendt's humankind may be subject to time, but that fact is overall a way to create political agency, and creative meaning, rather than something to despair over.

In her dissertation, later published as *Love and Saint Augustine*, Arendt identified the relation between being, or humankind, and a sense of creation as a temporal association between the no-more/

---

88. Arendt, *Between Past and Future: Eight Exercises in Political Thought* (New York: Penguin, 2006), 10–11.
89. Arendt, *Between Past and Future*, 217.
90. Magda King, *A Guide to Heidegger's Being and Time* (Albany: State University of New York Press, 2001), 171, emphases in the original.

not-yet and no-longer. This association repeatedly stands at the center of her work after 1945 as well, and it demonstrates the relations, in different contexts, between past, present, and future, memory and self, and history and politics. She began in 1928 by reading various concepts of time in Augustine: "For Augustine ... memory, the storehouse of time, is the presence of the 'no more' (*iam non*) as expectation is the presence of the 'not yet' (*nondum*)."[91] If memory mediates and translates our sense of time and self, then man's "own being lies before him and is accessible to him only as presented past."[92] But our sense of our past, as developed in memory, also points us toward the essence of our temporal relation to the world, for man—and his memory—is "'later' than his own being," and "'prior' to his creation."[93] In other words, time existed before the creation of humankind and will continue to exist after it. We come into being "after the world" (*post mundum*) was created and are born before we can formulate our being in the world. Augustine, according to Arendt, is always thinking about the transiency of the world as constituted by humankind, which he shows "most clearly by referring to this constituted world as *saeculum* ... in order to express its temporalization."[94] While Arendt acknowledges the eternal vision of a divinely created heaven and earth in Augustine, she stresses the transient, temporal existence she calls the "temporalization of the world" (*Verzeitlichung der Welt*).[95] The world mankind enters is "the world that man himself establishes in 'being of the world.' The end of this world (*terminus saeculi*) coincides with the end of the human race."[96]

The transient human world, or *saeculum*, thus occurs within the temporal and ontological point between no-more (*Schon-Nicht*) and

---

91. Arendt, *Love and Saint Augustine*, 15. Arendt would phrase the Augustinian "no more" as "Schon Nicht" (no longer) in later writings, especially when writing about Benjamin, Kafka, and Broch. This passage is from Arendt's handwritten addenda made during the revision of the dissertation. I thank Patchen Markell for this tip.
92. Arendt, *Love and Saint Augustine*, 68.
93. Arendt, *Love and Saint Augustine*, 68.
94. Arendt, *Love and Saint Augustine*, 68.
95. Arendt, *Der Liebesbegriff bei Augustin: Versuch philosophischen Interpretation* (Hildesheim: Georg Olms, 2006), 45.
96. Arendt, *Love and Saint Augustine*, 69.

not-yet (*Noch-Nicht*). The relation is structural and dynamic: it can be realized only in the now that ties together parts and whole, before and after. "If man," Arendt explains in the second part of her text, "[is] coming from the 'not yet,'" the creature is "heading for 'no more,' . . . [which] refers forward to death (*se refert ad findem*)."[97] As Arendt notes, every interpretation of reality begins with the now-time, or simultaneity of human relations, and shapes humankind's relation to the world. "Time exists," she writes, "because, for the part [unlike the whole], simultaneousness unfolds itself in the guise of a sequence."[98] Time exists because individuals experience the reality around them as a chronological series of events that join to create an image of a whole. This is the opposite of "destruction": "For although the universe has been created and had a beginning and thereby must also perish and come to an end, Augustine is by no means sure that 'a total destruction' will ever come to pass. . . . If sequence is the mode in which the whole appears to the parts, time is the mode in which man understands it."[99] In contrast to Paul's understanding of an eschatological eternal heaven, writes Arendt, Augustine envisions an eternity embedded in the present: "For a fleeting moment (the temporal now) it is as though time stands still, and it is this Now that becomes Augustine's model of eternity."[100] It is no surprise that a close reader would find here echoes of Benjamin's later "dialectics in standstill" or his notion of *Jetztzeit* (now-time).

Arendt's dissertation opens by linking Augustine and Paul, the two confessors who turned against both pagan culture and Jewish culture. Shortly thereafter, however, she separates Augustine not only

---

97. Arendt, *Love and Saint Augustine*, 70. For the German, see Arendt, *Liebesbegriff*, 46: "Das creatum esse hat die Struktur des fieri, des Gewordenseins, und damit die Struktur der Vergänglichkeit überhaupt. Jedes Kreatürliche kommt aus dem *Noch-nicht* und eilt zu dem *Nicht-mehr*. Entsprechend dem Kommen aus dem Noch-nicht macht es, sofern es sich überhaupt auf die Suche nach dem eigenen Sein beginnt, in der Frage nach dem ante den Rückbezug auf den eigenen Ursprung für sich auf Grund dieses vorgegebenen Bezugs ausdrücklich, und entsprechend dem Eilen zu dem Nicht-mehr bezieht es sich vor auf den Tod (se refert ad finem). Das Leben vom Noch-nicht zum Nicht-mehr verläuft in der Welt."
98. Arendt, *Love and Saint Augustine*, 59.
99. Arendt, *Love and Saint Augustine*, 59.
100. Arendt, *Love and Saint Augustine*, 15.

from Paul but also from Luther's adaptation of Paul. In contrast to Augustine, who brings authority (*auctoritas*) and reason (*ratio*) together, Paul and Luther separate the two.[101] Augustine, she notes, reads secular reason and religious authority together under one God, but Paul and Luther separate them. Augustine's self and world must be united in order to answer his inquiry, "I have become a question to myself."[102]

Scholars have pointed out the centrality of the Augustinian *amor mundi*, love of the world, in Arendt's thought, but they usually underplay the importance of temporal aspects in her sense of the world. Eric Gregory and Peter Iver Kaufman also note that Arendt turned her critical eye toward Augustine's theocentricity, or his exclusive notion of Christian love.[103] But such discussions focus on the theological and ethical aspects first and temporal arguments second. Agata Bielik-Robson has instead positioned temporal concepts before the theological by separating the principle of *principium* (beginning of the world) from *initium* (beginning of humanity). Although Augustine framed both in a Christian context, Bielik-Robson writes, Arendt favored the latter idea, for only the "beginning of man" promised a "creative disruption of the cosmic monotony, into which there suddenly enters a *novitas*, something radically new."[104] In other words, while commentators on Arendt's interpretation of Augustine agree on her political and critical reading of Augustine, they vary in their evaluation of the relation between the theological and the temporal. Both camps, however, agree that Arendt recognizes Augustine as the first representative of Christian-Jewish dialogue and as the thinker who reacted against the cyclical time of the Greek world, a subject later addressed by the revivers of pre-Christian cyclicality,

---

101. Arendt, *Love and Saint Augustine*, 5.
102. Arendt, *Love and Saint Augustine*, 7.
103. Peter Iver Kaufman, *On Agamben, Arendt, Christianity, and the Dark Arts of Civilization* (London: Bloomsbury, 2020), 104. "[Arendt] believed Augustine instructed the faithful to orient *caritas* exclusively to their creator and redeemer.... Augustine's theocentricity, as Arendt interprets it, all but shreds the social relevance of *caritas*." Eric Gregory, *Politics and the Order of Love: An Augustinian Ethic of Democratic Citizenship* (Chicago; Chicago University Press, 2008), 205–6.
104. Bielik-Robson, *Another Finitude*, 78.

Nietzsche and Heidegger. "It is evident that the idea of *eternal recurrence* is quite alien to Christian doctrine and that Augustine, a Catholic bishop, would see a need to intervene in the discussion... 'to combat the theory of cycles,'" Stephan Kampowski writes.[105]

By distinguishing between Augustine's monotheistic *principium* and his Roman *initium*, Arendt endowed the latter with a strong secular and political element; by reintegrating the two beginnings, she bridged the ancient and the modern, religious and secular, monotheistic and pagan into natality, the formation of consciousness in time. Indeed, every action is a birth in time and represents the start of a new memory. Living our life between the no-longer of birth and not-yet of death implies a gradual and growing remembrance. "The proper question we ask about action," suggests Kampowski, "is not 'what was its result?' but 'is it worthy of remembrance?'"[106] As Bielik-Robson noted, the stress falls on Arendt's being-toward-birth, the opposite of Heidegger's being-toward-death.[107]

Between No-Longer and Not-Yet, 1940s

Arendt's political theory is based on a single temporal principle: living equals the no-longer of the past and the not-yet of the future. The moment of every beginning is the action of giving birth and being born. In that respect, human life involves acting in the world in love and collaboration with other human beings. The in-betweenness of life is political and politics is life. Within that structure, the Jew is a test case for every political form, for the Jew always lives in the interstices of political systems. In her now-classic article "The Jew as Pariah" (1940), Arendt narrativized attempts by Heinrich Heine,

---

105. Stephan Kampowski, *Arendt, Augustine, and the New Beginning: The Action Theory and Moral Thought of Hannah Arendt in the Light of Her Dissertation on St. Augustine* (Grand Rapids, MI: Eerdmans, 2008), 48.

106. Kampowski, *Arendt, Augustine*, 212.

107. Bielik-Robson, *Another Finitude*, 87. Yet neither Bielik-Robson nor Kampowski explains exactly what makes Augustine's stress on new beginnings—cosmic or human—the very heart of Arendtian politics. Because he viewed Augustine principally as a Catholic, whereas Arendt saw him as a Roman humanist, Kampowski concludes that it was wrong to portray Augustine as setting the human person at the beginning of the world. Kampowski, *Arendt, Augustine*, 52.

Bernard Lazar, and Franz Kafka to come to terms with the problems of Jewish assimilation, each representing a different step in a political consciousness that embraced the figure of the pariah and sought to derive from it an answer to the political quandary of the Jew. According to her perspective, written during the darkest of times, the Jew—whether outcast or attempting to assimilate—was thrown into the midst of the storm and had to cope. "Today the bottom has dropped out of the old ideology," she wrote. "The pariah Jew and the parvenu Jew [i.e., those who have attempted to assimilate] are in the same boat, rowing desperately in the same angry sea. Both are branded with the same mark; both alike are outlaws."[108] Kafka, she tells us, helps us figure out the inherent in-betweenness of the Jew because he had understood that the Jew belongs to a conflicted situation in which one cannot take for granted things such as freedom, rights, or the lack of violence. Instead, anyone who makes these demands "is driven today into isolation like the Jew-stranger in the Castle. He gets lost—or dies from exhaustion."[109] Arendt took her diagnosis of this historical condition—namely, that individual rights were far from guaranteed in contemporary society—and developed it into a diagnosis of modern politics.

Her diagnosis began by describing what a lack of political agency might look like. In a short review written in 1948, Arendt responded to the translation of Stefan Zweig's best-known novel, *The World of Yesterday*, a book originally published in German in 1942, the same year Zweig committed suicide in Brazil. Her review contrasted Stefan Zweig and Hermann Broch as two literary responses to the political situation. Arendt expressed her frustration with Zweig's "boast of his unpolitical view; it never occurred to him," she observed, that "it might be an honor for him to stand outside the law when all men were no longer equal before it."[110] Zweig refused to

---

108. Hannah Arendt, "The Jew as Pariah," in Arendt, *Reflections on Literature and Culture*, ed. Susannah Young-ah Gottlieb (Stanford, CA: Stanford University Press, 2007), 89.
109. Arendt, "The Jew as Pariah," 90. The reference to "the Castle" is to Kafka's *The Castle*.
110. Arendt, "Stefan Zweig: Jews in the World of Yesterday," in *Reflections on Literature and Culture*, 59.

accept a Europe in which Jews "were and remained pariahs" and where "yesterday is not detached from today," a Europe in which the Jew cannot participate fully in the political conversation. "There is no doubt," she argued, "that this is precisely what Stefan Zweig, all his life, had trained himself for: to live at peace with the world and his surroundings; to abstain in a noble fashion from struggles and from all politics."[111] Arendt accused Zweig of a selective view of history that "could not prevent him from simply ignoring the greatest poets of the postwar period, Franz Kafka and Bertolt Brecht."[112]

In contrast to Zweig, Arendt saw in Hermann Broch a living advocate of Augustine's *initium* and Kafka's critical view of modern politics. (Arendt probably missed this fact, but Kafka studied Augustine's *Confessions* in the fall of 1917, shortly after being diagnosed with tuberculosis and breaking off his engagement with Felice Bauer.) Arendt met Broch in 1946, six years after Broch helped composing a utopian manifesto calling for the United States to lead the civilizationary fight against Nazi Germany by shaping democracy as a political religion. The Augustinian title of the manifesto was "The City of Man" and it invoked Augustine's City of God as a source of inspiration.[113] In the first letter of her correspondence with Broch, from May 1946, she wrote that she considered his *Death of Virgil* "the greatest poetic achievement since Kafka's death."[114] As Scott and Stark explain in the introduction to their translation of Arendt's *Love and Saint Augustine*, "as early as 1946, in one of her first pieces

---

111. Arendt, "Stefan Zweig," 68.
112. Arendt, "Stefan Zweig," 64.
113. Broch joined Thomas Mann and Reinhold Niebuhr. For more about the manifesto, see Adi Gordon and Udi Greenberg, "The City of Man, European Émigrés, and the Genesis of Postwar Conservative Thought," in *Religions* 3, no. 3 (2012): 681–698, https://www.mdpi.com/2077-1444/3/3.
114. Hannah Arendt to Hermann Broch, May 20, 1946, in *Hannah Arendt, Hermann Broch: Briefwechsel, 1946–1951* (Frankfurt: Jüdischer Verlag, 1996), 9. In a subsequent letter, Arendt wrote to Broch about a plan, which never materialized, to edit a collection of essays about translations, which was to include writings by Broch, Benjamin, and Rosenzweig. Arendt to Broch, September 9, 1946, in *Hannah Arendt, Hermann Broch*, 14. In the coming months the two corresponded about the translations of Kafka to English. From a letter she sent him the following year, it is obvious that Heidegger was another frequent topic of conversation. See Arendt to Broch, October 16, 1947, in *Hannah Arendt, Hermann Broch*, 52.

published in a non-Jewish journal, Arendt would borrow language and concepts directly from her dissertation to review Hermann Broch's *Death of Virgil*. The title of her review, 'No Longer and Not Yet,' is one of her many metaphors for the 'space' borrowed from the dissertation."[115]

Published in the *Kenyon Review* in 1949, Arendt's review discussed Broch's *Death of Virgil* as a form of modernist prose straddling poetry and philosophy, unfolding its investigation in a state of suspension.[116] Arendt sees Broch's philosophical emphasis in the narrative's "repeating insistence on words like Life, Death, Time, Space, Love ... [which] is like the speculative attempt to penetrate to the *one* word, ... [the] Word of God that was in the beginning and is 'beyond speech.'"[117] Broch's lyrical writing, coupled with the novel's philosophical speculation, implies that the reader must "surrender himself" to the in-between state in which the narrative unfolds. She continues, "Suspended between life and death, between the 'no longer' and the 'not yet,' life reveals itself in that all-meaningful richness which becomes visible only against the dark background of death."[118] Broch's correspondence with Arendt from that period shows that he accepted her interpretation in full and continued to develop it in his own poetic terms. The poems he copied out for her in his letters express this clearly, in a language that evokes the creation of poetic self and surrounding nothingness. In "L'être et le néant," a short poem on Jean-Paul Sartre's response to Heidegger, Broch wrote: "The It [*Es*] of the end, the end of weight / as the It and the Never of the eternal poem: / At the core, the I and around it, light, / This is nothingness."[119]

---

115. Joanna Vecchiarelli Scott and Judith Chelius Stark, introduction to Arendt, *Love and Saint Augustine*, 118.

116. Arendt, "The Achievement of Hermann Broch," *Kenyon Review* 11, no. 3 (1949): 478.

117. Arendt, "Achievement of Hermann Broch," 482.

118. Arendt, "Achievement of Hermann Broch," 482.

119. The poem accompanied a critical review of the translation of Sartre's *Being and Nothingness* into English. Broch understood Sartre's book as a particular, if "not as well-grounded ... as Heidegger's," response to the existentialist "spiritual movement." See Broch, "Jean-Paul Sartre: L'être et le néant," in *Philosophische Schriften*, vol. 1, *Kritik* (Frankfurt: Suhrkamp, 1977), 277. The full poem

In her later revision of the article, as well as in the chapter dedicated to Broch in *Men in Dark Times*, Arendt contrasted Broch with the unnamed forces of "intoxication of blood, the intoxication of death, and ... the intoxication of beauty."[120] Such Nietzschean intoxication (*Rausch*), she argued, had to do with the "self-idolatry" of the mob and the self-titled artist, which she contrasted with the German Jewish bridge "between the 'no longer' of the old laws and the 'not yet' of the new saving word, between life and death."[121] Broch presented a concept of death or nothingness that, historically and politically, was situated rather differently from that of Heidegger and pro-Nazi life philosophers, who embraced the totality of wholeness.

Arendt's texts follow a well-known path in modern philosophy, the same path Heidegger followed in his attempt to destroy the metaphysical tradition: from Aristotle, to Augustine, to Kant, to Nietzsche, to contemporary society and politics. Heidegger reevaluated those thinkers in order to depict, criticize, and reshape the temporal experience of being from an existential perspective. Arendt's course took her from the temporality of the *polis*, via Aristotle, to the post-Augustinian subject, concluding with Kantian self-cultivation. In contrast to Heidegger, the historical process she followed gave prominence to the perspective of the pariah, the interval, the standstill between the part and the whole, the testimony of the oppressed minority or the violent action against it.[122] Working through Aristotle's *Politics*, Augustine's *Confessions*, and Kant's

---

reads in German: "L'être et le néant: Im Reime genitivischen Gesichts / Besitzender Besitz- in ihm verflicht's / Dem Anfangs-Nie, dem Nein-Spruch des Gerichts / Das Es des Endes, Ende des Gewichts / Als Es und Nie des ewigen Gedichts: / Im Kern das Ich und drum des Lichts, / Das ist das Nichts." Included in the letter from July 1947 [day unspecified], *Hannah Arendt, Hermann Broch*, 43.

120. Hannah Arendt, "No Longer and Not Yet," in Arendt, *Reflections on Literature and Culture*, 124. Arendt, *Men in Dark Time*, 111–51.

121. Arendt, "No Longer and Not Yet," 125.

122. Roberto Esposito discusses Arendt's interpretation of politics on the basis of the move from ancient Greek and Roman models to modern democracy: "It is not by chance that within Arendt's overall schema, at the margins of the originacy bloc— ... [of] Troy, Athens, and Rome—all other beginnings have to reproduce the primate nexus with violence that the Greek polis and the Roman urbs appeared to have destroyed." Esposito, *The Origin of the Political: Hannah Arendt*

Critique of Judgment in the early 1970s, Arendt continued to refer or return to questions she had adopted from Heidegger but reframed from a German Jewish perspective. In the following pages I explore how Arendt allied herself with the notion of German Jewish exception and with Augustine's plea for a *novus ordo saeclorum*, a new order of the ages. Such a project implied a rejection of Heidegger and his passive response to the catastrophe she—like Franz Kafka, Hermann Broch, and Walter Benjamin—believed was always possible.[123]

The Temporality of Totalitarianism, 1951

In 1946, while working on what would become *The Origins of Totalitarianism*, Arendt wrote to her editor, Mary Underwood, "The coherence of this book which is essentially a book *against* should not be the coherence of continuity."[124] In the conclusion to the work, which she wrote half a decade later, Arendt cautioned against the allure of continuity in politics that totalitarianism promised: "Totalitarian government can be safe only to the extent that it can mobilize man's own willpower in order to force him into that gigantic movement of History or Nature which supposedly uses mankind as its material and knows neither birth nor death."[125] Totalitarianism erased dissent and disobedience by attacking human temporality itself, subordinating human life instead to the temporality of a grand narrative. It erased the distinction between self and the world, reality and fiction, facts and propaganda, and permitted change only when

---

or Simone Weil?, trans. Vincenzo Binetti and Gareth Williams (New York: Fordham University Press, 2017), 33.

123. Peter Fenves demonstrates that Heidegger made a similar choice after taking Rickert's seminar on Bergson's philosophy of time (in the winter of 1913–14). Interestingly, another student attending the seminar was Walter Benjamin. See Fenves, *The Messianic Reduction: Walter Benjamin and the Shape of Time* (Stanford, CA: Stanford University Press, 2011), 2, 6.

124. Hannah Arendt to Mary Underwood, September 25, 1946, Hannah Arendt Papers, Library of Congress, Correspondence; emphasis in the original.

125. Arendt, *The Origins of Totalitarianism* (New York: Meridian Books, 1966), 473.

dictated from above. In contrast, Arendt pointed toward a different form of continuity, one grounded in disruption and dissent from below, which she identified with an immanent thread of the Judeo-Christian tradition following Augustine: "Every end in history necessarily contains a new beginning.... Politically, it is identical with man's freedom. *Initium ut esset homo creatus est*, 'that a beginning be made, man was created,' said Augustine."[126]

Like Heidegger's conception of time, Arendt's was shaped in opposition to tautology and linearity. Unlike his, hers rejected the idea of infallibility. Following Heidegger, she diagnosed the modern world as suffering from "worldlessness," a troubling absence of actuality, and a deep sense of estrangement and alienation from the world.[127] Unlike Heidegger, she recognized alienation not with the effect of Kant and Western metaphysics, but with the total politicization of life under authoritarian regimes. Arendt pointed out, in different places, how totalitarian regimes formed a circular logic of infallibility by accusing modernity, liberalism, and state organization of alienation, while simultaneously fusing individuals and the world, the private and public spheres. In *The Origins of Totalitarianism*, Arendt positioned solidarity and cooperation against self-referentiality, and beginning or natality against the principle of infallibility (self-prophecy), which she identifies as the essence of dictatorial thinking: "Mass leaders in power have one concern which overrules all utilitarian consideration: to make their predictions come true.... The propaganda effect of infallibility... has encouraged in totalitarian dictators the habit of announcing their political intentions in the form of prophecy."[128] Arendt explains that the most famous example of infallibility was Hitler's speech to the German Reichstag on January 30,

---

126. Arendt, *The Origins of Totalitarianism*, 479.

127. Seyla Benhabib traces "world and worldlessness" as key motives, especially in Arendt's early writing. See Benhabib, *The Reluctant Modernism of Hannah Arendt* (Lanham, MD: Rowman and Littlefield, 1996), 49.

128. Arendt, *The Origins of Totalitarianism*, 349. Careful readers, such as Philip Gorsky, completely missed Arendt's warning against self-prophecy, as well as the context for her interpretation of Augustine. See Gorsky, *American Covenant: A History of Civil Religion from the Puritans to the Present* (Princeton, NJ: Princeton University Press, 2017), 147–48.

1939, where he predicted that "in case the Jewish financiers will succeed once again in hurling the people into a world war," the inevitable result will be "the annihilation of the Jewish race in Europe."[129] "As soon as the execution of victims has been carried out," Arendt explains, "the 'prophecy' becomes a retrospective alibi."[130]

The principle of infallibility, Arendt explained, was the most important characteristic of totalitarian regimes, and it unfolded a different form of temporality. It permitted the regimes to rely on crude propaganda and terror, which she presented as its two salient political characteristics. But temporal observation, much like the structural analysis, preceded political concerns and lessons:

> The form of infallible prediction in which these concepts were presented has become more important than their content. The chief qualification of a mass leader has become unending infallibility; he can never admit an error. The assumption of infallibility, moreover, is based not so much on superior intelligence as on the correct interpretation of the essentially reliable forces in history or nature, forces which neither defeat nor ruin can prove wrong because they are bound to assert themselves in the long run. Mass leaders in power have one concern which overrules all utilitarian considerations: to make their predictions come true.[131]

Infallibility stood at the center of totalitarian logic because it reversed the order of thought and action, consideration and decision. All actions and decisions were retroactively justified thanks to their origin. Analysis of any sort was superfluous. In other words, the moment of beginning, or what Arendt came to call natality, proved to be an ontological principle of existence (being-toward-birth or being-toward-death) as well as a hermeneutic principle.

As Roy Tsao has shown, it was while revising *The Origins of Totalitarianism* that Arendt first used the notion of *natality*, in her essay about "Ideology and Terror: A Novel Form of Government" (1953), before adopting it as a central term in *The Human Condition*

---

129. For Hitler's speech, see J. Noakes and G. Pridham, eds., *Nazism, 1919–1945: A Documentary Reader*, vol. 3 (Exeter: University of Exeter Press, 1988), 1049.
130. Arendt, *The Origins of Totalitarianism*, 349.
131. Arendt, *The Origins of Totalitarianism*, 349.

(1958).[132] Elisabeth Young-Bruehl writes that Arendt saw totalitarianism as "the complete denial of the spatial and temporal requirements of freedom. Totalitarian ideologies devoured both past and future, turned the past into myths of Nature or History, and erased the unpredictability of the future with millennial images of these myths' fulfillments."[133] I would go further: the principle of infallibility that lay at the heart of the Nazi propaganda machine erased the divide between public and private spheres, as well as the line between fact and fiction, truth and lie. It compelled individuals to stand for a collective principle and erased their autonomous mobility. Hitler's infallibility, which involved a self-affirming act of prophecy, introduced a temporal structure that removed worldly temporality from the public sphere and reduced public participation to its most passive and negative aspects.[134]

The infallible tyrant exposed a characteristic shared by all forms of modern politics, democracy included: "Democratic government had rested as much on the silent approbation and tolerance of the indifferent and inarticulate sections of the people as on the articulate and visible institutions and organizations of the country."[135] In other words, infallibility requires the complicity and silent cooperation of the average person. Once it is enabled, if only by nonparticipation, its logic swallows everything. It devours the principal divisions of thought, judgment, political action, and even life and death. "All debate about the truth or falsity of a totalitarian dictator's prediction is as weird as arguing with a potential murderer about whether his

---

132. Tsao, "Arendt's Augustine," 50. Tsao also provides a short history of natality in Arendt's writings at 39–57. Arendt's essay was originally published as "Ideology and Terror: A Novel Form of Government," *Review of Politics* 15, no. 3 (1953): 303–27. It was then added as the concluding chapter to the second edition of *The Origins of Totalitarianism* (1958).
133. Young-Bruehl, *Hannah Arendt*, 253.
134. This is the logic behind Giorgio Agamben's "total politicization of life." Agamben paraphrases ideas he extracts from Arendt and Löwith. See Agamben, *Homo Sacer: Sovereign Power and Bare Life*, trans. Daniel Heller-Roazen (Stanford, CA: Stanford University Press, 1998), 120–21.
135. Arendt, *The Origins of Totalitarianism*, 312. See also John McGowan, *Hannah Arendt: An Introduction* (Minneapolis: University of Minnesota Press, 1998), 16.

future victim is dead or alive."[136] Infallibility and propaganda take over the political realm and life more generally, erasing the distinctions between them. There is no life outside this new world order. The shape of infallibility is the shape of Ouroboros, the mythic serpent who devours itself with its tail in its mouth.

Arendt's observation concerning the temporal paradox that lies at the heart of totalitarianism was grounded in a dichotomy between right and wrong, reality and illusion. As John McGowan shows, it was not always an easy dichotomy to hold on to: "The success of such tactics of total obliteration [of the public sphere] points to a profound ambiguity in Arendt's ontology. She insists that the totalitarian world is 'fictitious,' yet that world manages to exist, manages to displace the 'real' world for a time."[137] The alleged ambiguity is in reality the outcome of Arendt's principle of infallibility. Arendt's ontology is not "grounded on the insistence that plurality is a fact," as McGowan declares, but that plurality is conditioned by ideology, propaganda, and self-fulfilling prophecies. This is a deeply suspicious view of politics, totalitarian and democratic alike, but it is also a view that insists on individuals' ability to choose. Arendt always assumes that human agency can resist the fictitious propaganda and political lies meant to turn a person into a passive follower. Amir Eshel explains: "It is precisely in the face of such recent end points as the unparalleled terror of the totalitarian state that Arendt emphasizes the constitutive nature of futurity ('there remains' a 'new beginning') and human agency."[138]

The Human Condition, 1958

For Arendt, the alternative to infallibility was the adoption of a post-Augustinian, German Jewish politics of life. She presented this view in *The Human Condition*, where she developed a temporal ontology

---

136. Arendt, *The Origins of Totalitarianism*, 350.
137. McGowan, *Hannah Arendt*, 28.
138. Amir Eshel, *Futurity: Contemporary Literature and the Quest for the Past* (Chicago: Chicago University Press, 2013), 17.

of the *vita activa*. This temporality fell back on a historical and structural observation: from the perspective of in-betweenness, only those trapped between the fall of one system—such as the fall of Jerusalem, Rome, or the Weimar Republic—and the rise of another could grasp how action related to multiple options in the public sphere.

Life under threat of collapse enabled a different view of everyday life. The historian Edward Baring concluded that in Heidegger's philosophy the foregrounding of temporality demonstrated how the potentiality of the Dasein or its existence as "*not yet be* something" foregrounds its existential structure.[139] While Heidegger's *Logik* envisioned the concept of work "as a structure of temporalization founded in the Care structure of the ... Volk,"[140] Arendt's interpretation of action, work, and labor concentrated on plurality and natality, as well as the dependence of change on "strangers." "Labor and work," she wrote, "as well as action, are also rooted in natality in so far as they have the task to provide and preserve the world for, to foresee and reckon with, the constant influx of newcomers who are born into the world as strangers."[141] It is hard to miss the clear German Jewish intonation of this passage, and the way it plays with Augustinian time in the service of creation and plurality, while setting aside notions such as "care" and "Volk." Turning Simmel's "stranger" (a Jew) into a universal principle of action shapes a temporal structure that opposes Heidegger's.

Arendt had already taken up the relationship between action and plurality in her dissertation and its later revisions and publication. When she returned to the subject in 1958, she coupled a consideration of plurality (the social condition of human existence) with a concrete understanding of action. "Plurality is specifically *the* condition ... of all political life," she wrote. "Thus the language of the

---

139. Baring, *Converts to the Real*, 112.
140. Bernhard Radloff, *Heidegger and the Question of National Socialism: Discourse and Gestalt* (Toronto: University of Toronto Press, 2007), 8. See also Martin Heidegger, *Logic: The Question of Truth*, trans. Thomas Sheehan (Bloomington: University of Indiana Press, 2010).
141. Arendt, *The Human Condition*, 9.

Romans, perhaps the most political people we have known, used the words 'to live' and 'to be among men' (*inter homines esse*) or 'to die' and 'to cease to be among men' (*inter homines esse desinere*) as synonyms.... Plurality is the condition of human action."[142] But the condition itself was grounded in a temporal order. The history of both Greeks and Romans demonstrates it: Although the Greeks thought about the cosmos from the perspective of mythological immortality—in Arendt's words, "endurance in time, deathless life on this earth"[143] —they considered human life to be "distinguished from all other things by the rectilinear course of its movement, which, so to speak, cuts through the circular movements of biological life."[144] The Roman Republic politicized this rectilinear line, within the cosmic order, but with Rome's fall and the rise of Christianity, human life was launched into the metaphysical realm.

Michael Scanlon noted that Augustine's (and Arendt's) stress on the *novus ordo saeclorum* served to overcome the Greek understanding of cyclical time and replace it instead with Roman revivalism and Christian incarnation.[145] The rise of Christianity made "*vita activa* and *bios politikos* the handmaidens of contemplation."[146] Augustine, the first analyst of the self and the key theoretician of the witness doctrine, stood at the threshold between the world of Roman paganism and Christianity. Instead of viewing Augustine as the father of Christian metaphysics, as Heidegger had, Arendt considered him the last Roman thinker to adapt Roman politics to the Christian empire, setting the *bios politikos*—political life—within the individual life, rather than within a perishable external world:

---

142. Arendt, *The Human Condition*, 7–8, emphasis in original.
143. Arendt, *The Human Condition*, 18.
144. Arendt, *Between Past and Future*, 42. The Postclassicisms Collective explains that "Arendt does not treat antiquity as if it were timeless. Rather, she structures the encounter between ancient and modern as a *political* encounter.... The references to the Greeks function for Arendt as a kind of performative." Postclassicisms Collective, *Postclassicisms* (Chicago: Chicago University Press, 2020), 39, emphasis in original.
145. Michael J. Scanlon, "Arendt's Augustine," in *Augustine and Postmodernism: Confession and Circumfession*, ed. John D. Caputo and Michael J. Scanlon (Bloomington: Indiana University Press, 2005), 159.
146. Arendt, *The Human Condition*, 21.

> To find a bond between people strong enough to replace the world was the main political task of early Christian philosophy, and it was Augustine who proposed to found not only the Christian "brotherhood" but all human relationships on charity. But this charity, though its worldlessness clearly corresponds to the general human experience of love, ... [provided] that the world itself is doomed and that every activity in it is undertaken with the proviso *quamdiu mundus durat* ("as long as the world lasts"). The unpolitical, non-public character of the Christian community was early defined in the demand that it should form a *corpus,* a "body."[147]

In other words, Augustine worked to transcend all previous divisions in the ancient world by rejoining people, values, and world, or body. Augustine's future-oriented reform was anchored in transcending historical circumstances, not in an eschatological principle. Augustine taught that the heart of the political-theological is action. As mentioned above, Arendt repeated her call for action, grounded in Augustine's philosophy of time. She repeated the same sentence in *The Origins of Totalitarianism* (1951), *The Human Condition* (1958), *An Introduction into Politics* (1959) and *The Life of the Mind* (1974). In *The Human Condition* she explained that

> To act, in its most general sense, means to take an initiative ... said Augustine in his political philosophy, but then moved from the action to the actor and the principle of beginning: This beginning is not the same as the beginning of the world; it is not the beginning of something but somebody, who is a beginner himself. With the creation of man, the principle of beginning came into the world itself, which, of course, is only another way of saying that the principle of freedom was created when man was created but not before.[148]

What Arendt says here, repeating her analysis from The Introduction into Politics almost word for word, is that the principle of beginning came from a metaphysical principle but evolved into an ontological and phenomenological idea.[149] The principle of beginning does not

---

147. Arendt, *The Human Condition*, 53.
148. Arendt, *The Human Condition*, 177.
149. Arendt started working on *The Introduction into Politics* as a book-length project the same year as *The Human Condition* but never completed it. See Arendt, *The Promise of Politics* (New York: Schocken Books, 2005), 126. See also Elisabeth Young-Bruehl, "Reflections on Hannah Arendt's *The Life of the Mind*,"

create the world. It creates, rather, our notion of existence *in* the world, or in a world that has moved away from us. It creates human temporality—the condition of living, understanding, and dying. Birth and death are part of the same temporal order.

In *The Human Condition* Arendt developed a comprehensive argument about the nature of action versus contemplation and the difference between labor and work, based on an analysis of temporality and movement. Arendt believed in the close relationship between life and politics, or the temporal mechanism that connects the laborer (her deeds), political action (public impact), and thought or storytelling (meaning), which charges the deed with power and significance: "That deeds possess such an enormous capacity for endurance, superior to every other man-made product, could be a matter of pride if men were able to bear its burden, the burden of irreversibility and unpredictability, from which the action process draws its very strength."[150]

The "capacity for endurance" proposes continuity with the past, even a catastrophic past. For moderns, this capacity dwindled, as myth and trust in eternity evaporated and were replaced by industrial production. By breaking away from the world of myth, modern politics also abandoned its own metaphysical fount.

Between Past and Future, 1961, and *On Revolution*, 1962

As her biographer tells us, between 1952 and 1956 Arendt worked on a wide-ranging analysis of Marx, which was ultimately incorporated into three works: *The Human Condition* (1958), *Between Past and Future* (1961), and *On Revolution* (1962). Arendt scholars often portray *The Human Condition* as Arendt's greatest contribution to philosophy,[151] but in *Between Past and Future* and in *On Revolution*

Political Theory 10, no. 2 (1982): 277. As Patchen Markell noted in his comments on this manuscript, it is not clear what preceded what, as Arendt worked on these sections of the introduction after *The Human Condition* had been completed.

150. Arendt, *The Origins of Totalitarianism*, 233.

151. Karin A. Fry, *Arendt: A Guide for the Perplexed* (New York: Continuum, 2009), 34; Sahar Aurore Saeidnia, *An Analysis of Hannah Arendt's* The Human Condition (London: Routledge, 2017), 49.

Arendt unpacks the theme of temporality that stands at the center of her work.

Composed initially of six essays, *Between Past and Future* demonstrates how catastrophic or traumatic events interrupt the sequence of time, engendering both forgetfulness and a deep sense of loss. As Seyla Benhabib put it, "the events of the twentieth century . . . have created a 'gap' between past and future of such a magnitude that the past, while still present, is fragmented and can no longer be told as a unified narrative."[152] The opening essay is dedicated to a Benjaminian "break of tradition," and how "to most people today this culture looks like a field of ruins."[153] In the 1968 edition, Arendt added two further essays to the collection—"Truth and Politics" and "The Conquest of Space and the Stature of Man"—dedicated to that year's political upheavals. Between the ruins of tradition and the destruction of future mankind, she found one spark of hope. Memory, both Augustinian and German Jewish, *can* keep thinking alive if given a proper framework: "There seems to be no willed continuity in time and hence, humanly speaking, neither past nor future. . . . The loss, at any rate, perhaps inevitable in terms of political reality, was consummated by oblivion, by a failure of memory. . . . For remembrance, which is only one, though one of the most important, modes of thought, is helpless outside a pre-established framework of reference."[154]

Memory, history, thinking, and politics are all characteristics of life and, as such, characteristics of our experience of the past and horizon of expectations. They offer a sense of coherence and continuity. The interruption of Western metaphysical temporality, in contrast, signified to Arendt a moment of loss, forgetting, and deep individual sorrow. Benhabib explained that "the political actor, who is always caught in the uncertain moment between past and future, namely, in the present" shaped Arendt's "insistence upon the radical contingency of history" and its relation to "the methods

---

152. Benhabib, *Reluctant Modernism*, 91.
153. Arendt, *Between Past and Future*, 28.
154. Arendt, *Between Past and Future*, 5.

of social control, propaganda, surveillance, and extermination practiced by totalitarian regimes."[155]

On Revolution includes an entire chapter on Augustine's *novus ordo saeclorum* in which she explains that his idea of *initium* underlies her idea of natality.[156] What follows is Arendt's masterly explanation of successful beginnings (or revolutions). "The problem of beginning is solved through the introduction of a beginner whose own beginnings are no longer subject to question because he is 'from eternity to eternity.'"[157] A strong metaphysical scaffold holds natality in place. The arc of the book follows a modern political translation of this tradition, stretching from the creation of the world to the age of modern revolutions: the French Revolution (which Arendt believes failed) and the American Revolution (which succeeded). The French Revolution failed due to its destructive and cyclical-eschatological commitment; the American Revolution succeeded because it synthesized the Virgilian-republican and Judeo-Christian traditions and adopted natality as its driving force. "When the Americans decided," she writes, "to vary Virgil's line from *magnus ab integro saeclorum nascitur ordo* [The great cycle of periods is born anew] to *novus ordo saeclorum*, they had admitted that it was no longer a matter of founding 'Rome anew' but of founding 'a new Rome.'"[158]

Kafka: *Men in Dark Times*, 1968

The discussion of continuity and memory versus interruption and forgetting takes an unexpected turn when one considers the basis of Arendt's natality. As mentioned above, in her 1963 preface to *Between Past and Future*, Arendt declared that the framework of political analysis should be "the insertion of man into time."[159] In making this statement, however, she relies not only on Augustine but equally on Kafka: "Man is inserted into time.... It is this *insertion—*

---

155. Benhabib, *Reluctant Modernism*, 72.
156. Arendt, *On Revolution* (London: Penguin Books, 1963), 211.
157. Arendt, *On Revolution*, 206.
158. Arendt, *On Revolution*, 212.
159. Arendt, *Between Past and Future*, 10–11.

the beginning of a beginning, to put it into Augustinian terms—which splits up the time continuum into forces which then [are] acting upon man in the way Kafka describes.... Kafka describes how the insertion of man breaks up the unidirectional flow of time but, strangely enough, he does not change the traditional image according to which we think of time as moving in a straight line."[160] These lines clarify how closely Arendt sees her own and Kafka's mission. I mentioned above that Augustine's time disrupts human existence through sin and death, but memory and faith demonstrate an intimate relation to eternity and God. For Arendt, Kafka's modern "insertion into time" presents a dual course of disruption and continuity, based on modern culture rather than of faith. By linking the paradigmatic ancient theologian with the emblematic modern author—and both with a heavy stress on natality—Arendt puts forward an alternative to the failure of metaphysics as Heidegger saw it. Instead, she points to a constructive view shared by Augustine and German Jewish authors—that is, a strong opposition to solipsism and self-referentiality. In the last section of the closing essay in *Between Past and Future*, Arendt returns to her preface and to Kafka. Extending Kafka's observation that "man found the Archimedean point, but he used it against himself," she states, while thinking about deep space, "The only true Archimedean point would be the absolute void behind the universe."[161]

In *Men in Dark Times*, Arendt explained that she was analyzing Benjamin and Kafka together, for "Benjamin felt the closest personal affinity with Kafka, among contemporary authors."[162] In Arendt's view, Benjamin opened a path to see Kafka within "a field of ruins and the disaster area," and Kafka's texts opened a path to the mind of her brilliant friend.[163] Both, together, presented *the* answer to the catastrophic condition of time: the circular, infallible logic of

---

160. Arendt, *Between Past and Future*, 10–11.
161. See the conclusions to both *The Human Condition* and *Between Past and Future*. See also *The Human Condition*, 322.
162. Hannah Arendt, "Walter Benjamin, 1892–1940," in *Men in Dark Times* (New York: Harcourt, Brace and World, 1983 [1968]), 169.
163. Arendt, "Walter Benjamin," 169.

totalitarianism. Kafka unpacked the paradoxical logic of modern obsession with the self and demonstrated how this self—and his political and administrative representations—were the product of a circular order of time. Arendt believed that Kafka, and his close reader, confronted a hostile cultural and political world in which bourgeois continuity had ceded to a radical sense of the unknown and old language seemed bankrupt, and "exemplified this situation . . . by 'linguistic impossibilities.'"[164]

As I explained in chapter 3, during the early 1930s Benjamin had begun to write about the work of Franz Kafka, an author whom he admired and discussed with Gershom Scholem for years. Scholem understood Kafka as speaking to a post-mystical Jewish tradition, while Benjamin viewed Kafka as a literary critic of the Western tradition.[165] In his essay on Kafka (1934), Benjamin portrayed Kafka's literature as an experiment in a primordial or "pre-Adamite" language.[166] As Vivian Liska describes it, Benjamin believed that this linguistic experiment took place in settings of "'unbounded promiscuity,' the lowest stage of human existence."[167] Benjamin identified settings within Kafka as a prehistoric swamp (*Sumpfwelt*) "in which everyone is guilty and everyone is also a victim of the law," a world in which there is no decisionism in the form of clear sovereignty.[168] Benjamin saw in Kafka's works a duality, according to Beatrice Hanssen. On the one hand lay "a forgotten natural guilt-laden primeval and Amazonian world (*Vorwelt*)—akin to Bachofen's matriarchic 'hetaeric natural being'—and, on the other hand, Judaic law,"

---

164. Arendt, "Walter Benjamin," 187.
165. Walter Benjamin, *Benjamin über Kafka: Texte, Briefzeugnisse, Aufzeichnungen*, ed. Hermann Schweppenhäuser (Frankfurt: Suhrkamp, 1981).
166. This idea would become Jacques Derrida's springboard for his theory of deconstruction, which opens *Of Grammatology* with "writing before the letter." See Jacques Derrida, *Of Grammatology*, trans. Gayatri Chakravorty Spivak (Baltimore: Johns Hopkins University Press, 2016), 3.
167. Vivian Liska, *German-Jewish Thought and Its Afterlife: A Tenuous Legacy* (Bloomington: University of Indiana Press, 2017), 57.
168. Liska, *German-Jewish Thought*, 57. See also my reading of the swamp: Nitzan Lebovic, "Benjamins Sumpflogik: Ein Kommentar zu Agambens Kafka und Benjamin Lektüre," in *Profanes Leben*, ed. Daniel Weidner (Frankfurt: Suhrkamp, 2010), 190–212.

which broke the distinctions between male and female, human and creaturely, Halakha (law) and Haggadah (parable).[169]

Arendt's interest in Kafka paralleled her interest in Benjamin.[170] Her first piece for *The Partisan Review*, published in 1944, was titled "Franz Kafka: A Reevaluation," and it carried the signs of a Benjaminian analysis.[171] Her interpretation heeded Benjamin's advice from 1934: "There are two ways to miss the point of Kafka's works. One is to interpret them naturally; the other is to interpret them from a supernatural perspective. Both the psychoanalytic and the theological interpretations miss the essential points."[172] Arendt echoed Benjamin without mentioning him, repeating his warning that "people ... looked for other, seemingly deeper interpretations, and they found them, following the fashion of the day, in a mysterious depiction of religious reality, the expression of a terrible theology," or in "a misunderstanding as the psychoanalytical variety."[173] (The vague "people" referred to, among others, Gershom Scholem.)

In this early essay, as in later essays, Arendt approached Kafka as the author who best captured the zeitgeist of the German Jewish stranger. His poetics of in-betweenness were a source of inspiration for her political thought.[174] The crux of his poetics, and politics,

---

169. Beatrice Hanssen, *Walter Benjamin's Other History: Of Stones, Animals, Human Beings, and Angels* (Berkeley: University of California Press, 2000), 138.

170. The connection was obvious in Arendt's theoretical and administrative work. For example, as Elisabeth Young-Buehl reported, "before [Salman Schocken] hired her as an editor," Arendt "recommended to him both Walter Benjamin's unpublished manuscripts and the edition of the writings of Bernard Lazare." She began editing the German edition of Kafka's diaries during those years as well. Young-Buehl, *Hannah Arendt*, 189. I thank Patchen Markell for turning my attention to the exact place and phrasing of this reference.

171. Arendt, "Franz Kafka: A Reevaluation," *Partisan Review* 11, no. 4 (1944). Republished in Arendt, *Essays in Understanding*, 69–80.

172. Walter Benjamin, "Franz Kafka," in *Selected Writings*, vol. 2, trans. Harry Zohn, ed. Michael Jennings, Howard Eiland, and Gary Smith (Cambridge, MA: Harvard University Press, 2001), 806.

173. Arendt, "Franz Kafka," 72.

174. As Arendt noted, following Benjamin's "The Storyteller" (1936)—an essay she edited when she published Benjamin's *Illuminations*—that in modern capitalism the nature of action, work, and storytelling change to prevent honest communication, an actual relation between life and death, and a direct biological connection between human and animal, in favor of human-made technology. Arendt's solution was to find

was the failure of representation; no normative language could capture a paradox such as his paradox of identity: "What have I in common with Jews? I have scarcely anything in common with myself and should stand completely quietly in a corner, content that I can breathe."[175] As we shall see below, Arendt's emphasis on the "nonexisting language" or the "impossible linguistics" of German Jewish letters—for which Kafka and Benjamin are the principal representatives—gave a (negative) voice to how "catastrophe can be foreseen."[176] Arendt continued to think about Kafka and Benjamin until the end of her life, and she often related them, as Jewish thinkers, to Augustinian motifs. They gave her the right keys to open the doors of Western metaphysics. After criticizing different misinterpretations of Kafka, she explained the framework for a correct analysis: "Kafka depicted a society which had established itself as a substitute for God, and he described men who looked upon the laws of society as though they were divine laws—unchangeable through the will of men."[177] In other words, critics had often produced mistaken analyses of Kafka's stories by equating their subjects with Kafka's position. Instead of validating hidden theological structures in society, Kafka wanted to critique an attitude that took the theological seriously: "Kafka wants to destroy this world by exposing its hideous and hidden structure, by contrasting reality and pretense."[178]

Through Benjamin's reading, Arendt could see in Kafka "a dissolving society" that "blindly follows the natural course of ruin,

---

the anchor for her observations in storytelling in Kafka, Broch, and Benjamin. Benjamin's storytelling is for her the most obvious realm of in-betweenness, the keeper of time and natality, guardian of life. It is the political medium par excellence. If storytelling is the medium of in-betweenness, it is also anchored in an inherent understanding of beginning, middle, and end, as Aristotle demonstrated in the *Poetics*. By following the differentiation between beginning and end, or multiple perspectives within the story, we come to realize that ours is not the only valid time or perspective. Walter Benjamin, "The Storyteller," in *Illuminations*, trans. Harry Zohn, ed. and intro. by Hannah Arendt (Boston: Houghton Mifflin Harcourt, 2019 [1968]), 26–56.

175. Kafka, Diary entry from January 8, 1914, *The Diaries*, trans. Ross Benjamin (New York: Schocken Books, 2022), 327.
176. Arendt, "Franz Kafka," 74.
177. Arendt, "Franz Kafka," 65.
178. Arendt, "Franz Kafka," 65.

[and in which] catastrophe can be foreseen."[179] In this situation, she wrote, "Kafka's so-called prophecies were but a sober analysis of underlying structures which today have come into the open."[180] In short, Kafka's stories started with a stress similar to Benjamin's on the failure of communication, and they ended similarly, by opening up the possibility of political consciousness.

The notes Arendt kept in her *Denktagebuch* while she was beginning to work on *The Human Condition* show a consistent interest in Kafka's understanding of time, politics, and the "Archimedean point he found, but which he used against itself, and, in fact, allowed him to find it only under such conditions."[181] In May 1967, while beginning to work on *Men in Dark Times*, she noted that the Archimedean point represented the convergence of different timelines: "1. Cyclical Time. . . . Time is eternal (Nietzsche). 2. Nonlinear time: Beginning, Hebrew or Roman. The beginning is sacred, and man keeps himself balanced only by referring back to [a point] of beginning. Revolutions make an attempt to erase that point." She then points to Hegel and Heidegger as proponents of "the type of cyclical time" that "will come to a standstill," due to their stress on nothingness.[182] Time at a standstill (parallel to Benjamin's "dialectics at a standstill") was the opposite of Kafka and Benjamin's subversive nonlinearity, or the "'explosion' that Benjamin explicitly linked to political action."[183]

Breaking with tradition implied a breach in time, politics, and Judeo-Christian culture. As Vivian Liska put it, "Arendt derives

---

179. Arendt, "Franz Kafka," 74.
180. Arendt, "Franz Kafka," 74.
181. Arendt, *Denktagebuch: 1950–1973*, ed. Ursula Ludz and Ingeborg Nordmann (Munich: Piper, 2002), February 1956, bk. 22, sec. 9, my translation.
182. Arendt, *Denktagebuch*, May 1967, bk. 25, sec. 23.
183. In contrast to *stasis* or absolute *standstill*, Benjamin's "measure of time," John McCole explains, is "simultaneity that produces an 'explosion' in the present, an explosion that Benjamin explicitly linked to political action. . . . In this sense the dialectical image represents 'dialectics at a standstill.' It loads time into itself until the energies generated by the dialectic of recognition produce an irruption of discontinuity. This conception of time set Benjamin off from vitalism, idealism, and historicism alike." McCole, *Walter Benjamin and the Antinomies of Tradition* (Ithaca, NY: Cornell University Press, 1993), 249.

from literature, and from Kafka in particular, instructions for the right way of behaving politically in a world in which the transmission of the original message has been disrupted."[184] And Birgit Erdle has pointed out that Arendt's reference to Kafka in her last work, *The Life of the Mind*, served to describe the contemporary rift she saw in a post-1945 "groundless" reality with a "gap in time" that defines the "insertion of man" into reality.[185] Kafka supplied Arendt with a modern version of homo temporalis in his aphoristic "He," in which a protagonist battles a man behind him and one in front of him. "In Kafka, this scene is a battleground where the forces of past and future clash with each other. Between them we find the man Kafka calls 'He.'"[186] Arendt came to see Kafka as her literary compatriot, and, writing about "He" (*Er*): "Without 'him' there would be no difference between past and future, but only everlasting change. Or else these forces would clash head on and annihilate each other. But thanks to the insertion of a fighting presence, they meet at an angle, ... no longer beyond and above the world and human time."[187] Indeed, Kafka's storytelling seems to define for Arendt the mechanism of reflection itself. "The gap between past and future," she wrote, "opens only in reflection, whose subject-matter is what is absent—either what has already disappeared or what has not yet appeared. Reflection draws these absent 'regions' into the mind's presence."[188]

Arendt's analysis of Kafka's "He" is a poetic analysis of "our 'inner state' in regard to time," an inner state that expresses a sheer state of in-betweenness that correlates with Benjaminian nowness. "Seen from the viewpoint of man," explains Birgit Erdle, "at each single moment inserted and caught in the middle between his past

---

184. Vivian Liska, *When Kafka Says We: Uncommon Communities in German-Jewish Literature* (Bloomington: Indiana University Press 2009), 209.
185. Birgit R. Erdle, "Dis/Placing Thought: Franz Kafka and Hannah Arendt," in *Kafka and the Universal*, ed. Arthur Cools and Vivian Liska (Berlin: De Gruyter, 2016), 312.
186. Arendt, *The Life of the Mind*, vol. 1, *Thinking* (New York: Harcourt Brace Jovanovich, 1978), 203.
187. Arendt, *The Life of the Mind*, 1:208.
188. Arendt, *The Life of the Mind*, 1:206.

and his future, both aimed at the one who is creating his present, the battleground is an in-between, an extended Now on which he spends his life."[189] Roberto Esposito sees Arendt's interpretation of Benjamin and Kafka as focusing on "the 'gap,' the *nunc stans* or the Jetzt-Zeit, between the 'no longer' and the 'not yet.' This means that Ursprung [origins], unlike Genesis, both belongs to and does not belong to the sphere of history, . . . from what is *not yet* and what is *no longer* history."[190] In short, Arendt's view of temporality was inclusive, building on various traditions and sources from the Jewish and Christian world. But how open was it to a non-European world?

Arendt's closeness to Kafka and Benjamin and her sympathies for the struggles of their protagonists—always in the margins of society—did not always mean that she was open-minded toward the struggles of other minorities. Between 1957 and 1959 she weighed in on the events that unfolded in Little Rock, Arkansas. In September 1957 nine African American students enrolled in an all-white high school. When the Arkansas National Guard was called in to block the entrance to the school, the federal government under Dwight Eisenhower intervened, and troops were sent in to secure the black students and ensure that they could enter the school. The case caused an uproar, and many conservatives criticized the government's actions. One of those critics was Arendt, in an article first rejected by *Commentary* but later published in *Dissent*, notwithstanding internal debates among its editors.[191]

In her critique, Arendt argued that education belongs to the social sphere, in which people have the right to discriminate if they choose, and that therefore *Brown v. Board of Education*'s abolishment of segregation in schooling was unconstitutional. As I will argue in the conclusion to this book, Arendt's lack of support for struggles that

---

189. Arendt, *The Life of the Mind*, 1:205. Quoted in Erdle, "Dis/Placing Thought," 312.
190. Roberto Esposito, *Origin of the Political*, 21.
191. Chad Kautzer, "Political Violence and Race: A Critique of Hannah Arendt," *Comparative Literature and Culture* 21, no. 3 (2019): 5. For a comprehensive analysis of this episode and Arendt's mischaracterization of Black activism, see Kathryn T. Gines, *Hannah Arendt and the Negro Question* (Bloomington: Indiana University Press, 2014).

were not hers in part expresses her commitment to reform and change from within. An avowed critic of Marxism, anarchism, and revolutionary rhetoric, Arendt had an instinctive aversion to attempts to erase tradition as a whole, one aspect of which was her resistance to nihilism. The mirror image of her critique of nihilism was her resistance to Black activism, her ignorance about indigenous politics, Palestinian rights, and Jewish Mizrahi culture. Arendt's egalitarianism was ontological and structural, but because of that also dogmatic and distinctly European. I will return to such shortcomings in the conclusion to this book.

Novus Ordo Saeclorum: The Life of the Mind

In her lectures from the early 1970s, Arendt attempted to respond to a world turned upside down.[192] The danger Kant confronted during the heydays of revolution, absolutism, and democratic terror was the loss of control over human experience, a danger Arendt traced to "the gap between a time continuum of ordered succession and the spontaneous start of something new."[193] In historical terms she pinpointed such moments in the foundation of Rome and in the exodus of the Jews from Egypt, moving toward "the conquest of a new 'promised land.'"[194] Both stories opened "a hiatus between disaster and salvation, between liberation from the old order and the new freedom, embodied in a *novus ordo saeclorum*, a 'new order of the ages' with whose rise the world has structurally changed."[195] This new order was a concept embraced and passed on to us by Virgil and Augustine. Arendt used the expression repeatedly, usually in the context of Augustine's tolerant political-theological creed, his plea to preserve the Jewish minority as a testimony to the victory of Christianity. In other writings she explicitly compares Virgil's story of wandering and exile to the experience of Jewish politics. As Miguel

---

192. Hannah Arendt, *Lectures on Kant's Political Philosophy* (Chicago: University of Chicago Press, 1982), 16.
193. Arendt, *The Life of the Mind*, 2:206.
194. Arendt, *The Life of the Mind*, 2:204.
195. Arendt, *The Life of the Mind*, 2:204.

Vatter has shown, in contrast to Heidegger's return to the pre-Socratic Greeks, Arendt turned to "the Judeo-Roman parallel with which [she] began her political theorizing of a 'Jewish politics in general' during the late 1930s."[196] Virgil and Augustine formed two arcs within Roman history, which "presuppose[d] the wandering in the wilderness proper to the establishment of a new polity."[197] "A new order of the ages" was clearly the battle cry of those yearning for political and a metaphysical change. As Agata Bielik-Robson has shown, natality and transition for Arendt stress the value of transitive life.[198] In *The Life of the Mind*, Arendt contrasts Augustine's dynamic stress on men as *natals* with the static understanding of mortality found in Greek tragedy.[199]

Arendt believed that only the founders of the United States of America had correctly realized a transition through continuity because they were "well acquainted with Roman as well as Biblical antiquity.... Nowhere do they use the hiatus as a possible basis for explaining what they were doing."[200] The mistake made by other "men of action,"—she was thinking about the French revolutionaries—who did not privilege continuity, was that, instead of the Bible, "they ransacked the archives of Roman antiquity" and formed "a government 'of laws and not of men.' What they needed was not only an acquaintance with a new form of government but also a lesson in the art of foundation."[201]

Arendt's ontology of time stood in opposition to radical revolutionary powers such as the French Revolution, on the one hand, and Nietzsche and Heidegger's "active will to annihilate what was," on the other hand.[202] She preferred Augustine's approach, building itself

---

196. Vatter traces clear, if unstated, references to Buber: "Her interpretation of the biblical covenant is clearly drawn from Buber's an-archic interpretation of the *brit* [covenant]." Vatter, *Living Law*, 261.
197. Vatter, *Living Law*, 266.
198. Bielik-Robson, *Another Finitude*, 77.
199. Bielik-Robson, *Another Finitude*, 109.
200. Arendt, *The Life of the Mind*, 204.
201. Arendt, *The Life of the Mind*, 210.
202. Arendt, *The Life of the Mind*, 178.

on the foundations of Jewish scripture and Virgilian poetics, and using it to counter nationalistic and imperialistic logics of infallibility. As she puts it in the last paragraph of *The Life of the Mind*:

> The Christian philosopher of the fifth century AD was the only philosopher the Romans ever had.... In his great work on the *City of God*, he mentions, but does not explicate, what could have become the ontological underpinning for a truly Roman or Virgilian philosophy of politics. According to him, as we know, God created man as a temporal creature, *homo temporalis*; time and man were created together, and this temporality was affirmed by the fact that each man owed his life not just to the multiplication of the species, but to birth, the entry of a novel creation who *as* something entirely new appears in the midst of the time continuum of the world.[203]

In these final pages, Arendt returned to her Freiburg lecture and critical engagement with Heidegger, the Christian republic, natality, and homo temporalis. The plea for *novus ordo saeclorum*, a "new order of the ages," was heavily embedded in a reinterpretation of tradition and history, Jewish and Christian theology, ancient and modern philosophy. How radical, or how new, could it be? While Benjamin's critique of violence attempted to frame political boundaries, law, and violence from the outside, Arendt defended them as "positively established fences which hedge in, protect, and limit the space in which freedom is ... a living, political reality."[204] A temporal focus adds to this political reading a distinction between the temporality of majoritarian power and minority rights, the spectacle of infallibility and the free rhythm of individual life.

While agreeing with Benjamin that a temporal focus constituted the start of reflection, Arendt arrived at a more forcefully practical, political end point. Adopting the American republic as a model for a modern Augustinian "city on the hill," Arendt stressed its constitutional order as a dynamic view of revolution.[205] For her, a positive

---

203. Arendt, *The Life of the Mind*, 217, emphasis in the original.
204. Arendt, "Karl Jaspers: Citizen of the World?," in *Men in Dark Times*, 81–82.
205. "Neither the spirit of this [American] revolution nor the thoughtful and erudite political theories of the Founding Fathers had much noticeable impact upon the European continent." Arendt, *On Revolution*, 24.

political model stressed democracy as natality or "permanent revolution" that situated living time as a political principle between past and future. "Human beings in the process of becoming but not yet complete ... are thereby forced to expose themselves to the light of a public existence."[206]

After mapping the genus and development of political forms in the West since the Hebrew and the Roman "in the beginning," she explains: "The only trait that all these various forms and shapes of human plurality have in common is the simple fact of their genesis.... No matter how this 'we' [of politics] is first experienced and articulated, it seems that it always needs a beginning, and nothing seems too shrouded in darkness and mystery as that 'In the beginning,' not only of the human species as distinguished from other living organisms, but also of the enormous variety of indubitably human societies."[207] Focusing on beginnings, origins, and natality is not just a way to understand the mechanism that forms collectives ("we") but also the temporality of the many individuals that shape them in the everyday. "In the everyday world where we spend our own exiguous quotient of reality," wrote Arendt, "we can only be sure of a shrinkage of time behind us that is no less decisive than the shrinkage of spatial distances on the earth."[208] In short, *The Life of the Mind* attempts to demonstrate how time defines our essence as living organisms, while space defines our temporal organization in the polity.

Not Staying There

Arendt's analysis of time develops the conditions necessary for political action. Although many experts have commented on Arendt's stress on secularization and the public sphere as conditions for political action, few have noticed how her vision of politics, secularization, or revolution, owes its form to an ontology of time. Even

---

206. Arendt, *Between Past and Future*, 183.
207. Arendt, *The Life of the Mind*, 202.
208. Arendt, *The Life of the Mind*, 202.

fewer noticed how her vision rejects the Paulinian-Heideggerian *eschaton* and instead embraces its opposite, an Augustinian vision. As Karl Löwith put it in *Meaning in History* (1949), "Augustine rejected in principle any *world*-historical, i.e., political, eschatology."[209] Much like Löwith, Arendt contrasted an Augustinian "scattered" time to any "end of history."[210] Much like her friends Karl Löwith and Hans Jonas, Arendt began her life as a follower of Heidegger and gradually developed into a critic of his destructive, nihilistic, and eschatological philosophy. After 1933 she believed that Heidegger had failed to supply ethical categories to his understanding of time and being because he viewed man as "'the shepherd of being,' instead of listening to an obligation beyond himself, be it from the encounter with the Other"—as in Buber and Levinas, for example—or simply "in the inherent value of life," as in Jonas.[211] Arendt moved even further beyond Löwith's attack on Heidegger's "eschatological construction of world-history as his history of Being" by developing a democratic political theory.[212] Augustine's thoughts on time and community enabled Arendt to tie her interest in natality and the "moment of insertion" or creation to the necessary presence of the Jew in a Christian society—a revision of the witness doctrine for the sake of democratic plural order. In other words, she wrote in *Between Past and Future*, "plurality is the hallmark of action."[213]

She also moved beyond Jonas. In a long and unpublished letter to him, from June 5, 1964, she wrote, "I always understood Paul's position [in Romans 7:19] 'For the good that I *will* to do, I *do not* do

---

209. Karl Löwith, *Meaning in History* (Chicago: Chicago University Press, 1949), 168.

210. Arendt, "From Hegel to Marx," in *The Promise of Politics*, ed. Jerome Kohn (New York: Schocken Books 2005), 70.

211. Benjamin Lazier, *God Interrupted: Heresy and the European Imagination between the World Wars* (Princeton, NJ: Princeton University Press, 2008), 46. See also Wiese, *Hans Jonas*, 94.

212. Löwith, "Heidegger," 82.

213. Arendt, *Between Past and Future*, 163. Dana Villa notes that, on the basis of this principle, "the freedom of political action [is] essentially *worldly, limited, and nonsovereign*." See Dana R. Villa, "Beyond Good and Evil: Arendt, Nietzsche, and the Aestheticization of Political Action," *Political Theory* 20, no. 2 (1992): 277, emphasis in the original.

etc.' as an existential denial of freedom."[214] The letter was a long commentary on Jonas's *habilitation* from 1928, which he translated into English in 1964 and published the following year in German.[215] In her commentary Arendt warned Jonas, her lifelong friend and another Heidegger veteran, against excessively identifying with Paul. Arendt and Jonas in fact composed their dissertations during the same period (Löwith was older and already completing his *habilitation*), and both argued with and against Heidegger, starting with his readings of Augustine and Paul on time. It is in this context that on April 9, 1964—a few weeks before the aforementioned letter—Jonas publicly came out against Heidegger at an international conference at Drew University, identifying Heidegger as a nihilist and an opponent of Judeo-Christian ethics.[216]

Arendt identified democratic, individual rights with a Judeo-Christian value system that supported modern "common sense."[217] As the modern authoritative state attempted to turn politics into a magnificent celebration of "unappearance," where everything and nothing is political, Arendt made an effort to unpack and expose the conditions of political possibility; she insisted on retrieving the Jewish-Christian paradox—the Jew as exception to Christian rule—that has dominated the heart of Christian politics since Augustine.

---

214. Hannah Arendt to Hans Jonas, June 5, 1964. Hans Jonas Papers, Philosophical Archives of the University of Konstanz, HJ3-12-11; emphases in the original.

215. According to Jonas's own testimony, the paper originated in Heidegger's Augustine seminar. See Jonas, *Memoirs*, 146.

216. The incident frames Richard Wolin's chapter about Hans Jonas. See Wolin, *Heidegger's Children: Hannah Arendt, Karl Löwith, Hans Jonas, and Herbert Marcuse* (Princeton, NJ: Princeton University Press, 2001), 101–33.

217. The loss of common sense she describes in *The Human Condition* directs the individual into an extreme subjectivism, or "the prison of his own mind, into the limitations of patterns he himself created." Arendt, *The Human Condition*, 288. Needless to say, Arendt's cleavage to the Judeo-Christian tradition came at a high cost; she was blind to the problems of those on the margins of Judeo-Christian society. In spite of short excursions into the "Arab question" in Israel or the oppression of African Americans in the United States, her focus lay in other areas. For a critical and a fascinating discussion of the latter, see Gines, *Hannah Arendt and the Negro Question*. For a recent reassessment of the notion of Judeo-Christianity, see Emmanuel Nathan and Anya Topolski, "The Myth of Judeo-Christian Tradition: Introducing a European Perspective," in *Is There a Judeo-Christian Tradition? A European Perspective*, ed. Emmanuel Nathan and Anya Topolski (Berlin: De Gruyter, 2016), 1–16.

If, as Werner Hamacher put it, "democracy is the political form par excellence of Christianity," then it needs the Jew, the Arab, the African American as a pariah.[218] "The Christian state is, in its totality, from its very beginning, and at every moment, a state of exception," he writes. "It is a state against itself."[219] What Augustine taught Arendt, and what Arendt taught Lacoue-Labarthe, Nancy, Hamacher, Agamben, Rancière, and other thinkers of the last generation, is that a structural paradox has always been part of the temporal order of the Christian state: the status of the Jew as pariah and object of infallible political prophecy helped exclude the Jew yet also preserve the Jew's status as witness. It is the Jew who enables, thanks to her otherness, in abstract before the Holocaust and explicitly after it, a *novus ordo saeclorum*.[220]

From her first to her last work, Arendt refused to accept any models of (Western) politics that were not based on pluralism, otherness, and exception. This logic had the power to reform the existing order, rather than adopt a revisionist approach, as Heidegger had. As she explained in her analysis of Benjamin, Kafka, and Broch, humanity's "insertion into time"—an insertion that interrupts time, but does not stop or end it—enables a politics of permanent revolution and creation. Its condition of possibility is a reflective, living temporality of no-longer and not-yet.

"The creation of the world is reflected in the ritual celebrating the New Year," Sylvie Anne Goldberg wrote recently, "At Rosh-Ha-Shanah, the liturgical year begins, and with it, rereading the original

---

218. According to Hamacher, "Democracy pursues the structural depriviledging of Christianity as a confession." Werner Hamacher, "The Right to Have Rights (Four-and-a-Half Remarks)," trans. Kirk Wetters, *South Atlantic Quarterly* 103, no. 2 (2004): 345.

219. Hamacher, "The Right to Have Rights," 347.

220. "The right to have rights is therefore primarily and above all valid for those whom Arendt characterizes as absolutely deprived, alienated in every sense of the word, exploited and divested, for those who exist in 'the abstract nakedness of being human' . . . as a human being in general—without a profession, without citizenship, without an opinion, without a deed by which to identify and specify himself—and different in general, representing nothing but his own absolutely unique individuality which, deprived of expression within action upon a common world, loses all significance." Hamacher, "The Right to Have Rights," 299, 302.

text reiterates the creation by an intermediary in everyone's life."[221] For Arendt, the avowed secularist, the creation of the world could only be conceptualized in democratic, Judeo-Christian terms that always remained self-critical. That might have been "the Jew in her," as Jerome Kohn argued, to adapt the comment she made to Jonas about a potential source of his inspiration. For Arendt, temporality framed the human condition and turned humans into creatures that could act, become, and undertake the great project of forging a polis in the specific present granted to them, rather than succumb to despair over the inevitability of death. Unlike Heidegger, she did not wish to destroy metaphysics, but instead wished to recuperate it to save pluralism. Her goal was political rather than philosophical; as she explained in a 1964 TV interview with Günter Gaus, "I studied philosophy, but that does not mean I have to stay there."[222]

---

221. Sylvie Anne Goldberg, *Clepsydra: Essay on the Plurality of Time in Judaism*, trans. Benjamin Ivry (Stanford, CA: Stanford University Press, 2016), 51.

222. "A TV Conversation with Günter Gaus (1964)," in *Hannah Arendt: Ich will verstehen: Selbstauskünfte zu Leben und Werk*, ed. Ursula Ludz (Munich: Piper, 1996), 44.

5

PAUL CELAN

The Syntax of Time

Few twentieth-century poets have had as great a reputation in postwar philosophy, literature, and literary scholarship as Paul Celan. From Martin Heidegger to Jacques Derrida, Nelly Sachs to Ingeborg Bachmann, Hans-Georg Gadamer and Otto Pöggeler to Emanuel Levinas and Philippe Lacoue-Labarthe, Peter Szondi to Werner Hamacher—these philosophers and writers greatly admired Celan and identified his voice with the "shibboleth" of the post-Holocaust world. Celan's layered language helped his generation reconsider and reshape a new vocabulary that expressed the rupture of annihilation and total war.

Indeed, much of German, French, and Anglo-American thought after 1945 turned to Celan's poetry in order to understand what language "after Auschwitz" might look like. Paul Celan and Theodor Adorno, who coined the phrase "to write poetry after Auschwitz is barbaric," discussed poetry and the impact of the Holocaust in person as well as in writing.¹ The translator and poet Pierre Joris writes in an introduction to a selection of Celan's translated works, "All poetry, after this date, will have to be, at some level, a poetry of witnessing."² Indeed, Celan became the paradigmatic witness for post-1945 literature, "an iconic figure."³ His impact extended much further than a small number of poetry readers. Marjorie Perloff points out that "Continental philosophers . . . have read Celan's poetic oeuvre as a post–World War II Book of Wisdom." Yet Perloff continues by noting the danger of this approach: "The result, ironically, has been to place Celan in a kind of solitary confinement, a private cell where his every 'circumcised word' (Jacques Derrida's term) can be examined for its allegorical weight."⁴

Celan's rebellion, I argue in this chapter, can only be understood in the context of what I have called the temporal turn. Celan was a thoroughly engaged student of the canon of modern literature and philosophy in the classical languages of the previous centuries—German, French, Russian, English, Hebrew, and Yiddish—all of which served him well in finding alternatives to traditional forms of expression. More specifically, his analysis and poetic production provide a consistent and intensive engagement with the philosophy of time, and within it, the legacy German Jewish authors and thinkers engaged with. The marginalia he inscribed in his copies of Nietzsche, Heidegger, Buber, and Benjamin, in books of Russian and French literature and scholarship on Shakespeare—now held at the

---

1. For Adorno's actual expression, see Theodor Adorno, "Kulturkritik und Gesellschaft," in *Prisms* (London: Neville Spearman, 1967), 34. A lively debate about whether the expression is translated and understood in its right context is analyzed, succinctly, in Anthony Rowland, "Re-reading 'Impossibility' and 'Barbarism': Adorno and Post-Holocaust Poetics," *Critical Survey* 9, no. 1 (1997), 57–69; John Zilcosky, "Poetry after Auschwitz? Celan and Adorno Revisited," *Deutsche vierteljahrsschrift für Literaturwissenschaft und Geistesgeschichte* 79 (2005): 670–91.
2. Pierre Joris, introduction to *Paul Celan: Selections*, trans. Pierre Joris (Berkeley: University of California Press, 2005), 6.
3. Marjorie Perloff, "'Sound Scraps, Vision Scraps': Paul Celan's Poetic Practice," in *Radical Poetics and Secular Jewish Culture*, ed. Stephen Paul Miller and Daniel Morris (Tuscaloosa: University of Alabama Press, 2010), 287.
4. Perloff, "'Sound Scraps, Vision Scraps,'" 287.

German Literary Archive in Marbach—testifies to a body of careful scholarship that could still support many a doctorate. The comments prove a commitment to the unpacking of cultural, historical, and linguistic concerns German Jewish thinkers encountered, often against their will. His readings of Greek and Latin texts, Christian and Jewish scripture, mysticism, and science show a remarkably broad and consistently analytical eye that has astonished scholars, even those who prefer to frame Celan in romantic and identitarian terms of victimhood and trauma. Reading Celan with an eye toward his scholarship, not just his identity, reveals a new poetic vocabulary and syntax that came to terms with the conditions of post-Holocaust genocide and beyond to the conditions of life in modernity. For that purpose, Celan's readers have to research his poems synchronically, diachronically, and historically—in Pierre Joris's terms, "vertically."[5] Doing so exposes language that enabled the transformation from an premodern to a modern moment, and from the era that preceded industrialized killing to the post-1945 era. For Celan, thinking about the Holocaust required a reconsideration of human finality and temporal existence. His response in his poetics used the strategy of the caesura, a fissure that reconfigured continuity in life as a series of temporal breaks.[6] Indeed, some keen readers have suggested that "the development of Celan's work had little to do with a thematic

---

5. Pierre Joris, introduction to *Microliths They Are, Little Stones: Posthumous Prose*, by Paul Celan (New Yorrk: Contra Mundum Press, 2020), vi.

6. Joel Gold has said of caesuras that they "thematize temporal process as the mnemonic movement toward a traumatic past." See Joel Gold, "Reading Celan: The Allegory of 'Hohles Lebensgehöft,'" in *Word Traces: Readings of Paul Celan*, ed. Aris Fioretos (Baltimore: Johns Hopkins University Press, 1994), 191. In "Reading Celan," Gold refers to "Winfried Menninghaus's taxonomy of Celan's imaginary universe [of botanical and mineral metaphors]," and he concludes that Celan develops "a poetological movement, . . . telling a kind of story: that of the poem's own movement, or the writing of the poem, or, as I have described it, the poet's quest to master a traumatic past by evoking a utopian point of its recovery" (190). For the poetics of caesura, see also Shira Wolosky, who follows Stéphane Moses by arguing that "the caesura in Celan is at once linguistic and temporal, structural and sacral." Shira Wolosky, *Language Mysticism: The Negative Way of Language in Eliot, Beckett, and Celan* (Stanford, CA: Stanford University Press, 2013), 258.

plan as much as with the problem of time [*Zeitproblematik*]."[7] Time, from this perspective, is what charges language with the energy of testimony and memory.

Accordingly, in this chapter I engage with Celan's poetry as a poetic philosophy of time following the early twentieth-century discussions of temporality by Buber and Benjamin, and by Arendt's midcentury reconfiguration thereof. Indeed, Celan presents a literary equivalent to Arendt's political reflections on the "linguistic impossibilities of . . . German-Jewish letters."[8] I begin this chapter with a depiction of Celan's own stress on temporality—itself in dialogue with Buber and Adorno, Scholem and Benjamin, but also with Heidegger and the Augustinian tradition Heidegger rejected. I continue by focusing on Celan's use of temporal forms as a foundation for a new vocabulary and syntax, and conclude with a short analysis of the poem "Nah im Aortenbogen" (Close in the aorta, 1968), which conveys a German Jewish temporal turn as the most fitting language for the postwar era.[9]

Background: "What Reaches through Time"

Celan's friend, the literary scholar Peter Szondi, wrote that it was the rupture or caesura of time that organizes Celan's poems.[10] The caesura enabled Celan to recalibrate the mirrors of language so they reflect collective expressions and internal divisions between self and other, present and past, the gaze and the observed, the language of description and the object described, phenomenon and

---

7. Axel Gellhaus, "Das Datum des Gedichts: Textgeschichte und Geschichtlichkeit des Textes bei Celan," in *Lesarten: Beiträge zum Werk Paul Celans*, ed. Axel Gellhaus and Andreas Lohr (Cologne: Böhlau, 1996), 181, my translation.

8. Hannah Arendt, "Walter Benjamin, 1892–1940," in Arendt, *Men in Dark Times* (New York: Harcourt, Brace and World, 1983 [1968]), 187.

9. All German quotations from Celan are taken from Paul Celan, *Gesammelte Werke in fünf Bänden*, ed. Beda Allemann, Rudolf Bücher, and Stefan Reichert (Frankfurt: Suhrkamp, 1986).

10. Peter Szondi, "Reading 'Engführung': An Essay on the Poetry of Paul Celan," *Boundary 2* 11, no. 3 (1983): 231–64.

meaning, distance and proximity, signifier and signified.[11] Celan draws attention to those relationships via the ethics of encounter with otherness by developing a broken syntax of poetic language. One cannot talk about his poetry without "the other" or "self" and how they appear on the page. By organizing his syntax around the rhythm of ellipses and caesuras, dropping verbs and adding neologisms, Celan leads the reader in a circle or a loop.

In his notes Celan frequently referred to poetry as "never timeless" and as a type of language that "wants-to-reach-through-time" (*Durch-die-Zeit-hindurch-greifen-wollen*).[12] As I show below, the syntax of Celan's poems and speeches is circular. Looking at language as what "reaches through time" implies that language has an intention—a phenomenological concept—but also that it gains new meaning as it passes through time, hence accumulating different, paradoxical intonations borrowed from linguistic, historical, and literary contexts. Appearing often in Celan's poems, this form implies that the last line of a poem leads back to the first, but now charged with new layers of meaning, a deeper historical semantics. A perceptive reading of the poem would note that the circular motion also appears in single sentences and even words: verbs imply the beginning or end of movements, nouns the origins and ends of the name. Celan often breaks up German words, separating the prefixes and suffixes from nouns, verbs, and adjectives then reattaching them to form neologisms. Thus, in this broken but circular form, time functions as the dynamic force of Celan's poetics. In reading through Celan's earliest known letters, Sandro Zanetti notes that "the structure of Celan's sentence is the sign of precariousness and the attempt to recapture a moment in which the meaning of 'there is no time' is

---

11. Winfried Menninghaus shows how Celan disengaged *Sprachgestaltung* (language forming) from the semiological difference between the signified and the signifier. Menninghaus, *Paul Celan: Magie der Form* (Frankfurt: Suhrkamp, 1980), 35. See also the discussion in Krzystof Ziarek, *Inflected Language: Toward a Hermeneutics of Nearness—Heidegger, Levinas, Stevens, Celan* (Albany: SUNY Press, 1994), 143.

12. Notes for the Bremen speech in the Paul Celan Literary Archives, Deutsches Literaturarchiv in Marbach (DLA), file D90.1.3256a. See also Sandro Zanetti, *"Zeitoffen": Zur Chronographie Paul Celans* (Munich: W. Fink, 2006), 64n47; all quotes from this source are my translation.

reversed: 'I have then, if I may say so, no time'" (*Ich habe also, wenn ich so sagen darf, keine Zeit*).[13] What Zanetti describes in this early letter would become a central feature of Celan's writing and thought: the casual ontology of time ("I have") as the condition of its own negation ("no time").

Celan's unique ability as a designer and builder of word parts ensured that each sentence, and the closure of the poem as a whole, sends the reader back to its opening. The philosophical message accompanying such loops was, Celan experts have demonstrated, to point the reader toward the consistent use of living time—the time one has or not—through a system of interconnected texts.[14] In contrast to the mythic circle of nature or life, Celan's poetic movement circles around absences: the expulsion and deportation of his family and other Romanian Jews to the ghettos, labor camps, and extermination camps. Celan's parents were deported in the summer of 1942; his father died of typhus and his mother was shot shortly thereafter. Numerous friends and relatives disappeared without a trace. It was obvious to Celan, even before the full facts were known, that the Nazis had declared war not just on the physical body of the Jew, but also on the Jew's memory and culture. The disappearance of worlds, from the personal to the familial, social, and cultural, is evident in his circular poems. Each round deepens the reader's understanding of this absence; each turn adds further layers of references to what is no longer there. As Celan explains in the opening to a poem titled "It Is No Longer" (*Es ist nicht mehr*, 1963): "this / heaviness sunk / at times with you / Into this hour. It is / another one."[15]

Identifying absence as tragic, as many Celan interpreters have done, is a partial interpretation at best. The process that leads from

---

13. Zanetti quotes here from a letter Celan sent to Diet Kloos on August 23, 1949, shortly after his arrival in Paris. See Zanetti, *"Zeitoffen,"* 34.

14. Barbara Wiedemann, "'Lesen Sie! Immerzu nur Lesen,': Gellan-Lektüre und Celans Lektüren," *Poetica* 36, no. 1/2 (2004): 169–91; Axel Gellhaus, "Marginalien: Paul Celan als Leser," in *"Der glühende Leertext": Annährungen an Paul Celans Dichtung*, ed. Otto Pöggeler and Christoph Jamme (Munich: W. Fink, 1993), 41–65; Zanetti, *"Zeitoffen."*

15. Celan, "It Is No Longer," in *Memory Rose into Threshold Speech*, trans. Pierre Joris (New York: Farrar, Straus and Giroux, 2020), 282.

the fullness or "more" of the tragic hero to the "no more" of the hero's fall is not linear. Celan's philosophical message ends not only with death, eschatology, or disaster but with the witnessing act of "another one" (*eine andre*). Who is the other? "The other," Celan's partner in a poetic dialogue, is none other than the time of witnessing; his speaker talks, not to another person, but to another reality, another time. Celan, in other words, made time into the narrator of his poems.

Much like the other German Jewish thinkers he read carefully, Celan traced a dialectical process of *kinesis* and *kenosis* that he identified with German Jewish transgression. Buber identified the time of movement (kinesis) with the actualization of man and God or "the transition from the potential to the actual."[16] Scholem identified "emptying out" (kenosis) with the Kabbalist and Neoplatonist stress on a political theology of subtraction from the fullness of "the one" to the mystical *Zimzum* and absence. (*Zimzum*, literally "contraction" of divine presence in order to leave empty space for creation, has also been taken to mean, since the Middle Ages, a sign of "divine rupture.") Here, absence or rupture "is conceived not in terms of lack or absence or void, but in terms of an excess of being."[17] Benjamin developed a "kinetic and temporal manipulation . . . not subordinated to the chronological momentum of linear narrative."[18] Arendt, following Heidegger's interpretation of Nietzsche, searched for an alternative to the pessimistic movement of emptying out and the preference to "will nothingness [rather] than not will at all."[19] Celan followed suit: In "It Is No Longer," Celan depicts the emptiness that has no name but still

---

16. Martin Buber to Frederik van Eeden, October 1914, in Buber, *Briefwechsel aus Sieben Jahrzenten*, vol. 1, *1897–1918*, ed. Grete Schaeder (Heidelberg: Lambert Schneider, 1972), 380.

17. Gershom Scholem, "Das Ringen zwischen dem biblischen Gott und dem Gott Plotins in der alten Kabbala," in *Über einige Grundbegriffe des Judentums* (Frankfurt: Suhrkamp, 1970), 39–40. See the translation and analysis in Miguel Vatter, *Living Time* (New York: Oxford University Press, 2021), 165–66.

18. Miriam Hansen, "Benjamin, Cinema, and Experience: 'The Blue Flower in the Land of Technology,'" in *Walter Benjamin: Critical Evaluations in Cultural Theory*, vol. 2, *Modernity*, ed. Peter Osborne (London: Routledge, 2005), 254.

19. Arendt is referring here to Heidegger's critique of Nietzsche. See Arendt, *The Life of the Mind*, vol. 2, *Willing* (New York: Harcourt, 1978), 177.

names its subjects: "It is the weight that holds back the emptiness / that accom / panies you. / Like you, it has no name. Maybe / you are the same. Maybe / some day you'll call me that / too."[20] Who will name the speaker but has no name itself? Repeating the question above, who is the ultimate "other one"? The poem seems to suggest that it can be both the divine or the human, the still-alive survivor or the almost-dead, but life cannot be full and death is not the same as nothingness. Neither is it *Zimzum*, realization, the hidden face of the divine, or melancholic sovereignty—all concepts mentioned in this book. Celan rejects any form of divine transcendence, messianism, sovereignty, or deliverance. Instead, his "other" is someone able to "accompany" us in both life and death, in fullness and emptiness, in birth and in death. She is the voice of a poetic thinker who reconsiders the role of homo temporalis in the *Jetztzeit* (now-time).

In this chapter I argue not only that Celan consciously built a poetics of temporality and living-time within his grammar, syntax, and vocabulary, but also that he did so following closely other German Jewish thinkers, including Kafka, Buber and Rosenzweig, Löwith, Scholem, Benjamin, and Margarete Susman. Celan never refers to Arendt, even though he shares many of her assumptions concerning "the insertion of man" between past and future—Arendt's characterization of both Kafka's secret and Augustinian temporality. Celan, like Arendt, paid close hermeneutic attention to the not-yet and already-not, the no-longer that he placed at the heart of his paradigmatic "Meridian" speech in 1961.[21] Like other German Jews,

---

20. Celan, "It Is No Longer," in *Memory Rose*, 282.
21. The "Meridian" speech was given at the occasion of Celan's receiving Germany's premier literary award, the Georg Büchner Prize, on October 22, 1960. John Felstiner tells us that Celan composed *The Meridian* in three days, after nearly five months of preparation. Felstiner stresses the frequent use of the word "encounter," borrowed from Buber's interpretation of the dialogue between I and Thou as a metaphysical encounter. Celan prepared the speech while consulting Benjamin and Kafka, among others. See Felstiner, *Paul Celan: Poet, Survivor, Jew* (New Haven, CT: Yale University Press, 1995), 163–66. In a short essay about Celan's temporality, Jean Greisch discusses Celan's use of this "Dia-chronie" to mark the threshold between self and other, isolation and encounter, presence and absence, arrival and leaving. See Greisch, "Zeitgehöft und Anwesen: Zur Dia-chronie des Gedichts," in Pöggeler and Jamme *"Der glühende Leertext,"* 258.

Celan saw himself responding to a temporal standstill (stasis) of trauma, an in-betweenness that had to be reconciled with a changing world. As Zanetti has pointed out, Celan took an "intermediate position" (*Zwischenstellung*) between "a commitment to facticity and context ... and the possibility of future reading."[22] Such use of grammar and syntax was supposed to avoid teleology and ensure a dialogical, open-ended language.[23]

As his library demonstrates clearly, from the mid-1950s to the end of his life Celan carefully gathered an intertextual network of Jewish and Christian sources but rejected a Judeo-Christian embracing of victimhood and identitarian difference.[24] The "other" did not refer to himself, as it often does in the celebration of otherness.[25] In contrast to Buber's hopeful concept of dialogue and Arendt's revolutionary natality, Celan's poetry avoided stable entities such as self and another—"Into this hour. It is / another one"—in favor of unstable signs, linguistic traces that serve as testimonies for the remains of our world and the failure of representation. The comma, caesura, or "breathturn," as he called it, connected and separated languages, traditions, and parts of a sentence. Celan's poems make us aware that a simple comma can serve as a concealed visual key to presence and absence, or as a way to stress the mechanism of *Zimzum* in language. The comma separates as well as unites the two parts of the sentence; it marks where the worlds of presence and absence, life and death, past and present, creation and destruction meet. Celan's poems lay bare the inherent temporal quality of syntactical signs:

---

22. Zanetti, *"Zeitoffen,"* 11.
23. Zanetti, *"Zeitoffen,"* 41.
24. "Reading traces (dating, markings, commenting, etc.) in Celan's library prove the great interest Celan took specifically in texts dedicated to the philosophy of time." Zanetti, *"Zeitoffen,"* 13. For the remarkable work of cataloguing Celan's philosophical library and his various systems of dating, marking, and commenting, see Paul Celan, *La bibliothèque philosophique: Die philosophische Bibliothek*, ed. Alexandra Richter, Patrik Alac, and Bertrand Badiou (Paris: Rue d'Ulm, 2004).
25. Daniel Cohn-Bendit discussed himself, and the German Jew, half a century after May 1968, as an event: "In moral terms," he explained in a recent interview, "that was 1968's greatest event: Africans, Arabs—all the world called themselves 'undesirable' German Jews. That's when multiculturalism was born." Daniel Cohn-Bendit and Claus Leggewie, "1968: Power to the Imagination," *New York Review of Books*, May 10, 2018.

poetic syntax is the thread that holds together words and meaning, the signifier and the signified of time itself.

In the following pages I ground those claims by moving backward from the commentators to Celan's own words and from the present back to his poetry and the reflection of temporality in his syntax. Looking back as well as forward also implies a direct engagement with the "thou-ness" of poetry in a particular historical mode. Celan explains its potential in *The Meridian*: "The one who has been addressed ... becomes a thou, also brings its otherness along into the present, in this present.—In the here and now of the poem it is still possible—the poem itself, after all, has only this one, unique, limited present—only in this immediacy and proximity does it allow the most idiosyncratic quality of the Other, its time, to participate in the dialogue."[26] Poetry manifests its otherness by shaping an alternative syntax that leads forward—from the first to the last word—and back to the start, signaling the temporal core of language and testifying to the failure of language.

A German Jewish Philosophy

Celan's circular poetics demonstrated how deeply connected he was to German Jewish in-betweenness and its "linguistic impossibility." In a letter to Theodor and Gretel Adorno from May 23, 1960, he mentioned a "small piece of writing" that is "the 'prehistory' [*Vorgeschichte*] of the Meridian [speech] and that is German Jewish already in its title. It is *'assumons donc ce que l'on nous prête!'* [let us take upon ourselves that which is given to us], that is the crooked nose ... through which the third or the silent can materialize."[27]

---

26. Paul Celan, *The Meridian*, in the appendix to Jacques Derrida, *Sovereignties in Question: The Poetics of Paul Celan*, trans. Jerry Glenn (New York: Fordham University Press, 2005), 182. Derrida published *Shibboleth: Pour Paul Celan* first in French, in 1986, in (Paris: Galilée, 1986). It was published in full in English as "Shibboleth for Paul Celan," in Derrida, *Sovereignties in Question*, 1–64.

27. Paul Celan to Theodor Adorno, May 23, 1960, Paul Celan Literary Archive, DLA, D90.1.686/1–4; my translation. I thank Eric Badiou for his permission to examine and quote from this letter.

Mirjam Sieber notes that the exchange between Celan and Adorno expresses their mutual "critique of Enlightenment and care for the non-identical."[28] John Felstiner, Celan's biographer, argued that Celan's short piece "Gespräch im Gebirg" (Conversation in the mountains), echoes Büchner's Lenz, who identifies with "a wandering Jew," and Nietzsche's Zarathustra, who goes into the mountains and discovers the death of God.[29] The combination of the two, Felstiner shows, marks a typical German Jewish paradox, a position of eternal wandering in spite of the collapse of old religious and metaphysical boundaries. Celan identified this paradox, in his letter to Adorno, as leading to the position of "the third" or "the silent," who exists outside the usual social norms and metaphysical assumptions.[30] Celan's prose fragment referred also to the kabbalistic symbolism of Gershom Scholem and to Heidegger's reading of Nietzsche, but "above all," Felstiner wrote, "'Gespräch im Gebirg' owes to Martin Buber, whose philosophical writings and retellings of Hasidic tales Celan was reading during the late 1950s."[31] Buber similarly titled an essay in his book about *Daniel* "Gespräch in den Bergen" (Conversation in the mountains, 1913). In this early attempt to form a dialogical philosophy, Buber explored terms such as "dialogical living" [*dialogisch Lebende*], the dialectics of self and

---

28. Mirjam Sieber mentions the letter exchange in the context of *The Dialectic of Enlightenment* and Celan's short prose piece "Gespräch im Gebirg." See Sieber, *Paul Celans "Gespräch im Gebirg": Erinnerung an eine "Versäumte Begegnung"* (Tübingen: Max Niemeyer, 2007), 224.
29. Felstiner, *Paul Celan*, 140.
30. Celan refers here to Simmel and Adorno's "figure of the third," itself a sociological rebranding of Nietzsche's figure of "the third," in his well-known fragment from Zarathustra: "For the solitary the friend is always the third one: the third one is the cork that prevents the conversation of the two from sinking into the depths." See Friedrich Nietzsche, *Thus Spoke Zarathustra: A Book for Everyone and Nobody*, trans. Graham Parkes (New York: Oxford University Press, 2005), 49. Curiously, the great historian of German Jewry, George Mosse, referred to German Jews along the same lines, as a "third force," yet without mentioning Celan. Mosse, *Germans and Jews: The Right, the Left, and the Search for a "Third Force" in Pre-Nazi Germany* (Detroit: Wayne State University Press, 1970).
31. Felstiner, *Paul Celan*, 140. Felstiner pointed out that the piece was written after Celan avoided meeting Adorno in Sils-Maria in the Swiss Alps. Felstiner, *Paul Celan*, 140.

other, human and divine. The trope of wondering allows one to reflect about tradition, and the present realization of these relationships. As I demonstrated in chapter 2, the heart of Buber's argument concerned the function of promise and realization, immediacy and revival in both the Jewish tradition and German Jewish politics. Celan's text transformed Buber's prophetic tone into a poetic one.

Buber's *Daniel* opens with a conversation between Daniel and a woman, while climbing up a mountain. This unmistakably Nietzschean text is full of terms such as rhythm, ecstasy, living experience, and calls for "a liberation from the prison of direction" and space, but conditioned by the requirement to act in the world and realize ideals.[32] Celan's piece, written half a century later, is much less verbal. It follows two Jews named Klein (small) and Gross (big), who talk about the language of a third, unnamed Jew, who speaks "without I and without you." The third, unspecified Jew, is depicted as estranged from language itself.[33] Celan's constant reference to German Jews as a prototype of their desolated time placed German Jews between self and other, life and death, perpetrator and victim, murder and memory. The German Jew speaks the language of the murderer but is excluded from this language as a viable subject. She is, as a result, the speaker of a language that exists outside the usual I–Thou dialogical possibility. Indeed, the 1960 "Meridian" speech differentiates between "poetry committed to dialogue between I and thou, and poetry in which the other remains absolutely other, *Du*."[34] In other words, as the brief prose piece and the "Meridian" speech demonstrate, "Celan is not interested in approaching the other through the concepts of difference or identity," as Buber did, "but instead in exploring the glass trace of the silent con-sonant, which indicates a readiness, an openness of language of the other."[35]

The figure of the German Jew served not just Celan or political rebels such as "Dani the Red" (Daniel Cohn-Bendit's nickname as a student leader in 1968) but a whole post-1945 generation that

---
32. For a brief discussion of Buber's Daniel see Phil Huston, *Martin Buber's Journey to Presence* (New York: Fordham University Press, 2007), 110–11.
33. I follow here the reading offered in Ziarek, *Inflected Language*, 150.
34. Ziarek, *Inflected Language*, 155.
35. Ziarek, *Inflected Language*, 157.

attempted to comprehend the ethical, cultural, and political implications of industrialized genocide. Adorno's dictum and Sartre's critical engagement with Heidegger's German were characteristic of the questions asked by this generation of European intellectuals. A first and second wave of reception stressed Celan's identity and tragic fate, seeing him alternately as a poet working within the lyrical tradition and as a "representative" of post-Holocaust Jewry. Hence, philosophical analyses of his poetry usually adopt a melancholic-exilic register. Needless to say, Celan's depression, hospitalization, and suicide contributed to this reading as well. In this context, Celan was read as equally versed as "[an] apparent loud voice that spreads above the whole plateau of lyric tradition."[36] In a posthumous review of Celan's *Atemkristall*, in 1970, Hans-Georg Gadamer noted that "it is not clear in these poems by Celan who is the I and who is the you," but "whoever understands lyric poetry understands that the I is . . . not the poet but rather 'the single one' [*jener Einzelne*], as Kierkegaard called every one of us."[37] Readers such as Gadamer, Menninghaus, and Pöggeler frame Celan as a representative of a lyrical and existential or eschatological position. In his 1957 reading of Celan's poem "Tenebrae," a poem we will return to below, Gadamer had already revealed his preference for a Christological reading of Celan that was utterly blind to the Jewish context.[38] Gadamer was probably unaware of Celan's careful reading of Gershom Scholem's 1917 essay on the book of Lamentations—the basis of "Tenebrae"—as well as of Buber's "Question to the Single One" ("Frage an der Einzelnen," 1936), a response to Kierkegaard's understanding of Christian time and Schmitt's sovereignty.

While early critics were inclined to place Celan within the lyrical or "subjectivist" tradition, as Winfried Menninghaus put it, scholars

---

36. Horst Bienek, "Narben unserer Zeit" (1959), in *Über Paul Celan*, ed. Dietlind Meinecke (Frankfurt: Suhrkamp, 1970), 43.

37. Hans-Georg Gadamer, "Wer bin Ich und wer bist Du?," in Meinecke, *Über Paul Celan*, 260–61, my translation.

38. For a critical commentary on this interpretation, see Adam Lipszic, "Words and Corpses: Celan's 'Tenebrae' between Gadamer and Scholem," *Jewish Studies Quarterly* 21, no. 1 (2014): 55–66.

in the 1980s philosophized his position and counted him among the key thinkers of the twentieth century.[39] Otto Pöggeler was one of the first philosophers to pay homage, as early as the late 1950s, to Celan's Heideggerian vocabulary, and his full interpretation, published in 1986, analyzed Celan via Hölderlin and Heidegger. Pöggeler himself explained in an interview, "During the 1950s the simple question was how could one, as a German, return to the history of ideas [*Geistesgeschichte*] and work in an international philosophical context."[40] The answer, for Pöggeler, had to do with "the subtle poetry of Celan. Here, in the German language, is present what we are struggling for in public discourse: a Holocaust memorial, but one that every person can grapple with individually, in private."[41] Indeed, the mid-1980s, which also saw the German *Historikerstreit* (the historians debate) concerning the singularity of the Holocaust, gave birth to several key philosophical essays on Celan. The analyses usually focused on Celan's language as a reflection of the traumatic "inclination toward silence," as Celan put it in his "Meridian" speech, or what Derrida characterized as "the counter-logic of iterability" in his now-classic philosophical reflection on Celan.[42] Hans-Georg Gadamer, who studied with Heidegger, explained his interest in Celan in 1973 (revised and published in 1986) in somewhat evasive terms that echo Heidegger's own use of language. Gadamer wrote that his interest in Celan's poetry had to

---

39. Menninghaus, *Paul Celan*.

40. Andreas Grossmann and Gerhard Unterthurner, "'Ich schwimme lieber': Ein Gespräch mit Otto Pöggeler," interview, *Journal Phänomenologie* 11 (1999), my translation. The interview can be read in full online at https://www.journal-phaenomenologie.ac.at/texte/11/interview/.

41. "Ich habe immer gemeint, daß hier [in Celan] in deutscher Sprache da ist, worum man gegenwärtig in der Öffentlichkeit ringt: ein Holocaust-Mahnmal, aber eines, mit dem sich jeder einzelne und in Stille für sich auseinandersetzen kann." Grossmann and Unterthurner, "'Ich schwimme Lieber,'" my translation.

42. Paul Celan, *The Meridian: Final Version—Drafts—Materials*, ed. Bernhard Böschenstein and Heino Schmull, trans. Pierre Joris (Stanford, CA: Stanford University Press, 2011), 8; Celan, *Gesammelte Werke*, 3:197: "das Gedicht heute ... zeigt ... eine starke neigong zum Verstummen." Jacques Derrida, "Shibboleth: For Paul Celan," in Derrida, *Acts of Literature*, ed. Derrick Attridge (New York: Routledge, 1992), 371.

do with his "hermeneutics of hermeneutics" or how "word-creation and word-discovery aris[e] like a confession from a specific life circumstance."[43] French interpreters paid closer attention to the language of silence, even if Philippe Lacoue-Labarthe argued that same year (1986), much as Pöggeler had a few decades earlier, that Celan's poetics "is, in its entirety, a dialogue with Heidegger's thought."[44]

Within literary studies and theory, Derrida's reflections on Celan, beginning in the mid-1980s, were a turning point for both Derrida's own mission of de- and reconstructing language and for anyone interested in the reception and philosophical application of Celan. In October 1984, in a lecture on Celan's poetry at the University of Washington,[45] Derrida emphasized Celan's language, or the shibboleth that "forges and seals, in a single idiom, *in eins*, the poetic event, a multiplicity of languages of equally singular dates."[46] According to Derrida, Celan's poetics reflects the tie that binds the event as it is remembered and the way it changes the moment of perception (Benjamin's now-time) in the present or "the *double edge* of a *shibboleth*. The mark of a covenant or alliance, it also *intervenes*, it interdicts, it signifies the sentence of exclusion, of discrimination, indeed, of extermination."[47] The implications are broad and important not only for the discussion of self and tradition, but also for any disciplinary division. Derrida's own rhetoric became decisive at this point, warning us against the heaviest sin committed against Celan—namely, to separate the theoretical implications of his poetry from his poetic practice. "To trust in the partition [*partage*] between a theoretical, philosophical, hermeneutic, even poeticist discourse on

---

43. Hans-Georg Gadamer, *Gadamer on Celan: "Who Am I and Who Are You?" and Other Essays*, trans. Richard Heinemann and Bruce Krajewski (Albany: SUNY Press, 1997), 131.

44. Philippe Lacoue-Labarthe, *Poetry as Experience*, trans. Andrea Tarnowski (Stanford, CA: Stanford University Press, 1999), 33. Lacoue-Labarthe's focus is on the poetic relations between Celan and Hölderlin, which he connects to Celan's reading of Heidegger's interpretations of Hölderlin.

45. Derrida, *Sovereignties in Question*, 29.

46. Derrida, *Sovereignties in Question*, 29.

47. Derrida, *Sovereignties in Question*, 63, emphases in the original.

the phenomenon of the date, on the one hand, and, on the other hand, a poetic implementation of dating is to no longer read him."[48]

The current reception of Paul Celan's work reveals that when considering Celan today, one must write about the second half of the twentieth century from the perspective of "futurity,"[49] "the temporality of 'a time to come,'"[50] or "Jewish modernity"[51] after the Holocaust. Jacques Derrida identified the paradox of talking about absence and unrepresentability as "the German-Jewish phenomenon."[52] In his introduction to Celan's biography, John Felstiner notes the inability to separate Celan as a representative German-speaking Jew from his work as a poet, for "every day he felt his era's and his own history pressing on the poems he wrote, which 'had to pass' (as he said of the German language itself) 'through the thousand darknesses of death-bringing speech.'"[53] Charles Bambach has noted that the challenges Celan confronted did not stop at the confrontation between his own personal history and the history of his time. This confrontation also involved revising his expectations of present language vis-à-vis the expectations inherited from past millennia. In contrast to the hermeneutic and eschatological message, "the poet can no longer speak with the voice of the prophet and call for the return of the gods to come. In the post-Nietzschean, post-Auschwitz era of the

---

48. Derrida, *Sovereignties in Question*, 4.
49. "Futurity... draws on Walter Benjamin and Hannah Arendt's view of what constitutes meaning... [these are] issues of the present and future responsibility." See Amir Eshel, *Futurity: Contemporary Literature and the Quest for the Past* (Chicago: Chicago University Press, 2014), 254–55.
50. Michael G. Levine, *A Weak Messianic Power: Figures of a Time to Come in Benjamin, Derrida, and Celan* (New York: Fordham University Press, 2014), 5.
51. Vivian Liska explained Jewish modernity as a set of relations corresponding to tradition, law, messianism, and remembrance. "The transmission of tradition focuses on Arendt; the interaction between law and narrative on Kafka; the conception of a messianic language on Benjamin; and the interrelated notions of exile, remembrance, and exemplarity on Celan." See Liska, *German-Jewish Thought*, 7.
52. Jacques Derrida, "Interpretations at War: Kant, the Jew, the German," in Derrida, *Acts of Religion*, ed. Gil Anidjar (New York: Routledge, 2002), 150.
53. John Felstiner, *Paul Celan*, xv. Felstiner quotes here from Celan, "Anlässlich der Entgegennahme des Literaturpreises der Freien Hansestadt Bremen," in *Gesammelte Werke*, 3:186.

'world's night,' the eschatological idiom of coming salvation reveals itself only in/as a repetitive, doubling, and ambiguous language of stammering, stuttering, babbling."⁵⁴ Celan's proposition, according to Bambach, was to stress the unorthodox function of language, its silence.

Felstiner and Bambach are two of the leading voices in a crowded field. The scholarly thirst for Celan's poetics, especially since the mid-1980s, is still not quenched. This is not surprising, considering that "we experience Celan's pathos as a loss of any final 'ground' to our subjective judgment."⁵⁵ For the most part, scholars have followed Celan's biography and principal themes, producing a rich field of research on personal-historical tension, the failure of language, the urgency of testimony and memory, and the hopelessness in face of genocidal murder, alongside many other topics. For the most part, however, these scholars miss the underlying semantic layer that holds together both historical and poetic observations: the temporal order in general and the temporal order of German Jewish in-betweenness in particular.

Close readers of poetry have understood the "vertical" intertextual layer within Celan's work as the key that unlocks the "German-Jewish phenomenon."⁵⁶ In his 2001–2003 seminar at the École des hautes études en sciences sociales, Derrida shifted his earlier stress on the shibboleth of language to an emphasis on temporality and the ontology of witnessing at the center of Celan's poetics: "What the poem lets speak at the same time . . . is the time of the other, its time in what it has as its most proper: the most proper, and thus most untranslatably other, of the time of the other. . . . It

---

54. Charles Bambach, *Thinking the Poetic Measure of Justice: Hölderlin-Heidegger-Celan* (Albany: SUNY Press, 2011), 211.

55. Joel Gold, "Reading Celan," 192.

56. Liska, *German-Jewish Thought*, 127. See also interpretations by Ulrich Baer, *Remnants of Song: Trauma and the Experience of Modernity in Charles Baudelaire and Paul Celan* (Stanford, CA: Stanford University Press, 2000); Bernhard Böschenstein, *Leuchttürme: Von Hölderlin zu Celan* (Frankfurt am Main: Insel Verlag, 1977); Galili Shahar, *Haeven vehamilah: 'al shirat Paul Celan* (Jerusalem: Mossad Bialik, 2019); Shira Wolosky, *Language Mysticism: The Negative Way of Language in Eliot, Beckett, and Celan* (Stanford, CA: Stanford University Press, 1995).

is not only a matter of letting the other speak, but of letting time speak, its time, what its time, the time of the other, has as its most proper."[57]

What is the time of the other? Buber considered it an ecstatic time of *Erlebnis* (lived experience) that unites humans with one another and with the divine. For Derrida it is a broken linguistic phenomenon. It is a caesura in language as a referent of reality, the break at the heart of testimony about the impossible historical event: "Ellipsis and caesura and the cut-off breath no doubt designate here, as always in Celan, that which, in the body and the rhythm of the poem, seems most *decisive. A decision*, as its name indicates, always appears as interruption.... What matters most is the strange limit between what can and cannot be determined or decided in *this poem's bearing witness to bearing witness*."[58] For Derrida and Felstiner, Celan molded an existing break—historical and ontological—into a new condition of expression.[59] Derrida's interest in Celan's use of language, his system of de- and reconstructing language, and the unique system of temporal in-betweenness allows Derrida to frame poetry—against Heidegger's emphasis on poetry as a higher form of philosophical speculation—as an ethical system that opens a door to "the time of the other." "Speaking with the other or to the other, even before speaking alone," he writes, "is the time of the other."[60]

---

57. Derrida, *Sovereignties in Question*, 120–21.
58. Derrida, *Sovereignties in Question*, 69–70, emphases in the original.
59. Following Derrida, Werner Hamacher in 1985 characterized Celan's language as the poetry of time: "Celan's poem attempts to speak from the negativity of time itself." But unlike the process I follow in this book, Hamacher characterized the "movement of time" in Celan's poetics as a Hegelian "continuum of negativity referring to itself and, furthermore, as the negative unity of difference." Hamacher's essay was published first as "The Second of Inversion: Movements of a Figure through Celan's Poetry," in *The Lessons of Paul de Man*, trans. William D. Jewett, *Yale French Studies*, no. 69 (1985): 285. The original German text was published three years later as "Die Sekunde der Inversion: Bewegungen einer Figur durch Celans Gedichte," in *Paul Celan*, eds. Werner Hamacher and Winfried Menninghaus (Frankfurt: Suhrkamp, 1988), 81–127. See also Hamacher, "The Second Inversion," in *Premises: Essays on Philosophy and Literature from Kant to Celan*, trans. Peter Fenves (Stanford, CA: Stanford University Press, 1996), 356.
60. Derrida, *Sovereignties in Question*, 120.

A careful reading of Celan's "time of the other," in his speeches, poems, and marginalia, demonstrates that Celan, like other German Jewish critics, identified those principles of critical and temporal hermeneutics with his own sense of Jewishness. In a letter to Margarete Susman, in June 1963, Celan wrote, "What you wrote, dear Margarete Susman, and what you still write, tells me about the unique conditions of the encounter [*Begegnung*] in which man lives. Let me tell you, please, that you are to me an instance [*eine Instanz*], a person [*Mensch*] whose shape and word I look up to—*a Jewish person*."[61] For Celan, "an encounter" had far more to do with the politics of temporality than with personal or collective identity, as Pöggeler and Gadamer had argued. Furthermore, Celan's deep investment in "the time of the other" demonstrates how he unfolded his notion of egalitarian politics. "Celan's texts," argues Krzystof Ziarek, "become an accusation of the totalizing tendency of Western thinking to subordinate alterity and difference to sameness."[62] In *The Meridian* Celan plays on antisemitic idioms, such as the slur "*Verjuden*" (to "Judaize") used by antisemites to mark what they perceived as Jewish characteristics contaminating German culture. Celan turns the idiom upside down by declaring "verjuden: es is Anderswerden und dessen Geheimnis stehn" (Judaizing: that is, becoming the other and his standing secret)."[63] About this interpretation

---

61. Paul Celan to Margarete Susman, June 7, 1963, in "Paul Celan-Margarete Susman: Der Briefwechsel aus den Jahren 1963–1965," in *Celan-Jahrbuch* 8 (2001/2), ed. Hans Michael Speier (Heidelberg: Heidelberg University Press, 2003), 42; my translation, emphasis in the original. What made Celan see in Susman the epitome of Jewishness? In their correspondence, Susman and Celan exchanged views about Buber's concept of encounter (*Begegnung*); Celan's poems, which he attached to his letters; Susman's essays on Spinoza (originally published in Buber's *Vom Judentum*, which is where, Celan admitted, he had come across her writing); Buber himself; and Simmel; as well as the notion of "absolute poetry" inspired by Stefan George. In her answer to Celan's compliments, Susman admits to be thinking about this last topic in connection with Celan's poetry, especially after reading *Absolute Poetry* by Michael Landmann, a German Jewish (Swiss-born) follower of Stefan George who was inspired by George's understanding of total language and a "secret Germany."
62. Ziarek, *Inflected Language*, 147.
63. Paul Celan, *Der Meridian: Endfassung, Vorstufen, Materialien*, ed. Bernhard Böschenstein and Heino Schmull (Frankfurt: Suhrkamp, 1999), 130. See also the commentary by Steven Aschheim, "The Jew Within: The Myth of Judaization

Derrida commented, "The secret is the very essence of otherness," which poetry and testimony must also strive to disclose.[64]

Since Derrida, there has been an interesting, albeit strange, return to the earlier hermeneutic and eschatological trend. The question of the poems' ability to serve as testimony receives a different interpretation in Giorgio Agamben's *Remnants of Auschwitz* (1998), where Celan turns into a source of a new philosophy of testimony. For Agamben, the paradox of testimony, the position that "the survivors are not the true witnesses, . . . [for] those who saw the Gorgon have not returned to tell about it or have returned mute,"[65] parallels the paradox of sovereignty. In the Muselmann, we note the inability to distinguish sovereignty and law, except when it silences or excludes the witness.[66] In this paradoxical reality where (moral) language must keep silent, Celan testifies by not testifying: "Celan the poet must be considered and mourned rather than imitated. If his is a message, it is lost in the 'background noise.'"[67]

In a more recent essay, Agamben has continued to develop this paradox by propagating an active silencing of Celan. In exploring

---

in German," in *Culture and Catastrophe: German and Jewish Confrontations with National Socialism and Other Crises* (New York: NYU Press, 1996), 45–68; Amir Eshel, "Paul Celan's Other: History, Poetics, and Ethics," *New German Critique* 91 (2004): 57–77; and Liska, *German-Jewish Thought*, 125.

64. Derrida, *Sovereignties in Question*, 164–65. See also Pajari Räsänen, "Counter-Figures: An Essay on Anti-Metaphoric Resistance—Paul Celan's Poetry and Poetics at the Limits of Figurality" (diss., University of Helsinki, 2007), 347.

65. Giorgio Agamben, *Remnants of Auschwitz: The Witness and the Archive*, trans. Daniel Heller-Roazen (New York: Zone Books, 1999), 33.

66. The Yad Vashem Resource Center defines "Muselmann" as "[a] German [term] widely used among concentration camp inmates to refer to prisoners who were near death due to exhaustion, starvation, or hopelessness. The word Muselmann literally means 'Muslim,'" https://www.yadvashem.org/odot_pdf/Microsoft%20Word%20-%206474.pdf. "[In the Muselmann] a law seeks to transform itself entirely into life, finds itself confronted with a life that is absolutely indistinguishable for law, and it is precisely this indiscernibility that threatens the *lex animate* of the camp." Agamben, *Homo Sacer: Sovereign Power and Bare Life*, trans. Daniel Heller-Roazen (Stanford, CA: Stanford University Press, 1998), 185. See also the analysis of David M. Seymour, "The Purgatory of the Camp: Political Emancipation and the Emancipation of the Political," in *Giorgio Agamben: Legal, Political, and Philosophical Perspectives*, ed. Tom Frost (New York: Routledge, 2013), 97–118.

67. Agamben, *Remnants of Auschwitz*, 37.

Celan's poetics as a paradigmatic case of the exile who chose to stay in exile (the metaphoric Egypt), Agamben identifies Celan's Egypt with an "*a*topia" and with "Easter."[68] Curiously, in his interpretation Agamben chooses to retain the Christian parallel of a sacred Jewish holiday that served also as Celan's Jewish name: "Celan, who was registered in his birth certificate as Paul, received eight days later the secret name Pesach.... This connection [to Egypt as a *topia*] becomes even more evident if we recall the particular importance that the term Pesach, 'Easter,' had for Celan."[69] Agamben, in contrast to Felstiner's interpretation, and in accordance with Gadamer's (and his own of Benjamin), reads Celan as an exemplary Pauline figure, indeed a Paul, or "a 'foreigner' who ... will somehow become the foundation of and justification for writing poetry in Egypt."[70] Such an understanding contrasts with Celan's emphasis on the "silent" or "the third," in his letter to Adorno. The letter reads "Egypt" not as a mission or an attempt of conversion but as a metaphorical space where silence overrules language. But hasn't Celan's poetry worked to shape an alternative to silence? By giving the silence a rhythm and a time, Egypt becomes a temporal metaphor.

Paying Attention to Time

As the marginalia in his books show, since the early 1950s Celan was engaged in intensive readings of Martin Buber, Gershom Scholem, Walter Benjamin, Franz Rosenzweig, Karl Löwith, and, of course, Martin Heidegger. He had already studied Heidegger's earlier *Being and Time* and *What Is Metaphysics?* in 1952 and went back to Buber's *Hasidic Tales* shortly after. His detailed comments in the margins of Heidegger's *Introduction to Metaphysics* were written between September 23 and October 7, 1954, when Celan was on vacation with his wife in La Ciotat in the French Riviera. As he did

---

68. In Italian, "Pasqua" refers both to Easter and Passover, but the translator's choice to limit the translation to Easter is consistent with the rest of the argument.
69. Agamben, *Remnants of Auschwitz*, 75.
70. Giorgio Agamben, "Easter in Egypt," in *The Fire and the Tale*, trans. Lorenzo Chiesa (Stanford, CA: Stanford University Press, 2017), 75.

with other crucial texts, Celan signed each segment of reading with the date and the place of reading. The marginalia show not only a deep understanding of Heidegger's and German Jewish philosophy, but also an advanced and coherent sense of their poetic and political implications.

In contrast to how most of the philosophical interpreters discussed it, Celan read Heidegger always alongside German Jewish critics such as Scholem, Buber, or Karl Löwith. The Löwith work that Celan paired with Heidegger's *Introduction to Metaphysics* was Löwith's damning "Martin Heidegger: Thinker in a Destitute Time" (1952).[71] This essay analyzed Heidegger's thought in conjunction with political authoritarianism, Stefan George's poetics of the "New Reich," and, most importantly, Heidegger's own Christian background. Löwith writes, "The fascination with Heidegger's thinking is based primarily on this religious undertone of an epochal and eschatological consciousness. In fact, he thinks Being on the basis of time, as a thinker 'in a destitute time' whose destitution consists (according to his interpretation of Hölderlin) in its standing under a twofold lack: 'in the no-longer of the gods who have fled, and in the not-yet of the one to come.'"[72] Löwith, one of the few scholars to confront Heidegger about his Nazi sympathies, extended his reading of Heidegger's philosophy to support a political and a theological interpretation of Heidegger's oeuvre, in which Heidegger regressed from both Jewish-Christian and Nietzschean understanding of the sacredness of life.[73]

---

71. The essay appeared first as Karl Löwith, "Martin Heidegger—Denker in durftiger Zeit," *Die Neue Rudschau* 1 (1952).

72. Löwith refers here to Heidegger's own quote from Hölderlin. Quoted in Karl Löwith, "Martin Heidegger: Thinker in a Destitute Time," in *Heidegger and European Nihilism*, trans. Gary Steiner (New York: Columbia University Press, 1995), 133. The title for Löwith's article is taken from Heidegger's discussion of Hölderlin's question in his Bread and Wine cycle: "und wozu Dichter in dürftiger Zeit?" (and who wants poets in lean years?) See Friedrich Hölderlin, *Selected Poems and Fragments*, trans. Michael Hamburger (Harmondsworth: Penguin, 1998), 157.

73. In reading Löwith in conjunction with Rosenzweig (and Husserl and Blumenberg), Rodolphe Gasché debates Peter Gordon's *Rosenzweig and Heidegger: Between Judaism and German Philosophy* (Berkeley: University of California Press, 2003), and demonstrates that "the similarity of both Heidegger and Rosenzweig's starting point ... did not prevent both thinkers from developing their

Celan had a different take on the time between the no-longer and not-yet. Poetry, rather than the presence or expectation of the sublime, is what defines the present moment. He frames *The Meridian* in the interim temporal zone of not-yet and no-longer; a poem, he argues, "ceaselessly calls and hauls itself back ... from its now no-longer into its still-now."[74] Most interpreters connect Celan's interest in the idiomatic relation between the not-yet (*Noch nicht*) and no-longer (*Schon nicht*) to Heidegger and his "proclivity to use hyphenated compounds for time-space designations."[75] However, this idiom served Celan—as it had Arendt before him—to mark the point of meeting and separation between Heidegger's philosophy of time and the German Jewish critique of it. Heidegger follows Hölderlin in order to imagine a mythic, triumphant Germany "as a nation standing spatially and temporally in the middle, caught between past and future, lying between East and West,"[76] but for the German Jews in-betweenness (*Zwiesprache*) means *getting caught* between languages, cultures, and the national struggles that nations project back onto their Jewish minorities. Like other German Jewish thinkers, Celan's language is a commentary on this sense of entrapment. Krzystof Ziarek writes, "Celan's poems separate themselves from themselves," and, as such, contrast with Heidegger's "self-referentiality."[77] In contrast to those jockeying for social superiority, German Jewish thinkers were interested in the interim or liminal zone extending between the *Schon nicht* and *Noch nicht* as a time of radical change. For this reason, Arendt

---

thought in thoroughly opposite directions." Gasché, "On the Eastward Trajectory toward Europe: Karl Löwith's Exiles," in *Escape to Life: German Intellectuals in New York: A Compendium on Exile after 1933*, ed. Eckart Goebel and Sigrid Weigel (Berlin: De Gruyter, 2012), 315.

74. Paul Celan, *The Meridian: Final Version—Drafts—Materials*, ed. Bernhard Böschenstein and Heino Schmull, trans. Pierre Joris (Stanford, CA: Stanford University Press, 2011), 9. "Es ruft und holt sich ... unausgesetzt aus seinem Schon-nicht-mehr in sein Immer-noch zurück." Celan, *Gesammelte Werke*, 3:197.

75. James Lyon, *Paul Celan and Martin Heidegger: An Unresolved Conversation, 1951–1970* (Baltimore: Johns Hopkins University Press, 2006), 130.

76. Charles Bambach, "The Geo-Politics of Heidegger's Mitteleuropa," in *Heidegger's Roots: Nietzsche, National Socialism, and the Greeks* (Ithaca, NY: Cornell University Press, 2003), 139.

77. Ziarek, *Inflected Language*, 141.

portrayed the oeuvres of Kafka, Benjamin, and Hermann Broch as extending a bridge "between the 'no longer' of the old laws and the 'not yet' of the new saving word, between life and death."[78]

Celan produced a critical poetics of silence, breaks, and neologisms in the early 1950s, utilizing egalitarian idioms borrowed from the Jewish prophets, Spanish civil war fighters, and communist surrealists.[79] Felstiner writes that Celan's poetics of this period, which concluded with the collection *Von Schwelle zu Schwelle* (Threshold to threshold), "sounds forward-looking, unless this wanderer, like Franz Kafka or Walter Benjamin, is reaching thresholds but cannot cross them."[80] Celan, like Arendt, read back from a postwar revolutionary climate and German Jewish critique to the conditions of both Jewish identity and revolutionary politics of the period. In 1946, for example, he responded to news about antisemitic incidents in Romania and a racist article in a French communist magazine deploring the influence of "black literature" by translating four of Kafka's stories into Romanian.[81] Like Buber, Benjamin, and Arendt before him, Celan shaped a new language of postwar temporality; his tools came not just from religious studies, critical thought, or political thought but from the history of literature.

Eyeing Time

Celan's poetics reveal extraordinary coherence and consistency in his use of temporal concepts and forms. After escaping the Nazi murderers and their Romanian collaborators, Celan left his hometown Czernowitz to Bucharest, and from there to Paris via Vienna, where he found temporary resident in 1947–1948. In Vienna he met Ingeborg Bachmann, who was herself engaging with writing a dissertation about the philosophy of Martin Heidegger. During his time in Vienna Celan wrote "Corona," the opening line of which alludes

---

78. Hannah Arendt, "No Longer and Not Yet," in *Reflections on Literature and Culture* (Stanford, CA: Stanford University Press, 2007), 125.
79. Felstiner, *Paul Celan*, 81–82.
80. Felstiner, *Paul Celan*, 82.
81. Felstiner, *Paul Celan*, 46.

to Rilke's "Autumn," "Lord, it is time" (*Herr, es ist Zeit*). The title of the poem refers to the heart of the living body (coronary), to a neo-Platonist and Kabbalist notion of light, and a gentle ironic gesture to the German Romantic tradition. Celan will return to the metaphor of "corona" in one of his last poems, also concluding our discussion below, "Near, in the aorta's arch." In the early "Corona" Celan sheds the authoritative, metaphysical address, "Lord," and makes Rilke's first line into his last. "Corona" opens instead with a description of the poem's condition of possibility: "autumn nibbles its leaf right from my hand: we're friends. / We shell time from the nuts and teach it to walk: / time turns back into its shell."[82] The opening line explains how time works for the speaker, but it deliberately keeps the "we" indeterminate: Is the speaker talking about himself and a loved one, or himself and autumn?

The syntax reverses the well-known logic of Rilke's poem. Instead of setting time as a primary declarative condition—Rilke's "it is time" alludes to the pathos-filled time of decision, the last moments of warmth before winter—"Corona" offers a list of unsteady signifiers. It uses unconventional metaphors of the season: autumn as a shell, as nuts, as mirrors; and most importantly, the time of autumn as a time of self-conscious observation, with and against the other. "My eye goes down to my lover's loins: / we gaze at each other, / we say dark things. . . . It's time it came time. / It is time."[83] Celan reverses Rilke's romanticism and his time of realization to a time of longing; loins and dark things lead, this time, to the union of physical bodies.

Yet what seems at first like a magnificent love song preoccupied with the realization and frustration of love is in fact a negative evaluation of its conditions—"it's time it came time" implies an expectation and lack of realization—or a work of disintegration of desire: the *noch nicht* (not yet) and *schon nicht* (already not) of love. Undoubtedly, Ingeborg Bachmann saw the poem as a (sad)

---

82. Felstiner, *Paul Celan*, 54. For the original German, see Celan, *Gesammelte Werke*, 1:37: "Aus der Hand frisst der Herbst mir sein Blatt: wir sind Freund. / Wir schälen die Zeit aus den Nüssen und lehren sie gehn: / die Zeit kehrt zurück in die Schale."

83. Felstiner, *Paul Celan*, 54.

product of lost love between herself and Celan. Marjorie Perloff suggests exactly that: "Rather than reading 'Corona' as a passionate love poem, Bachmann takes 'it is time' as a moment of unfortunate closure when 'everything turns to marble.'"[84] But an end of time, freezing everything in marble—the material of great sculptures and tombstones—ignores the ontological "it is"-ness of Celan's time, in which Celan *reverses* stasis and finality.[85] "It is time" concludes the poem, but the last line sends us back to the first line: It is the time of autumn, or the beginning of the end of time that may never arrive, or not in that form. How will it arrive?

In the subsequent poems of the 1950s, Celan continued to play with similar rhythms and themes. In "The Jars" he depicts the biblical tablets of the law as "the long tables of time" and as "God's jars."[86] The eye is a repeating motif for him—inspired by Heidegger's reading of Rilke and Hölderlin—as a temporal relation. The eye in Celan's poems examines not only the objects it sees but also the relationship between self and other, or between past, present, and future. In a short poem titled "Eye of Time," Celan describes the function of the eye: "the world warms up, / and the dead / bud and bloom."[87] Much like the play on "it is time" in "Corona," here Celan again uses Romantic vocabulary to make a darker comment about time as a fundamental condition of life: rotting in death also means budding and blooming that will support the birth of new life. By following the state of decline as a cycle of life and death, Celan explodes the temporality of life-toward-death that is also death-toward-life. To the Greek cycle of nature, the Romantic aestheticization of nature or its modern restructuring, Celan adds a concrete absence that is not about nature, metaphysics, or the modern techne; instead it assumes

---

84. Marjorie Perloff, *Edge of Irony: Modernism in the Shadow of the Habsburg Empire* (Chicago: Chicago University Press, 2016), 142.

85. I thank Ethan Kleinberg for his private comment that marble is used for both classic sculptures and modern tombstones.

86. Celan, *Selections*, 48.

87. For the complete English translation: Celan, "Eye of Time," in *Memory Rose*, 139. For the German: "es wird warm in der Welt, / und die Toten / knospen und blühen": Celan, "Auge der Zeit," in *Von Schwelle zu Schwelle: Vorstufen-Textgenese-Endfassung* (Frankfurt: Suhrkamp, 2002), 89.

all of those as the condition to an absolute force, the destruction of living time itself: "This is the eye of time.... Its lid washed by fires, its tear is steam."[88] During the 1950s, Celan's metaphors of the eye register "an alien time." Everyday life became, after the Holocaust, estranged from its own rhythm of living. The life of the third is the life of silence within speech.

Gadamer located Celan's motif of the eye at the intersection between the Hölderlin tradition of mythic-lyrical poetry and Christian symbols, the metaphysical and the phenomenon, the latter grounded in Heidegger's philosophy.[89] But Celan's interpretation of the relationship between the eye and reality is not metaphysical or phenomenal. Rather, it aims to clarify the simultaneity and circularity of perception. This is the work of poetry, flickering between different tenses of time. Rochelle Tobias notes that Celan's notion of time "remains allusive because it is not space. It is neither the distance a body travels nor the stages a body goes through" but instead is the simultaneity of both.[90] In simple words, one's life and movement are always relational.

The connection between eyes and times repeats again and again in Celan's poems. What the eye sees is not the actual movement of a body but an estimate of movement in time. In Celan we know that the condition for this movement is its own negation. For example, in "The Vintagers" ("Die Winzer," 1953) he opens by bringing the weeping eyes together with the night, the wall and the stone, the silence and the fall, to reach the horrid action of squashing the

---

88. Celan, "Eye of Time," 139. Heidegger identifies Hölderlin's resistance to metaphysics and techne with his rejection of spatiotemporal "locality" or his Romantic "acknowledgment of darkness" and sensitivity to light. See Martin Heidegger, *Hölderlin's Hymn "The Ister,"* trans. William McNeill and Julia Davis (Bloomington: Indiana University Press, 1996), 47–48.

89. Gadamer, *Gadamer on Celan*, 146. Shira Wolosky argues against this perception, claiming that "Celan's is finally not a poetic of individual consciousness only. It shows consciousness as structured through history." Wolosky, *Language Mysticism*, 148.

90. Rochelle Tobias refers here to Celan's "*Nacht*" (Night) from his *Sprachgitter* (Speech grill) but the claim is a general one. Rochelle Tobias, *The Discourse of Nature in the Poetry of Celan: The Unnatural World* (Baltimore: Johns Hopkins University Press, 2006), 45. Tobias translates or modifies existing translations. For a recent translation, see Celan, *Memory Rose*, 194.

grape-shaped eyes: "they press down on time like their eye ... with night-toughened hands."[91] In "Remembrance" ("Andenken," 1954) he writes of the "almond eye of the dead." In "Confidence" ("Zuversicht," 1955) from his collection *Speech-Grille* (*Sprachgitter*), the eye "will be yet one eye, / a strange one," and in "Streak" ("Schliere," 1956) it is the "streak of the eye: ... sign, / livened by sand—or ice?—of / an alien time for a more alien always."[92] Many interpreters have noted the centrality of the eye to Celan's metaphorology, but few have noticed how closely the visual and temporal interact, connecting life and death, the familiar and the alien, or how this weaving together of image and temporality shapes a negative grammar of time: "I have, then ... no time."

In the second half of the 1950s, Celan plunged even deeper into the poetics of time. The origins of "This Evening Also" ("Auch Heute Abend") is sketched out on the back cover of Löwith's book on Heidegger. The poem repeats Celan's usual natural metaphors: snow, ice, sand, sea in the first stanza, the impossible return to a nonexistent home in the second one, identifying the speaker with the evening that "also wants to be fed / out of the trickling hour."[93] We do not know more about the poem's source of inspiration, except that it pertained to the self-relation to object and to Kafka's amorphic body. When Löwith writes about Hegel's use of "Meinen" (opinions) and "the possessive pronouns," Celan notes in the margins, "compare [to] Kafka: 'Sein Leib / im Dunkel'" (his body in the dark).[94]

---

91. Felstiner, *Paul Celan*, 85. Felstiner, who identifies here an allusion to Hölderlin's "Brot und Wein," chose to turn the single "hand" to plural "hands," in order to strengthen the dramatic effect, thereby obscuring the biblical allusion to God's "strong hand, and with an outstretched arm" (Psalm 136:12). In the original German: "Sie herbsten, sie keltern den Wein, / sie pressen die Zeit wie ihr Auge ... mit nachtstarker Hand." Celan, *Gesammelte Werke*, 1:140.

92. Felstiner, *Paul Celan*, 97; Celan, *Gesammelte Werke*, 1:159.

93. Celan, "This Evening Also," in *Poems of Paul Celan*, trans. Michael Hamburger (London: Anvil Press Poetry, 1998), 89. Celan, "Tonight Too," in *Memory Rose*, 114.

94. See Celan, *La bibliothèque philosophique*, 498. Celan probably thinks about Kafka's "Description of a Struggle." Celan himself dated the poem to October 19, 1954, and related it to a direct comment about the Nazi "brown shirts"; but as Jean Bollack showed, "This Evening Also" revolves around the sensation of the sand, which was present all around Celan during a family vacation on the beach

Said differently, for Celan neither the phenomenon, nor the physical body, can be separated from past or present circumstances.

On March 10, 1957, Celan wrote "Tenebrae," a work he regarded, as he put it in a letter to Otto Pöggeler, as "one of [my] favorite poems." The poem opens with a declaration that alludes to Rilke and his own "Corona": "We are near, Lord."[95] Nearness to the divine implies proximity to the end of life or an ecstatic experience, not a measurement of distance from an object. "Nearness," a key term for Celan, follows Walter Benjamin's understanding of nearness as a temporal rather than a spatial category.[96] More specifically, the poem refers to a realization about the end of time, to the lamentations of Jeremiah during the siege of Jerusalem, and the Gospel's vision of "darkness over all the earth" (Matthew 27:45).[97] After asking God to pray for the survivors and "cast your image into our eyes," the poem concludes by declaring again. "Pray, Lord. / We are near." The handwritten version of the poem bore the title *Leçons de ténèbres* (Lessons of darkness), emphasizing the pedagogical nature of the Catholic service.[98] Celan's critical tone in this poem led Pöggeler to advise him against "rebellious subjectivism."[99] Gadamer responded to Celan's poem by transforming his earlier understanding of Celan's "Who Am I and Who Are You" into the "theology of the *Deus absconditus*," the Gnostic "hidden God," or the notion that

---

when he wrote it. According to Bollack, for Celan the poem "denoted the amorphic character of time. . . . The sand comes from the night, from 'somewhere else,' everywhere on the coast, or the deserts of death." Bollack, *Dichtung wider Dichtung: Paul Celan und die Literatur* (Göttingen: Wallstein, 2006), 445, my translation.

95. I use Richard Heinemann and Bruce Krajewski's translation of the poem, published in Gadamer, *Gadamer on Celan*, 168.

96. Eli Friedlaender has argued that "near and far, insofar as they determine life, are manifest by two states that Benjamin identifies as 'spell' and 'yearning.' Spell is the magic of nearness: being immediately attracted or bound to the near, . . . far from being in control of the near." Friedlaender, *Walter Benjamin: A Philosophical Portrait* (Cambridge, MA: Harvard University Press, 2012), 87–88.

97. Felstiner, *Paul Celan*, 101.

98. See the development of the different versions in Paul Celan, *Sprachgitter: Vorstuffen-Textgenese-Endfassung* (Frankfurt: Suhrkamp, 1996), 30–31. *Leçons de ténèbres* is also a term used during the French baroque period in which Couperin, Charpentier, and others composed in a polyphonic style.

99. Felstiner, *Paul Celan*, 102.

"this is not a flowing message of salvation, but rather a painstakingly extorted word."[100] In other words, Gadamer interprets Celan's rejection of revelation as a personal and confessional mode: "Celan's poetry is a kind of word-creation and word-discovery arising like a confession from a specific life circumstance."[101] Gadamer and Pöggeler saw this mode of poetry as a form of lyrical, secularized confessionalism. As he explains toward the end of his text, Gadamer identifies Celan's poetry with a universal and Christian temporal order anchored in Paul's understanding of *parousia* (the second coming): "It is an affirmation of distress. By taking death seriously and accepting it as the destiny of human beings, . . . the poem approaches the ultimate intention of the Christian doctrine of the incarnation."[102] Gadamer's interpretation traces the roots and background of Celan's hermeneutics of time but utterly misses its "inversion."

"Tenebrae" ("darkness" in Latin and in Celan's poem without the addition of "lessons of") was published in 1959 in the third cycle included in *Sprachgitter*. The cycle led from silence in the early part to, says Felstiner, a "reconsideration of the voice" in the fourth cycle of the collection." The voice, Felstiner argues, is not just any voice but "the reversal of [Christian] passion," for it emphasized the reflection—"It was blood, . . . it shined" (*es glänzte*)—of violence and its Jewish victim. "We are near," Felstiner suggests, echoes not a nearness to God in the state of reincarnation but a nearness to death, destruction, and the gleam (*Glanz*) of blood as a last sign of life.[103]

In "Tenebrae," "Lord, we are near," can be seen as another comment on Rilke's "Lord, it is time." Unlike "Corona" from a few years

---

100. Gadamer, *Gadamer on Celan*, 80. *Deus absconditus* is Latin for "the hidden God," a concept in Gnostic theology and adapted later by Luther and Martin Buber, among others.
101. Gadamer, *Gadamer on Celan*, 131.
102. Gadamer, *Gadamer on Celan*, 176.
103. Flestiner, *Paul Celan*, 103–4. Pöggeler admits as much in spite of framing the intertext from the perspective of Heidegger and Hölderlin. Poems that allude to God's distance "can be God's nearness. Are the thoughts of the Prophet Jeremiah not also incorporated in that the voice of a wrathful God roars even in the very snorting of the steed of an enemy army which falls upon Jerusalem?" See Otto Pöggeler, "Mystical Elements in Heidegger's Thought and Celan's Poetry," in Fioretos *Word Traces*, 94.

before, "Tenebrae" acknowledges the existence of the "Lord" (eleven times!), but does so only to emphasize the negligence, ignorance, hiddenness, and cruelty of the divine. "It was blood, it was / what you shed, Lord." "Pray, Lord. / We are near" (*Bete, Herr. / Wir sind nah*) is how the poem ends, making "nearness" the remainder of life, that which is wasted by the divine. God, if there is one, is nothing but an ironist, reflecting on his own absence and the destruction of those who are near to him.

Many of these same motifs appear in Celan's work right up to his last poems. The temporal condition of our gaze unites us as human beings beyond ethnic and cultural divisions, beyond nearness and distance. If anything, the themes of "eyeing" time and of the temporality of limited human observation only strengthen and deepen in later years. In Celan, the temporality of time is communicated through broken syntax, neologisms, and distorted meaning.[104] His 1962 poem "Tübingen, January" is the subject of multiple interpretations because of its explicit debt to Heidegger. Celan opens it, as usual, with a paradox: "Eyes talked in- / to blindness." Interpretations since Philippe Lacoue-Labarthe and Charles Bambach focus on the clear allusions to Hölderlin in this poem, and through him to Heidegger's analysis of Hölderlin's hymns. The poem's direct engagement with temporality transposes the mythic and historical allusions in Hölderlin and Heidegger into an ironic commentary about the German obsession with the Greeks, as well as an expression of broken existence: "he could, / if he spoke of this / time, he / could / only babble and babble, / ever- ever- / moremore [*immer-, immer-,/ zuzu*].[105]

Many commentators have focused on the last two words of the poem, which allude to Hölderlin's "madness," yet few have noted in this context the temporal—as well as locative and causal—preposition (*zu*) that follows it, or its doubling (*zuzu*). Both Felstiner ("ever- ever / moremore") and Joris ("always, always / again") chose to play with

---

104. See Shira Wolosky's analysis of Celan's poems in terms of "[what is] fragmented to an extreme, both in syntax and in highly neologistic word forms." Wolosky, *Language Mysticism*, 213.
105. Felstiner, *Paul Celan*, 172. Celan, "Tübingen, Jänner," in *Gesammelte Werke*, 1:226.

the temporal semantics in their translations, but they ignored the syntactical function of *zu* as pointing toward itself, as well as back to the beginning of the poem: From "Eyes talked in- / to blindness" they talked into the always of "to- to." The condition set by "this time" is historical and an ironic commentary on the discrepancy between romantic vocabulary and the annihilation of the Jews, but it is also a way to turn time into the temporal condition of language as such. The last line of the poem integrates both past ("spoke") and the movement of *zuzu* ("to-to") toward the future—and by implication sets the expectation created by the speech-act apart from its realization, which degenerates into nonsense. The babbling lays bare the failure of the signifier-signified relation. "To-to" can only refer to its own hope of creating meaning and not to an external, independent meaning in the world. Separating time and the third person ("he") from both action and speech also demonstrates that closure comes in the form of the *in*completeness of time—ever (*immer*). In other words, logical speech or the relationship between signifier and signified can only end in fragmentation. The mad Hölderlin, in his last years, makes more sense than any modern commentator. The eye with its in-built blindness no longer aspires to capture outside reality as orderly or logical. The mad *zuzu* sends us back to the first line. Where to-to? "Lord, we are near": We must go to another, alien time we cannot see.

German Jewish Intertexts: The Early 1960s

At the center of his "Meridian" speech Celan interrogates one of the fundamental problems of representation: Art threatens, like death, to freeze life and love, death and birth, and transform their memory into a textual or visual image. (Emmanuel Levinas explains that death turns a face into a mask in which the expression disappears.)[106] For Celan, however, time moves in loops: it's time it came. Time does not have a telos outside itself and can only come to terms with its

---

106. Emmanuel Levinas, *God, Death, and Time*, trans. Bettina Bergo (Stanford, CA: Stanford University Press, 2000), 12.

own existence. Therefore, "it is time" is not the full, declarative state Rilke addresses to the Lord, nor the kind of memorial that bespeaks "the self-understanding of the poem as an inclined messianic speech [Heme-messianischer Tendenz]," as Hamacher argues.[107] Instead it is a multivalent operation of living time, often expressed in human terms such as "experience" and "expectation."

In the "Meridian" speech Celan encounters experience ("already-no-longer") and expectation ("always-still" or "not-yet") with the poetic occupation. "Certainly, the poem—the poem today," he explains in his notes, "calls and brings itself, in order to be able to exist, ceaselessly back from its already-no-longer into its always-still."[108] In the following passage of the speech, Celan brings together the "always-still" of poetic speech and the question of "attention." Attention to what? In *Being and Time* Heidegger explains that everyday language, since Kant, "[is] not paying specific attention to [things]."[109] Western metaphysics in general, and Kantian thinking in particular, "do not even pay any attention to it [the thing], [which] hides in itself enigma upon enigma existentially and ontologically."[110] Instead, we

---

107. Werner Hamacher, "HÄM: Ein Gedicht Celans mit Motiven Benjamins," in *Keinmaleins: Texte zu Celan* (Frankfurt: Vittorio Klostermann, 2019), 24. Hamacher plays with the idea of "Heme-messianism [*Hememessianischen*]," "a messianity without messianism, a messianity that has no names, only failed or half names." Hamacher, "HÄM: Ein Gedicht Celans," 36. For Celan, time is instead a state of paradoxical and meaningless entrapment that circles human folly. Hamacher's emphasis on Rilke's ninth elegy from the *Duino Elegies* is spot-on where it concerns the silence that falls on speech ("Here is the time for the sayable, . . . an act under a shell"), but he misses the emphasis on time ("*des Säglichen Zeit*") as well as the connection to Rilke's "Es ist Zeit," and Celan's "Corona" ("We shell time from the nuts and teach it to walk"). Furthermore, while tracing the lines that lead back from Celan's reading in Benjamin's interpretation of Kafka, Hamacher sticks to his Heideggerian understanding of temporality and ignores the fact that Celan reverses Heidegger's "Die Zeit des Weltbildes" into the Jewish imperative "Ohnebild" (No image). In contrast to Hamacher's broken relation of *Freiraum* to a messianic language, the caesura pushes the temporal dimension to the fore, ensuring that the gap between the verses bespeaks the evaporating movement of lost time, not a future spatial redemption. Hamacher, "HÄM: Ein Gedicht Celans mit Motiven Benjamins," 28.

108. Celan, *The Meridian*, 8.

109. Martin Heidegger, *Being and Time*, trans. Joan Stambaugh (Albany: State University of New York Press, 1996), 70.

110. Heidegger, *Being and Time*, 390.

should realize that "if we pay attention to the derivation of now-time from temporality we are justified in addressing temporality as *primordial time*."[111] Celan answers the question of attention by turning the reader's gaze to the solutions offered by a tradition, not as "primordial time" but as a tradition of conversation, dialogue, and relation: "Attention—permit me to quote here a phrase by Malebranche, via Walter Benjamin's essay on Kafka—'Attention is the natural prayer of the soul.'" Giving the right attention enables "a dialogue" with an addressee who has "become a you, brings its otherness into this present. Even in this here and now of the poem."[112] Giving attention to the temporal aspect of language enables Celan to express the trauma of the Holocaust while acknowledging the failure of language to express it. The best indication for this failure is the suspended and recurring time of "always-still"—and it leads Celan to realize that the poem is a desperate conversation with time itself. In that realization he was not alone. He acknowledged the debt to Buber's immediacy and to Benjamin's "now-time."

But the history of German Jewish in-betweenness does not stop with German Jews themselves. As I argued in this chapter, their hermeneutics of time was later taken up by radical voices within the second generation of Heideggerian philosophers, especially Gadamer and Pöggeler, as well as representatives of deconstruction and biopolitics. Celan put it in *The Meridian*:

> Only in the real of this dialogue does that which is addressed take form and gather around. . . . But the one who has been addressed, and, by virtue of having been named, has, as it were, become a Thou, also brings its otherness along into the present, into this present. In the here and now of the poem it is still possible—the poem itself, after all, has only this one, unique, punctual present—only in this immediacy and proximity it lets speak what the Other has that is most proper to it: its time.[113]

---

111. Heidegger, *Being and Time*, 405.
112. Celan, *The Meridian*, 9.
113. Quoted in Derrida, *Sovereignties in Question*, 120. This passage is quoted again in the full translation of *The Meridian* in the appendix to Derrida, *Sovereignties in Question*, 182.

250   Chapter 5

"Nah im Aortenbogen": The Late 1960s

I opened this chapter by arguing that Celan's poetic syntax stresses a temporal logic beyond ethnic or cultural separations. The logic of Celan's language and of his political message became more apparent with every collection of poems. To a large degree, it developed out of his close dialogue with German Jewish authors, from Buber and Landauer to Kafka, Susman, Scholem, Benjamin, and Löwith. Equally, it drew from the legacy of German poetry and Jewish thought, especially in relation to its language of time. In "Breathturn" ("Atemwende," 1967) Celan defined the ontology of witnessing in relation to the "time crevasse" and the "unnullable witness": "Deep in the time crevasse, / by / honeycomb-ice / there waits, a breathcrystal, / your unnullable / witness."[114] Felstiner explains this poem as the end of a process that began in 1952 with "Count up the Almonds." In fact, Celan recited these two poems as the bookends, the beginning and ending poems, of a reading he did in Freiburg before he met with Heidegger in the summer of 1967.[115] For Felstiner, the core of Celan's thought was his identity as a German Jew and his conflicted relationship with Heidegger. But Felstiner reads Celan as a poet who assumes a normative Jewish position and identity; in his words, "The alien Hebrew 'shibboleth' serves as password for the poet himself."[116]

In contrast, reading Celan in a wider context of German Jewish critique—rather than identity—shows a thinker who united his radical notion of language with his critical view of politics. Vivian Liska explains that, for Celan, "The German-Jewish pair becomes the very site of self-difference, a mode of being, thinking, and writing that invokes Jews but is not necessarily embodied by them."[117] My own argument takes this claim one step further: Celan, like

---

114. Celan, *Selected Poems and Prose of Paul Celan*, trans. John Felstiner (New York: W. W. Norton, 2001), 247.
115. Felstiner, *Paul Celan*, 245.
116. Felstiner, *Paul Celan*, 82.
117. Liska, *German-Jewish Thought*, 127.

other German Jews who embodied the notion of self-difference—that is, the "shibboleth"—utilized the ontological force of time, a common "breathturn" he was attempting to create out of the ashes of the Holocaust.[118]

The best demonstration of Celan's unique understanding of a German Jewish breathturn is obvious in one of Celan's best-known poems, "Near, in the Aorta's Arch" (Close, in the aortic arch):

Nah, im Aortenbogen,
im Hellblut:
das Hellwort.
Mutter Rachel
weint nicht mehr.
Rübergetragen
alles Geweinte.
Still, in den Kranzarterien,
unumschnürt
Ziw, jenes Licht. (*Gesammelte Werke*, 2: 202)

Close, in the aortic arch,
in the bright blood:
the bright word.
Mother Rachel
weeps no more.
Carried across,
all that was wept.

---

118. Derrida recaptures this principle—whether from Benjamin, Celan, or Lacoue-Labarthe's discussion of their responses to Heidegger as "a notion of temporality" (rather than a scheme of temporality)—as the principle of caesura, which he contrasts with the logic of sameness and identity. Derrida's genealogy leads from Greek tragedy, via Hölderlin, Benjamin's *Trauerspiel*, Heidegger's Hölderlin lectures, and Celan's poetry, to deconstruction: "When in Sophoclean tragedy, it marks the withdrawal of the divine and turning back of man toward the earth, the caesura, gap or hiatus plays at and undoes mourning. A *Trauerspiel* plays at mourning. It doubles the work.... Gap or hiatus: the open mouth. To give and receive. The caesura sometimes takes your breath away. When luck is with it, it's to let you speak." Jacques Derrida, "Introduction: Desistance," in Philippe Lacoue-Labarthe, *Typography: Mimesis, Philosophy, Politics*, trans. Christopher Fynsk (Stanford, CA: Stanford University Press, 1998), 42.

> Quiet, in the coronary arteries,
> unconstricted:
> *Ziv*, that light.[119]

The poem describes a sick body during its last breaths of life and follows the medical process of death in the first stanza (Celan studied medicine before shifting to literature).[120] The process follows the logic of *Zimzum*, or the gradual narrowing of life to its most fundamental, singular essence. Notes in Celan's marginalia show he was referring to Gershom Scholem's and Martin Heidegger's interpretations of those traditions, as well as to a modern Yiddish interpretation of a canonical liturgical reference: "Mother Rachel / weeps no more." The allusion refers to a Jewish prayer that is borrowed from Jeremiah 31: "A voice is heard in Ramah, mourning and great weeping, Rachel weeping for her children and refusing to be comforted because they are no more." The poem changes the focus from the prophecy of destruction to its aftermath, and from mourning to the silence that follows it. Celan jotted down this passage in the margins of a book by Gershom Scholem, where Scholem framed the prayer as a key to his discussion of Kabbalist *Zimzum* and messianic redemption.[121] Celan's "vertical" allusion to Jeremiah's prophecy of destruction is a bitter one, for the poem's end point is not consolation or redemption but negation. The only consolation is the individual's own moment of death. Indeed, the third and final stanza casts a critical eye on the physiological and mystical concentration of the body.

In the third stanza, Celan alludes to the opening line of the poem, "Close, in the aortic arch," but this time stresses the temporal moment not the spatial category "close" that is present in the first line. In the first line of the third stanza nearness is transformed into a

---

119. John Felstiner, "'Ziv, that light': Translation and Tradition in Paul Celan," *New Literary History* 18, no. 3 (1987): 614.

120. For Celan's study of medicine and how it contributed to his poetry, see Felstiner, *Paul Celan*, 23; Lyon, *Paul Celan and Martin Heidegger*, 25.

121. This section relies on a much longer, detailed interpretation of the poem. See Nitzan Lebovic, "Near the End: Paul Celan between Scholem and Heidegger," *German Quarterly* 83, no. 4 (2010): 465–84.

moment of stillness before death: "Quiet, in the coronary arteries." With the final line, "*Ziv*, that light," the poem invokes *Ziv*, a mystical Hebrew term that means "glow" that often marks the glow of secret, mystical realization (similarly, *Glanz*, or glow, is a prominent term in the poem "Tenebrae"). To the Hebrew word Celan adds the German literal explanation and indication, "that light." The most important element in this concluding line is the comma that separates and connects the Hebrew and the German, the mystical and the physiological, the Jewish and the Christian. The comma is itself a syntactical representation of the breathturn. The choice of "*jenes*" rather than the more obvious "*dieses*" implies a displacement of light, and thus the action of reaching toward the light "over there" rather than "here." Both choices demonstrate how the syntax of German Jewish life marks the end of one world (the dying body) and the beginning of another (that light). This is a poetic form that "wants-to-reach-through-time," and its touch is simultaneously warm and cold, animated and spectral. Celan's last line not only leads us back to the first, shaping his familiar loop form, it also shows us the way out: one last deep breath, before turning the page.

6

LIFE-FORM

After the Turn

> One must imagine the transformation of epic forms occurring in rhythms comparable to those of the change that has come over the earth's surface in the course of thousands of years.
> —Walter Benjamin, "The Storyteller"

> A Brechtian maxim: to not build on the good old days, but on the bad new ones.
> —Walter Benjamin, "Conversations with Brecht"

After a century of technological, economic, political, cultural, and social acceleration, time seems to be collapsing all around us.[1] Dipesh

---

1. For scholarship on time in the twenty-first century, see Bernard Tschumi, introduction to *A Landscape of Events*, by Paul Virilio, trans. Julie Rose (Cambridge, MA: MIT Press, 2000), vii: "Time, rather than space, is the theme of this book: the collapse of time, the acceleration of time, the reversal of time, the simultaneity of all times." See also Virilio, *The Futurism of the Instant: Stop-Eject*, trans.

Chakrabarty, a historian of the Anthropocene, talks about "the collapse of multiple chronologies, of species history and geological times within living memory."[2] Surveying the scholarly and popular works on this theme, the influence of German Jewish thinkers from the early twentieth century can be found everywhere. Whether one reads about post-1945 democracy or genocide, neoliberal acceleration or neofascist nihilism, the post-Freudian self or the Anthropocene, the names and ideas of Buber, Benjamin, Arendt, and Celan recur repeatedly. There are good reasons for this. Following the failure of assimilation and the rise of antisemitism, German Jewish thinkers were among the first to identify the "collapse of time" at the heart of democratic politics, free markets, and modern art and philosophy. They noted the temporal turn in the early 1900s, a sense of rupture between 1933 and 1945, and an accelerating rate of social and technological change after 1945. In this concluding chapter I trace two principal threads out of this genealogy, while leaving others aside. I follow, first, the centrality of life philosophy in Buber's stress on living experience, and second, Benjamin, Arendt, and Celan's accents on post-Nietzschean critical thought. I choose to set aside Franz Rosenzweig's critique of idealism and Ernst Bloch's messianic eschatology, which are, however, just as important for this story. Choosing to follow the political implications of the three temporal turns along these lines necessarily means moving past major works of critical studies dedicated to Adorno and Horkheimer's sway in post-1945 critical thought, the impact of Husserl's phenomenology and Blumenberg's analysis of world-time and life-time (*Lebenszeit*), and the critical reception of Heidegger's existentialism in Derrida's work. Additionally, I do not have the space to explore the specific reception of this German Jewish genealogy and its reception and integration by critical thinkers in related fields. Joseph Winters's

---

Julie Rose (Cambridge, MA: Polity, 2010); Hartmut Rosa, *Social Acceleration: A New Theory of Modernity*, trans. Jonathan Trejo-Mathys (New York: Columbia University Press, 2013); Robin Mackay and Armen Avenassian, eds., *#Accelerate* (Falmouth, UK: Urbanomic, 2014); Benjamin Noys, *Malign Velocities: Accelerationism and Capitalism* (Alresford: Zero Books, 2014).

2. Dipesh Chakrabarty, *The Climate of History in a Planetary Age* (Chicago: Chicago University Press, 2021), 14.

critique of the doctrine of racial progress and Lee Edelman's framing of queer temporality as a rebellion against "the logic that always serves to 'straighten' it out, and thus proclaims the universality of reproductive futurism." Both are theories inspired by Benjamin's critique of capitalist progress and therefore participate in the temporal turn initiated by this set of German Jewish thinkers.[3]

Why insist on this particular story, then? As I explain below, after 1945 German Jewish interpretations of life concerned not only the sources of living language and the exclusion of specific life-forms, but also the first open discussion of the environmental destruction of our planet. For German Jewish thinkers who survived the Holocaust, the concept of time allowed them to give meaning to the catastrophe they had experienced. Thanks to a deep understanding of temporality as the basis of all life-forms, critical disciplines in the humanities took inspiration from the thinkers I discuss in this book. The failed promise of emancipation meant that borders became rigid once again and the space of life (*Lebensraum*) more circumscribed, but time offered an alternative way of reframing life. What German Jewish thinking shared, I have argued, was an unequivocal belief in the living time of minorities and the belief that life can be shared beyond spatial and identitarian differences, as a fundamental, endangered life-form. And this intersection is also where their projects met their anthropocentric limit. In his recent books Chakrabarty discusses Kafka, Benjamin, and Arendt, in particular, as sources of inspiration for every discussion of natality and an analysis of our "moment of danger." It is only when we "get thrown into the abyss of deep time that an alternative history of modernity 'flashes up' before our eyes."[4] This final chapter will recall the key threads that have guided our reading thus far and attempt to frame them in the

---

3. Quotation from Lee Edelman, *No Future: Queer Theory and the Death Drive* (Durham, NC: Duke University Press, 2004), 26. Winters and Edelman both ground their critiques of progress, reproduction, and instrumental use of history in Walter Benjamin's thought. See Joseph R. Winters, *Hope Draped in Black: Race, Melancholy, and the Agony of Progress* (Durham, NC: Duke University Press, 2016), 13. For a specific reference to Benjamin's critique of history, see Edelman, 134–35.

4. Chakrabarty, *The Climate of History*, 183.

broad course of the three temporal turns that accompany the story of the twentieth- and twenty-first-century "moment of danger." Having assessed the contributions our quartet of thinkers made to the first two temporal turns of the twentieth century, I discuss how their thought can help us address the one we face today, in the twenty-first century.

"Expound the Nineteenth Century"

The concept of the life-form allows us to understand how German Jewish thinkers responded to the rise of life philosophy and to the political and philosophical crisis of their time.[5] They used the concept in order to transgress the limitations of identity while advocating a minoritarian position I identify in this book as *egalitarian ontology*. The concept of life, egalitarian and ontological, allowed them to consider the time of life as a door to both the philosophical and the political. But what is life-form? The concept of life-form shows up in a variety of contexts since the mid-nineteenth century. The philosopher Rahel Jaeggi explains that it originated in the German concept of *Lebensform*; that it can be translated as "way of life," "habit of life," "lifestyle," or "life-form"; and that the phrase became fashionable in the 1920s.[6] The concept had already appeared in the Grimm dictionary (1838) in the context of "the physical condition of heavenly bodies" and the "poetry of mental urge."[7] The concept gained in popularity after the life philosopher Eduard Spranger used it to analyze characters as anchored in the "life-style" of modern social life, but

---

5. Walter Benjamin, Conv. K1, 4, in *The Arcades Project*, trans. Howard Eiland and Kevin McLaughlin (Cambridge, MA: Belknap Press of Harvard University Press, 2002), 389; Benjamin, *Gesammelte Schriften*, 7 vols., ed. Rolf Tiedemann and Harald Schweppenhäuser (Frankfurt: Suhrkamp, 1991–2012), 5:492: "um das XIX Jahrhundert ... als die Folge seiner Traumgeschichte zu deuten."
6. Rahel Jaeggi, *Critique of Forms of Life*, trans. Ciaran Cronin (Cambridge, MA: Harvard University Press, 2018), 36, and see also Jaeggi's "Note on Translation."
7. Jesùs Padilla Gálvez and Margit Gaffal, eds., *Forms of Life and Language Games* (Heusenstamm: Ontosverlag, 2011), 8.

even more so after Rudolf Kjellén, a Swedish scholar who published in German, used it for his theory of geopolitics.[8] In his *Grundriss zu einem System der Politik* (A plan for a system of politics, 1920), Kjellén mentions the concept as an integral part of the German discourse of life-forms, additionally coining the concept of biopolitics. "The characteristic tension of life," he wrote "is called biopolitics [*Biopolitik*], ... [for] it suggests to me a [political] analogy to disciplines concerned with life sciences, for example biology."[9] As I mentioned in chapter 1, the concept did not disappear even when its context changed. Chakrabarty considers the many "form[s] of life" beyond the anthropocentric and "minoritarian forms of political thought, of the kind that Arendt or Deleuze on Kafka have educated us in, thought that would avoid 'majoritarian' ... dreams of domination."[10] In other words, the reception of the concept since the early 1930s shows a dual course, not unlike the course of twentieth-century life-philosophy; one road led toward a reactionary, immanent understanding of life as "Aryan" and affirmatively geopolitical and biopolitical. The other was taken by radical critics, mostly German-speaking Jews, and recaptured by recent critics of chauvinist language—nationalist, racist, or anthropogenic. Buber depicted a utopian Zionism as an alternative language of life-forms in 1914. Four decades later, Ludwig Wittgenstein stressed the use of different languages as plural life-forms that could be the basis for action, speech, and democratic politics.[11]

---

8. Jaeggi, *Critique of Forms of Life*, 36; Gálvez and Gaffal, *Forms of Life*, 8.

9. Kjellén's quote in the original German: "Diese Spannung, die für das Leben selbst charakteristisch ist, ... brachte mich dazu, eine solche Disziplin, die der Lebenswissenschaft, also Biologie, analog ist, Biopolitik zu nennen." Rudolf Kjellén, *Grundriss zu einem System der Politik* (Leipzig: Hirzel, 1920), 3–4, cited in Roberto Esposito, *Bíos: Biopolitics and Philosophy*, trans. Timothy C. Campbell (Minneapolis: University of Minnesota Press, 2008), 17n1.

10. Dipesh Chakrabarty, *One Planet, Many Worlds: The Climate Parallax* (Waltham, MA: Brandies University Press, 2023), 39. Recent histories demonstrate that majoritarian decision-making is following closely the forming of a consensual and procedural discourse. See William Bulman, *The Rise of Majority Rule in Britain and Its Empire* (Cambridge: Cambridge University Press, 2021), 18.

11. Hans-Joachim Glock, "Philosophical Investigations: Principles of Interpretation," in *Wittgenstein: Eine Neubewertung: Akten des 14. internationalen*

The four thinkers discussed in this book participated in the critical legacy of post-Nietzschean life philosophy and thus joined earlier German Jewish thinkers, such as Rahel Varnhagen, in advocating for alternative life-forms since the early 1800s. Varnhagen, Arendt tells us, saw how time cuts across the stream of temporal life. A century later, Georg Simmel—a source of inspiration for all four thinkers studied in this book—wrote about life and living experience as a "*secret king* of the intellectual epoch."[12] This "jargon of life"—a favorite, too, of rebellious post-Nietzschean radicals from both ends of the political spectrum—undermined telos, industrialization, and liberal ideology. In the early 1900s it helped empower both nationalists and opponents of nationalism, racists, and socialists, who rebelled against both the imperialist legacy of Bismarck and the Liberal state. What can we deduce from this dual course of life images and living-language? In the coming pages I consider the reasons for the German Jewish legacy that came to be identified with the previous two temporal turns and the German Jewish commitment to life-forms: Buber's hope to revive a Jewish time; Benjamin's hope to crack open now-time (*Jetztzeit*); Arendt's hope to reach a new democratic culture, grounded in Natality; and Calen's hope to shape a new grammar of life-forms. All four move the concept of life from its initial nineteenth-century context to a post-catastrophe understanding of life after 1945.

The four thinkers shared a wider understanding of life-forms and egalitarian politics. Close colleagues and friends, such as Margarete Susman, used the term to depict the work of German-Jewish thinkers who "self-consciously tried to break through the conventional life forms [*Lebensformen*], and expected the same from every human being whom [they] recognized as kindred."[13] Here I

Wittgenstein-Symposiums, ed. Rudolf Haller and Johannes Brandl (Vienna: Hölder-Pichler-Tempsky, 1990), 152–62.

12. Georg Simmel, *Der Konflikt der modernen Kultur: Ein Vortrag* (Munich: Duncker und Humblot, 1918), 13, my translation, emphasis in the original. See also the discussion in Adam Y. Stern, *Survival: A Theological-Political Genealogy* (Philadelphia: University of Pennsylvania Press, 2021), 95.

13. Quoted in Rabinbach, *Shadow of Catastrophe*, 47. As Susanne Hillman put it, "Like so many of her contemporaries, Susman at some point fell under the

briefly indicate some areas of interest that deserve more attention. First, a brief discussion of the limitations of the four thinkers and their disciplinary interests; a discussion of Günther Anders and Hans Jonas will demonstrate that the four cases I followed in this book were part of a far larger context and that a deep commitment to temporal egalitarianism received a variety of interpretations between 1900 and 1975. Second, a more general discussion of biopolitical critique and the theory of the Anthropocene, as two current fields that follow the four thinkers, and their contribution to the two temporal turns of the early and mid-twentieth century.

Estrangement and Nuclear Catastrophe: Günther Anders

The scholar Mara Benjamin has recently pointed out "the reluctance, or perhaps refusal, of most contemporary Jewish thinkers to reckon with the existential, ecological catastrophe that faces human and non-human life on Planet Earth."[14] The legacy of the thinkers I have discussed, however, provides a good starting point from which to re-engage with life-forms and confront the thanatopolitics of climate catastrophe and ecological crisis. Since the 1940s, Hannah Arendt had advocated a new perspective that adapts Kafka's Archimedean perspective, watching earth as if from "the absolute void behind the universe."[15] Her point was that a Kafkaesque, negative, and planetary view would enable humans to reconsider ancient prejudices. Dipesh Chakrabarty explained that the current references to

---

spell of Nietzsche. . . . She had been gripped by the 'overwhelming beauty' of *Also Sprach Zarathustra*, a work that seemed to illuminate all life like a 'golden dusk.'" See Hillman, "'A Germ So Tiny': Margarete Susman's Messianism of Small Steps," *Soundings: An Interdisciplinary Journal* 96, no. 1 (2013): 44.

14. Mara H. Benjamin, "There Is No 'Away': Ecological Fact as Jewish Theological Problem," *Religions* 13, no. 4 (2022), https://static1.squarespace.com/static/5c3694c4cc8feda148ec1e5b/t/63cf26635e2dbe02b923371a/1674520163228/Benjamin%2C+There+is+No+%27Away%2C%27+2022.pdf.

15. See the conclusion to Hannah Arendt, *The Human Condition* (Chicago: University of Chicago Press, 1969), also 322; and the conclusion to Arendt, *Between Past and Future: Eight Exercises in Political Thought* (New York: Penguin, 2006).

"the planetary" are often originated in Heidegger's *The Age of the World Picture* (1938), "which has influenced much recent thinking on images of earth taken from space." "The planetary," Chakrabarty explains, "refers here to the earth as a single planet taken by itself, not studied in comparison to other planets."[16] For Heidegger, "the planetary" served as an image of total uniformity shaped by destructive technology. In considering a post-1945 world, the author and thinker Günther Anders (born Günther Stern, 1902–92), Walter Benjamin's cousin and Arendt's first husband (1931–37), sought a similar challenge but from the opposite political end: to comprehend the historical break brought about by the war from a sober perspective that overcomes old dichotomies and empty slogans. Like Arendt, he searched for an "Archimedean perspective" beyond imperialism and globalism. Unlike Arendt, however, he considered Kafka only partially successful in achieving this goal. As the philosopher Babette Babich has shown, Anders belonged to the age of the Nietzschean "death of God" and of the rise of the post-human condition.[17] During the 1920s Anders had studied with Cassirer, Heidegger, Husserl, Max Scheler, and Paul Tillich, and he was acquainted with Benjamin, Brecht, Grosz, Löwith, and many members of the Frankfurt School.[18]

Like many of his intellectual contemporaries, Anders also engaged with Kafka, but he worried that the preoccupation of so many German Jewish thinkers with Kafka's writings would make them insensitive to real political matters. Anders lectured on Kafka as early as 1934, in Paris, and wrote two versions of the lecture in 1946 and 1951.[19] In 1951 he published *Kafka, Pro and Contra: The Trial*

---

16. Dipesh Chakrabarty, *The Climate of History in a Planetary Age*, 74.
17. Babette Babich, *Günther Anders' Philosophy of Technology: From Phenomenology to Critical Theory* (London: Bloomsbury Academic, 2023), 4. I am grateful to Prof. Babich for sharing her manuscript with me.
18. For a fascinating article about Anders's work in Germany, and especially in postwar Austria, see Jason Dawsey, "Where Hitler's Name Is Never Spoken: Günther Anders in 1950s Vienna," in *Austrian Lives*, ed. Günter Bischof, Fritz Plasser, and Eva Maltschnig (New Orleans: University of New Orleans Press, 2012), 212–39.
19. For more about Anders's intensive interest in Kafka, see Kata Gellen, "Kafka, Pro and Contra: Günther Anders's Holocaust Book," in *Kafka and the Universal*, ed. Arthur Cools and Vivian Liska (Berlin: De Gruyter, 2016), 283–306.

Documents, in which he criticized the popularity of Kafka among German Jewish authors. Anders warned that Kafka's work might prevent others from recognizing the real dangers of a fascist and a post-fascist world, because of its repetitive, almost fatalistic, emphasis on modern bureaucracy. Reflecting on those years in a later introduction, he wrote, "Even K. [the protagonist of *The Trial*] would not, under these circumstances, have read Kafka."[20] This critical creed can be seen as the start of the rebellion against the anti-totalitarian movement of the 1970s.[21]

Anders joined the antinuclear movement in 1947, while revising his critique of Kafka and his reception. Yet in spite of his sharp critical tone, Anders's intensive interest in Kafka and other German Jewish thinkers seems less of a turn away than a constructive critique from within. In his literary and philosophical texts, Anders developed a phenomenological hermeneutics of uncertainty, arguing that one can never know what tomorrow will be like or who will be master tomorrow.[22] This phenomenology of time had to do with how he viewed his own Jewish identity. Being a Jew, he explained in "Mein Judentum" (My Judaism) "meant a firm rejection of the guilt internalized by Christians and imposed by them onto Jews."[23] Anders felt that Kafka had internalized this guilt and therefore represented a continuation rather than a break in a misleading Christian tradition. A more relevant contemporary conflict to address, Anders felt, had to do with the technology of destruction and a solipsistic understanding of human life and human time as Heidegger represented them. In short, one needed to tackle both Kafka and Heidegger in order to come to terms with the era of total destruction.

---

20. Günther Anders, *Mensch ohne Welt: Schriften zur Kunst und Literatur* (Munich: C. H. Beck, 1984), xxxiii. Translated in Gellen, "Kafka, Pro and Contra," 284.

21. For more about the anti-totalitarian movement of the 1970s, see, for example, Pierre Rosanvallon, *Democracy Past and Future*, ed. Samuel Moyn (New York: Columbia University Press, 2006), 51.

22. Günther Anders, "The Émigré," in *The Life and Work of Günther Anders*, ed. Günther Bischopf, Jason Dawsey, and Bernhard Fetz (Innsbruck: Studien, 2014), 171–86.

23. Günther Anders, "Mein Judentum," in *Das Günther Anders Lesebuch*, ed. Bernhard Lassahn (Zurich: Diogenes, 1984), 235–36, discussed in Gellen, "Kafka, Pro and Contra," 293.

The editors of Anders's correspondence explained that it was Hans Jonas who introduced Anders to Heidegger's *History of the Concept of Time* in 1925, and that Anders fell prey to the "demonic spell" of Heidegger's existential phenomenology.[24] The letters expose a problematic relationship to Heidegger's philosophy, especially where Anders understood Heidegger to stand for the "un-, no, *anti*-natural sciences" and philosophical anthropology.[25] This understanding ultimately led to his influential work, "On the Pseudo-Concreteness of Heidegger's Philosophy" (1943) and a series of essays opposing the use of atomic bombs (late 1950s), declaring resistance to the Vietnam War (mid-1960s), and reflecting on catastrophe and "Endzeit und Zeitende" (End-time and time of the end, 1972). One of his last texts was titled *Die Antiquiertheit des Menschen: Über die Zerstörung des Lebens im Zeitalter der dritten industriellen Revolution* (The obsolescence of human beings: Destruction of life in the era of the third Industrial Revolution, 1980).[26] In public talks and journalistic essays, Anders identified the atomic bomb with the legacy of the Industrial Revolution and a new age of *modo negativo*, a time defined as "not yet being non-existing."[27] He asked his listeners and readers to reevaluate modern history in light of something utterly new: "the power to transform any given place on our planet, and even our planet itself, into a Hiroshima," and he warned that "atomic warfare disturbed the order of the universe."[28] Extending the temporal perspective from the Nazi genocide to the

---

24. Reinhard Ellensohn and Krestin Putz, epilogue to Günther Anders, *Gut, dass wir einmal die hot potatoes ausgraben: Briefwechsel mit Theodor W. Adorno, Ernst Bloch, Max Horkheimer, Herbert Marcuse, und Helmuth Plessner* (Munich: C. H. Beck, 2022), 354, 407.

25. Anders to Helmuth Plessner, July 8, 1977, in Anders, *Gut, dass wir einmal die hot potatoes ausgraben*, 237 (Anders-Plessner section, letter 66), emphasis in original.

26. Anders, *Die Antiquiertheit des Menschen: Über die Zerstörung des Lebens im Zeitalter der dritten industriellen Revolution* (Munich: C. H. Beck, 1965). This was volume 2, dedicated to "The Outdatedness of Human Beings." The first volume was dedicated to "The Soul in the Era of the Second Industrial Revolution."

27. See Günther Anders, "Theses on the Atomic Age," *Massachusetts Review* 3, no. 3 (1962): 493. In February 1959 Anders held a two-day seminar at the Free University in Berlin; this is his later publication of the lecture he delivered there.

28. Anders, "Theses on the Atomic Age," 493.

industrial conditions that enabled the bomb and the post-1945 triumph of capitalism in Western Europe, Anders talked, in 1956, about "the obsolescence of man."[29] The historian Enzo Traverso explains, "For Anders, far from plunging humanity back into ancestral barbarism, Auschwitz and Hiroshima herald the arrival of a new era for the human species, which has now become 'obsolete' in a world dominated by technology and thus susceptible to being totally wiped out."[30] The philosopher Susan Neiman determined, after the likes of Anders, that after the Holocaust and the atomic bomb, "a complete and total destruction of life itself threatened the human soul."[31] Indeed, Anders's short essay has become a key text for disaster studies and researchers of the Anthropocene. In his recent book, *Chronos: The West Confronts Time*, the historian François Hartog notes that Anders "evokes 'lords of the Apocalypse' who possess the power to 'destroy one another.'"[32] This is not a rejection of Anders, however, for Hartog stresses how Anders "drew a practical lesson. He called for a change in the relation between humanity and time, for adopting a 'broader temporal horizon'" while viewing this very instant as apocalyptic.[33]

Anders's critique of the opposition between morality and nature allowed him to view the destruction of the soul (Auschwitz) alongside the destruction of life (Hiroshima) as twin attacks on humanity. These attacks amounted to an assault on human time, the times of the individual body and public memory. Those who read his book on the bomb noticed his broader interest in time and life and his implied links between a fascist takeover and planetary annihilation.[34] For Anders, the "afterlife" of fascism manifested itself in two

---

29. Anders, *Die Antiquiertheit des Menschen*, vol. 1, *Über die Seele im Zeitalter der zweiten industriellen Revolution* (Munich: C. H. Beck, 1992).

30. Enzo Traverso, *Understanding the Nazi Genocide: Marxism after Auschwitz*, trans. Peter Drucker (London: Pluto Press, 1999), 48.

31. Susan Neiman, *Evil in Modern Thought: An Alternative History of Philosophy* (Princeton, NJ: Princeton University Press, 2002), 251.

32. François Hartog, *Chronos: The West Confronts Time*, trans. S. R. Gilbert (New York: Columbia University Press, 2022), 188.

33. Hartog, *Chronos*, 188.

34. See, for example, Holger Nehring, "Cold War, Apocalypse, and Peaceful Atoms: Interpretations of Nuclear Energy in the British and West German Anti-

factors: a growing estrangement from the world (*Weltfremdheit*) and environmental catastrophe.[35] Like Heidegger and Arendt, he believed that technological progress and capitalist industrialization had corrupted modern persons' view of the world, blinding them to the basic truth that they are part of the world and nature. But unlike Heidegger, and in close alignment with his Jewish students, he believed that a committed understanding of life implied a fundamental notion of equality, where humans are not just equal with one another, but are just one among many other natural life-forms. As mentioned, this brought him close to another close interlocutor of Arendt: Hans Jonas.

The Ethics of Living Experience: Hans Jonas

Born in 1903 to an assimilated Jewish family living in North Rhine–Westphalia, Hans Jonas (1903–93) was another of Heidegger's students whose critique of his teacher's philosophy of time "continues to reward careful study in the twenty-first century."[36] His interest in phenomenology and the philosophy of life led him to Freiburg University, where he studied under Husserl and Heidegger and met Anders. Initially he planned to work on the history and philosophy of the Wissenschaft des Judentums, but he changed his mind and followed Heidegger to Marburg in 1924.[37] There he met Hannah

---

Nuclear Weapons Movements, 1955–1964," *Historical Social Research* 29, no. 3 (2004): 150–70.

35. Anders and Arendt coauthored an interpretation of Rilke's *Duino Elegies*, which they published in 1930. The two interpreted the growing sense of estrangement as a process extending from Augustine's "organ of awareness" to the modern "loss of hearing" (*Echolosigkeit*). See Hannah Arendt and Günther Anders, "Rilkes Duineser Elegien," in *Schreib doch mal hard facts über dich: Briefe 1939–1975* (Munich: Piper, 2018), 105–27.

36. Lawrence Vogel, foreword to *The Phenomenon of Life: Toward a Philosophy of Biology*, by Hans Jonas (Evanston, IL: Northwestern University Press, 2001), xi.

37. Wissenschaft des Judentums (Science of Judaism) was a nineteenth-century movement in Germany that focused on the study of Jewish literature and culture, and which has now become identified with Jewish studies. For a broad and suggestive discussion of its sources and legacy, see *Jewish Historiography between*

Arendt, who became a lifelong friend, and he continued to correspond with both Anders and Arendt until their deaths. Jonas is best-known for his interpretation of Gnosticism, a topic he began investigating under Heidegger's tutelage. After 1945, he turned to the philosophical underpinnings of the phenomenon of life, publishing in 1966 the groundbreaking work *The Phenomenon of Life: Toward a Philosophical Biology*, which today is considered a precursor to environmental ethics.[38]

After the Holocaust, Jonas turned toward an investigation of ethical life and away from Heidegger's "wholesale dismissal of the entire tradition of Western philosophy."[39] In *The Phenomenon of Life* he advocated for an ethics of life-forms as an absolute equalizer: "Let us consider . . . this new element of freedom that appears in organism, with special reference to form. Form, we have seen, is an essential and a real, that is efficacious, characteristic of life."[40] In *The Imperative of Responsibility* (1979) he pleaded for a consideration of "temporal life" next to "eternal life," as well as the temporariness of all life-forms next to technological and political abstractions.[41] Jonas criticized Heidegger and his German Jewish disciples in their reduction of life, as well as Heidegger's dismissal of responsibility at the core of political life.

In both books Jonas discussed at great length "the problem of life" in relation to the "problem of death," and the environment (*Umwelt*) that encapsulates both. From this perspective all life-forms are equal, for "most of what we now know to be inanimate is so intimately intertwined with the dynamics of life that it seems to

---

Past and Future: 200 Years of Wissenschaft des Judentums, ed. Paul Mendes-Flohr, Rachel livneh-Freudenthal, and Guy Miron (Berlin: De Gruyter, 2019).

38. Hans Jonas, *The Phenomenon of Life*. On Jonas's ontology of life and environmental ethics, see Lawrence Troster, "Caretaker or Citizen: Hans Jonas, Aldo Leopold, and the Development of Jewish Environmental Ethics," in *The Legacy of Hans Jonas: Judaism and the Phenomenon of Life*, ed. Hava Tirosh-Samuelson and Christian Wiese (Leiden: Brill, 2008), 373–96; Theresa Morris, *Hans Jonas's Ethic of Responsibility: From Ontology to Ecology* (Albany: SUNY Press, 2013).

39. Chistopher Macann, ed., *Critical Heidegger* (London: Routledge, 1996), 3.

40. Jonas, *The Phenomenon of Life*, 80.

41. Hans Jonas, *The Imperative of Responsibility: In Search of an Ethics for the Technological Age* (Chicago: Chicago University Press, 1984), 37.

share its nature."[42] Accordingly, plant, animal, and human life relate to each other because they share traits in a common environment (*Umwelt*) and move in different rhythms within it due to "the temporal continuity or discontinuity between need and satisfaction."[43]

The written texts were not Jonas's first attack on Heidegger. He had already criticized him in 1952, albeit in a coded form, when he lambasted Heidegger's replication of nihilistic Gnostic categories.[44] On April 9, 1964, Jonas verbally attacked Heidegger at an international conference at Drew University, where a group of Protestant theologians had gathered to pay their respects to Heidegger. The older philosopher could not make the transatlantic trip, and Jonas was asked to replace him. In his speech, Jonas called Heidegger an opponent of Judeo-Christian ethics and accused him of driving moral values to the brink of nihilism.[45] In his memoirs, Jonas described the event as "a sensation, and a disaster for Heidegger," one Jonas was only too happy to inflict.[46] The historian and Jonas expert Christian Wiese sees this attack as a turning point for Jonas, who had never forgiven Heidegger for his sympathy to the Nazi regime, though until then he had avoided criticizing him in public.[47]

A broad understanding of life at the core of Western metaphysics lies at the heart of Jonas's dissertation, before he moved to analyze Gnosticism in his *habilitation* (second dissertation). He published *Augustin und das paulinische Freiheitsproblem (Augustine and the Pauline Problem of Freedom)* in 1965, in a revised version, in German and in English. The terminology he developed in his dissertation came out of a critical engagement with Heidegger and his other

---

42. Jonas, *The Phenomenon of Life*, 7.
43. Jonas, *The Phenomenon of Life*, 104.
44. See Benjamin Lazier, "Pauline Theology in the Weimar Republic: Hans Jonas, Karl Barth, and Martin Heidegger," in *Legacy of Hans Jonas*, 111.
45. The incident frames a chapter Richard Wolin devoted to Jonas. See Wolin, *Heidegger's Children: Hannah Arendt, Karl Löwith, Hans Jonas, and Herbert Marcuse* (Princeton, NJ: Princeton University Press, 2001), 101–33.
46. Hans Jonas, *Memoirs*, trans. Krishna Winston (Waltham, MA: Brandeis University Press, 2008), 190.
47. Christian Wiese, *The Life and Thought of Hans Jonas: Jewish Dimensions*, trans. Jeffrey Grossman and Christian Wiese (Waltham, MA: Brandeis University Press, 2007), 70–74.

mentor, the Protestant theologian Rudolf Bultmann (1884–1976), who was Heidegger's closest philosophical ally in Freiburg. Jonas's monograph devotes little space to demythologization—the task Bultmann assigned to modern theology—and instead delivers a critique of Heideggerian temporality and decisionism through an examination of the question of freedom.[48] As his biographer explains, for Jonas the question of freedom in the 1920s was at the heart of modern ethics: freedom of thought, freedom to act, and freedom to consider an "initial creative will" that avoids the dichotomy between good and evil.[49] After 1945 Jonas argued against what he saw as a general nihilistic break with Western ethics.[50] The revised dissertation offers both a clear critique of the Enlightenment's emphasis on free will and the Heideggerian stress on existential "thrownness" and letting be, which Jonas identifies with "the decision ... [which] is the condition of possibility for both indifference and its opposite."[51] Jonas thus accused Heidegger of a political and philosophical mistake: opportunism. According to Jonas, Heidegger ignored the political implications of his theory when it did not serve him but embraced them when it did. Jonas took his critique one step further by tracing the mistake as far back as Augustine and Paul. Like the fathers of Christian dogma, he contended, Heidegger had created a dualistic course that enabled a pagan form of nihilism and decisionism to rule over both philosophy and politics.

From this perspective, the correct philosophical response to the Holocaust was not the wholesale rejection of technology and embrace of a mythic *Seyn* (translated as *Beyng*), as Heidegger had suggested, but a new philosophy and theology of time inspired by

---

48. Hans Jonas, *Augustin und das paulinische Freiheitsproblem: Eine philosophische Studie zum pelagianischen Streit* (Göttingen: Vandenhoeck und Ruprecht, 1965). Jonas followed Heidegger in reevaluating the role of the "Judeo-Christian interpretation of Dasein" (*die jüdisch-christliche Daseinsauslegung*), a tradition he considered central to Heideggger's "factical experience and horizon of living experience." Jonas, *Augustin*, 25, my translation.
49. Christian Wiese, *Life and Thought of Hans Jonas*, 124.
50. Wiese believes that Jonas underwent a change after 1945, when he took Heidegger to task for abandoning a "responsible" approach to freedom. Wiese, *Life and Thought of Hans Jonas*, 60.
51. Jonas, *Augustin*, 95.

Christian and Jewish concepts.⁵² Jonas proposed a Judeo-Christian temporality shaped by all lived experiences (*Erlebnis*) in the world.⁵³

In Arendt's response to Jonas's manuscript, which he had sent her in 1964 asking for honest feedback, she noted that while moving forward depended on overthrowing Heidegger's system, Jonas remained too sympathetic to Paul. Evidently she felt that overcoming Heidegger involved overcoming the impact of Paulinian thought, including his thoughts about Judaism.⁵⁴ Every exchange between Jonas and Arendt concerned the political repercussions of totalitarianism and the Holocaust. They armed themselves with temporal concepts to confront both passive complicity and active nihilism (the latter embodied in Heidegger's reception of Nietzsche), the principal lessons from the era of "obsolete man."

After 1945: No-Longer and Not-Yet

After the Holocaust, Anders, Jonas, Arendt, and Celan offered a post-catastrophe language of time. For Arendt, the first lesson—integral to her work on totalitarianism and later in *The Human*

---

52. Jonas sought the sources of Western dualism in Augustine and Pascal. See Hans Jonas, *Mortality and Morality: A Search for the Good after Auschwitz*, ed. Lawrence Vogel (Evanston, IL: Northwestern University Press, 1996), 47.

53. Jonas's thinking on temporality precedes Reinhart Koselleck's theory of time by a good twenty years. In Koselleck's "Does History Accelerate?" (written in 1976, published in 1985), one finds Jonasian concepts such as experience and expectation and a Judeo-Christian "temporal foreshortening" coterminous with an "overcoming of time itself." See Koselleck, *Sediments of Time: On Possible Histories*, trans. Sean Franzel and Stefan-Ludwig Hoffmann (Stanford, CA: Stanford University Press, 2018), 94.

54. In a reference to Romans 7:19, Arendt wrote, "I always understood Paul's position 'For the good that I *will* to do, I *do not* do etc.' as an existential denial of freedom." She felt that Jonas went too far when he argued that "Paul understands the situation of man better than Jesus." After tartly commenting, "This claim cannot be substantiated," she added parenthetically, "I wonder whether the 'Jew' in you fully agrees with Paul, the 'extreme Christian.'" Arendt cast Jonas—alongside Paul and Heidegger—as a radical critic of the legalistic and normative tradition of rabbinic Judaism. For her, Jonas was stuck in a Jewish in-betweenness, unable to free his politics from the chains of identity. Hannah Arendt to Hans Jonas, June 5, 1964, Hans Jonas Papers, HJ3-12-11; all emphases in the original.

Condition—was the fundamental egalitarianism of temporality, beginning with creation or birth. The fundamental condition of life is birth into a world. Celan, in turn, emphasized that language gave birth to a new notion of absence. Next, Arendt reframed the Judeo-Christian tradition since Augustine as a *novus ordo saeclorum*, a "new order of the ages," in order to offer a democratic and a pluralist theory of natality. Anders and Jonas reached similar conclusions from different perspectives.

In Arendt's case, a new order was grounded in a politics of natality, "between the 'no longer' of the old laws and the 'not yet' of the new saving word, between life and death."[55] Celan, for his part, built a poetic syntax that he identified in the tension between the "already-no-longer" and the "always-still."[56] German Jewish thinkers after 1945 incorporated this sense of "in-betweenness" into their reexaminations of history, particularly the history of Christian–Jewish and German–Jewish relations. Reinhart Koselleck frames the story of modernity as a time of "in-betweenness"—from Augustine's "experience of the past" to an enlightened "horizon of expectations"—but German Jewish thinkers focus less on the Enlightenment as a teleological high point of history, instead looking toward catastrophe.[57] After the Holocaust every life-form was seen as a form of in-betweenness. For Anders, Jonas, Arendt, and Celan, Heidegger's emphasis on finitude and the frailty of human existence only served his own will to power, as Arendt explained in a letter to Karl Jaspers.[58] Her own politics of natality was a politics of equality: "Every

---

55. Hannah Arendt, "No Longer and Not Yet," in Arendt, *Reflections on Literature and Culture*, ed. Susannah Young-ah Gottlieb (Stanford, CA: Stanford University Press, 2007), 125.

56. Paul Celan, *The Meridian: Final Version—Drafts—Materials*, ed. Bernhard Böschenstein and Heino Schmull, trans. Pierre Joris (Stanford, CA: Stanford University Press, 2011), 8.

57. Reinhart Koselleck, "History, Histories, and Formal Structures of Time," in *Future Past: On the Semantics of Historical Time*, trans. Keith Tribe (Cambridge, MA: MIT Press, 2005), 94. Augustine's *ordo temporum*, continues Koselleck, is inherently tied to the "'not yet' and the 'no longer,' the 'earlier' or 'later than,'" or the "doctrine of the three phases before, during, and after the Law." Koselleck, "History, Histories," 100.

58. Arendt to Jaspers, July 20, 1963, in Elisabeth Young-Bruehl, *Hannah Arendt: For Love of the World* (New Haven, CT: Yale University Press, 1982), 304–5.

end in history necessarily contains a new beginning.... Politically, it is identical with man's freedom. *Initium ut esset homo creatus est,* 'that a beginning be made, man was created,' said Augustine."[59] By contrasting Augustine's *initium* with being-toward-death, Arendt found a way to join, rather than juxtapose, the Jewish and Christian continuity. As Dana Villa has noted, Arendt "used Heidegger against Heidegger in the service of ideas he would have condemned."[60] Buber, Benjamin, and Celan, in turn, expanded this thinking beyond politics: the idea of emergence in the in-between pointed to a broader, more fundamental form of life that wove together humans, nature, and planetary dimensions. "The stones in the womb of the earth and the planets at celestial heights were still concerned with the fate of men," wrote Benjamin.[61] Or, as Celan wrote, "The stone, you say, can speak."[62]

Biopolitics and the Anthropocene

Biopolitical Critique

A recent roundtable discussion on queer time mentioned the impact that Benjamin, especially, has had on the perception of "heteronormative time" and its notion of space, "as an entity that nations and nationalisms have tried to bring into national and nationalist time."[63] Benjamin's examination of conventions, from an Archimedean perspective he and Arendt identified with Kafka and "the womb of time," enables critics of chauvinism and capitalism—such as those at

---

59. Arendt, *The Origins of Totalitarianism* (New York: Meridian Books, 1966), 479.
60. Dana R. Villa, "Apologist or Critic?," in *Hannah Arendt in Jerusalem*, ed. Steven E. Aschheim (Berkeley: University of California Press, 2001), 328.
61. Walter Benjamin, "The Storyteller," in *Selected Writing*, vol. 3, *1935–1938*, ed. Michael Jennings et al. (Cambridge, MA: Belknap Press of Harvard University Press, 1996), 153.
62. Paul Celan, "Conversation in the Mountain," in *Paul Celan: Poet, Survivor, Jew,* trans. John Felstiner (New Haven, CT: Yale University Press, 1995), 143.
63. Hendrik Ferguson, "Theorizing Queer Temporalities: A Roundtable Discussion," *GLQ* 13, no. 2–3 (2006): 185.

this roundtable—to expose manipulative uses of norms. In fact, the reception of German Jewish thought in recent decades has been heavily shaped by theories of temporal hermeneutics, an academic phenomenon I call the third temporal turn. Both biopolitical critique and discussions of the Anthropocene rely largely on this recognition.

Biopolitical critique, particularly as articulated in the work of Foucault in the mid-1970s, has been taken up by Giorgio Agamben and, following him, Michael Hardt, Antonio Negri, Roberto Esposito, Judith Butler, Bonnie Honig, Eric Santner, and Achille Mbembe, among others. While Foucault expounded on Nietzschean genealogy and Heideggerian *Dasein*, Agamben integrated their interpreters and critics. Agamben never discusses the German Jewish theory of life as a separate issue, though a survey of his output shows his profound debt to the strain of thought that extends from Nietzsche to Benjamin and Arendt, Kafka and Celan.[64] Benjamin's understanding of Nietzsche's flash and shock led to his standstill, rhythm, and *Jetztzeit*, and those three concepts are central in Agamben's critical take on modernity. Agamben has acknowledged his debt to both Benjamin and Arendt in various essays, as well as in an admiring letter he sent Arendt in February 1970, not long after attending a seminar by Heidegger.[65] But the biopolitical reliance on German Jewish thought, particularly its analysis of time, extends further than this.

Agamben and other thinkers working in the biopolitical tradition also rely on the political-theological tradition to which Heidegger, Schmitt, Buber, Benjamin, Arendt, and other German and German Jewish thinkers were indebted.[66] In that sense, biopolitical critics

---

64. Adam Kotsko identified Agamben's two sources of inspiration as Heidegger and Benjamin, positing that the latter's influence "is, if anything, even more decisive." See Adam Kotsko, "Giorgio Agamben (1942–)," in *Religion and European Philosophy: Key Thinkers from Kant to Žižek*, ed. Philip Goodchild and Hollis Phelps (New York: Routledge, 2017), 452.

65. One of his essays, for example, builds on Benjamin and Arendt's theory of violence as a springboard for a biopolitical theory of violence. The editors of the issue in which his essay appeared added a photo of Agamben's letter to Arendt in his text. See Giorgio Agamben, "On the Limits of Violence," *Diacritics* 39, no. 4 (2009): 103–11.

66. Agamben assumes, in various works, a close affiliation between Benjamin and Scholem's stress on deferral, their rejection of linearity, and the assumption

were returning to familiar philosophical-political grounds, well-trodden since the 1920s. These thinkers, however, failed to contextualize this tradition, and as a result failed to grasp the precise function of temporal concepts in German Jewish thought and their own use of it.

The concept of the life-form stands at the heart of biopolitical critique. After Kjellen's introduction of the concept of *Lebensform* in 1920 (as described earlier in this chapter), it was taken by German Jewish critics, during the 1950s and 1960s, and by Foucault in the mid-1970s. Foucault connected life-form and biopolitics, via Nietzsche and Heidegger, to the Nazis and modern genocide but did not address the word's genealogy.[67] As Chloë Taylor has shown, Foucault understood biopower as the modern existence of death in the midst of lived experience (*Erlebnis*), but he did not dig further.[68]

Agamben, Hardt, Negri, and others have tried to update this view for the post-1945 and post-9/11 era. Their theories explain modern power through insights pioneered in German—often German Jewish—thought in general, and in particular in theories that address the Christian struggle with the Jew, the stranger, and the exception. For Agamben, contemporary interpretations of power, on both the right and the left, originate with the political stress on life and sovereignty. He turns to critics of liberalism like Benjamin's *Jetztzeit*, Schmitt's state of exception, and Kafka's understanding of the law. Roberto Esposito, another representative of biopolitical critique, argues that the 1920s—by which he specifically means the struggle between German nationalists and German Jewish critics of a "nucleus of biopolitical semantics"—set the tone for the rest of the twentieth century, in its obsession with sovereignty and political exception.[69] From another angle, Eric Santner perceptively notes that

---

that capitalism drives acceleration instead. Agamben, *The Time That Remains: A Commentary on the Letter to the Romans*, trans. Patricia Dailey (Stanford, CA: Stanford University Press, 2005), 144.

67. Foucault, *The History of Sexuality*, vol. 1, *The Will to Knowledge*, trans. R. J. Hurley (New York: Penguin, 1978), 137.

68. Chloë Taylor, "Biopower," in *Michel Foucault: Key Concepts*, ed. Dianna Taylor (Durham, NC: Acumen, 2011), 48.

69. Esposito, *Bíos*, 16–17.

German Jewish thought "always includes an immanent reference to a state of exception."[70]

How is biopolitical critique shaped by German Jewish temporal concepts? Temporal terms lend biopolitical critique its revolutionary edge. In an essay published in 1973, Agamben explained the attraction of a "revolutionary concept of history and a traditional experience of time" associated with the Western understanding of change.[71] As the editor of Benjamin's oeuvre in Italian, he often related to Benjamin as "the antidote that allowed me to survive Heidegger."[72] Agamben warned against embracing a "vulgar representation of time," which "Benjamin had already warned of... in his 'Theses on the Philosophy of History.'"[73] Instead, Agamben's essay examines models of exception and otherness, beginning with Greco-Roman cyclical time (according to Aristotle, an accumulation of instants) founded on the premise that "now is always 'other'... [yet] always the same; and in this is the basis of the radical 'otherness' of time, and of its 'destructive' character."[74]

Whereas Agamben's work in the 1980s and early 1990s was concerned with critiques of liberalism, political-theological terminology, and radical aestheticism, from the mid-1990s he narrowed his hermeneutics to focus on "bare life" (*blosses Leben*) and modern, secularized economy (*oikonomia*). The first concept is borrowed from Georg Simmel's discussion of life-form (Lebensform) and its "mere nowness" (Das blosse Jetzt-Sosein); the second is a Greek term adapted by the Church fathers to help convey a Christian universal notion of life.[75] Modern commodification and the absolute

---

70. Eric L. Santner, *On Creaturely Life: Rilke, Benjamin, Sebald* (Chicago: University of Chicago Press, 2006), 12.
71. Giorgio Agamben, "Time and History: Critique of the Instant and the Continuum," in *Infancy and History: The Destruction of Experience*, trans. Liz Heron (London: Verso, 1993), 99.
72. Quoted in Leland de la Durantaye, *Giorgio Agamben: A Critical Introduction* (Stanford: Stanford University Press, 2009), 53.
73. Agamben, "Time and History," 99.
74. Agamben, "Time and History," 102.
75. Simmel popularized the term "bare life" (*blossen Leben*), with its immanent stress on immediacy and "nowness," in his *Lebensanschauugen* (1918). See Georg Simmel, *Lebensanschauungen: Vier metaphysisiche Kapitel* (Berlin: Duncker

notion of sovereignty, Agamben contended, were responsible for the reduction of human beings to the "bare life" of the *Muselmann* in the concentration camp.[76] Eva Geulen has remarked that Agamben's separation of bare life (*zoe*) from the good life (*bios*) "follows not the Greek unqualified concept of life, but the reverse, a qualified notion of life or life-form, for example as theoretical life."[77] Simply put, Agamben understands ancient life through the eyes of a critical Benjamin. In that respect, Geulen explains, Benjamin's understanding of "sacredness of life, crosses the boundaries between life, death, and afterlife [*Nachleben*], and marks for Benjamin a shared understanding of bare life as creaturely life."[78] Whereas Benjamin utilizes life, life-form, or the sacredness of life in order to break away from tradition and norms, Agamben, who followed Benjamin's use of the concept of life-form, understands the concept as "what develops in relation to a political form or philosophical existence."[79]

Humans who exist solely as "bare life," such as the *Muselmann*, recast the Western tradition from the perspective of a critical, excluded, or incorporated minority. For Agamben, biopolitical critique enables a revolutionary reappreciation of the Western canon on the basis of marginal positions and dialectics at a standstill. As an alternative to the authoritarian use of sovereign control, Agamben introduced the notion of the "*in*operative" and "weak messianic" Pauline

---

und Humblot, 1994), 108. Simmel understands life as an immanent force that transcends every conceptualization. He explains in that context that "it is silly to try to turn life into an art-work. Life has its norms embedded in it, [as] ideal requirements which could be realized only in living forms, not imported from art, which has it own [norms]." See Simmel, *Fragmente und Aufsätze aus dem Nachlass* (Munich: Drei Massken, 1923), 24, my translation. For a detailed analysis of *Oikonomia*, see the second chapter of Giorgio Agamben, *The Kingdom and the Glory: For a Theological Genealogy of Economy and Government (Homo Sacer II, 2)*, trans. Lorenzo Chiesa (Stanford, CA: Stanford University Press, 2011), 17–49.

76. Giorgio Agamben, *Remnants of Auschwitz: The Witness and the Archive*, trans. Daniel Heller-Roazen (New York: Zone, 1999).

77. In the original German: "Bios meint aber im Griechischen gerade nicht ein allgemeines, unqualifiziertes Leben, sondern genau umgekehrt ein qualifiziertes Leben oder eine Lebensform, zum Beispiel das theoretische Leben." Eva Geulen, *Giorgio Agamben zur Einführung* (Hamburg: Junius Verlag, 2005), 83, my translation.

78. Geulen, *Agamben zur Einführung*, 87.

79. Geulen, *Agamben zur Einführung*, 107.

concept of *hōs mē* ("as not"). Agamben explains, while updating Paul via Benjamin, how "to deny authoritarian figures their legitimacy" by using alternative temporalities.[80] By this he meant that applying the inoperative to modern politics required the assistance of Benjamin's "dialectics in standstill," "weak messianic force," and Scholem's *Zimzum* (contraction).[81] In short, by hybridizing Benjamin and Scholem with Paul, Schmitt, and Heidegger, Agamben challenged liberal conceptions of sovereignty through a radical hermeneutics of time.

Recent commentary on biopolitical critique underlined its limitations but often adapted the German Jewish egalitarian temporality at its core. Saidiya Hartman, Joseph Winters and Alexander Weheliye discuss the relevance of biopolitical critique to critical race studies; they reflect on the central role that alternative concepts of time, proposed by Walter Benjamin and Hannah Arendt, play in critical race studies and a critique of liberal progress.[82] Vivian Liska and Adam Y. Stern have dwelt on the Judeo-Christian history of biopolitics and its reception. Liska, who is quite critical of Agamben's Christianized terminology, argues that the idea of a caesura was present in German Jewish writing far before Agamben's adoption of the term.[83] She does not focus on the impact of a post-Nietzschean life philosophy, or Foucauldian critique of biopower, but instead puts a stronger emphasis on Jewish hermeneutics. In her view, Agamben's eschatological modernity "collapses end and beginning into a single, spaceless spot and becomes a herald of history's end."[84] Stern, by contrast, focuses on the political stakes that led from the catastrophe of modernity, as

---

80. Agamben, *The Time That Remains*, 24.

81. "Metanomasia realizes the intransigent messianic principle articulated firmly by the apostle, in which those things that are weak and insignificant will, in the days of the Messiah, prevail over those things the world considers to be strong and important." Agamben, *The Time That Remains*, 10.

82. Alexander Weheliye, *Habeus Viscus: Racializing Assemblages, Biopolitics, and Black Feminist Theories of the Human* (Durham, NC: Duke University Press, 2014); Joseph R. Winters, *Hope Draped in Black: Race, Melancholy, and the Agony of Progress* (Durham, NC: Duke University Press, 2016).

83. Vivian Liska, *German-Jewish Thought and Its Afterlife: A Tenuous Legacy* (Bloomington: Indiana University Press, 2017), 27.

84. Liska, *German-Jewish Thought*, 34.

it was taken by Kafka and Arendt, to the catastrophic present, and he explains how the legacy "of the 'last man,' ideas about 'population,' and slogans like 'survival of the fittest' have offered vocabulary and conceptual resources for the emergence of biopolitics and catastrophic thinking in the time of the anthropocene."[85]

The Anthropocene

German Jewish ideas about time can be helpful in establishing a historical grammar of current temporal concepts. Dipesh Chakrabarty explained in a recent interview, "German-Jewish thought informs [my thinking] in many ways.... My critique of the empty notion of time... owes a direct and major debt to Walter Benjamin's last important piece of writing, *Theses on the Philosophy of History*." He then went on to discuss Kafka and Arendt.[86]

The intellectual transition from the earlier twentieth century to the early twenty-first century, however, has not always been smooth. Concepts such as living experience, natality, now-time, and breath-turn do not always extend to biopolitical critique and the Anthropocene.[87] After all, as the German Jewish thinkers realized, understanding time and life required a definition of the Other, and the time of life cannot be understood without a concrete conception of lived time. Their lived time helped them pinpoint the first temporal turn after their experience as an oppressed minority in Germany over a century ago.

In historicizing their temporal concepts as analytical categories, we can theorize the efficacy of older concepts and their current, revised forms. One clear advantage of the twentieth-century use of temporal concepts is that they enabled minorities, whose lives diverge from those of the majority, to transcend essential social and

---

85. Stern, *Survival*, 8.
86. "An Interview with Dipesh Chakrabarty," in *Unacknowledged Kinship: Postcolonial Studies and the Historiography of Zionism*, ed. Derek Penslar, Arieh Saposnik, and Stefan Vogt (Waltham, MA: Brandeis University Press, 2023), 8.
87. Stern, *Survival*, 11. The following section owes some of its language to Nitzan Lebovic, "Homo Complexus: The Historical Future of Complicity," *History and Theory* 60, no. 3 (2021): 409–24.

political divides. As I mentioned in the chapter 4, Hannah Arendt identified Rahel Varnhagen, as a woman and as a German Jew, as an ideal mediator between minority and majority, past, present, and future. Two centuries after Varnhagen, and a century after Arendt's depiction, those temporal concepts serve to extend the concept of "minority" itself in order to transcend interhuman categories. "The geobiological history of the planet," writes Chakrabarty, "makes us realize that we [humans] are a minority form of life and that the majority forms of life on the planet are microbial."[88] Once we can see ourselves as a minority form of life among many others, "this realization calls on us to develop minoritarian forms of thinking with regards to other forms of life."[89] One lesson is the need to transition from the discussion of otherness to a plural understanding of life, which must support social equality and the multiplicity of life-forms in the age of the Anthropocene.[90]

The term *Anthropocene*, coined in the early 2000s by Paul Crutzen and Eugene Stoermer, marks the moment when human effects on the planet came to rival the scale of change through geological "deep time."[91] German Jewish thought, in contrast, is usually focused on human time, or the time since humans first appeared on the planet. I am reminded of Arendt's reaction to the launch of Sputnik in 1957: she took it as a sign of growing worldlessness.[92] Our human experiences bore witness to "an interval in time which is altogether determined by things that are no longer and by things that are not yet."[93] Said differently, "an interval" wins different size and proportion when viewed from the perspective of "deep time." And yet, in

---

88. Chakrabarty, *One Planet, Many Worlds*, 5.
89. Chakrabarty, *One Planet, Many Worlds*, 5.
90. See Chakrabarty's discussion of Déborah Danowski and Eduardo Viveiros de Castro, *The Ends of the World*, trans. Rodrigo Nunes (Cambridge: Polity, 2017), in Chakrabarty, *One Planet, Many Worlds*, 81–91.
91. Paul J. Crutzen and Eugene F. Stoermer, "The Anthropocene," *Global Change Newsletter* 41 (2000): 1–20; Paul J. Crutzen, "Geology of Mankind," *Nature* 415 (2002): 23; Will Steffen, Paul J. Crutzen, and John R. McNeill, "The Anthropocene: Are Humans Now Overwhelming the Great Forces of Nature?," *Ambio* 36, no. 8 (2007): 614–21.
92. Arendt, *The Human Condition*, 1.
93. Arendt, *Between Past and Future*, 9.

spite of her original concentration on anthropogenics, what Arendt diagnosed as a potential problem, a specific "interval" at the end of the 1950s, has helped us to acknowledge the full-blown planetary catastrophe that threatens to change our notion of "deep past" and "deep future."[94]

Since the popular adoption of the term in the early 2000s, the Anthropocene has become more than the designation of a period of time; the word also implies that our age may soon end. Not only do geologists and climate scientists acknowledge this fact, but many philosophers, legal theorists, and critical theorists do as well. Anne Fremaux and John Barry, for example, write, "The Anthropocene represents a radical break, a point of no return, a dangerous upheaval that calls for the rethinking of our paradigms of thought and action."[95]

The Anthropocene has forced us to consider modes of temporality different from those of early modernism or the post-Holocaust era. If modern history was focused on the "hermeneutic of futurity," as Amir Eshel argued, the Anthropocene envisions the human past.[96] German Jewish thinkers offer, in that context, an arbitrating voice, leading from the catastrophe of the twentieth century to the age of the Anthropocene. Clive Hamilton has observed that "the Moderns are like Walter Benjamin's Angel of History, flying into the future but facing backwards, fleeing from a horrible past of suffering and oppression but unable to see the destruction that lies ahead."[97] Recent works by Elizabeth DeLoughrey, Thomas Ford, and Tobias Menely

---

94. On "deep past," see Joe D. Burchfield, "Darwin and the Dilemma of Geological Time," *Isis* 65, no. 3 (1974): 300–21; on "deep future," see Curt Stager, *Deep Future: The Next 100,000 Years of Life on Earth* (New York: Thomas Dunne, 2011), 62. See also Dipesh Chakrabarty, *The Climate of History*, 243, 268.

95. Anne Fremaux and John Barry, "The 'Good Anthropocene' and Green Political Theory: Rethinking Environmentalism, Resisting Ecomodernism," in *Anthropocene Encounters: New Directions in Green Political Thinking*, ed. Frank Biermann and Eva Lövbrand (Cambridge: Cambridge University Press, 2019), 172.

96. Amir Eshel, *Futurity: Contemporary Literature and the Quest for the Past* (Chicago: Chicago University Press, 2013), 258.

97. Clive Hamilton, "Human Destiny in the Anthropocene," in *The Anthropocene and the Global Environmental Crisis: Rethinking Modernity in a New Epoch*, ed. Clive Hamilton, Christophe Bonneuil, and François Gemenne (New York: Routledge, 2015), 43.

have explored in more detail the connection between the Anthropocene and Benjamin's theory of history or Arendt's worldlessness. DeLoughrey argues that "Benjamin has laid the groundwork for theorizing Anthropocene discourse in that [he] also remarks on a disjuncture between humans (history) and the planet (nature)." For her, Benjamin's understanding of history and nature is always framed in relation to decline, which is "represented in Benjaminian allegory and Anthropocene scholarship as ruins."[98] Thomas Ford and Tobias Menely also discuss the importance of decline, focusing on Benjamin's understanding of the aura, a "strange weave of space and time" that appears in times of decline.[99] All three scholars focus on the cautionary tale embedded in Benjamin's anti-linear history, yet, in spite of their different emphases, they identify decline with the Anthropocene catastrophe of the twenty-first century.

In contrast to DeLoughrey, Ford, and Menely, environmental historians and theorists such as Chakrabarty and Hamilton engage with German Jewish thought as an overarching discourse of

---

98. Elizabeth M. DeLoughrey, *Allegories of the Anthropocene* (Durham, NC: Duke University Press, 2019), 6.

99. Thomas H. Ford, "Aura in the Anthropocene," *Symploke* 21, no. 1 (2013): 71. Ford was quoting from Walter Benjamin, "Little History of Photography," in *Selected Writings*, vol. 2, part 2, *1931–1934*, ed. Michael Jennings, Howard Eiland, and Gary Smith, trans. Rodney Livingstone (Cambridge, MA: Harvard University Press, 2005), 518. Ford sees the concept of the Anthropocene as having originated at the time of industrial reproduction, when the aura was in decline. Fundamental to Ford is the convergence and collapse of time frames when "discrepant temporal scales suddenly intersect, and distinct ways of telling time are folded, concretely, into each other." Ford, "Aura in the Anthropocene," 66. The decline was due to end, according to Nietzsche and Benjamin, with "a star without atmosphere"—without aura, breath, or time. Ford shows that Nietzsche mentions "the star without atmosphere" twice and that Benjamin read both of the passages (77). Benjamin repeated the image in "On Some Motifs in Baudelaire," in *Selected Writings*, vol. 4, *1938–1940*, trans. Edmund Jephcott et al., ed. Howard Eiland and Michael W. Jennings (Cambridge, MA: Harvard University Press, 2003), 343. In contrast to the usual modern understanding of crisis as a rift or decline, as a "break with the past," the decline of the aura shows "the accretion of the past, a thickening of the air," and the way "the temporality of the Anthropocene [is] the delayed and disaggregated effect of fossil capitalism, the accumulation of greenhouse gases, the acidification and heating of the oceans." Ford, "Aura in the Anthropocene," 100.

temporality, rather than as a single disciplinary system or a mode of intellectual thought specific to a given "other."

The Many Endings of German Jewish Time

Benjamin believed it necessary to "expound the nineteenth century," an age that for him stood for the legacy of the Enlightenment, the critical reception of historicism, and the rise of nationalism and a commodified society. He and the other three thinkers I focus on in this book are the children of the first two temporal turns: the turn into modernity at the beginning of the twentieth century and the turn that concluded early modernity in 1945 and (as Frederick Jameson has described) encompassed the transition from industrial to late capitalism.[100] From Buber's declaration of a Jewish renaissance in 1900 to Arendt's death in 1975, the period covered is marked by the "double asymmetry" of "a break in the regular passage of time" that Bruno Latour has found characteristic of modernity.[101] The evolution of modernity from a small cultural rebellion against the *ancien régime* to mass mobilization and mass killing shaped not just the first half of the twentieth century but the second as well. This is when the German Jewish critique of idealism and liberalism came to serve new critical methods.

In contrast to the asymmetry of modernity, the Anthropocene proposes a nonanthropogenic asymmetry between human time and planetary time, also known as "post-human time."[102] As Eileen Crist has noted, Hans Jonas explained as early as 1974 that in the post-1945 world, "a silent plea for sparing [nature's] integrity seems to issue from the threatened plenitude of the living world."[103] The

---

100. Jameson, whose emphasis on "late capitalism" places the full transformation in the 1950s and 1960s. See Frederick Jameson, *Postmodernism, or the Cultural Logic of Late Capitalism* (Durham, NC: Duke University Press, 1991), 2.

101. Bruno Latour, *We Have Never Been Modern*, trans. Catherine Porter (Cambridge, MA: Harvard University Press, 1993), 10.

102. Bruno Latour, *Facing Gaia: Eight Lectures on the New Climatic Regime*, trans. Catherine Porter (Cambridge, MA: Polity, 2017), 117.

103. Hans Jonas, *Philosophical Essays* (Englewood Cliffs, NJ: Prentice Hall, 1974), 126. Quoted in Eileen Crist, "On the Poverty of Our Nomenclature," in

German Jewish attempt to "expound" previous times, rather than destroy them, can guide us toward a planetary perspective. This intellectual tradition spurs a reconsideration of Nietzsche's theory of the last man and the transformative stage between humanism and the nonhuman. Anything that succeeds humanism belongs to a different temporal logic, a logic without metaphysics, that also reaches beyond the metaphysical notion of life.[104] Nietzsche referred to the last man in aesthetic terms, as a stage before the rise of the superman, but Benjamin politicized him in admitting to his fear of becoming the "good European" and the "last man."[105] From this angle, as Günther Anders said, modernity is the bedrock of the last man, or a "*modo negativo*," time defined as "not yet being nonexisting."[106]

In the age of the Anthropocene, our impulse to divide life from nonlife has been undermined by climate change and the appeal to revise our understanding of the planet, where human life is just one life-form among many. Historians and philosophers of climate have pointed out the need for a historical and philosophical revolution that would bring together a new understanding of life, body, and environment.[107] After all, as the environmental historian Nancy Langston has noted, the womb was discussed, in the

---

Anthropocene or Capitalocene? Nature, History, and the Crisis of Liberalism, ed. Jason W. Moore (Oakland, CA: Kairos Books, 2016), 21.

104. Chakrabarty, *The Climate of History*, 184.

105. Walter Benjamin to Stephan Lackner, May 5, 1940, in Benjamin, *Gesammelte Briefe*, vol. 6, *1938–1940*, ed. Christoph Gödde and Henri Lonitz (Frankfurt: Suhrkamp, 2000), 441, my translation. The quote is from this passage: "Is it possible that history is forging an ingenious synthesis of two Nietzschean concepts, which are 'the good Europeans' and 'the last man'? The result could be 'the last European.' We are struggling to not become that." "On se demande si l'histoire n'est pas en train de forger une synthèse ingénieuse de deux conceptions nietzschéenes, à savoir des guten Europäers et des letzten Menschen. Cela pourrait donner den letzten Europäer. Nous tous nous luttons pour ne pas le devenir."

106. Anders, "Theses on the Atomic Age," 493.

107. Andreas Malm, "Who Lit This Fire? Approaching the History of the Fossil Fuel Economy," *Critical Historical Studies* 3, no. 2 (2016): 215–48. See also Marc Dorpema, "Narrative, Emplotment, Power: On Agency and the Environment," *Rethinking History* 27, no. 3 (2023): 511–36.

past, as "inviolate" and separate from the outside world—until recently.[108] Benjamin's historiosophic revolution helped change that notion by explaining how our historical imagination since Hegel grasps time shaped in the womb. As scholars have shown, Benjamin came to identify an anti-historicist, anti-idealist historical understanding with the underrepresented, the vanquished, the supposedly "inviolate," or the "[pre-life and] afterlife of that which has been understood."[109] Starting with the effect of the event, this afterlife allows us to find traces of lost potentials, imagining Hegel's womb of time giving birth to alternate temporalities. This view of temporality, for Benjamin—as for Buber, Arendt, and Celan—is where one finds the creaturely, pre-enlightened, pre- and post-linear womb of time. As some thinkers have noted, shifting from a linear notion of time to a "matrixial," mother-child "co-eventness," allows us to understand human temporality as a form of living present rather than a utilitarian form of self-realization.[110] The image of the womb as giving birth to time itself is something quite different from mankind creating time as an expression of technological progress, economic gain, and power over earth; it avoids one of the central assumptions of Western time—namely, that it began with Adam and revolves around human

---

108. Nancy Langston, "The Retreat from Precaution: Regulating Diethylstilbestrol (Des), Endocrine Disruptors, and Environmental Health," *Environmental History* 13, no. 1 (2008): 53.

109. Benjamin, *The Arcades Project*, Conv. N, 3, 460. See also Harry D. Harootunian, "The Benjamin Effect: Modernism, Repetition, and the Path to Different Cultural Imaginaries," in *Walter Benjamin and the Demands of History*, ed. Michael P. Steinberg (Ithaca, NY: Cornell University Press, 1996), 71; Daniel Weidner, "Fort-, Über-, Nachleben: Zu einer Denkfigur bei Benjamin," in *Benjamin-Studien*, vol. 2, ed. Daniel Weidner and Sigrid Weigel (Munich: Wilhelm Fink, 2011), 161–78; Caroline Disler, "Benjamin's 'Afterlife': A Productive Mistranslation in Memoriam Daniel Simeoni," *Du système en traduction: Approches critiques* 24, no. 1 (2011): 183–221.

110. The psychoanalyst Bracha Ettinger discussed the fetus in the womb as living in symbiosis with the mother and in a state of trans-subjective "co-event." The symbiosis is based on a "rhythmic bipolarity of inside/outside" that expands the boundaries of the self. See Bracha L. Ettinger, *The Matrixial Borderspace* (Minneapolis: University of Minnesota Press, 2006), 80–82.

reproduction. Benjamin stresses instead the role of language in shaping our immediate experience.[111]

Scholars of time and temporality in the Anthropocene have noted that critiques of modernity have so far failed to stop the "social acceleration" of late capitalism, as described by Hartmut Rosa, or have simply exchanged the Enlightenment notion of progress for one of crisis, as Helga Jordeim and Einar Wigen propose.[112] The thinker Claire Sagan has identified the current climate crisis with what she calls *uchronia*, "the abstract, non-time temporality."[113] Sagan contends, following Emilie Hache's critique of Hans Jonas, that a contemporary notion of the present and the future must extend beyond capitalism and patriarchy. Hache and Sagan are critical about Jonas's naïveté but also return to his "precaution principle," which "utilized the European law to suspend the commercialization or use of certain products suspected of damaging ecological effect."[114] Donna Haraway coupled this thought to Hannah Arendt's "banality of evil, of the particular sort that could make the disaster of the Anthropocene, with its ramped-up genocides and speciescides, come true."[115]

Another recent example of the impact of twentieth-century German Jewish thought on Anthropocene formulations is Elizabeth Povinelli's work on "geontologies," entities that defy their division into life and nonlife and that take inspiration from Arendt and Foucault's critiques of power. Applying the post-human temporal-

---

111. The language of a "blissful Adamite" stands between man and his invented God, or between the immediate and the mediated notion of language. See Walter Benjamin, "On Language as Such and on the Language of Man," in Benjamin, *Selected Writings*, vol. 1, *1913–1926*, ed. Marcus Bullock and Michael W. Jennings (Cambridge, MA: Harvard University Press, 2002), 71.

112. Hartmut Rosa, *Social Acceleration*, 4; Helge Jordheim and Einar Wigen, "Conceptual Synchronisation: From *Progress* to *Crisis*," *Millennium* 46, no. 3 (2018): 421–39.

113. Claire Sagan, "Capitalist Temporalities as Uchronia," *Theory and Event* 22, no. 1 (2019): 153–54.

114. Sagan, "Capitalist Temporalities," 161. See also Émilie Hache, *Ce à quoi nous tenons: Propositions pour une écologie pragmatique* (Paris: Les empêcheurs de penser en rond, 2010).

115. Donna Haraway, "Staying with the Trouble: Anthropocene, Capitalocene, Chthulucene," in Moore, *Anthropocene or Capitalocene?*, 39.

ity cultivated by Benjamin in the 1930s to the "nonlife of the present," Povinelli proposes the perspective of "afterlife" and "after finitude."[116] For her, a critical understanding of the present involves recoupling life and nonlife to question the biopolitical government of life and death.[117] Povinelli sees the explicit division of entities into nonlife and life as a mechanism of political and juridical power. "The sovereign people of geontopower are those who abide by the fundamental separation of Life and Nonlife with all the subsequent implications of this separation on intentionality, vulnerability, and ethical implication."[118] What Arendt deemed "the lost contact 'between the world of the senses and the appearances and the physical worldview'" is for Povinelli an invitation to reconsider vitalist forms retroactively, beyond their separation into life and nonlife.[119] From this perspective, an animist such as Nietzsche or Buber might "insist that the difference between Life and Nonlife is not a problem because all forms of existence have within them a vital animating, affecting force."[120] Paul Celan's post-1945 perspective serves that effort as literary imagination: realizing that the Nazi language was revolving around the separation of life (Aryan) and death (Jew), he moved to reconstruct a syntax that re-integrated the two. From this perspective, a new language of life must allow us to understand how to incorporate both rupture and absence, human life and a new afterlife. Even a theory of the post-human, or a completely alternate planetary temporality, thus reclaims a vitalist discourse, borrowed from the first half of the twentieth century and adapted to our present circumstances and needs.

---

116. Povinelli follows here the work of Eugene Thacker and Quentin Meillasoux. See Elizabeth A. Povinelli, *Geontologies: A Requiem to Late Liberalism* (Durham, NC: Duke University Press, 2016), 51–53, 71–75.
117. Povinelli, *Geontologies*, 9.
118. Povinelli, *Geontologies*, 35.
119. Povinelli, *Geontologies*, 10.
120. Povinelli, *Geontologies*, 17.

Epilogue

In 1940, the year of Walter Benjamin's death, Virginia Woolf observed that "the nineteenth century ended; but the same conditions went on."[121] Just like the nineteenth century bled into the twentieth and created the mechanisms that enabled the first industrialized genocide, the destructive forces of the twentieth century are bleeding into the twenty-first. The continuity that Woolf observed confused scholars interested in clean lines of separation between periods, disciplines, and identities. Despite the differences among them, each of the Jewish thinkers we have read succeeded in making sense of these continuities. Their projects shared certain assumptions, such as a stress on birth and creation from an anthropogenic, not environmental or planetary, perspective. Accordingly, all upheld forms of continuity, even when their analyses were founded on particular disruptions or contrasts, such as the rejection of idealism and historicism.

The four thinkers and their collaborators looked to different ideological or political realizations. For instance, Buber's cultural Zionism originated from the same Nietzschean, anti-idealist source that inspired the other three, but it gave birth to an optimistic plea to "engage in talk with another," which was essential "if the devastated life of the earth [is to] renew itself."[122] Benjamin and Arendt's rejection of Zionism stemmed from the same source—their rejection of nationalism—but led to two different interpretations of democracy. Benjamin's utter resistance to capitalist progress and his deconstructive stress on critical language contrasted with Arendt's stress on natality as the starting point of common sense and plurality. And

---

121. Virginia Woolf, "The Leaning Tower," in *A Twentieth-Century Literature Reader: Texts and Debates*, ed. Suman Gupta and David Johnson (London: Routledge, 2005), 73.

122. The quotation is from the speech Buber delivered at the Frankfurt Book Fair in 1953 upon receiving the Peace Prize of the Book Fair. See Martin Buber, "Genuine Dialogue and the Possibilities of Peace," *CrossCurrents* 5, no. 4 (1955): 234–35. See also Paul Mendes-Flohr, "Martin Buber and Martin Heidegger in Dialogue," *Journal of Religion* 94, no. 1 (2014): 12.

Arendt's natality had little in common with Buber's notion of renaissance: for her, the answer lay in the power of constitutional revolution, not in the internal qualities of a certain people. After 1945 Celan brought all four "linguistic impossibilities" to their most radical end with his insistence on the language of living absence, a language that "ceaselessly calls and hauls itself back ... from its now-no-longer into its still-now."[123] At the most fundamental level, all four thinkers shared a commitment to vitalist discourse, even when they rejected its political, philosophical, and aesthetic conclusions. Even though this commitment formed the basis of their temporal egalitarianism and their nonanthropocentric humanism, it also defined the anthropogenic limit of all their projects.

The sociologist Zygmunt Bauman has argued that modern concepts such as natality render "a modern way of being-in-the-world both possible and inescapable."[124] But he insists that "there is no return to natality," for "the past has not been stored in a warehouse until such times as it may be taken out, dusted, and restored to its former beauty."[125] If the most radical concepts of the twentieth century no longer suffice, we must find a new language that serves our present and future horizons. Indeed, in this book I followed the courageous advice of the German Jews who escaped their homes and left their lives behind but pleaded with us to engage fearlessly with the conditions of the time. I did my best to follow a sentiment expressed by Brecht, which Benjamin wrote down in his diary: "[Don't] build on the good old days, but on the bad new ones."[126]

Rosh HaShana, September 15, 2023

---

123. Paul Celan, *Gesammelte Werke*, vol. 3, ed. Beda Alemann, Stefan Reichert, and Rolf Bücher (Frankfurt: Suhrkamp, 1986), 197.

124. Zygmunt Bauman, *Liquid Modernity* (Cambridge, MA: Polity, 2012), 21.

125. Zygmunt Bauman, *Life in Fragments: Essays in Postmodern Morality* (Oxford: Blackwell, 1995), 136–37.

126. Walter Benjamin, "Conversations with Brecht," in Benjamin, *Reflections: Essays, Aphorisms, Autobiographical Writings*, ed. Peter Demetz, trans. Edmund Jephcott (New York: Harcourt Brace Jovanovich, 1978), 219. For a slightly different translation, see Benjamin, "Diary Entries, 1938," in *Selected Works*, 3:340.

Bibliography

Archives / Collections

Hannah Arendt Collection. Digital Marginalia, https://blogs.Bard.edu/arendt collection/marginalia/.
Hannah Arendt Papers. Library of Congress.
Hans Jonas Papers. Philosophical Archives of the University of Konstanz.
Hugo Bergmann Literary Remains, National Library, Jerusalem.
Martin Buber Archive. National Library in Jerusalem. Martin Buber Literary Remains.
Paul Celan Literary Archives. Deutsches Literaturarchiv in Marbach (DLA).
Yad Vashem Resource Center. https://www.yadvashem.org/odot_pdf/Microsoft%20Word%20-%206474.pdf.

Works Cited

Adeyemi, Femi. *Covenant Torah in Jeremiah and Paul: The Law of Christ in Paul*. New York: Peter Lang, 2006.

Adorno, Theodor. "Critique." In *Critical Models: Interventions and Catchwords*, translated by Henry W. Pickford. New York: Columbia University Press, 1998.

Adorno, Theodor. "Kulturkritik und Gesellschaft." In *Prisms*. London: Neville Spearman, 1967.

Agamben, Giorgio. "Easter in Egypt." In *The Fire and the Tale*, translated by Lorenzo Chiesa. Stanford, CA: Stanford University Press, 2017.

Agamben, Giorgio. *Homo Sacer: Sovereign Power and Bare Life*. Translated by Daniel Heller-Roazen. Stanford, CA: Stanford University Press, 1998.

Agamben, Giorgio. *The Kingdom and the Glory: For a Theological Genealogy of Economy and Government (Homo Sacer II, 2)*. Translated by Lorenzo Chiesa. Stanford, CA: Stanford University Press, 2011.

Agamben, Giorgio. "The Messiah and the Sovereign: The Problem of Law in Walter Benjamin." In *Potentialities*, translated by Daniel Heller-Roazen. Stanford, CA: Stanford University Press, 1999.

Agamben, Giorgio. "On the Limits of Violence," *Diacritics* 39, no. 4 (2009): 103–11.

Agamben, Giorgio. *Remnants of Auschwitz: The Witness and the Archive*. Translated by Daniel Heller-Roazen. New York: Zone Books, 1999.

Agamben, Giorgio. "Time and History: Critique of the Instant and the Continuum." In *Infancy and History: The Destruction of Experience*, translated by Liz Heron. London: Verso, 1993.

Agamben, Giorgio. *The Time That Remains: A Commentary on the Letter to the Romans*. Translated by Patricia Dailey. Stanford, CA: Stanford University Press, 2005.

Altmann, Alexander. *Moses Mendelssohn: A Biographical Study*. Tuscaloosa: University of Alabama Press, 1973.

Anders, Günther. *Die Antiquiertheit des Menschen: Über die Zerstörung des Lebens im Zeitalter der dritten industriellen Revolution*. Munich: C. H. Beck, 1965.

Anders, Günther. "The Émigré." In *The Life and Work of Günther Anders*, edited by Günther Bischopf, Jason Dawsey, and Bernhard Fetz. Innsbruck: Studienverlag, 2014.

Anders, Günther. "Mein Judentum." In *Das Günther Anders Lesebuch*, edited by Bernhard Lassahn. Zurich: Diogenes, 1984.

Anders, Günther. *Mensch ohne Welt: Schriften zur Kunst und Literatur*. Munich: C. H. Beck, 1984.

Anders, Günther. "Theses on the Atomic Age." *Massachusetts Review* 3, no. 3 (1962): 493.

Anderson, Benedict. *Imagined Communities: Reflections on the Origin and Spread of Nationalism*. London: Verso Books, 2006.

Arendt, Hannah. "The Achievement of Hermann Broch." *Kenyon Review* 11, no. 3 (1949): 476–83.

Arendt, Hannah. "Augustine and Protestantism." In *Essays in Understanding, 1930–1954*. New York: Harcourt Brace, 1994.

Arendt, Hannah. *Between Past and Future: Eight Exercises in Political Thought*. New York: Penguin, 2006.

Arendt, Hannah. *Denktagebuch: 1950–1973*. Edited by Ursula Ludz and Ingeborg Nordmann. Munich: Piper, 2002.
Arendt, Hannah. *Der Liebesbegriff bei Augustin: Versuch philosophischen Interpretation*. Hildesheim: Georg Olms, 2006.
Arendt, Hannah. "Franz Kafka: A Reevaluation." *Partisan Review*, 11, no. 4 (1944): 412–22.
Arendt, Hannah. "A Guide for Youth: Martin Buber." In Arendt, *The Jewish Writings*, edited by Jerome Kohn and Ron H. Feldman. New York: Schocken, 2007.
Arendt, Hannah. *Hannah Arendt / Hermann Broch Briefwechsel, 1946–1951*. Edited by Paul Michael Lützeler. Frankfurt: Jüdischer Verlag, 1996.
Arendt, Hannah. *The Human Condition*. Chicago: University of Chicago Press, 1969.
Arendt, Hannah. "The Jew as Pariah." In Arendt, *Reflections on Literature and Culture*, edited by Susannah Young-ah Gottlieb. Stanford, CA: Stanford University Press, 2007.
Arendt, Hannah. "Karl Jaspers: Citizen of the World?" In *Men in Dark Times*. New York: Harcourt Brace Jovanovich, 1983.
Arendt, Hannah. *Lectures on Kant's Political Philosophy*. Chicago: University of Chicago Press, 1982.
Arendt, Hannah. *The Life of the Mind*. Boston: Houghton Mifflin Harcourt, 1981.
Arendt, Hannah. *Love and Saint Augustine*. Chicago: Chicago University Press, 1996.
Arendt, Hannah. "No Longer and Not Yet." In *Reflections on Literature and Culture*, edited by Susannah Young-ah Gottlieb. Stanford, CA: Stanford University Press, 2007.
Arendt, Hannah. *On Revolution*. London: Penguin Books, 1963.
Arendt, Hannah. "Original Assimilation: An Epilogue to the One Hundredth Anniversary of Rahel Varnhagen's Death." In *The Jewish Writings*. New York: Schocken, 2007.
Arendt, Hannah. *The Origins of Totalitarianism*. New York: Meridian Books, 1966.
Arendt, Hannah. *The Promise of Politics*. New York: Schocken Books, 2005.
Arendt, Hannah. *Rahel Varnhagen: The Life of a Jewess*. Edited by Liliane Weissberg. Translated by Richard and Clara Winston. Baltimore: Johns Hopkins University Press, 1997.
Arendt, Hannah. *Reflections on Literature and Culture*. Edited by Susannah Young-ah Gottlieb. Stanford, CA: Stanford University Press, 2007.
Arendt, Hannah. "Stefan Zweig: Jews in the World of Yesterday." In *Reflections on Literature and Culture*, edited by Susannah Young-ah Gottlieb. Stanford, CA: Stanford University Press, 2007.
Arendt, Hannah. "Walter Benjamin, 1892–1940." In *Men in Dark Times*. New York: Harcourt Brace Jovanovich, 1983(1968).
Arendt, Hannah. "What Is Existential Philosophy?" *Partisan Review* 13 (1946): 34–56.

Arendt, Hannah, and Günther Anders. "Rilkes Duineser Elegien." In *Schreib doch mal hard facts über dich: Briefe 1939–1975*. Munich: Piper, 2018.

Aschheim, Steven E. *Beyond the Border: The German-Jewish Legacy Abroad*. Princeton, NJ: Princeton University Press, 2007.

Aschheim, Steven E. *In Times of Crisis: Essays on European Culture, Germans, and Jews*. Madison: University of Wisconsin Press, 2001.

Aschheim, Steven E. "The Jew Within: The Myth of Judaization in German." In *Culture and Catastrophe: German and Jewish Confrontations with National Socialism and Other Crises*. New York: NYU Press, 1996.

Aschheim, Steven E. *The Nietzsche Legacy in Germany: 1890–1990*. Berkeley: University of California Press, 1992.

Asman, Carrie L. "Theater and *Agon* / *Agon* and Theater: Walter Benjamin and Florens Christian Rang." *MLN* 107, no. 3 (1992): 606–24.

Avnon, Dan. *Martin Buber: The Hidden Dialogue*. Lanham, MD: Rowan and Littlefield, 1998.

Ayres, Lewis. "Being (esse/essentia)." In *Augustine through the Ages: An Encyclopedia*, edited by Allan D. Fitzgerald. Cambridge: Eerdmans, 1999.

Babich, Babette. *Günther Anders' Philosophy of Technology: From Phenomenology to Critical Theory*. London: Bloomsbury Academic, 2023.

Babich, Babette. "Who Is Nietzsche's Archilochus? Rhythm and the Problem of the Subject." In *Philosophers and Their Poets*, edited by Charles Bambach and Theodore George. Albany: SUNY Press, 2019.

Balfour, Ian. *The Rhetoric of Romantic Prophecy*. Stanford, CA: Stanford University Press, 2002.

Bambach, Charles. *Heidegger's Roots: Nietzsche, National Socialism, and the Greeks*. Ithaca, NY: Cornell University Press, 2003.

Bambach, Charles. *Thinking the Poetic Measure of Justice: Hölderlin-Heidegger-Celan*. Albany: SUNY Press, 2011.

Barash, Jeffrey Andrew. "Heidegger's Ontological 'Destruction' of Western Intellectual Traditions." In *Reading Heidegger from the Start*, edited by Theodore Kisiel and John van Buren. Albany: SUNY Press, 1994.

Baring, Edward. *Converts to the Real: Catholicism and the Making of Continental Philosophy*. Cambridge, MA: Harvard University Press, 2019.

Barouch, Lina. *Between German and Hebrew: The Counterlanguages of Gershom Scholem, Werner Kraft, and Ludwig Strauss*. Berlin: De Gruyter Oldenbourg, 2016.

Baschet, Jérôme. *Défaire la tyrannie du présent: Temporalités èmergentes et futurs inédits*. Paris: La Découverte, 2018. Translated in Marek Tamm, "How to Reinvent the Future?," *History and Theory* 59, no. 3 (2020): 448–58.

Bashir, Shahzad. "On Islamic Time: Rethinking Chronology in the Historiography of Muslim Societies." *History and Theory* 53, no. 4 (2014): 519–44.

Batnitzky, Leora. *Idolatry and Representation: The Philosophy of Franz Rosenzweig Reconsidered*. Princeton, NJ: Princeton University Press, 2000.

Batnitzky, Leora. "Revelation and *Neues Denken*: Rethinking Buber and Rosenzweig on the Law." In *New Perspectives on Martin Buber*, edited by Michael Zank. Tübingen: Mohr Siebeck, 2006.

Batnitzky, Leora. "Translation as Transcendence: A Glimpse into the Workshop of the Buber-Rosenzweig Bible Translation." *New German Critique* 70 (1997): 87–116.

Bauman, Zygmunt. *Life in Fragments: Essays in Postmodern Morality*. Oxford: Blackwell, 1995.

Bauman, Zygmunt. *Liquid Modernity*. Cambridge, MA: Polity, 2012.

Beiser, Frederick C. *German Idealism: The Struggle against Subjectivism, 1781–1801*. Cambridge, MA: Harvard University Press, 2009.

Beiser, Frederick C. *Hermann Cohen: An Intellectual Biography*. Oxford: Oxford University Press, 2018.

Benhabib, Seyla. *The Reluctant Modernism of Hannah Arendt*. Lanham, MD: Rowman and Littlefield, 1996.

Benjamin, Andrew. *Present Hope: Philosophy, Architecture, Judaism*. London: Routledge, 1997.

Benjamin, Mara H. "There Is No 'Away': Ecological Fact as Jewish Theological Problem." *Religions* 13 (2022): 290.

Benjamin, Walter. *The Arcades Project*. Translated by Howard Eiland and Kevin McLaughlin. Cambridge, MA: Harvard University Press, 2002.

Benjamin, Walter. "Aufzeichnungen zu einem ungeschriebenen Essay und zum Vortrag von 1931." In *Benjamin über Kafka: Texte, Briefzeugnisse, Aufzeichnungen*, edited by Hermann Schweppenhäuser. Frankfurt: Suhrkamp, 1981.

Benjamin, Walter. *Briefe*, vol. 1. Edited by Gershom Scholem and Theodor W. Adorno. Frankfurt: Suhrkamp, 1966.

Benjamin, Walter. "Carl Albrecht Bernoulli, Johann Jakob Bachofen, und das Natursymbol: Ein Würdigungsversuch." In *Gesammelte Schriften*, edited by Rolf Tiedemann and Hermann Schweppenhäuser. Frankfurt: Suhrkamp, 1991.

Benjamin, Walter. "Categories of Aesthetics." In *Selected Writings*, vol. 1, *1913–1926*, edited by Marcus Bullock and Michael W. Jennings. Cambridge, MA: Harvard University Press, 1996.

Benjamin, Walter. "Central Park." In *Selected Writings*, vol. 4, *1938–1940*, edited by Howard Eiland and Michael W. Jennings. Cambridge, MA: Harvard University Press, 2003.

Benjamin, Walter. "The Concept of Criticism in German Romanticism." In *Selected Writings*, vol. 1, *1913–1926*, edited by Marcus Bullock and Michael W. Jennings. Cambridge, MA: Harvard University Press, 1996.

Benjamin, Walter. "Conversations with Brecht." In *Reflections: Essays, Aphorisms, Autobiographical Writings*, edited by Peter Demetz, translated by Edmund Jephcott. New York: Harcourt Brace Jovanovich, 1978.

Benjamin, Walter. *The Correspondence of Walter Benjamin*. Translated Manfred R. Jacobson and Evelyn M. Jacobson. Chicago: Chicago University Press, 1994.

Benjamin, Walter. "The Critique of Violence." In *Selected Writings*, vol. 1, *1913–1926*, edited by Marcus Bullock and Michael W. Jennings. Cambridge, MA: Harvard University Press, 1996.

Benjamin, Walter. "Diary Entries, 1938." In *Selected Writings*, vol. 3, *1935–1938*, edited by Howard Eiland and Michael W. Jennings. Cambridge, MA: Harvard University Press, 2002.

Benjamin, Walter. "Franz Kafka." In *Gesammelte Schriften*, edited by Rolf Tiedemann and Hermann Schweppenhäuser. Frankfurt: Suhrkamp, 1991.

Benjamin, Walter. "Franz Kafka." In *Selected Writings*, vol. 2, *1927–1934*, translated by Rodney Livingstone. Cambridge, MA: Harvard University Press, 1999.

Benjamin, Walter. "A German Institute for Independent Research." In *Selected Writings*, vol. 3, *1935–1938*, edited by Howard Eiland and Michael W. Jennings. Cambridge, MA: Harvard University Press, 2002.

Benjamin, Walter. *Gesammelte Briefe*, vol. 1, *1910–1918*, edited by Christoph Gödde and Henri Lonitz. Frankfurt: Suhrkamp, 1999.

Benjamin, Walter. *Gesammelte Briefe*, vol. 2, *1919–1924*, edited by Christoph Gödde and Henri Lonitz. Frankfurt: Suhrkamp, 1996.

Benjamin, Walter. *Gesammelte Briefe*, vol. 5, *1935–193*, edited by Christoph Gödde and Henri Lonitz. Frankfurt: Suhrkamp, 1999.

Benjamin, Walter. *Gesammelte Briefe*, vol. 6, *1938–1940*, edited by Christoph Gödde and Henri Lonitz. Frankfurt: Suhrkamp, 2000.

Benjamin, Walter. "Goethe's *Elective Affinities*." In *Selected Writings*, vol. 1, *1913–1926*, edited by Marcus Bullock and Michael W. Jennings. Cambridge, MA: Harvard University Press, 1996.

Benjamin, Walter. "Introduction to the *Urspring des Deutschen Trauerspiel*." In *Gesammelte Schriften*, edited by Rolf Tiedemann and Hermann Schweppenhäuser. Frankfurt: Suhrkamp, 1991.

Benjamin, Walter. "Introductory Remarks on a Series for *L'Humanité*." In *Selected Writings*, vol. 2, *1927–1934*, translated by Rodney Livingstone. Cambridge, MA: Harvard University Press, 1999.

Benjamin, Walter. "Johann Jakob Bachofen." In *Selected Writings*, vol. 3, *1935–1938*, edited by Howard Eiland and Michael W. Jennings. Cambridge, MA: Harvard University Press, 2002.

Benjamin, Walter. "Karl Kraus." In *Selected Writings*, vol. 2, *1927–1934*, translated by Rodney Livingstone. Cambridge, MA: Harvard University Press, 1999.

Benjamin, Walter. "The Life of Students." In *Early Writings: 1910–1917*, translated by Howard Eiland et al., edited by Howard Eiland. Cambridge, MA: Harvard University Press, 2011.

Benjamin, Walter. "Little History of Photography." In *Selected Writings*, vol. 2, *1927–1934*, translated by Rodney Livingstone. Cambridge, MA: Harvard University Press, 1999.

Benjamin, Walter. "Little Tricks of the Trade." In *Selected Writings*, vol. 2, *1927–1934*, translated by Rodney Livingstone. Cambridge, MA: Harvard University Press, 1999.

Benjamin, Walter. "May–June 1931." In *Selected Writings,* vol. 2, *1927–1934,* translated by Rodney Livingstone. Cambridge, MA: Harvard University Press, 1999.

Benjamin, Walter. "The Metaphysics of Youth." In *Early Writings: 1910–1917,* translated by Howard Eiland et al., edited by Howard Eiland. Cambridge, MA: Harvard University Press, 2011.

Benjamin, Walter. "Moscow." In *Selected Writings,* vol. 2, *1927–1934,* translated by Rodney Livingstone. Cambridge, MA: Harvard University Press, 1999.

Benjamin, Walter. "Naples." In *Selected Writings,* vol. 1, *1913–1926,* edited by Marcus Bullock and Michael W. Jennings. Cambridge, MA: Harvard University Press, 1996.

Benjamin, Walter. "On Language as Such and on the Language of Man." In *Selected Writings*, vol. 1, *1913–1926,* edited by Marcus Bullock and Michael W. Jennings. Cambridge, MA: Harvard University Press, 1996.

Benjamin, Walter. "On Some Motifs in Baudelaire." In *Selected Writings,* vol. 4, *1938–1940,* edited by Howard Eiland and Michael W. Jennings. Cambridge, MA: Harvard University Press, 2003.

Benjamin, Walter. "On the Concept of History." In *Selected Writings,* vol. 4, *1938–1940,* edited by Howard Eiland and Michael W. Jennings. Cambridge, MA: Harvard University Press, 2003.

Benjamin, Walter. "One-Way Street." In *Selected Writings,* vol. 1, *1913–1926,* edited by Marcus Bullock and Michael W. Jennings. Cambridge, MA: Harvard University Press, 1996.

Benjamin, Walter. *Origins of the German Drama.* Translated by John Osborne. London: Verso, 1998.

Benjamin, Walter. "Painting and the Graphic Arts." In *Selected Writings,* vol. 1, *1913–1926,* edited by Marcus Bullock and Michael W. Jennings. Cambridge, MA: Harvard University Press, 1996.

Benjamin, Walter. "Review of the Mendelssohns' *Der Mensch in der Handschrift.*" In *Selected Writings,* vol. 2, *1927–1934,* translated by Rodney Livingstone. Cambridge, MA: Harvard University Press, 1999.

Benjamin, Walter. "Riddle and Mystery." In *Selected Writings,* vol. 1, *1913–1926,* edited by Marcus Bullock and Michael W. Jennings. Cambridge, MA: Harvard University Press, 1996.

Benjamin, Walter. "The Right to Use Force." In *Selected Writings,* vol. 1, *1913–1926,* edited by Marcus Bullock and Michael W. Jennings. Cambridge, MA: Harvard University Press, 1996.

Benjamin, Walter. "Romanticism: An Undelivered Address to Students." In *Early Writings: 1910–1917,* translated by Howard Eiland et al., edited by Howard Eiland. Cambridge, MA: Harvard University Press, 2011.

Benjamin, Walter. "The Storyteller." In *Illuminations,* translated by Harry Zohn, edited and with an introduction by Hannah Arendt. Boston: Houghton Mifflin Harcourt, 2019 [1968]).

Benjamin, Walter. "The Storyteller." In *Selected Writings*, vol. 3, *1935–1938*, edited by Howard Eiland and Michael W. Jennings. Cambridge, MA: Harvard University Press, 2002.

Benjamin, Walter. "Surrealism." In *Selected Writings*, vol. 2, *1927–1934*, translated by Rodney Livingstone. Cambridge, MA: Harvard University Press, 1999.

Benjamin, Walter. "The Task of the Translator." In *Selected Writings*, vol. 1, *1913–1926*, edited by Marcus Bullock and Michael W. Jennings. Cambridge, MA: Harvard University Press, 1996.

Benjamin, Walter. "Theological-Political Fragment." In *Selected Writings*, vol. 3, *1935–1938*, edited by Howard Eiland and Michael W. Jennings. Cambridge, MA: Harvard University Press, 2002.

Benjamin, Walter. "*Trauerspiel* and Tragedy." In *Selected Writings*, vol. 1, *1913–1926*, edited by Marcus Bullock and Michael W. Jennings. Cambridge, MA: Harvard University Press, 1996.

Benjamin, Walter. "World and Time." In *Selected Writings*, vol. 1, *1913–1926*, edited by Marcus Bullock and Michael W. Jennings. Cambridge, MA: Harvard University Press, 1996.

Bergmann, Hugo. *Dialogical Philosophy from Kierkegaard to Buber*, translated by Arnold A. Gerstein. Albany: SUNY Press, 1991.

Bergmann, Hugo. "Ha'Hashiva Ha'Du-Sichit shel M. M. Buber." In *Anashim u'Drachim* [Men and ways]. Jerusalem: Mosad Bialik, 1967.

Bergmann, Hugo. "Proslov." *Zidovske Zpravy*, December 1919, 1–3.

Bergmann, Hugo. *Tagebücher und Briefe*, vol. 1. Edited by Miriam Sambursky. Königstein: Jüdischer Verlag bei Athenäum, 1985.

Bergmann, Hugo. *Tagebucher und Briefe*, vol. 2. *1948–1975*. Edited by Miriam Sambursky. Konigstein: Judischer Verlag bei Athenaum, 1985.

Bergson, Henri. *Matter and Memory*. Translated by Nancy Margaret Paul and W. Scott Palmer. New York: Zone Books, 1996.

Berman, Lila Corwin. "Jewish History beyond the Jewish People." *AJS Review* (2018): 1–24.

Berman, Marshall. *All That Is Solid Melts into Air: The Experience of Modernity*. New York: Simon and Schuster, 1982.

Bhabha, Homi K. "Unpacking My Library Again." *Journal of the Midwest Modern Language Association* 28, no. 1 (Spring 1995): 14.

Biale, David. *Blood and Belief: The Circulation of a Symbol between Jews and Christians*. Berkeley: University of California Press, 2007.

Biale, David, ed. *Cultures of the Jews: A New History*. New York: Schocken Books, 2002.

Biale, David. "Experience vs. Tradition: Reflections on the Origins of the Buber-Scholem Controversy." *Simon Dubnov Institute Yearbook* 15 (2016): 33–47.

Biale, David. *Gershom Scholem: Master of the Kabbalah*. New Haven, CT: Yale University Press, 2018.

Bielik-Robson, Agata. *Another Finitude: Messianic Vitalism and Philosophy*. New York: Bloomsbury Academic, 2019.

Biemann, Asher. "Revival as Imperative: Reflections on the Normativity of Jewish Renaissance." In *Jewish Revival Inside Out: Remaking Jewishness in a Transnational Age*, edited by Daniel Monterescu and Rachel Werczberger. Detroit: Wayne State University Press, 2022.

Bienek, Horst. "Narben unserer Zeit" (1959). In *Über Paul Celan*, edited by Dietlind Meinecke. Frankfurt: Suhrkamp, 1970.

Blanton, Ward. "Paul's Secretary: Heidegger's Apostolic Light." In *Displacing Christian Origins: Philosophy, Secularity, and the New Testament*. Chicago: University of Chicago Press, 2006.

Bollack, Jean. *Dichtung wider Dichtung: Paul Celan und die Literatur*. Göttingen: Wallstein, 2006.

Bourel, Dominique. *Martin Buber: Was es heisst, ein Mensch zu sein*. Gütersloh: Gütersloher Verlagshaus, 2017.

Bowie, Andrew. "Critiques of Culture." In *The Cambridge Companion to Modern German Culture*, edited by Eva Kolinsky and Wolfried van der Will. Cambridge: Cambridge University Press, 1998.

Boyarin, Daniel. *A Radical Jew: Paul and the Politics of Identity*. Berkeley: Universiyy of California Press, 1994.

Braiterman, Zachary. *The Shape of Revelation: Aesthetics and Modern Jewish History and Culture*. Stanford, CA: Stanford University Press, 2007.

Breckman, Warren. *Adventures of the Symbolic: Post-Marxism and Radical Democracy*. New York: Columbia University Press, 2013.

Brenner, Michael. *The Renaissance of Jewish Culture in Weimar Germany*. New Haven, CT: Yale University Press, 1996.

Broch, Hermann. "Jean-Paul Sartre: L'être et le néant." In *Philosophische Schriften*, vol. 1, *Kritik*. Frankfurt: Suhrkamp, 1977.

Brod, Max. *Heidentum, Christentum, Judentum: Ein Bekenntnisbuch*. Munich: Kurt Wolff, 1921.

Brod, Max. "Judaism and Christianity in Buber's Work." In *The Philosophy of Martin Buber*, edited by Paul Arthur Schilpp and Maurice Friedman. La Salle, IL: Open Court, 1967.

Brody, Samuel Hayim. *Martin Buber's Theopolitics*. Bloomington: Indiana University Press, 2018.

Buber, Martin. *Believing Humanism: My Testament, 1902–1965*. Translated by Maurice Friedman. New York: Simon and Schuster, 1967.

Buber, Martin. *Between Man and Man*. Translated by Ronald Gregor Smith. New York: Macmillan, 1965.

Buber, Martin. "Bewegung: Aus einem Brief an einen Holländer," *Der Neue Merkur* 1, no. 10 (1915).

Buber, Martin. *Briefwechsel aus Sieben Jahrzenten*, vol. 1, *1897–1918*. Edited by Grete Schaeder. Heidelberg: Lambert Schneider, 1972.

Buber, Martin. *Broschüre*. Berlin: Lambert Schneider, 1930.

Buber, Martin. *Daniel: Dialogues on Realization*. Translated by Maurice Friedman. New York: Holt, Rinehart and Winston, 1964.

Buber, Martin. *Daniel: Gespräche von der Verwirklichung*. Wiesbaden: Insel, 1913.
Buber, Martin. *Der heilige Weg: Ein Wort an die Juden und an die Völker*. Frankfurt: Rütten und Loening, 1920.
Buber, Martin. "Die Forderung des Geistes und die geschichtliche Wirklichkeit." In *Werkausgabe*, vol. 11, part 2, *Schriften zur politischen Philosophie und zur Sozialphilosophie*, edited by Francesco Ferrari, Stefano Franchini, and Massimiliano De Villa. Gütersloh: Gütersloher, 2019.
Buber, Martin. "Die Schaffenden, das Volk und die Bewegung." In *Jüdischer Almanach*, edited by Berthold Feiwel and E.M. Lilien, 19–24. Berlin: Jüdische Verlag, 1902.
Buber, Martin. *Drei Reden über das Judentum*. Frankfurt: Rütten und Loening, 1920.
Buber, Martin. *The Eclipse of God*. Princeton, NJ: Princeton University Press, 2016.
Buber, Martin. *Ecstasy and Confession: The Heart of Mysticism*. Translated by Esther Cameron. Syracuse, NY: Syracuse University Press, 1996.
Buber, Martin. "Ein geistiges Zentrum," *Ost und West* 2, no. 10 (1902): cols. 663–72. Translated in Martin Buber, *The First Buber: Youthful Zionist Writings of Martin Buber*, translated by Gilya G. Schmidt. Syracuse, NY: Syracuse University Press, 1999.
Buber, Martin. "Ein Heidenbuch." In *Die Jüdische Bewegung: Gesammelte Aufsätze und Ansprachen*, vol. 2. Berlin: Jüdischer Verlag, 1920.
Buber, Martin. "Elements of the Interhuman." In *Martin Buber on Psychology and Psychotherapy: Essays, Letters, and Dialogue*, edited by Judith Buber Agassi. Syracuse, NY: Syracuse University Press, 1999.
Buber, Martin. "Genuine Dialogue and the Possibilities of Peace." *CrossCurrents* 5, no. 4 (1955): 234–35.
Buber, Martin. *Good and Evil: Two Interpretations*. Translated by Ronald Gregor Smith. Upper Saddle River, NJ: Prentice Hall, 1997.
Buber, Martin. *I and Thou*. Translated by Walter Kaufmann. New York: Touchstone, 1996.
Buber, Martin. *Ich und Du*. Gütersloh: Gütersloher Verlagshaus, 2010.
Buber, Martin. "Jüdische Renaissance." In *Die Jüdische Bewegung: Gesammelte Aufsätze und Ansprachen*. Berlin: Jüdischer Verlag, 1920.
Buber, Martin. *Knowledge of Man: Selected Essays*. Edited by Maurice Friedman. Amherst, MA: Humanity Books, 1988.
Buber, Martin. *Königtum Gottes*. Berlin: Schocken, 1936.
Buber, Martin. *The Letters of Martin Buber: A Life of Dialogue*. Translated by Richard Winston, Clara Winston, and Harry Zohn. New York: Schocken, 1991.
Buber, Martin. *Moses: The Revelation and the Covenant*. New York: Harper Books, 1958 [1946].
Buber, Martin. "On Word Choice in Translating the Bible." In *Martin Buber and Franz Rosenzweig, Scripture and Translation*, translated by Lawrence Rosenwald and Everett Fox. Bloomington: Indiana University Press, 1994.

Buber, Martin. *Paths in Utopia*. Translated by R. F. C. Hull. Boston: Beacon Press, 1949.
Buber, Martin. *Pfade in Utopia: Über Gemeinschaft und deren Verwirklichung*. Heidelberg: L. Schneider, 1985.
Buber, Martin. *The Prophetic Faith*. [Based on the 1949 translation bay Carlyle Litton-Davies.] Princeton, NJ: Princeton University Press, 2016.
Buber, Martin. "The Renewal of Judaism." In *On Judaism*, edited by Nahum N. Glatzer. New York: Schocken, 1967.
Buber, Martin. "The Spirit of the Orient and Judaism." In *On Judaism*, edited by Nahum N. Glatzer. New York: Schocken, 1967.
Buber, Martin. *Torat Ha-nevi'im* [*The Prophetic Faith*]. Tel-Aviv: Dvir, 1942.
Buber, Martin. *Two Types of Faith*. Translated by Norma P. Goldhawk. Syracuse, NY: Syracuse University Press, 2003.
Buber, Martin. "The Validity and Limitations of Political Principle." In *Pointing the Way*, translated by Maurice Friedman. New York: Harper, 1957.
Buber, Martin. "Wann Denn." In *Werkausgabe*, vol. 21, *Schriften zur zionistischen Politik und zur jüdisch-arabischen Frage*, edited by Samuel Hayim Brody and Paul Mendes-Flohr. Gütersloh: Gütersloher, 2019.
Buber, Martin. *Werkausgabe*, vol. 3, *Frühe jüdische Schriften, 1900–1922*. Edited by Barbara Schäfer. Gütersloher: Gütersloher Verlaghaus, 2007.
Buber, Martin. "What Is Man?" In *Between Man and Man*, translated by Ronald Gregor-Smith. London: Routledge, 2002.
Buber, Martin. "Zarathustra." In *Werkausgabe*, vol. 1, *Frühe kulturkritische und philosophische Schriften*, edited by Martin Treml. Gütersloh: Gütersloher Verlagshaus, 2001.
Bulman, William. *The Rise of Majority Rule in Britain and Its Empire*. Cambridge: Cambridge University Press, 2021.
Burchfield, Joe D. "Darwin and the Dilemma of Geological Time." *Isis* 65, no. 3 (1974): 300–21.
Burrus, Virginia. "Augustine, Rosenzweig, and the Possibility of Experiencing Miracle." In *Material Spirit: Religion and Literature Intranscendent*, edited by Gregory C. Stallings, Manuel Asensi, and Carl Good. New York: Fordham University Press, 2013.
Calcagno, Antonio. "The Role of Forgetting in Our Experience of Time: Augustine of Hippo and Hannah Arendt." *Parrhesia* 13 (2011): 14–27.
Canales, Jimena. *The Physicist and the Philosopher: Einstein, Bergson, and the Debate That Changed Our Understanding of Time*. Princeton, NJ: Princeton University Press, 2015.
Carlebach, Elisheva. *Palaces of Time: Jewish Calendar and Culture in Early Modern Europe*. Cambridge, MA: Harvard University Press, 2011.
Celan, Paul. "Auge der Zeit." In *Von Schwelle zu Schwelle: Vorstufen-Textgenese-Endfassung*. Frankfurt: Suhrkamp, 2002.
Celan, Paul. "Conversation in the Mountain." In *Paul Celan: Poet, Survivor, Jew*, translated by John Felstiner. New Haven, CT: Yale University Press, 1995.

Celan, Paul. *Der Meridian: Endfassung, Vorstufen, Materialien*. Edited by Bernhard Böschenstein and Heino Schmull. Frankfurt: Suhrkamp, 1999.

Celan, Paul. "Eye of Time." In *Memory Rose into Threshold Speech*, translated by Pierre Joris. New York: Farrar, Straus and Giroux, 2020.

Celan, Paul. *Gesammelte Werke in fünf Bänden*. Edited by Beda Allemann, Rudolf Bücher, and Stefan Reichert. Frankfurt: Suhrkamp, 1986.

Celan, Paul. "It Is No Longer." In *Memory Rose into Threshold Speech*, translated by Pierre Joris. New York: Farrar, Straus and Giroux, 2020.

Celan, Paul. *La bibliothèque philosophique: Die philosophische Bibliothek*. Edited by Alexandra Richter, Patrik Alac, and Bertrand Badiou. Paris: Rue d'Ulm, 2004.

Celan, Paul. "The Meridian." In the appendix to Derrida, *Sovereignties in Question: The Poetics of Paul Celan*, translated by Jerry Glenn. New York: Fordham University Press, 2005.

Celan, Paul. *The Meridian: Final Version—Drafts—Materials*. Edited by Bernhard Böschenstein and Heino Schmull. Translated by Pierre Joris. Stanford, CA: Stanford University Press, 2011.

Celan, Paul. "Paul Celan–Margarete Susman: Der Briefwechsel aus den Jahren 1963–1965." In *Celan-Jahrbuch* 8 (2001/2), edited by Hans Michael Speier. Heidelberg: Heidelberg University Press, 2003.

Celan, Paul. *Sprachgitter: Vorstuffen—Textgenese—Endfassung*. Frankfurt: Suhrkamp, 1996.

Celan, Paul. "This Evening Also." In *Poems of Paul Celan*, translated by Michael Hamburger. London: Anvil Press Poetry, 1998.

Celan, Paul. "Tonight Too." In *Memory Rose into Threshold Speech*, translated by Pierre Joris. New York: Farrar, Straus and Giroux, 2020.

Cesana, Andreas. *Johann Jakob Bachofens Geschichtsdeutung: Eine Untersuchung ihrer geschichtsphilosophischen Voraussetzungen*. Basel: Birkhäuser, 1983.

Chakrabarty, Dipesh. "The Climate of History: Four Theses." *Critical Inquiry* 35, no. 2 (2009): 197–222.

Chakrabarty, Dipesh. *The Climate of History in a Planetary Age*. Chicago: Chicago University Press, 2021.

Chakrabarty, Dipesh. *The Ends of the World*. Translated by Rodrigo Nunes. Cambridge: Polity, 2017.

Chakrabarty, Dipesh. "An Interview with Dipesh Chakrabarty." In *Unacknowledged Kinship: Postcolonial Studies and the Historiography of Zionism*, edited by Derek Penslar, Arieh Saposnik, and Stefan Vogt, Waltham, MA: Brandeis University Press, 2023.

Chakrabarty, Dipesh. *One Planet, Many Worlds: The Climate Parallax*. Waltham, MA: Brandeis University Press, 2023.

Clark, Christopher. "Revisiting Augustine's Doctrine of Jewish Witness." *Journal of Religion* 89, no. 4 (2009): 564–78.

Clark, Christopher. *Time and Power: Visions of History in German Politics, from the Thirty Years' War to the Third Reich*. Princeton, NJ: Princeton University Press, 2019.

Coe, Cynthia. *Levinas and the Trauma of Responsibility: The Ethical Significance of Time*. Bloomington: Indiana University Press, 2018.
Cohen, Hermann. *Religion of Reason out of the Sources of Judaism*. Translated by Simon Kaplan. New York: Ungar, 1972.
Cohen, Jeremy. *Living Letters of the Law: Ideas of the Jew in Medieval Christianity*. Berkeley: University of California Press, 1999.
Cohen, Uri. *Ha'har ve'ha'giva: Ha'universita ha'ivrit bi'tekufat terom ha'atzma'ut* [The mountain and the hill: The Hebrew University of Jerusalem during the pre-independence period]. Tel-Aviv: Am Oved, 2006.
Cohn-Bendit, Daniel, and Claus Leggewie. "1968: Power to the Imagination." *New York Review of Books*, May 10, 2018.
Cooper, Andrea Dara. *Gendering Modern Jewish Thought*. Bloomington: Indiana University Press, 2021.
Coyne, Ryan. *Heidegger's Confessions: The Remains of Saint Augustine in Being and Time and Beyond*. Chicago: University of Chicago Press, 2015.
Crist, Eileen. "On the Poverty of Our Nomenclature." In *Anthropocene or Capitalocene? Nature, History, and the Crisis of Liberalism*, edited by Jason W. Moore. Oakland, CA: Kairos Books, 2016.
Crutzen, Paul J., and Eugene F. Stoermer. "The Anthropocene." *Global Change Newsletter* 41 (2000): 1–20.
Crutzen, Paul J., and Eugene F. Stoermer. "Geology of Mankind." *Nature* 415 (2002): 23.
Davies, Peter. "Myth and Maternalism in the Work of Johann Jakob Bachofen." *German Studies Review* 28, no. 3 (2005): 501–18.
Dawsey, Jason. "Where Hitler's Name Is Never Spoken: Günther Anders in 1950s Vienna." In *Austrian Lives*, edited by Günter Bischof, Fritz Plasser, and Eva Maltschnig. New Orleans: University of New Orleans Press, 2012.
de la Durantaye, Leland. *Giorgio Agamben: A Critical Introduction*. Stanford, CA: Stanford University Press, 2009.
DeLoughrey, Elizabeth M. *Allegories of the Anthropocene*. Durham, NC: Duke University Press, 2019.
Deroo, Neal, and John Panteleimon Manoussakis, eds. *Phenomenology and Eschatology: Not Yet in the Now*. Burlington, VT: Ashgate, 2009.
Derrida, Jacques. *The Animal That Therefore I Am*. Translated by Marie-Louise Mallet. New York: Fordham University Press, 2008.
Derrida, Jacques. "Interpretations at War: Kant, the Jew, the German." In *Acts of Religion*, edited by Gil Anidjar. New York: Routledge, 2002.
Derrida, Jacques. "Introduction: Desistance." In Philippe Lacoue-Labarthe, *Typography: Mimesis, Philosophy, Politics*, translated by Christopher Fynsk. Stanford, CA: Stanford University Press, 1998.
Derrida, Jacques. Introduction to Philippe Lacoue-Labarthe, *Typography: Mimesis, Philosophy, Politics*, translated by C. Fynsk. Cambridge, MA: Harvard University Press, 1989.
Derrida, Jacques. *Of Grammatology*. Translated by Gayatri Chakravorty Spivak. Baltimore: Johns Hopkins University Press, 2016.

Derrida, Jacques. "Shibboleth: For Paul Celan." In *Acts of Literature*, edited by Derrick Attridge. New York: Routledge, 1992.

Derrida, Jacques. *Shibboleth: Pour Paul Celan*. Paris: Galilée, 1986.

Derrida, Jacques. "Shibboleth for Paul Celan." In *Sovereignties in Question: The Poetics of Paul Celan*. New York: Fordham University Press, 2005.

Diner, Dan. *Zivilisationsbruch: Denken nach Auschwitz*. Frankfurt: Fischer, 1988.

Disler, Caroline. "Benjamin's 'Afterlife': A Productive Mistranslation in Memoriam Daniel Simeoni." *Du système en traduction: Approches critiques* 24, no. 1 (2011): 183–221.

Dodaro, Robert. "Fear of Death in the Thought of Augustine of Hippo." In *The Influence of Augustine on Heidegger: The Emergence of an Augustinian Phenomenology*, edited by Craig J. N. de Paulo. Lewiston, NY: Edwin Mellen Press, 2006.

Dorpema, Marc. "Narrative, Emplotment, Power: On Agency and the Environment." *Rethinking History* 27, no. 3 (2023): 511–36.

Dubbels, Elke. *Figuren des Messianischen in Schriften deutsch-jüdischer Intellektueller, 1900–1933*. Berlin: De Gruyter, 2011.

Durkheim, Émile. *Elementary Forms of Religious Life*. Oxford: Oxford University Press, 2008 [1912].

Duttlinger, Carolin. "Studium, Aufmerksamkeit, Gebet: Walter Benjamin und die Kontemplation." In *Profanes Leben: Walter Benjamins Dialektik der Säkularisierung*, edited by Daniel Weidner. Berlin: Suhrkamp, 2010.

Edelman, Lee. *No Future: Queer Theory and the Death Drive*. Durham, NC: Duke University Press, 2004.

Eiland, Howard, and Michael W. Jennings. *Walter Benjamin: A Critical Life*. Cambridge, MA: Harvard University Press, 2014.

Ellensohn, Reinhard, and Krestin Putz. Epilogue to *Gut, dass wir einmal die hot potatoes ausgraben: Briefwechsel mit Theodor W. Adorno, Ernst Bloch, Max Horkheimer, Herbert Marcuse, und Helmuth Plessner*, by Günther Anders. Munich: C. H. Beck, 2022.

Emundts, Dina. "The Refutation of Idealism and the Distinction between Phenomena and Noumena." In *The Cambridge Companion to Kant's Critique of Pure Reason*, edited by Paul Guyer. Cambridge: Cambridge University Press, 2010.

Erdle, Birgit R. "Dis/Placing Thought: Franz Kafka and Hannah Arendt." In *Kafka and the Universal*, edited by Arthur Cools and Vivian Liska. Berlin: De Gruyter, 2016.

Erlewine, Robert. *Judaism and the West: From Hermann Cohen to Joseph Soloveitchik*. Bloomington: Indiana University Press, 2016.

Eshel, Amir. *Futurity: Contemporary Literature and the Quest for the Past*. Chicago: Chicago University Press, 2013.

Eshel, Amir. "Paul Celan's Other: History, Poetics, and Ethics." *New German Critique* 91 (2004): 57–77.

Esposito, Roberto. *Bíos: Biopolitics and Philosophy*. Translated by Timothy C. Campbell. Minneapolis: University of Minnesota Press, 2008.

Esposito, Roberto. *The Origin of the Political: Hannah Arendt or Simone Weil?* Translated by Vincenzo Binetti and Gareth Williams. New York: Fordham University Press, 2017.

Ettinger, Bracha L. *The Matrixial Borderspace*. Minneapolis: University of Minnesota Press, 2006.

Felstiner, John. *Paul Celan: Poet, Survivor, Jew*. New Haven, CT: Yale University Press, 1995.

Felstiner, John. "'Ziv, that light': Translation and Tradition in Paul Celan." *New Literary History* 18, no. 3 (1987): 611–31.

Fenves, Peter. *The Messianic Reduction: Walter Benjamin and the Shape of Time*. Stanford, CA: Stanford University Press, 2011.

Ferguson, Hendrik. "Theorizing QueerTemporalities: A Roundtable Discussion." *GLQ* 13, no. 2/3 (2006): 177–95.

Fonrobert, Charlotte Elisheva. "The New Spatial Turn in Jewish Studies." *AJS Review* 33, no. 1 (2009): 155–64.

Ford, Thomas H. "Aura in the Anthropocene." *Symploke* 21, no. 1 (2013): 65–82.

Foucault, Michel. *The History of Sexuality*, vol. 1, *The Will to Knowledge*. Translated by R. J. Hurley. New York: Penguin, 1978.

Fredriksen, Paula. *Augustine and the Jews: A Christian Defense of Jews and Judaism*. New York: Doubleday, 2008.

Fremaux, Anne, and John Barry. "The 'Good Anthropocene' and Green Political Theory: Rethinking Environmentalism, Resisting Ecomodernism." In *Anthropocene Encounters: New Directions in Green Political Thinking*, edited by Frank Biermann and Eva Lövbrand. Cambridge: Cambridge University Press, 2019.

Frey, Christopher. "Eschatology and Ethics: Their Relation in Recent Continental Protestantism." In *Eschatology in the Bible in Jewish and Christian Tradition*, edited by Henning Graf Reventlow. Sheffield: Sheffield Academic, 1997.

Friedlaender, Eli. *Walter Benjamin: A Philosophical Portrait*. Cambridge, MA: Harvard University Press, 2012.

Friedman, Maurice. *Martin Buber's Life and Work: The Early Years: 1878–1923*. Detroit: Wayne State University Press, 1988.

Friedman, Maurice. *Martin Buber: The Life of Dialogue*. New York: Harper, 1960.

Friese, Heidrun, ed. *The Moment: Time and Rupture in Modern Thought*. Liverpool: Liverpool University Press, 2001.

Fritzsche, Peter. *Stranded in the Present: Modern Time and the Melancholy of History*. Cambridge, MA: Harvard University Press, 2004.

Fry, Karin A. *Arendt: A Guide for the Perplexed*. New York: Continuum, 2009.

Fry, Karin A. "Natality." In *Hannah Arendt: Key Concepts*, edited by Patrick Hayden. London: Routledge, 2014.

Gadamer, Hans-Georg. *Gadamer on Celan: 'Who Am I and Who Are You?' and Other Essays*. Translated by Richard Heinemann and Bruce Krajewski. Albany: SUNY Press, 1997.

Gadamer, Hans-Georg. "Heidegger and the Language of Metaphysics." In *Philosophical Hermeneutics*, translated by David E. Linge. Berkeley: University of California Press, 1976.

Gadamer, Hans-Georg. "Wer bin Ich und wer bist Du?" In *Über Paul Celan*, edited by Dietlind Meinecke. Frankfurt: Suhrkamp, 1970.

Gálvez, Jesùs Padilla, and Margit Gaffal, eds. *Forms of Life and Language Games*. Heusenstamm: Ontosverlag, 2011.

Gardner, Sebastian. *Routledge Guidebook to Kant and the Critique of Pure Reason*. New York: Routledge, 1999.

Gasché, Rodolphe. "On the Eastward Trajectory toward Europe: Karl Löwith's Exiles." In *Escape to Life: German Intellectuals in New York: A Compendium on Exile after 1933*, edited by Eckart Goebel and Sigrid Weigel. Berlin: De Gruyter, 2012.

Gasché, Rodolphe. *The Stelliferous Fold: Toward a Virtual Law of Literature's Self-Formation*. New York: Fordham University Press, 2011.

Gaus, Günter. "A TV Conversation with Günter Gaus (1964)." In *Hannah Arendt: Ich will verstehen: Selbstauskünfte zu Leben und Werk*, edited by Ursula Ludz. Munich: Piper, 1996.

Gelber, Mark H. *Stefan Zweig, Judentum und Zionismus*. Vienna: Studien, 2014.

Gellen, Kata. "Kafka, Pro and Contra: Günther Anders's Holocaust Book." In *Kafka and the Universal*, edited by Arthur Cools and Vivian Liska. Berlin: De Gruyter, 2016.

Gellhaus, Axel. "Das Datum des Gedichts: Textgeschichte und Geschichtlichkeit des Textes bei Celan." In *Lesarten: Beiträge zum Werk Paul Celans*, edited by Axel Gellhaus and Andreas Lohr. Cologne: Böhlau, 1996.

Gellhaus, Axel. "Marginalien: Paul Celan als Leser." In *Der glühende Leertext: Annährung an Paul Celans Dichtung*, edited by Otto Pöggeler and Christoph Jamme. Munich: W. Fink, 1993.

Geulen, Eva. *Giorgio Agamben zur Einführung*. Hamburg: Junius, 2005.

Geulen, Eva. "Toward a Genealogy of Gender in Walter Benjamin's Writing." *German Quarterly* 69, no. 2 (1996): 161–80.

Gines, Kathryn T. *Hannah Arendt and the Negro Question*. Bloomington: Indiana University Press, 2014.

Glock, Hans-Joachim. "Philosophical Investigations: Principles of Interpretation." In *Wittgenstein: Eine Neubewertung: Akten des 14. internationalen Wittgenstein-Symposiums*, edited by Rudolf Haller and Johannes Brandl. Vienna: Hölder-Pichler-Tempsky, 1990.

Goetschel, Willi. *The Discipline of Philosophy and the Invention of Modern Jewish Thought*. New York: Fordham University Press, 2013.

Gold, Joel. "Reading Celan: The Allegory of 'Hohles Lebensgehöft.'" In *Word Traces: Readings of Paul Celan*, edited by Aris Fioretos. Baltimore: Johns Hopkins University Press, 1994.

Goldberg, Sylvie Anne. *Clepsydra: Essay on the Plurality of Time in Judaism*. Translated by Benjamin Ivry. Stanford, CA: Stanford University Press, 2016.

Golomb, Jacob. *Nietzsche and Zion*. Ithaca, NY: Cornell University Press, 2004.
Gordon, Adi. *Toward Nationalism's End: An Intellectual Biography of Hans Kohn*. Waltham, MA: Brandeis University Press, 2017.
Gordon, Adi and Greenberg, Udi. "The City of Man, European Émigrés, and the Genesis of Postwar Conservative Thought." *Religions* 3, no. 3 (2012): 681–698. https://www.mdpi.com/2077-1444/3/3.
Gordon, Peter. *Continental Divide: Heidegger, Cassirer, Davos*. Cambridge, MA: Harvard University Press, 2010.
Gordon, Peter. *Rosenzweig and Heidegger: Between Judaism and German Philosophy*. Berkeley: University of California Press, 2003.
Gordon, Peter. "Weimar Theology: From Historicism to Crisis." In *Weimar Thought: A Contested Legacy*, edited by Peter E. Gordon and John P. McCormick. Princeton, NJ: Princeton University Press, 2015.
Gorsky, Philip. *American Covenant: A History of Civil Religion from the Puritans to the Present*. Princeton, NJ: Princeton University Press, 2017.
Gossman, Lionel. *Orpheus Philologus: Bachofen versus Mommsen on the Study of Antiquity*. Philadelphia: American Philosophical Society, 1983.
Gregory, Eric. *Politics and the Order of Love: An Augustinian Ethic of Democratic Citizenship*. Chicago: Chicago University Press, 2008.
Greisch, Jean. "Zeitgehöft und Anwesen: Zur Dia-chronie des Gedichts." In *"Der glühende Leertext": Annäherungen an Paul Celans Dichtung*, edited by Otto Pöggeler and Christoph Jamme. Munich: W. Fink, 1993.
Gribetz, Kattan, and Lynn Kaye. "The Temporal Turn in Ancient Judaism and Jewish Studies." *Currents for Biblical Research* 17, no. 3 (2019): 332–95.
Gross, Raphael. *Carl Schmitt and the Jews: The "Jewish Question," the Holocaust, and German Legal Theory*. Translated by Joel Golb. Madison: University of Wisconsin Press, 2000.
Grunenberg, Antonia. *Hannah Arendt and Martin Heidegger: History of Love*. Translated by Peg Birmingham, Kristina Lebedeva, and Elizabeth von Witzke Birmingham. Bloomington: Indiana University Press, 2017.
Gumbrecht, Hans Ulrich. *Our Broad Present: Time and Contemporary Culture*. New York: Columbia University Press, 2014.
Günther, Friederike Felicitas. *Rhythmus beim frühen Nietzsche*. Berlin: De Gruyter, 2008.
Hache, Émilie. *Ce à quoi nous tenons: Propositions pour une écologie pragmatique*. Paris: Les empêcheurs de penser en rond, 2010.
Hadad, Yemima. "Feminism, Nashim ve'Nashiut: Nochechutan ve'Trumatan la'Hagut Ha'Buberianit" [Feminism, women, and femininity: Their presence and contribution to Buberian thought], *Alpaim ve'Od*, no. 3 (2021): 151–64.
Hahn, Barbara. *The Jewess Pallas Athena: This Too a Theory of Modernity*. Translated by James McFarland. Princeton, NJ: Princeton University Press, 2002.
Hamacher, Werner. "Die Sekunde der Inversion. Bewegungen einer Figur durch Celans Gedichte." In *Paul Celan: Materialien*, edited by Werner Hamacher and Winfried Menninghaus. Frankfurt: Suhrkamp, 1988.

Hamacher, Werner. "HÄM: Ein Gedicht Celans mit Motiven Benjamins." In *Keinmaleins: Texte zu Celan*. Frankfurt: Vittorio Klostermann, 2019.

Hamacher, Werner. "'Now': Walter Benjamin on Historical Time." In *The Moment: Time and Rupture in Modern Thought*, edited by Heidrun Friese. Liverpool: Liverpool University Press, 2001.

Hamacher, Werner. "The Right to Have Rights (Four-and-a-Half Remarks)," translated by Kirk Wetters. *South Atlantic Quarterly*, 103, no. 2 (2004): 343–56.

Hamacher, Werner. "The Second Inversion." In *Premises: Essays on Philosophy and Literature from Kant to Celan*, translated by Peter Fenves. Stanford, CA: Stanford University Press, 1996.

Hamacher, Werner. "The Second of Inversion: Movements of a Figure through Celan's Poetry." In *The Lessons of Paul de Man*, translated by William D. Jewett, *Yale French Studies* no. 69 (1985): 276–311.

Hamilton, Clive. "Human Destiny in the Anthropocene." In *The Anthropocene and the Global Environmental Crisis: Rethinking Modernity in a New Epoch*, edited by Clive Hamilton, Christophe Bonneuil, and François Gemenne. London: Routledge, 2015.

Hansen, Miriam. "Benjamin, Cinema, and Experience: 'The Blue Flower in the Land of Technology.'" In *Walter Benjamin: Critical Evaluations in Cultural Theory*, vol. 2, *Modernity*, edited by Peter Osborne. London: Routledge, 2005.

Hanssen, Beatrice. *Walter Benjamin's Other History: Of Stones, Animals, Human Beings, and Angels*. Berkeley: University of California Press, 1998.

Haraway, Donna. "Staying with the Trouble: Anthropocene, Capitalocene, Chthulucene." In *Anthropocene or Capitalocene? Nature, History, and the Crisis of Liberalism*, edited by Jason W. Moore. Oakland, CA: Kairos Books, 2016.

Hardt, Michael, and Antonio Negri. *Empire*. Cambridge, MA: Harvard University Press, 2000.

Harootunian, Harry D. "The Benjamin Effect: Modernism, Repetition, and the Path to Different Cultural Imaginaries." In *Walter Benjamin and the Demands of History*, edited by Michael P. Steinberg. Ithaca, NY: Cornell University Press, 1996.

Hartman, Saidiya. *Scenes of Subjection: Terror, Slavery, and Self-Making in Nineteenth-Century America*. New York: Oxford University Press, 1997.

Hartog, François. *Chronos: The West Confronts Time*. Translated by S. R. Gilbert. New York: Columbia University Press, 2022.

Hartog, François. "Chronos, Kairos, Krisis: The Genesis of Western Time," translated by Samuel Gilbert. *History and Theory* 60, no. 3 (2021): 425–39.

Hartog, François. *Regimes of Historicity: Presentism and Experiences of Time*. Translated by Saskia Brown. New York: Columbia University Press, 2015.

Hatfield, Gary. "Kant on the Perception of Space (and Time)." In *The Cambridge Companion to Kant and Modern Philosophy*, edited by Paul Guyer. Cambridge: Cambridge University Press, 2007.

Hegel, G. W. F. *The Philosophy of History*. Translated by J. Sibree. New York: Colonial Press, 1956.

Heidegger, Martin. Appendices to *Kant and the Problem of Metaphysics*. Translated by Richard Taft. Bloomington: Indiana University Press, 1997.
Heidegger, Martin. *Becoming Heidegger: On the Trail of His Early Occasional Writings, 1910–1927*. Edited by Theodore Kisiel and Thomas Sheehan. Evanston, IL: Northwestern University Press, 2007.
Heidegger, Martin. *Being and Time*. Translated by Joan Stambaugh. Albany: SUNY Press, 2010.
Heidegger, Martin. *Elucidations of Hölderlin's Poetry*. Translated by Keith Hoeller. Amherst, NY: Humanity Books, 2000.
Heidegger, Martin. *Gesamtausgabe*, vol. 75, *Unveröffentlichte Abhandlungen: Zu Hölderlin/ Griechenlandreisen*. Frankfurt: Vittorio Klostermann, 2000.
Heidegger, Martin. *Hölderlin's Hymn "The Ister."* Translated by William McNeill and Julia Davis. Bloomington: Indiana University Press, 1996.
Heidegger, Martin. *Logic: The Question of Truth*. Translated by Thomas Sheehan. Bloomington: University of Indiana Press, 2010.
Heidegger, Martin. *The Phenomenology of Religious Life*. Translated by Matthias Fritsch and Jennifer Anna Gosetti-Ferencei. Bloomington: Indiana University Press, 2010.
Heidegger, Martin. *Sein und Zeit*. Tübingen: Neomarius, 1949.
Heidegger, Martin. *Was heisst Denken? Vorlesungen Wintersemester 1951/2*. Stuttgart: Reclam, 1992.
Heidegger, Martin. *What Is Called Thinking?* Translated by J. Glenn Gray. New York: Harper and Row, 1968.
Herdt, Jennifer A. *Putting on Virtue: The Legacy of the Splendid Vices*. Chicago: Chicago University Press, 2012.
Herf, Jeffrey. *Reactionary Modernism: Technology, Culture, and Politics in Weimar and the Third Reich*. Cambridge: Cambridge University Press, 1984.
Herskowitz, Daniel M. "Between Exclusion and Intersection: Heidegger's Philosophy and Jewish Volkism." *Leo Baeck Institute Yearbook* 65, no. 1 (2020): 135–36.
Herskowitz, Daniel M. *Heidegger and His Jewish Reception*. Cambridge: Cambridge University Press, 2021.
Heschel, A. J. *The Sabbath: Its Meaning for Modern Man*. New York: Farrar, Straus and Giroux, 1951
Heschel, Susannah. *The Aryan Jesus: Christian Theologians and the Bible in Nazi Germany*. Princeton, NJ: Princeton University Press, 2021.
Hillman, Susanne. "'A Germ So Tiny': Margarete Susman's Messianism of Small Steps." *Soundings: An Interdisciplinary Journal* 96, no. 1 (2013): 40–84.
Hölderlin, Friedrich. *Selected Poems and Fragments*. Translated by Michael Hamburger. Harmondsworth: Penguin, 1998.
Hollander, Dana. "Buber, Rosenzweig, and the Politics of Cultural Affirmation." *Jewish Studies Quarterly* 13, no. 1 (2006): 87–103.
Hollander, Dana. "'Plato Prophesied the Revelation': The Philosophico-Political Theology of Strauss's Philosophy and Law and the Guidance of Hermann

Cohen." In *Judaism, Liberalism, and Political Theology*, edited by Randi Rashkover and Martin Kavka. Bloomington: Indiana University Press, 2014.

Holste, Christine. "'Menschen von Potsdam': Der Forte-Kreis (1910–1915)." In *Der Potsdamer Forte-Kreis: Eine utopische Intellektuellenassoziation zur europäischen Friedenssicherung*, edited by Richard Faber and Christine Holste. Würzburg: Königshausen und Neumann, 2001.

Horwitz, Rivka. *Buber's Way to I and Thou: An Historical Analysis and the First Publication of Martin Buber's Lectures "Religion als Gegenwart."* Heidelberg: Schneider, 1978.

Howard, Thomas Albert. *Protestant Theology and the Making of the Modern German University*. New York: Oxford University Press, 2006.

Husserl, Edmund. *On the Phenomenology of Consciousness of Internal Time*. Translated by John Barnett Brough. Dordrecht: Springer, 1991.

Huston, Phil. *Martin Buber's Journey to Presence*. New York: Fordham University Press, 2007.

Idel, Moshe. *Old Worlds, New Mirrors: On Jewish Mysticism and Twentieth-Century Thought*. Philadelphia: University of Pennsylvania Press, 2010.

Imdahl, Georg. *Das Lebens-Verstehen: Heideggers formal anzeigende Hermeneutik in den frühen Freiburger Vorlesungen*. Würzburg: Königshausen und Neumann, 1997.

Isenberg, Noah. *Between Redemption and Doom: The Strains of German-Jewish Modernism*. Lincoln: University of Nebraska Press, 1999.

Jacobs, Andrew S. *Remains of the Jews: The Holy Land and Christian Empire in Late Antiquity*. Stanford, CA: Stanford University Press, 2004.

Jaeggi, Rahel. *Critique of Forms of Life*. Translated by Ciaran Cronin. Cambridge, MA: Harvard University Press, 2018.

Jameson, Frederick. *Postmodernism, or The Cultural Logic of Late Capitalism*. Durham, NC: Duke University Press, 2003.

Jantzen, Grace. "Eros and the Abyss: Reading Medieval Mystics in Postmodernity." *Literature and Theology* 17, no. 3 (2003): 244–64.

Jay, Martin. *Songs of Experience: Modern American and European Variations on a Universal Theme*. Berkeley: University of California Press, 2005.

Jennings, Michael W. *Walter Benjamin: A Critical Life*. Cambridge, MA: Harvard University Press, 2014.

Jennings, Michael W. "The Will to *apocatastasis*: Media, Experience, and Eschatology in Walter Benjamin's Late Theological Politics." In *Walter Benjamin and Theology*, edited by Colby Dickinson and Stéphane Symons. New York: Fordham University Press, 2016.

Jonas, Hans. *Augustin und das paulinische Freiheitsproblem: Eine philosophische Studie zum pelagianischen Streit*. Göttingen: Vandenhoeck und Ruprecht, 1965.

Jonas, Hans. *The Imperative of Responsibility: In Search of an Ethics for the Technological Age*. Chicago: Chicago University Press, 1984.

Jonas, Hans. *Memoirs*. Translated by Krishna Winston. Waltham, MA: Brandeis University Press, 2008.

Jonas, Hans. *Mortality and Morality: A Search for the Good after Auschwitz.* Edited by Lawrence Vogel. Evanston, IL: Northwestern University Press, 1996.
Jonas, Hans. *The Phenomenon of Life: Toward a Philosophy of Biology.* Evanston, IL: Northwestern University Press, 2001.
Jonas, Hans. *Philosophical Essays.* Englewood Cliffs, NJ: Prentice Hall, 1974.
Jordheim, Helge, and Einar Wigen. "Conceptual Synchronisation: From *Progress* to *Crisis.*" *Millennium* 46, no. 3 (2018): 421–39.
Joris, Pierre. Introduction to *Paul Celan: Selections*, translated by Pierre Joris. Berkeley: University of California Press, 2005.
Jungk, Peter Stephan. *Franz Werfel: A Life in Prague, Vienna, and Hollywood.* Translated by Anselm Hollo. New York: Grove Weidenfeld, 1991.
Kafka, Franz. "Before the Law." In *Complete Stories*, edited by Nahum Glatzer. New York: Schocken Books, 1971.
Kafka, Franz. *The Diaries.* Translated Ross Benjamin. New York: Schocken Books, 2022.
Kafka, Franz. *Letters to Felice.* Translated by James Stern and Elisabeth Duckworth. New York: Schocken, 1973.
Kaiser, Corinna R. *Gustav Landauer als Schriftsteller: Sprache, Schweigen, Musik.* Berlin: De Gruyter Oldenbourg, 2014.
Kampowski, Stephan. *Arendt, Augustine, and the New Beginning: The Action Theory and Moral Thought of Hannah Arendt in the Light of Her Dissertation on St. Augustine.* Grand Rapids, MI: Eerdmans, 2008.
Kaufman, Peter Iver. *On Agamben, Arendt, Christianity, and the Dark Arts of Civilization.* London: Bloomsbury, 2020.
Kautzer, Chad. "Political Violence and Race: A Critique of Hannah Arendt." *Comparative Literature and Culture* 21, no. 3 (2019): 2–12.
Kavka, Martin. *Jewish Messianism and the History of Philosophy.* Cambridge: Cambridge University Press, 2004.
Kepnes, Steven. "Rosenzweig's Liturgical Reasoning as Response to Augustine's Temporal Aporias." In *Liturgy, Time, and the Politics of Redemption*, edited by Randi Rashkover and C. C. Picknold. Cambridge: Eerdmans, 2006.
Kern, Stephen. *The Culture of Space and Time, 1880–1918.* Cambridge, MA: Harvard University Press, 1983.
Keval, Hillel. *Languages of Community: The Jewish Experience in the Czech Lands.* Berkeley: University of California, 2000.
Killen, Andreas. *Berlin Electropolis: Shock, Nerves, and German Modernity.* Berkeley: University of California Press, 2006.
King, Magda. *A Guide to Heidegger's Being and Time.* Albany: SUNY Press, 2001.
King, Richard. *Arendt and America.* Chicago: University of Chicago Press, 2015.
Kisiel, Theodore. "Situating Augustine in Salvation History, Philosophy's History, and Heidegger's History." In *The Influence of Augustine on Heidegger: The Emergence of an Augustinian Phenomenology*, edited by Craig J. N. de Paulo. Lewiston, NY: Edwin Mellen Press, 2006.
Kjellén, Rudolf. *Grundriss zu einem System der Politik.* Leipzig: Hirzel, 1920.

Kleinberg, Ethan. *Emmanuel Levinas's Talmudic Turn: Philosophy and Jewish Thought*. Stanford, CA: Stanford University Press, 2021.

Kohn, Jerome. Preface to *The Jewish Writings*, by Hannah Arendt. New York: Schocken, 2007.

Koselleck, Reinhart. "Does History Accelerate?" In *Sediments of Time: On Possible Histories*, translated by Sean Franzel and Stefan-Ludwig Hoffmann. Stanford, CA: Stanford University Press, 2018.

Koselleck, Reinhart. *Futures Past: On the Semantics of Historical Time*. Translated by Keith Tribe. New York: Columbia University Press, 2004.

Koselleck, Reinhart. "History, Histories, and Formal Structures of Time." In *Futures Past: On the Semantics of Historical Time*, translated by Keith Tribe, 93–104. New York: Columbia University Press, 2004.

Koselleck, Reinhart. "'Space of Experience,' and 'Horizon of Expectation': Two Historical Categories." In *Futures Past: On the Semantics of Historical Time*, translated by Keith Tribe, 255–275. New York: Columbia University Press, 2004.

Koselleck, Reinhart. "Time and History." In *The Practice of Conceptual History: Timing History, Spacing Concepts*, translated by Todd Samuel Presener et al. Stanford, CA: Stanford University Press, 2002.

Kotsko, Adam. "Giorgio Agamben (1942–)." In *Religion and European Philosophy: Key Thinkers from Kant to Žižek*, edited by Philip Goodchild and Hollis Phelps. New York: Routledge, 2017.

Kracauer, Siegfried. "Die Bibel auf Deutsch." In *Werke*, vol. 5, part 1: *Essays, Feuilletons, Rezensionen, 1906–1923*, edited by Inka Mülder-Bach. Frankfurt: Suhrkamp, 1990.

Krell, David Farrell. *Daimon Life: Heidegger and Life-Philosophy*. Bloomington: Indiana University Press, 1992.

LaCapra, Dominick. *Writing History, Writing Trauma*. Baltimore: Johns Hopkins University Press, 2014.

Lacoue-Labarthe, Philippe. *Poetry as Experience*. Translated by Andrea Tarnowski. Stanford, CA: Stanford University Press, 1999.

Landauer, Gustav. *Die Revolution*. In *Gesellschaft*, vol. 13. Frankfurt: Rütten und Leoning, 1907.

Landauer, Gustav. "Jewishness Is an Inalienable Spiritual Sensibility." In *The Jew in the Modern World: A Documentary History*, 2nd ed., edited by Paul R. Mendes-Flohr and Jehuda Reinharz. New York: Oxford University Press, 1995.

Landauer, Gustav. "Martin Buber." In *Der werdende Mensch: Aufsätze über Leben und Schrifttum*. Potsdam: Kiepenheuer, 1921.

Landauer, Gustav. "Sind das Ketzergedanken?" In *Vom Judentum: Ein Sammelbuch*, edited by Hans Kohn. Leipzig: Kurt Wolff, 1913.

Langbehn, Julius. *Rembrandt als Erzieher*. Leipzig: C. L. Hirschfeld, 1896.

Langston, Nancy. "The Retreat from Precaution: Regulating Diethylstilbestrol (Des), Endocrine Disruptors, and Environmental Health." *Environmental History* 13, no. 1 (2008): 41–65.

Lappin, Eleonore. *Der Jude, 1916–1928: Jüdische Moderne zwischen Universalismus und Partikularismus.* Tübingen: Mohr Siebeck, 2000.
Latour, Bruno. *Facing Gaia: Eight Lectures on the New Climatic Regime.* Translated by Catherine Porter. Cambridge, MA: Polity, 2017.
Latour, Bruno. *We Have Never Been Modern.* Translated by Catherine Porter. Cambridge, MA: Harvard University Press, 1993.
Lavsky, Hagit. *Before Catastrophe: The Distinctive Path of German Zionism.* Detroit: Wayne State University Press, 1996.
Lazier, Benjamin. *God Interrupted: Heresy and the European Imagination between the World Wars.* Princeton, NJ: Princeton University Press, 2008.
Lazier, Benjamin. "Pauline Theology in the Weimar Republic: Hans Jonas, Karl Barth, and Martin Heidegger." In *The Legacy of Hans Jonas: Judaism and the Phenomenon of Life*, edited by Hava Tirosh-Samuelson and Christian Wiese. Leiden: Brill, 2008.
Lebovic, Nitzan. "The Beauty and Terror of *Lebensphilosophie*: Ludwig Klages, Walter Benjamin, and Alfred Baeumler." *South Central Review* 23, no. 1 (2006): 23–39.
Lebovic, Nitzan. "Benjamin's Nihilism: Rhythm and Political Stasis." In *Benjamin-Studien 2*, edited by Daniel Weidner and Sigrid Weigel. Munich: W. Fink, 2011.
Lebovic, Nitzan. "Benjamins Sumpflogik: Ein Kommentar zu Agambens Kafka und Benjamin Lektüre." In *Profanes Leben*, edited by Daniel Weidner. Frankfurt: Suhrkamp, 2010.
Lebovic, Nitzan. "The Jerusalem School: The Theopolitical Hour." *New German Critique* 35, no. 3 (2008): 97–120.
Lebovic, Nitzan. "Near the End: Paul Celan between Scholem and Heidegger." *German Quarterly* 83, no. 4 (2010): 465–84.
Lebovic, Nitzan. *The Philosophy of Life and Death: Ludwig Klages and the Rise of a Nazi Biopolitics.* New York: Palgrave Macmillan, 2013.
Lebovic, Nitzan, and Daniel Weidner. Introduction to *Special Issue on Prophetic Politics, Political Theology* 21, no. 2 (2020): 1–8.
Lefebvre, Henri. *Rhythmanalysis.* Translated by Stuart Elden and Gerald Moore. London: Continuum, 2004.
Leibovici, Martine. "Hannah Arendt (1906–1975): Being in the Present." In *Makers of Jewish Modernity: Thinkers, Artists, Leaders, and the World They Made*, edited by Jacques Picard et al. Princeton, NJ: Princeton University Press, 2016.
Lepenies, Wolf. *The Seduction of German Culture in German History.* Princeton, NJ: Princeton University Press, 2006.
Levin, Thomas Y. Introduction to *The Mass Ornament: Weimar Essays*, by Siegfried Kracauer, translated by Thomas Y. Levin. Cambridge, MA: Harvard University Press, 1995.
Levinas, Emmanuel. *God, Death, and Time.* Translated by Bettina Bergo. Stanford, CA: Stanford University Press, 2000.
Levine, Michael G. *A Weak Messianic Power: Figures of a Time to Come in Benjamin, Derrida, and Celan.* New York: Fordham University Press, 2014.

Liberles, Robert. "Was There a Jewish Movement for Emancipation in Germany?" *Leo Baeck Institute Year Book* 31, no. 1 (1986): 35–49.

Lievens, Matthias. "Carl Schmitt's Concept of History." In *The Oxford Handbook of Carl Schmitt*, edited by Jens Meierhenrich and Oliver Simons. New York: Oxford University Press, 2016.

Lindroos, Kia. *Now-Time Image-Space: Temporalization of Politics in Walter Benjamin's Philosophy of History and Art*. Jyväskylä: University of Jyväskylä, 1998.

Linse, Ulrich. "'Poetic Anarchism' versus 'Party Anarchism': Gustav Landauer and the Anarchist Movement in Wilhelmian Germany." In *Gustav Landauer: Anarchist and Jew*, edited by Paul Mendes-Flohr and Anya Mali. Berlin: De Gruyter Oldenbourg, 2015.

Lipszic, Adam. "Words and Corpses: Celan's 'Tenebrae' between Gadamer and Scholem." *Jewish Studies Quarterly* 21, no. 1 (2014): 55–66.

Liska, Vivian. "Denkfiguren des Neuanfangs im 20. Jahrhundert (Heidegger, Benjamin, Arendt, Agamben—und Kafka)." In *Renaissances: Über ein Muster der Aneignung von Tradition*, edited by Jürgen Fohrmann. Göttingen: Wallstein, 2022.

Liska, Vivian. *German-Jewish Thought and Its Afterlife: A Tenuous Legacy*. Bloomington: University of Indiana Press, 2018.

Liska, Vivian. *When Kafka Says We: Uncommon Communities in German-Jewish Literature*. Bloomington: Indiana University Press 2009.

Löwith, Karl. "Heidegger: Thinker in a Destitute Time." In *Martin Heidegger and European Nihilism*, translated by Gary Steiner. New York: Columbia University Press, 1995.

Löwith, Karl. *Martin Heidegger and European Nihilism*. Translated by Gary Stiner. New York: Columbia University Press, 1992.

Löwith, Karl. *Meaning in History*. Chicago: Chicago University Press, 1949.

Löwith, Karl. *Nietzsche's Philosophy of the Eternal Recurrence of the Same*. Translated by J. Harvey Lomax. Berkeley: University of California Press, 1997 [1935].

Löwy, Michael. *On Changing the World: Essays in Political Philosophy, from Karl Marx to Walter Benjamin*. Chicago: Haymarket Books, 2013.

Löwy, Michael. "Romantic Prophets of Utopia: Gustav Landauer and Martin Buber." In *Gustav Landauer: Anarchist and Jew*, edited by Paul Mendes-Flohr and Anya Mali. Berlin: De Gruyter Oldenbourg, 2015.

Lyon, James. *Paul Celan and Martin Heidegger: An Unresolved Conversation, 1951–1970*. Baltimore: Johns Hopkins University Press, 2006.

Macann, Christopher, ed. *Critical Heidegger*. London: Routledge, 1996.

Mackay, Robin, and Armen Avenassian, eds. *#Accelerate*. Falmouth, UK: Urbanomic, 2014.

Magid, Shaul. "Defining Christianity and Judaism from the Perspective of Religious Anarchy: Martin Buber on Jesus and the Ba'al Shem Tov." In *Martin Buber: His Intellectual and Scholarly Legacy*, edited by Sam Berrin Shonkoff. Leiden: Brill, 2018.

Mahmood, Saba. *Religious Difference in a Secular Age: A Minority Report.* Princeton, NJ: Princeton University Press, 2016.

Malm, Andreas. "Who Lit This Fire? Approaching the History of the Fossil Fuel Economy." *Critical Historical Studies* 3, no. 2 (2016): 215–48.

Marx, Karl. *Capital: A Critique of Political Economy.* Translated by Ben Fowkes. London: Penguin Classics, 1992.

Marx, Ursula, et al., eds. *Walter Benjamin's Archive: Images, Texts, Signs.* Translated by Esther Leslie. London: Verso, 2007.

Mbembe, Achille. *Necropolitics.* Translated by Steve Corcoran. Durham, NC: Duke University Press, 2019.

Mbembe, Achille. *On the Postcolony.* Berkeley: University of California Press, 2001.

McAfee, Noëlle. *Julia Kristeva.* New York: Routledge, 2004.

McCole, John. *Walter Benjamin and the Antinomies of Tradition.* Ithaca, NY: Cornell University Press, 1993.

McFarland, James. *Constellation: Friedrich Nietzsche and Walter Benjamin in the Now-Time of History.* New York: Fordham University Press, 2012.

McGowan, John. *Hannah Arendt: An Introduction.* Minneapolis: University of Minnesota Press, 1998.

Mendes-Flohr, Paul. "Buber's Rhetoric." In *Martin Buber: A Contemporary Perspective*, edited by Paul Mendes-Flohr. Syracuse, NY: Syracuse University Press, 2002.

Mendes-Flohr, Paul. *Divided Passions: Jewish Intellectuals and the Experience of Modernity.* Detroit: Wayne State University Press, 1991.

Mendes-Flohr, Paul. *From Mysticism to Dialogue: Martin Buber's Transformation of German Social Thought.* Detroit: Wayne State University Press, 1989.

Mendes-Flohr, Paul. *German Jews: A Dual Identity.* New Haven, CT: Yale University Press, 1999.

Mendes-Flohr, Paul. Introduction to Martin Buber, *Ecstatic Confessions: The Heart of Mysticism*, translated by Esther Cameron. Syracuse, NY: Syracuse University Press, 1996.

Mendes-Flohr, Paul. *Martin Buber: A Life of Faith and Dissent.* New Haven, CT: Yale University Press, 2019.

Mendes-Flohr, Paul. "Martin Buber and Martin Heidegger in Dialogue." *Journal of Religion* 94, no. 1 (2014): 2–25.

Mendes-Flohr, Paul, Rachel Livneh-Freudenthal, and Guy Miron, eds. *Jewish Historiography between Past and Future: 200 Years of Wissenschaft des Judentums.* Berlin: De Gruyter, 2019.

Mendoza-de Jesús, Ronald. "Index and Image: Benjamin, Héring, Heidegger, and the Phenomenology of History." *Qui Parle* 30, no. 2 (2021): 293–335.

Menninghaus, Winfried. *Paul Celan: Magie der Form.* Frankfurt: Suhrkamp, 1980.

Moran, Brendan. "Nature, Decision, and Muteness." In *Towards the Critique of Violence: Walter Benjamin and Giorgio Agamben*, edited by Brendan Moran and Carlo Salzani. London: Bloomsbury Academic, 2015.

Morris, Theresa. *Hans Jonas's Ethic of Responsibility: From Ontology to Ecology.* Albany: SUNY Press, 2013.

Mosès, Stéphane. *The Angel of History: Rosenzweig, Benjamin, Scholem.* Stanford, CA: Stanford University Press, 2009.

Moss, Kenneth E. *An Unchosen People: Jewish Political Reckoning in Interwar Poland.* Cambridge, MA: Harvard University Press, 2021.

Mosse, George. *German Jews beyond Judaism.* Bloomington: Indiana University Press, 1985.

Mosse, George. *Germans and Jews: The Right, the Left, and the Search for a "Third Force" in Pre-Nazi Germany.* Detroit: Wayne State University, 1987.

Moyn, Samuel. "Hannah Arendt on the Secular." *Critical Inquiry* 105 (2008): 71–96.

Moynihan, Thomas. "The End of Us." *Aeon*, August 7, 2019, https://aeon.co/essays/to-imagine-our-own-extinction-is-to-be-able-to-answer-for-it.

Munslow, Alun. *Narrative and History.* New York: Palgrave Macmillan, 2007.

Myers, David N. *Resisting History: Historicism and Its Discontents in German-Jewish Thought.* Princeton, NJ: Princeton University Press, 2003.

Myers, David N., and David B. Ruderman, eds. *The Jewish Past Revisited: Reflections on Modern Jewish Historians.* New Haven, CT: Yale University Press, 1998.

Nathan, Emmanuel, and Anya Topolski. "The Myth of Judeo-Christian Tradition: Introducing a European Perspective." In *Is There a Judeo-Christian Tradition? A European Perspective*, edited by Emmanuel Nathan and Anya Topolski. Berlin: De Gruyter, 2016.

Nehring, Holger. "Cold War, Apocalypse, and Peaceful Atoms: Interpretations of Nuclear Energy in the British and West German Anti-Nuclear Weapons Movements, 1955–1964." *Historical Social Research* 29, no. 3 (2004): 150–70.

Neiman, Susan. *Evil in Modern Thought: An Alternative History of Philosophy.* Princeton, NJ: Princeton University Press, 2002.

Ng, Karen. *Hegel's Concept of Life: Self-Consciousness, Freedom, Logic.* New York: Oxford University Press, 2020.

Nietzsche, Friedrich. *Thus Spoke Zarathustra: A Book for Everyone and Nobody.* Translated by Graham Parkes. New York: Oxford University Press, 2005.

Nirenberg, David. *Anti-Judaism: The Western Tradition.* New York: W. W. Norton, 2013.

Nirenberg, David. "Slay Them Not." *New Republic*, May 17, 2009.

Noakes, J., and G. Pridham, eds. *Nazism, 1919–1945: A Documentary Reader*, vol. 3. Exeter: University of Exeter Press, 1988.

Norton, Robert. *Secret Germany: Stefan George and His Circle.* Ithaca, NY: Cornell University Press, 2002.

Noys, Benjamin. *Malign Velocities: Accelerationism and Capitalism.* Alresford: Zero Books, 2014.

Nur, Ofer. *Eros and Tragedy: Jewish Male Fantasies and the Masculine Revolution of Zionism.* Boston: Academic Studies Press, 2014.

O'Byrne, Anne. *Natality and Finitude*. Indianapolis: Indiana University Press, 2010.

Osborne, Peter. *The Politics of Time: Modernity and Avant-Garde*. London: Verso Books, 1995.

Paipais, Vassilios. "'Already/Not Yet': St. Paul's Eschatology and the Modern Critique of Historicism." *Philosophy and Social Criticism* 44, no. 9 (2018): 1015–38.

Pardes, Ilana. *The Biography of Ancient Israel: National Narratives in the Bible*. Berkeley: University of California Press, 2000.

Peretz, Dekel. *Zionism and Cosmopolitanism: Franz Oppenheimer and the Dream of a Jewish Future in Germany and Palestine*. Munich: De Gruyter Oldenbourg, 2022.

Perloff, Marjorie. *Edge of Irony: Modernism in the Shadow of the Habsburg Empire*. Chicago: Chicago University Press, 2016.

Perloff, Marjorie. "'Sound Scraps, Vision Scraps': Paul Celan's Poetic Practice." In *Radical Poetics and Secular Jewish Culture*, edited by Stephen Paul Miller and Daniel Morris. Tuscaloosa: University of Alabama Press, 2010.

Peskowitz, Miriam, and Laura Lewitt, eds. *Judaism since Gender*. New York: Routledge, 1997.

Pippin, Robert B. *Hegel on Self-Consciousness: Desire and Death in the Phenomenology of Spirit*. Princeton, NJ: Princeton University Press, 2011.

Pöggeler, Otto. "'Ich schwimme lieber': Ein Gespräch mit Otto Pöggeler." Interview by Andreas Grossmann and Gerhard Unterthurner. *Journal Phänomenologie* 11 (1999).

Pöggeler, Otto. "Mystical Elements in Heidegger's Thought and Celan's Poetry." In *Word Traces: Reading of Paul Celan*. Baltimore: Johns Hopkins University Press, 1994.

Polt, Richard. *Heidegger: An Introduction*. London: Routledge, 1999.

Poma, Andrea. "Hermann Cohen: Judaism and Critical Idealism." In *The Cambridge Companion to Modern Jewish Philosophy*, edited by Michael L. Morgan and Peter Eli Gordon. Cambridge: Cambridge University Press, 2007.

Postclassicisms Collective. *Postclassicisms*. Chicago: Chicago University Press, 2020.

Povinelli, Elizabeth A. *Geontologies: A Requiem to Late Liberalism*. Durham, NC: Duke University Press, 2016.

Presner, Todd Samuel. "'The Fabrication of Corpses': Heidegger, Arendt, and the Modernity of Mass Death." *Telos* 135 (2006): 84–108.

Rabinbach, Anson. *The Human Motor: Energy, Fatigue, and the Origins of Modernity*. Berkeley: University of California Press, 1992.

Rabinbach, Anson. *In the Shadow of Catastrophe: German Intellectuals between Apocalypse and Enlightenment*. Berkeley: University of California Press, 1997.

Radloff, Bernhard. *Heidegger and the Question of National Socialism: Discourse and Gestalt*. Toronto: University of Toronto Press, 2007.

Räsänen, Pajari. "Counter-Figures: An Essay on Anti-Metaphoric Resistance: Paul Celan's Poetry and Poetics at the Limits of Figurality." PhD dissertation, University of Helsinki, Helsinki, Finland, 2007.

Reill, Peter Hans. *Vitalizing Nature in the Enlightenment*. Berkeley: University of California Press, 2005.

Rickert, Heinrich. *Die Philosophie des Lebens: Darstellung und Kritik der philosophischen Modeströmung unserer Zeit*. Tübingen: J. C. B. Mohr, 1920.

Ricoeur, Paul. *Time and Narrative*. Vol. 1. Translated by David Pellauer and Kathleen McLaughlin. Chicago: University of Chicago Press, 1990.

Riskin, Jessica. *The Restless Clock: A History of the Centuries-Long Argument over What Makes Living Things Tick*. Chicago: University of Chicago Press, 2014.

Robinson, James T. "Al-Farabi, Avicenna, and Averroes in Hebrew: Remarks on the Indirect Transmission of Arabic-Islamic Philosophy in Medieval Judaism." In *Judeo-Christian-Islamic Heritage: Philosophical and Theological Perspectives*, edited by Richard C. Taylor and Irgan A. Omar. Milwaukee, WI: Marquette University Press, 2011.

Roemer, Nils. "Between Hope and Despair: Conceptions of Time and the German-Jewish Experience in the Nineteenth Century." *Jewish History* 14 (2000): 345–63.

Rosa, Hartmut. *Social Acceleration: A New Theory of Modernity*. Translated by Jonathan Trejo-Mathys. New York: Columbia University Press, 2013.

Rosanvallon, Pierre. *Democracy Past and Future*. Edited by Samuel Moyn. New York: Columbia University Press, 2006.

Rose, Gillian. "Reply from 'The Single One.'" In *Martin Buber: A Contemporary Perspective*, edited by Paul Mendes-Flohr. Syracuse, NY: Syracuse University Press, 2022.

Rosenstock-Huessy, Eugen. *Ja und Nein: Autobiographische Fragmente*. Heidelberg: L. Schneider, 1968.

Rosenwald, Lawrence. "On the Reception of Buber and Rosenzweig's Bible." *Prooftexts* 14, no. 2 (1994): 141–65.

Rosenzweig, Franz. "Das Formgeheimnis der biblischen Erzählung." In Martin Buber and Franz Rosenzweig, *Die Schrift und ihre Verdeutschung*. Berlin: Schocken, 1936.

Rosenzweig, Franz. *Gesammelte Schriften*, vol. 3. The Hague: Martinus Nijhoff, 1984.

Rosenzweig, Franz. *Star of Redemption*. Translated by Barbara E. Galli. Madison: University of Wisconsin Press, 2005.

Rosenzweig, Franz. "Vom Geist der hebräischen Sprache." In *Der Mensch und Sein Werk*, vol. 3, *Zweistromland: Kleinere Schriften zu Glauben und Denken*. The Hague: Nijhoff, 1984.

Rothberg, Michael. *Multidirectional Memory*. Stanford: Stanford University Press, 2009.

Rovelli, Carlo. *The Order of Time*. Translated by Simon Carnell and Erica Segre. New York: Penguin, 2018.

Rowland, Anthony. "Re-reading 'Impossibility' and 'Barbarism': Adorno and Post-Holocaust Poetics." *Critical Survey* 9, no. 1 (1997): 57–69.

Rudavsky, Tamar. *Time Matters: Time, Creation, and Cosmology in Medieval Jewish Philosophy*. Albany: SUNY Press, 2000.

Sachar, Howard M. *A History of the Jews in the Modern World*. New York: Vintage Books, 2006.

Saeidnia, Sahar Aurore. *An Analysis of Hannah Arendt's The Human Condition*. London: Routledge, 2017.

Safranski, Rüdiger. *Zeit: Was sie mit uns macht und was wir aus ihr machen*. Munich: Carl Hanser, 2015.

Sagan, Claire. "Capitalist Temporalities as Uchronia." *Theory and Event* 22, no. 1 (2019): 153–54.

Santner, Eric L. *On Creaturely Life: Rilke, Benjamin, Sebald*. Chicago: University of Chicago Press, 2006.

Satia, Priya. *Time's Monster: How History Makes History*. Cambridge, MA: Harvard University Press, 2020.

Scanlon, Michael J. "Arendt's Augustine." In *Augustine and Postmodernism: Confession and Circumfession*, edited by John D. Caputo and Michael J. Scanlon. Bloomington: Indiana University Press, 2005.

Schmidt, Gilya Gerda. *Martin Buber's Formative Years: From German Culture to Jewish Renewal, 1897–1909*. Tuscaloosa: University of Alabama Press, 1995.

Schmitt, Carl. *The Concept of the Political*. Translated by Georg Schwab. Chicago: University of Chicago Press, 1996.

Schmitt, Carl. *Political Theology: Four Chapters on the Concept of Sovereignty*. Translated by George Schwab. Chicago: University of Chicago Press, 1985.

Schmitt, Carl. *Political Theology II: The Myth of the Closure of Any Political Theology*. Translated by Michael Hoelzl and Graham Ward. Cambridge, MA: Polity, 2014.

Scholem, Gershom. "Das Ringen zwischen dem biblischen Gott und dem Gott Plotins in der alten Kabbala." In *Über einige Grundbegriffe des Judentums*. Frankfurt: Suhrkamp, 1970.

Scholem, Gershom. *From Berlin to Jerusalem: Memories of My Youth*. Translated by Harry Zohn. Philadelphia: Paul Dry, 2012.

Scholem, Gershom. "On Jonah and the Concept of Justice," translated by Eric J. Schwab. *Critical Inquiry* 25, no. 2 (1999): 353–61.

Scholem, Gershom. "On Lament and Lamentation," translated by Lina Barouch and Paula Schwebel. *Jewish Studies Quarterly* 21, no. 1 (2014): 4–12.

Scholem, Gershom. "Walter Benjamin." *Neue Rundschau* 76, no. 1 (1965): 19.

Scholem, Gershom. *Walter Benjamin: The Story of a Friendship*. Translated by Harry Zohn. New York: New York Review Books, 2001.

Scholem, Gershom, and Theodor W. Adorno, eds. *The Correspondence of Walter Benjamin*. Translated by Manfred R. Jacobson and Evelyn M. Jacobson. Chicago: University of Chicago Press, 1994.

Schumacher, Eric. "Heidegger on the Relationship between Sterēsis and Kairos." *International Journal of Philosophy and Theology* 3, no. 1 (2015): 8–84.

Schwartz, Yossef. "The Politicization of the Mystical in Buber and His Contemporaries." In *New Perspectives on Martin Buber*, edited by Michael Zank. Tübingen: Mohr Siebeck, 2006.

Schwebel, Paula. "Monad and Time: Reading Leibniz with Heidegger and Benjamin." In *Sparks Will Fly: Benjamin and Heidegger*, edited by Andrew Benjamin and Dimitris Vardoulakis. Albany: SUNY Press, 2016.

Scott, Joanna Vecchiarelli, and Judith Chelius Stark. Introduction to Hannah Arendt, *Love and Saint Augustine*. Chicago: Chicago University Press, 1996.

Sehnhav, Ghilad H. "Abyss and Messiah: Gershom Scholem and the Question of Language." PhD dissertation, Tel-Aviv University, Tel-Aviv, Israel, 2021.

Seymour, David M. "The Purgatory of the Camp: Political Emancipation and the Emancipation of the Political." In *Giorgio Agamben: Legal, Political, and Philosophical Perspectives*, edited by Tom Frost. New York: Routledge, 2013.

Shapira, Avraham. *Hope for Our Time: Key Trends in the Thought of Martin Buber*. Translated by Jeffrey M. Green. Albany: SUNY Press, 1999.

Shapira, Anita. *Land and Power: The Zionist Resort to Force, 1881–1948*. Translated by William Templer. Stanford, CA: Stanford University Press, 1992.

Shapiro, Michael. *Politics and Time: Documenting the Event*. Malden, MA: Polity Books, 2016.

Shapiro, Susan. "A Matter of Discipline: Reading for Gender in Jewish Philosophy." In *Judaism since Gender*, edited by Miriam Peskowitz and Laura Lewitt. New York: Routledge, 1997.

Shenhav, Ghilad H. "Abyss and Messiah: Gershom Scholem and the Question of Language." PhD dissertation, Tel-Aviv University, Tel-Aviv, Israel, 2021.

Sheppard, Eugene R. *Leo Strauss and the Politics of Exile: The Making of a Political Philosopher*. Waltham, MA: Brandeis University Press, 2006.

Shonkoff, Sam. "Gender in Martin Buber's Hasidic Tales." *Leo Baeck Institute Year Book* 86, no. 1 (2023): 1–17.

Shraub, David. "White Jews: An Intersectional Approach." *AJS Review* 43, no. 2 (2019): 379–407.

Shumsky, Dimitry. *Ben Prague Li-Yerusalaim*. Jerusalem: Leo Baeck Institute and Zalman Shazar Center, 2010.

Shumsky, Dimitry. *Zweisprachigkeit und binationale Idee: Der Prager Zionismus, 1900–1930*. Translated by Dafna Mach. Göttingen: Vandenhoeck und Ruprecht, 2013.

Shuster, Martin. *How to Measure a World? A Philosophy of Judaism*. Bloomington: Indiana University Press, 2021.

Sieber, Mirjam. *Paul Celans "Gespräch im Gebirg": Erinnerung an eine "Versäumte Begegnung."* Tübingen: Max Niemeyer, 2007.

Silberstein, Laurence J. *Martin Buber's Social and Religious Thought: Alienation and the Quest for Meaning*. New York: NYU Press, 1990.

Simmel, Georg. "Brücke und Tür." In *Das Individuum und die Freiheit: Essais*. Frankfurt: Suhrkamp, 1993.

Simmel, Georg. *Der Konflikt der modernen Kultur: ein Vortrag.* Munich: Duncker and Humblot, 1918.
Simmel, Georg. *Fragmente und Aufsätze aus dem Nachlass.* Munich: Drei Massken, 1923.
Simmel, Georg. *Lebensanschauungen: Vier metaphysisiche Kapitel.* Berlin: Duncker und Humblot, 1994.
Simmel, Georg. "The Metropolis and Mental Life." In *On Individuality and Social Forms: Selected Writings,* edited by Donald N. Levine. Chicago: University of Chicago Press, 1971.
Simmel, Georg. *The Philosophy of Money.* Translated by Tom Bottomore and David Frisby. New York: Cambridge University Press, 2005.
Simmel, Georg. *The Problems of the Philosophy of History: An Epistemological Essay.* Translated and edited by Guy Oakes. New York: Free Press, 1977.
Sloterdijk, Peter. *Nietzsche Apostle.* Translated by Steven Corcoran. Madison: University of Wisconsin, 2013.
Smith, Zadie. "Meet Justin Bieber!" In *Feel Free.* New York: Penguin, 2018.
Smolin, Lee. *Einstein's Unfinished Revolution: The Search for What Lies Beyond the Quantum.* New York: Penguin Press, 2019.
Sorkin, David. *The Transformation of German Jewry, 1780–1840.* Detroit: Wayne State University Press, 1999.
Spector, Scott. *Modernism without Jews? German-Jewish Subjects and Histories.* Bloomington: Indiana University Press, 2017.
Spector, Scott. *Prague Territories: National Conflict and Cultural Innovation in Franz Kafka's Fin de Siècle.* Berkeley: University of California Press, 2000.
Stager, Curt. *Deep Future: The Next 100,000 Years of Life on Earth.* New York: Thomas Dunne, 2011.
Steffen, Will, Paul J. Crutzen, and John R. McNeill, "The Anthropocene: Are Humans Now Overwhelming the Great Forces of Nature?" *Ambio* 36, no. 8 (2007): 614–21.
Steiner, Uwe. *Walter Benjamin: An Introduction to His Work and Thought.* Translated by Michael Winkler. Chicago: University of Chicago Press, 2010.
Steizinger, Johannes. *Revolte, Eros und Sprache: Walter Benjamins "Metaphysik der Jugend."* Berlin: Kulturverlag Kadmos Berlin, 2013.
Stern, Adam. *Survival: A Theological-Political Genealogy.* Philadelphia: University of Pennsylvania Press, 2021.
Strong, Tracy. Foreword to Carl Schmitt, *Political Theology: Four Chapters on the Concept of Sovereignty.* Translated by George Schwab. Chicago: University of Chicago Press, 1985.
Stünkel, Knut Martin. "Eugen Rosenstock-Huessy's Early Symblysmatic Experiences: The Sociology of *Patmos* and *Die Kreatur.*" *Culture, Theory and Critique* 56, no. 1 (2015): 13–27.
Sufrin, Claire E. "Buber, the Bible, and Hebrew Humanism: Finding a Usable Past." *Modern Judaism* 38, no. 1 (2018): 29–43.
Sutcliffe, Adam. *What Are Jews For? History, Peoplehood, and Purpose.* Princeton, NJ: Princeton University Press, 2020.

Szondi, Peter. "Reading 'Engführung': An Essay on the Poetry of Paul Celan." *Boundary 2* 11, no. 3 (1983): 231–64.

Taubes, Jacob. *Occidental Eschatology*. Translated by David Ratmoko. Stanford, CA: Stanford University Press, 2009.

Taubes, Jacob. *The Political Theology of Paul*. Translated by Dana Hollander. Stanford, CA: Stanford University Press, 2004.

Taylor, Chloë. "Biopower." In *Michel Foucault: Key Concepts*, edited by Dianna Taylor. Durham, NC: Acumen, 2011.

Taylor, Marc C. *Abiding Grace: Time, Modernity, Death*. Chicago: University of Chicago Press, 2018.

Thompson, D'Arcy Wentworth. *On Growth and Form*. New York: Dover, 1992.

Tillich, Paul. "Jewish Influences on Contemporary Christian Theology." *Cross-Currents* 2/3 (Spring 1952): 38.

Tirosh-Samuelson, Hava. "Human Flourishing and History: A Religious Imaginary for the Anthropocene." *Journal of the Philosophy of History* 14, no. 3 (2020): 382–418.

Tobias, Rochelle. *The Discourse of Nature in the Poetry of Celan: The Unnatural World*. Baltimore: Johns Hopkins University Press, 2006.

Traverso, Enzo. *Understanding the Nazi Genocide: Marxism after Auschwitz*. Translated by Peter Drucker. London: Pluto Press, 1999.

Troster, Lawrence. "Caretaker or Citizen: Hans Jonas, Aldo Leopold, and the Development of Jewish Environmental Ethics." In *The Legacy of Hans Jonas: Judaism and the Phenomenon of Life*, edited by Hava Tirosh-Samuelson and Christian Wiese. Leiden: Brill, 2008.

Tsao, Roy T. "Arendt's Augustine." In *Politics in Dark Times: Encounters with Hannah Arendt*, edited by Seyla Benhabib. Cambridge: Cambridge University Press, 2010.

Tschumi, Bernard. Introduction to Paul Virilio, *A Landscape of Events*, translated by Julie Rose. Cambridge, MA: MIT Press, 2000.

Valdez, Damien. "Bachofen's Rome and the Fate of the Feminine Orient." *Journal of the History of Ideas* 70, no. 3 (2009): 421–43.

Vatter, Miguel. *Living Law: Jewish Political Theology from Hermann Cohen to Hannah Arendt*. Oxford: Oxford University Press, 2021.

Vatter, Miguel. *Living Time*. New York: Oxford University Press, 2021.

Verene, Donald Phillip. *The History of Philosophy: A Reader's Guide*. Evanston, IL: Northwestern University Press, 2008.

Villa, Dana. "Apologist or Critic?" In *Hannah Arendt in Jerusalem*, edited by Steven E. Aschheim. Berkeley: University of California Press, 2001.

Villa, Dana. *Arendt and Heidegger: The Fate of the Political*. Princeton, NJ: Princeton University Press, 1996.

Villa, Dana. "Beyond Good and Evil: Arendt, Nietzsche, and the Aestheticization of Political Action." *Political Theory* 20, no. 2 (1992): 274–308.

Virilio, Paul. *The Futurism of the Instant: Stop-Eject*. Translated by Julie Rose. Cambridge, MA: Polity, 2010.

Virilio, Paul. *Speed and Politics*. Translated by Mark Polizzotti. New York: Semiotext(e), 1986.
Vogel, Lawrence. Foreword to *The Phenomenon of Life: Toward a Philosophy of Biology*, by Hans Jonas. Evanston, IL: Northwestern University Press, 2001.
Volovici, Marc. *German as a Jewish Problem: The Language Politics of Jewish Nationalism*. Stanford, CA: Stanford University Press, 2020.
Weber, Samuel. *Benjamin's -abilities*. Cambridge, MA: Harvard University Press, 2008.
Weheliye, Alexander. *Habeus Viscus: Racializing Assemblages, Biopolitics, and Black Feminist Theories of the Human*. Durham, NC: Duke University Press, 2014.
Weidner, Daniel. *The Father of Jewish Mysticism: The Writings of Gershom Scholem*. Translated by Sage Anderson. Bloomington: Indiana University Press, 2022.
Weidner, Daniel. "Fort-, Über-, Nachleben: Zu einer Denkfigur bei Benjamin." In *Benjamin-Studien 2*, edited by Daniel Weidner and Sigrid Weigel. Munich: W. Fink, 2011.
Weidner, Daniel. "Mächtige Worte: Zur Politik der Prophetie in der Weimarer Republik." In *Prophetie und Prognostik: Verfügungen über Zukunft in Wissenschaften, Religionen und Künsten*, edited by Daniel Weidner and Stefan Willer. Munich: W. Fink, 2013.
Weidner, Daniel. "The Political Theology of Ethical Monotheism." In *Judaism, Liberalism, and Political Theology*, edited by Randi Rashkover and Martin Kavka. Bloomington: Indiana University Press, 2014.
Weidner, Daniel. "Prophetic Criticism and the Rhetoric of Temporality: Paul Tillich's *Kairos* Texts and Weimar Intellectual Politics." *Political Theology* 21, no. 2 (2020): 71–88.
Weigel, Sigrid. *Body and Image-Space*. Translated by Georgina Paul et al. New York: Routledge, 2003.
Wellmann, Janina. *The Form of Becoming: Embryology and the Epistemology of Rhythm, 1760–1830*. Translated by Kate Sturge. New York: Zone, 2017.
Wiedemann, Barbara. "'Lesen Sie! Immerzu nur Lesen': Gellan-Lektüre und Celans Lektüren." *Poetica* 36, no. 1/2 (2004): 169–91.
Wiese, Christian. *The Life and Thought of Hans Jonas: Jewish Dimensions*. Translated by Jeffrey Grossman and Christian Wiese. Waltham, MA: Brandeis University Press, 2007.
Winter, Ernst Karl. "Bachofen-Renaissance." *Zeitschrift für die gesamte Staatswissenschaft* 85, no. 2 (1928): 316–42.
Winters, Joseph R. *Hope Draped in Black: Race, Melancholy, and the Agony of Progress*. Durham, NC: Duke University Press, 2016.
Wistrich, Robert S. "Stefan Zweig and the 'World of Yesterday.'" In *Stefan Zweig Reconsidered: New Perspectives on His Literary and Biographical Writings*, edited by Mark H. Gelber. Tübingen: Max Niemeyer, 2000.
Wolfe, Judith. *Heidegger and Theology*. London: Bloomsbury, 2014.

Wolfe, Judith. *Heidegger's Eschatology: Theological Horizons in Martin Heidegger's Early Work*. Oxford: Oxford University Press, 2013.

Wolfson, Elliot R. "Light Does Not Talk but Shines: Apophasis and Visions in Rosenzweig's Theopoetic Temporality." In *New Directions in Jewish Philosophy*, edited by Elliot R. Wolfson and Aaron W. Hughes. Bloomington: Indiana University Press, 2010.

Wolin, Richard. *Heidegger's Children: Hannah Arendt, Karl Löwith, Hans Jonas, and Herbert Marcuse*. Princeton, NJ: Princeton University Press, 2001.

Wolin, Richard. *Walter Benjamin: An Aesthetic of Redemption*. Berkeley: University of California Press, 1994.

Wolosky, Shira. *Language Mysticism: The Negative Way of Language in Eliot, Beckett, and Celan*. Stanford, CA: Stanford University Press, 2013.

Woolf, Virginia. "The Leaning Tower." In *A Twentieth-Century Literature Reader: Texts and Debates*, edited by Suman Gupta and David Johnson. London: Routledge, 2005.

Wycoff, Asher. "Between Prophecy and Apocalypse: Buber, Benjamin, and Socialist Eschatology." *Political Theory* 49, no. 3 (2020): 354–79.

Young, Julian. *Friedrich Nietzsche: A Philosophical Biography*. Cambridge: Cambridge University Press, 2010.

Young-Bruehl, Elisabeth. *Hannah Arendt: For Love of the World*. New Haven, CT: Yale University Press, 1982.

Young-Bruehl, Elisabeth. "Reflections on Hannah Arendt's *The Life of the Mind*." *Political Theory* 10, no. 2 (1982): 277–305.

Zanetti, Sandro. *"Zeitoffen": Zur Chronographie Paul Celans*. Munich: W. Fink, 2006.

Zerubavel, Yael. *Recovered Roots: Collective Memory and the Making of Israeli National Identity*. Chicago: Chicago University Press, 1995.

Ziarek, Krzystof. *Inflected Language: Toward a Hermeneutics of Nearness: Heidegger, Levinas, Stevens, Celan*. Albany: SUNY Press, 1994.

Zilcosky, John. "Poetry after Auschwitz? Celan and Adorno Revisited." *Deutsche Vierteljahrsschrift für Literaturwissenschaft und Geistesgeschichte* 79 (2005): 670–91.

Zipperstein, Steven J. *Elusive Prophet: Ahad Ha'am and the Origins of Zionism*. Berkeley: University of California Press, 1993.

Zweig, Stefan. *Briefe zum Judentum*. Edited by Stefan Litt. Frankfurt: Suhrkamp, 2020.

Zweig, Stefan. *Jeremias: Eine dramatische Dichtung in neun Bildern*. Leipzig: Insel, 1919.

Index

Adorno, Gretel, 225
Adorno, Theodor: on Benjamin, 111; correspondence with Celan, 225–26, 226n28, 236; on figure of the third, 226n30; on political action, 80n125; post-Holocaust poetry and, 8, 216, 217n1, 228; post-war critical thought, 255
Agamben, Giorgio: Arendt and, 214, 272, 272n65; on Benjamin, 272n64, 272n65; biopolitical critique, 29, 272–76; caesura and, 276; on Celan, 235–36; on Heidegger, 174, 272n64, 272n65; on Schmitt, 174; temporal concepts and, 16, 29, 274; on total politicization of life, 193n134
Ahad Ha'am: Buber and, 117; cultural Zionism and, 48, 67
Altmann, Alexander, 10n18

Anders, Günther: on afterlife of fascism, 264–65; antinuclear movement and, 262–64; Archimedean perspective, 261; critique of Kafka, 261, 261n19, 262; on *modo negativo*, 263, 282; on not yet being nonexisting, 15–16; on obsolescence of man, 264–65
Anthropocene: anthropogenics and, 278–79, 281; not yet being nonexisting, 16; plurality of life-forms, 157, 278, 282; post-human time, 281; temporal turn and, 109, 260, 272, 277
antisemitism: Arendt and, 180; blood as racial signifier, 79; Buber and, 46, 58, 67, 90n159; Celan and, 234, 239; German Jewish thinkers and, 3, 5–6, 37, 255; Jewish and German origins in, 5; Paulinian anti-Judaism, 90n159, 91; racial rhetoric and, 78–79; witness doctrine, 171

apocatastasis, 133, 133n88
Arendt, Hannah: on action and plurality, 169, 172, 194–96, 209, 211, 214–15; anti-totalitarianism, 165, 180, 190–94, 269; on Augustine, 167–70, 170n45, 170n46, 171–72, 172n50, 174n64, 178, 181–82, 182n91, 183–84, 184n103, 200, 210, 212, 214; being-toward-birth, 167, 185, 192; on Benjamin, 18, 111, 154–56, 182n91, 201–3, 203n170, 203n174, 207, 214; Buber and, 209n196; on continuity, 190–91, 198–202, 209; critique of Heidegger, 14, 162, 162n15, 165, 165n27, 176, 178–80, 190, 201, 212, 222n19, 271; on disruption of existence, 184, 191, 201, 206; on emptying out (*kenosis*), 222; on Hebrew Bible translation, 82–83; Heidegger and, 160–61, 212; on *homo temporalis*, 14, 180–82, 206, 210; on in-betweenness, 11, 185–86, 206; on infallibility (self-prophecy), 191, 191n128, 192–95; *initium* (beginning of humanity), 184–85, 187, 200; Jonas and, 15, 159–61, 212–13, 215, 265–66, 269; on Kafka, 14, 43, 182n91, 187n114, 200–203, 203n170, 204–7, 214, 223; Löwith and, 160, 212; on Marx, 198, 208; on natality, 14, 162, 166–67, 167n33, 169, 185, 191–92, 193n132, 195, 197–98, 200, 204n174, 209–12, 224, 270–71, 286–87; not-yet and no-longer, 29, 182–83, 238–39; *novus ordo saeclorum*, 196, 200, 208–10, 214, 270; on Varnhagen, 165, 180–81, 278; on womb of time, 115; on worldlessness, 191, 191n127, 278–80; on Zweig, 186–87
Aristotle: cyclical time and, 274; Heidegger and, 28, 176–77, 179, 189; *Poetics*, 204n174; *Politics*, 189
Aschheim, Steven, 4, 4n7, 11n22, 56, 117, 121

Augustine: *City of God*, 76n107, 210; *Confessions*, 76, 77n111, 168–69, 170n46, 172n50, 173, 174n64, 176, 178, 189; *De Libero Arbitrio*, 168; *De Trinitate*, 168
Avnon, Dan, 47n9, 61

Babich, Babette, 261
Bachmann, Ingeborg, 216, 239–41
Bachofen, Johann Jakob: Benjamin on, 140–42, 142n118, 143, 143n122, 144–45, 147, 147n135; critique of patriarchy, 140–41, 147n135; Klages and, 141–42; matriarchy and, 141–42, 144, 202–3; Nietzsche and, 141, 141n116; Romantic politics, 144; swamp world, 142–43, 143n122, 144–45
Badiou, Eric, 225n27
Baeck, Leo, 86
Baeumler, Alfred, 58
Bambach, Charles, 231–32, 246
Barash, Jeffrey Andrew, 178n77
Baring, Edward, 177, 177n71, 195
Bar Kochba, 63, 64n69, 66–67, 71
Barry, John, 279
Barth, Karl, 5, 69n88, 74, 75n103
Baschet, Jérôme, 156
Bashir, Shahzad, 42n92
Baudelaire, Charles, 114n21, 154
Bauer, Felice, 187
Bauman, Zygmunt, 287
Ben Gurion, David, 73, 99
Benhabib, Seyla, 191n127, 199
Benjamin, Andrew, 149n142
Benjamin, Mara, 260
Benjamin, Walter: Arendt on, 18, 111, 154–56, 182n91, 201–3, 203n170, 203n174, 207, 214; on art, 111n13; aura and, 111, 113, 280, 280n99; on Bachofen, 140–42, 142n118, 143, 143n122, 144–45, 147, 147n135; bare life (*blosses Leben*), 275; biopolitical critique, 12, 111; Buber and, 13, 61, 81n125, 118, 122; on catastrophe, 37, 190; Derrida on, 12; dialectics at a standstill, 14, 35, 113,

Index 325

133, 139, 183, 205n183; on Heidegger, 116, 125, 125n63; interval (*Abstand*), 11, 114, 116, 120–22, 137, 151, 153; on Kafka, 140–41, 144–47, 155, 202, 248n107, 249; Klages and, 119–20, 123n55, 142n118; on lived experience, 8, 13, 118–20, 130–31; on now-time, 14, 39–40, 111, 139, 150, 150n146, 151, 154, 156–57, 183, 249, 259; "one-timeness," 113; on progress, 29–30, 108, 112–14, 116, 118, 131, 145, 151; Rang and, 70, 75n105; Rosenzweig and, 81n125; Scholem and, 5, 116–17, 120, 125–26, 202; womb metaphor, 114, 114n21, 115–16, 121, 138–39, 145n127, 146–50, 155, 271, 283
Bergmann, Hugo: Bar Kochba group, 63, 64n69; Ben Gurion and, 99; Benjamin and, 155; Buber and, 51, 61–64, 66–69, 72–73, 88, 101; cultural Zionism and, 62–63; *Dialogical Philosophy from Kierkegaard to Buber*, 104; dialogism, 68; on Kafka, 103; Prague circle and, 53, 63, 63n65;
Bergmann, Martin, 68
Bergson, Henri: duration (*durée*), 24, 78n113, 137; humanism and, 27; living time and, 24–25; *Matter and Memory*, 137, 137n103; on plurality of time, 26, 124n59, 190n123; temporal turn and, 21; translation into German, 25, 25n30; on uncertainty, 29; value of life and, 28; vitalism, 24, 116, 137
Berman, Lila, 12n25
Bernoulli, Carl Albrecht, 127, 142
Bhabha, Homi K., 12
Biale, David, 79
Bielik-Robson, Agata, 15, 184–85, 185n107, 209
Biemann, Asher, 48n11
biopolitics: Agamben on, 29; Benjamin on, 12, 111; catastrophe and, 276–77; critical race studies and, 276; German Jewish thinkers and, 15, 249, 272–76; Judeo-Christian history of, 276; Kjellén on, 258; life-form (*Lebensform*), 258, 273; Mbembe on, 12
Blanqui, Louis Auguste, 154
Bloch, Ernst, 127, 129, 142n118, 255
Blumenberg, Hans, 255
Bollack, Jean, 243n94
Bourel, Dominique, 55n33, 56–57
Bowie, Andrew, 33
Brecht, Bertolt, 149, 187, 287
Brith Shalom (Covenant of Peace), 49, 51, 72
Broch, Hermann: Arendt on, 14, 182n91, 186–89, 214; on catastrophe, 190; "The City of Man," 187, 187n113; correspondence with Arendt, 187n114, 188; *Death of Virgil*, 187–88; on Sartre, 188, 188n119
Brod, Max, 11, 63, 92, 92n165, 103, 142
Brody, Samuel, 52n20, 61, 96
Brunner, Emil, 69n88, 75n103
Buber, Martin: anarchism and, 52n20, 53, 58, 61; anti-fascism, 91–92, 95, 97, 101; Ben Gurion and, 99; Benjamin and, 81n125, 155; Bergmann and, 51, 62–64, 67–69, 72–73, 88, 101; betweenness and, 11, 100, 105, 271; Cohen and, 47n8; on the creaturely, 4, 74, 145; cultural Zionism and, 8, 53, 55, 60, 76, 79, 122, 286; dialogism, 47, 47n9, 48, 50–51, 56, 61–62, 64, 68–70, 76–77, 91, 95, 101, 105–6, 224, 226; on eclipse of God, 104, 104n205; on ecstasy, 45, 55–57, 60, 67, 71, 227; encounter and, 90, 234n61; Forte circle, 49, 73–74, 74n100; on Goethe, 76n108; Hasidic tradition and, 52, 55–56, 67, 226; Hebrew Bible translation, 40, 80–82, 82n132, 83–84; Hebrew University and, 46, 49, 50n14, 72; on Heidegger, 84, 84n139, 102, 104; on immediacy, 8, 45–47, 70–71, 79,

Buber, Martin (*continued*)
84; influence of Nietzsche on, 2, 2n4, 13, 33–34, 45–46, 48n9, 49, 52–53, 57–58, 60, 64, 87, 101, 115, 117, 121n48, 123; on I-Thou relations, 77–78, 103, 223n21; on Jeremiah, 45, 87, 92, 92n164, 101; Jewish revivalism and, 44, 46–48, 48n11, 49, 65, 68, 73, 83, 86, 90, 96, 101, 103, 119, 122, 227; on Kafka, 51, 101, 101n195, 102; on Kierkegaard, 94, 94n171; Landauer and, 34, 51–61, 61n57, 62, 101; lectures on Judaism, 46, 46n6, 53, 63–64, 64n67, 64n69, 65–66, 72, 117n32; lived experience (*Erlebnis*), 2, 8, 13, 45, 47n9, 65, 84, 101, 103, 233, 255; Nietzschean Lebensphilosophie, 13, 48, 56–58, 65, 118–19; not-yet and no-longer, 29, 54, 80, 100; Prague circle and, 53, 62–67; prophetic thinking, 45–46, 46n5, 47, 47n8, 49–50, 52, 70n93, 84–96, 98, 100–101, 105, 105n210, 106n211, 227; renewal (*Erneuerung*), 65–66; revolutionary change and, 54, 57–58; Rosenzweig and, 51, 62, 73–75, 75n104, 77–78, 80, 101; on Schmitt, 102, 104; Simmel and, 13, 50, 53, 57; Taubes and, 95n173, 105; theopolitics, 45, 47, 49–50, 83–88, 90–101, 159, 272; on time of movement (*kinesis*), 59, 222; Werfel and, 51, 73, 91–92; Zweig and, 51, 73, 91–92, 92n164

Bultmann, Rudolf, 42n94, 161, 178n77, 268

Burrus, Virginia, 76n107

Butler, Judith, 272

Calcagno, Antonio, 159n3

Canales, Jimena, 25–26

Cassirer, Ernst: history of philosophy, 27n38; neo-Kantianism, 26–27, 178, 178n77; temporal concepts and, 26–28; on value of life, 28

Cavanaugh, William, 174

Celan, Paul: Agamben on, 235–36; already-no-longer, 223, 248, 270; attention and, 248–49; breath-turn, 40, 224, 250–51, 253; caesura and, 41, 218, 218n6, 219–20, 224, 233, 238, 246, 248n107, 251, 251n118, 252; correspondence with Adorno, 225–26, 226n28, 236; Derrida on, 216–17, 225n26, 229–31, 233, 235; Georg Büchner Prize, 223n21; German Jewish critique and, 250–51; German-Jewish in-betweenness, 225–27, 238, 271; Hölderlin and, 229, 230n44, 246–47; influence of Heidegger, 219, 226, 229–30, 236–37, 246; *kinesis* and *kenosis*, 222–23; life-form (*Lebensform*), 259; on living time, 221, 223, 242, 248; not-yet and no-longer, 29, 223, 237–40, 248; ontology of witnessing, 216–17, 222, 232–33, 235, 250; otherness and, 219–23, 223n21, 224–25, 227, 233–35, 249; Pöggeler and, 228–30, 234, 244–45; *Sprachgestaltung* (language forming), 220n11; temporal in-betweenness, 233; on time of the other, 232–34, 240; use of "Dia-chronie," 223n21

Clark, Christopher, 17

clocks: growth of capital and, 22, 22n20; ordained rhythm of, 151; regulation of work, 22; scientific explanation of, 25; simultaneity and, 26; synchronization of, 24; world history, 35

Coe, Cynthia D., 79n119

Cohen, Hermann: on being, 98n184; cultural German Jewish symbiosis, 59, 60n54; Jewish tradition and, 33n60; neo-Kantianism, 160, 160n7, 178; prophetic thinking, 47n8; "The Style of the Prophets," 86

Cohen, Jeremy, 6n13, 171n47

Cohen, Uri, 50n14

Cohn-Bendit, Daniel, 224n25, 227

Cooper, Andrea Dara, 79n118

Courbet, Gustave, 154–55

Coyne, Ryan, 7n15, 174, 174n64, 175, 177
Crist, Eileen, 281
critical race studies, 108, 276
Crutzen, Paul, 278

Däubler, Theodor, 74n100
deferral: Benjamin on, 3, 15, 126, 150, 272n66; German Jewish thinkers and, 36, 39; infinity and, 126; Jewish language as temporal, 34–35; messianism and, 15; Paul's philosophy of, 174; Scholem on, 3, 15, 35, 126, 272n66
Deleuze, Gilles, 154
DeLoughrey, Elizabeth, 279–80
Derrida, Jacques: on Benjamin, 12, 113; on caesura, 251n118; on Celan, 216–17, 225n26, 229–31, 233, 235; deconstruction and, 202n166, 230, 251n118; deferral and, 15; on German Jewish understanding of life, 15, 15n31; *Of Grammatology*, 202n166; Heidegger's existentialism and, 255; Jewish tradition and, 33n60; on poetry as ethical system, 233; on rhythm, 113; *Shibboleth*, 225n26; *Sovereignties in Question*, 249n113; temporal concepts and, 16, 29, 232–33
dialogism: Buber and, 47, 47n9, 48, 50–51, 56, 61–62, 64, 68–70; I-it relation, 59n48, 72; immediacy and, 13, 70; between individual and God, 77; intrahuman, 76–77; I-Thou relation, 59n48, 70, 72, 75–77, 227
Die Kreatur, 49, 74, 90
Dilthey, Wilhelm: on Augustine, 173n53; Buber and, 53; Heidegger on, 29n44, 163, 173n53; humanism and, 176; life philosophy, 71, 176n70; lived experience and, 53; temporal turn and, 18n2, 21
dual identity: German Jewish thinkers and, 9–10; German Jews and, 9–10, 10n18, 11n22, 40
Durkheim, Emil, 135

Duttlinger, Carolin, 139n107
Duvernoy, Sophie, 80n122

Eckhart, Meister, 52, 54
ecstacy (*Rausch*): Benjamin and, 123; Buber on, 45, 55–57, 60, 67, 227; Hasidism and, 67; Nietzsche and, 57, 122, 227; Scholem on, 34
Edelman, Lee, 256, 256n3
Eeden, Frederik Willem van, 74n100
Ehrenberg, Hans, 74
Eiland, Howard, 118n36
Einstein, Albert, 24–27
Emundts, Dina, 19n7
environment: common (*Umwelt*), 267; cultural critique and, 13; destruction of, 15, 108, 256, 265–66; ethics of, 266, 266n38; historians of, 280, 282; swamp world, 131, 145; temporality and, 109, 131
Erdle, Birgit, 206
Erlewine, Robert, 106n211
Eshel, Amir, 10n18, 279
Esposito, Roberto, 189n122, 207, 272–73
Ettinger, Bracha, 283n110

Felstiner, John: on Celan, 232–33, 236, 246; on Celan and Adorno, 226n31; on Celan as German Jew, 231; on Celan's poetics, 239, 250; on "Gespräch im Gebirg," 226; on *The Meridian*, 223n21; on *Sprachgitter*, 243n91, 245
Fenves, Peter, 130, 130n78, 130n79, 190n123
Feuerbach, Ludwig, 33
Fichte, Johann Gottlieb, 122
Ford, Thomas, 279–80, 280n99
Forte circle, 49, 73–74, 74n100, 75n105
Foucault, Michel, 123n54, 272–73, 284
Fredriksen, Paula, 6n13, 171
Fremaux, Anne, 279
Freud, Sigmund, 91
Friedlaender, Eli, 244n96

Friedman, Maurice, 2n4, 46, 56
Fritzsche, Peter, 19

Gadamer, Hans-Georg: on Celan, 216, 228–29, 234, 236, 242, 244–45; on Heidegger, 160; temporal concepts and, 249
Gardner, Sebastian, 19n7
Gasché, Rodolphe, 142n118, 237n73
Gaus, Günter, 215
Gelber, Mark, 91
George, Stefan: on breathing units, 83, 83n136; Nietzschean Lebensphilosophie, 57; post-Nietzschean poets, 117; response to Buber, 66; *Rhythmus*, 105n208; Simmel and, 13; translatability and, 81
Geulen, Eva, 275
Gogarten, Friedrich, 69n88, 75n103, 85, 85n142, 178n77
Gold, Joel, 218n6
Goldberg, Sylvie Anne, 30, 78, 139, 214
Golomb, Jacob, 46n5, 47n9, 56
Gordon, Peter E., 10n18, 27n38, 75n103, 237n73
Gorsky, Philip, 191n128
Gossman, Lionel, 144
Gregory, Eric, 184
Greisch, Jean, 223n21
Gross, Raphael, 93n166
Gumbrecht, Hans Ulrich, 131n81, 157
Gutkind, Erich, 74n100

Hache, Emilie, 284
Hahn, Barbara, 10n18
Hamacher, Werner: on Benjamin, 156; on Celan, 216, 233n59, 248; on democracy and Christianity, 214, 214n218; on heme-messianism, 248n107; on nihilism, 132n84; on now-time, 152; on Rilke, 248, 248n107; on time of the unfinished, 112, 112n14
Hamilton, Clive, 109, 157, 279–80
Hanssen, Beatrice, 135n96, 202
Haraway, Donna, 284

Hardt, Michael, 22n20, 272–73
Harnack, Adolph von, 86, 173n53
Hart, Heinrich, 53
Hart, Julius, 53
Hartman, Saidiya, 108–9, 113, 149, 276
Hartog, François: on the Anthropocene, 157; on Benjamin's historical thinking, 108; on Christian eschatology, 156n175; on Christian historicity, 3n5; on Christian order of time, 168; *Chronos*, 264; critique of presentism, 45n2; on empty time, 16; on history and time, 156–57; *Regimes of Historicity*, 108; on Western progress, 109
Hebrew University, 46, 49, 50n14, 68, 72
Hegel, Georg: cyclical time and, 205; dialectics of internal and external, 121n46; historicism and, 21, 40, 84, 112, 115, 123, 169, 283; idealist approach, 121; *Lectures on the Philosophy of History*, 114, 121; life philosophy, 36; notion of self, 121n47, 122; on theater of history, 127, 128n71; use of "Meinen" (opinions), 243
Heidegger, Martin: Arendt and, 160–61, 190, 271; on Augustine, 172–73, 173n53, 174, 174n64, 175–79; on becoming, 37; on being-in-the-world, 14–15, 165n25, 165n26; being-toward-death, 15, 40, 162, 185; Benjamin and, 116, 125; Buber and, 84, 84n139, 102; on care (*Sorge, Cura*), 165, 165n26, 166; on Celan, 216; cyclical time and, 205; existential temporality, 172, 177, 255, 263; finality and, 11, 29–30, 270; on Hölderlin, 230n44; on *kairos* and *sterēsis*, 175, 175n66, 176; Löwith on, 161, 161n12, 162, 212, 243; nihilism and, 37–38, 41, 162n15, 178, 213, 267–69; Paulinian concepts and, 7, 7n15, 163–64, 172, 174–76, 179–80;

Index   329

phenomenology, 125n63, 177n71, 179; on the planetary, 261; self-referentiality, 14, 162n15, 165, 165n25, 166, 176–77, 179–80, 201, 238; on task of philosophy, 26–27, 27n38; on thrownness, 41, 181, 268
Heine, Heinrich, 20, 185
Heisenberg, Werner, 30n48
Herf, Jeffrey, 25
Herrmann, Leo, 64
Herskowitz, Daniel, 64n70, 105n208, 162n15, 174
Herzl, Theodor, 48, 48n12, 55, 67
Heschel, Abraham J., 1, 43, 106n211, 162n15
Hillach, Ansgar, 132n84
Hillman, Susanne, 129n74
Hitler, Adolf, 191–93
Hölderlin, Friedrich: "Brot und Wein," 237n72, 243n91; Celan and, 229, 230n44, 241, 246–47; Heidegger on, 41, 229, 230n44, 237, 237n72, 238, 242n88; mythic-lyrical poetry and, 242; prophetic thinking, 87
Holste, Christine, 74n100
homo temporalis, 14, 180–82, 206, 210
Honig, Bonnie, 272
Horkheimer, Max, 255
Horwitz, Rivka, 75n104
Husserl, Edmund: Heidegger and, 28–29; *Lectures on the Structure of Internal Time*, 28; phenomenology, 28n41, 116, 161, 178n77, 255; temporal concepts and, 21, 28; on uncertainty, 29; universalism and, 28
Huxley, Aldous, 29

Ibn Ezra, Abraham, 31
Imdahl, Georg, 176n70
infallibility, 191–95, 201–2

Jaeggi, Rahel, 257
Jameson, Frederick, 22n20, 281, 281n100
Jantzen, Grace, 115
Jaspers, Karl, 270

Jennings, Michael W., 118n36, 132n84
Jonas, Hans: Anders and, 263; Arendt and, 15, 159–61, 212–13, 215, 265–66, 269; critique of Heidegger, 161–62, 179, 212–13, 265–69; on ethics of life-forms, 266, 268; on Gnosticism, 266–67; *habilitation*, 213; influence of Bultmann, 43n94, 161; intellectual development of, 265; on Judeo-Christian temporality, 269; life-form (*Lebensform*), 266–67; lived experience (*Erlebnis*), 269; on obsolescence of man, 269; Paulinian concepts and, 267–69, 269n54; post-catastrophe language of time, 269–70, 281; precaution principle, 284; temporal egalitarianism, 260; on temporality, 269n53; on totalitarianism, 269; Western dualism and, 269, 269n52
Jordeim, Helga, 284
Joris, Pierre, 217–18, 246

Kafka, Franz: Arendt on, 14, 43, 182n91, 186–87, 187n114, 200–203, 203n170, 204–7, 214; Benjamin on, 140–41, 144–47, 202, 248n107, 249; Bergmann and, 103; Buber and, 51, 61, 63, 66, 101–2; on catastrophe, 190; on circular order of time, 201–2, 205–6; Hadad, Yemima, 51n18; immobile assault, 35; in-betweenness of, 203, 206; on man's insertion in time, 200–201; Prague circle and, 53, 63; as prophet, 142; prophetic thinking, 103; Scholem on, 143, 202; swamp world, 143, 143n122, 146, 202;
Kampowski, Stephan, 185, 185n107
Kant, Immanuel: *Critique of Judgment*, 190; Heidegger on, 248; on the intersubjective, 48; long experience, 122; philosophy of time, 19, 19n7; temporal concepts and, 20
Karplus, Gretel, 111n13
Kaufman, Peter Iver, 184
Kaufmann, Walter, 76n109, 78n113, 96

330 Index

Kavka, Martin, 33n60
Kepnes, Steven, 77n111
Kern, Stephen, 19, 21, 24, 135
Kierkegaard, Søren, 94, 94n171, 228
Killen, Andreas, 25, 30
Kisiel, Theodore, 163, 172, 176–79
Kjellén, Rudolf, 258, 258n9, 273
Klages, Ludwig: Bachofen and, 141–42; Benjamin and, 119–20, 123n55, 142n118; dream imagery and, 119n41; on ego, 122, 122n50; on historicism, 121–22; Nietzschean Lebensphilosophie, 119–20, 122n50, 123; post-Nietzschean critique, 119n41; ur-images (*Urbilder*) and, 122n50
Kleinberg, Ethan, 241n85
Kloos, Diet, 221n13
Kohn, Hans, 13, 61, 63, 65, 71
Kohn, Jerome, 158–59, 215
Koselleck, Reinhart: "Does History Accelerate?," 269n53; experience of modern, 38; horizon of expectation, 174; on in-betweenness, 270, 270n57; on modes of temporal experience, 151; regulation of time, 22, 269n53; on semantics of historical time, 168, 168n36; on space and time, 38n81
Kotsko, Adam, 272n64
Kracauer, Siegfried, 23, 82
Kraus, Karl, 11, 114n20
Krell, David Farrell, 176n70
Kristeva, Julia, 155
Kulturkritik (cultural critique), 2, 4n7

LaCapra, Dominick, 41n89
Lackner, Stephan, 153
Lacoue-Labarthe, Philippe, 214, 216, 230, 230n44, 246
Landauer, Gustav: anarchism and, 52n20, 53, 55, 58, 104; assassination of, 62, 79, 88; Buber and, 34, 51–61, 61n57, 62, 87; Forte circle, 74n100; in-betweenness of, 54; influence of Nietzsche on, 52, 55,

58; Meister Eckhart translation, 52, 54; Nietzschean Lebensphilosophie, 13, 33, 58, 65; *The Revolution*, 54; revolutionary change and, 54, 57–58, 65; *Skepticism and Mysticism*, 54;
Landmann, Michael, 234n61
Langbehn, Julius, 87
Langston, Nancy, 282
Latour, Bruno, 20
Lazare, Bernard, 186, 203n170
Lebensraum (living space), 4, 37, 120, 125n64, 256
Lefebvre, Henri, 23
Leibniz, Gottfried, 152n159
Lepenies, Wolf, 86
Leskov, Nikolai, 147
Levennson, Jon D., 86n144
Levinas, Emmanuel: on Celan, 216; on death, 247; immediacy and, 79n119; Jewish tradition and, 33n60; principle of life, 15n31; response to Heidegger, 161n12
Levine, Michael, 10n18
Lewitt, Laura, 113n15
Liberles, Robert, 32n59
life-form (*Lebensform*): alternative, 258–59, 278; Anders and, 265; bare life (*blosses Leben*), 274, 274n75; Benjamin and, 135–36; biopolitical critique and, 258, 273; Buber and, 56, 258–59; egalitarianism and, 4, 138, 259, 266–67; ethics of, 266; Jonas and, 266–67; languages and, 258; minoritarian perspective, 258, 277–78; plurality of, 278; temporality of, 256, 283;
life philosophy (*Lebensphilosophie*): Buber and, 13, 56; fascism and, 140; Heidegger and, 29n44; history and sources of, 21n16; post-Nietzschean, 3, 9, 259, 276; revolutionary change and, 65; Scholem and, 4n7; secular German, 48. *See also* Nietzsche, Friedrich
life-time (*Lebenszeit*), 3, 47
life-world (*Lebenswelt*), 3, 47
Lindroos, Kia, 150n146

Liska, Vivian, 10n18, 35, 142n120, 202, 205, 231n51, 250, 276
lived experience (*Erlebnis*): Benjamin and, 130–31; biopower and, 273; Buber on, 2, 8, 13, 45, 47n9, 61, 101, 103; Dilthey and, 53; Jewish temporality and, 65; Jews and, 60–61; Judeo-Christian temporality, 269; Nietzsche and, 34; post-Nietzschean, 56
living space (*Lebensraum*), 4, 120, 125n64
living time: Bergmann on, 104; Bergson on, 24–25; Celan on, 221, 223, 242, 248; democracy and, 211; egalitarianism and, 4, 20; individual experience of, 24–25; Kafka on, 145; minorities and, 256; modernity and, 21, 24; production and labor, 20; Simmel on, 25; womb symbolism, 147
Löwith, Karl: Arendt and, 160, 212; on Hegel, 243; on Heidegger, 34, 160–62, 162n15, 177, 212, 237, 237n72, 237n73, 243; *Meaning in History*, 212; on Nietzsche's eternal recurrence, 154; temporal concepts and, 34, 159, 162, 223
Löwy, Michael, 52
Luther, Martin, 82

Mahmood, Saba, 36n72
Maimon, Salomon, 19
Maimonides, Moses, 31, 33n60
Mann, Thomas, 187n113
Markell, Patchen, 170n45, 172n50, 182n91, 198n149
Marx, Karl, 20–22, 38, 39n83
Mauthner, Fritz, 11, 57
Mbembe, Achille, 12, 12n27, 272
McCole, John, 205n183
McFarland, James, 118
McGowan, John, 194
memory, 166, 173, 199–200, 219
Mendelssohn, Moses, 10n18, 19, 82
Mendes-Flohr, Paul, 11n22, 44n1, 53, 56, 61

Menely, Tobias, 279–80
Menninghaus, Winfried, 218n6, 220n11, 228
Mosès, Stéphane, 10n18, 218n6
Mosse, George, 10n18, 11n22, 226n30
Moyn, Samuel, 169n43
Munslow, Alun, 17
Myers, David, 10n18, 86n145

Nancy, Jean-Luc, 214
natality: Bauman on, 287; betweenness and, 166; democracy as, 8, 211; German Jewish thinkers and, 2, 256; humanity and, 14, 162. *See also* Arendt, Hannah
Negri, Antonio, 22n20, 272–73
Neiman, Susan, 264
Neoplatonism, 87n149, 173, 222, 240
Ng, Karen, 121n47
Niebuhr, Reinhold, 69n88, 187n113
Nietzsche, Friedrich: Bachofen and, 141, 141n116; Buber on, 45; critique of historicism, 118, 118n36; on ecstasy, 57, 122, 227; *Erlebnis* (lived experience) philosophy, 34, 45, 75n105; eternal recurrence, 34, 36n70, 154–55; Foucault on, 123n54; *Kulturkritik* (cultural critique), 2, 4n7; on last man, 114n21, 282, 282n105; life philosophy (*Lebensphilosophie*), 3, 9, 13, 15, 36, 45, 47, 53, 56–58, 71, 116–17, 122n50, 127
Nirenberg, David, 6n13, 7n14, 171, 171n47
Nordau, Max, 37
nowness (*Jetztzeit*), 8, 14, 206, 274, 274n75
now-time: Benjamin on, 40, 111, 139, 150, 150n146, 151, 154, 156–57, 183, 249, 259; German Jewish thinkers and, 20; as an interval, 151; messianism and, 15, 151–52; rhythm and, 151

O'Byrne, Anne, 167n33
Opitz, Michael, 111

Oppenheimer, Franz, 42
Osborne, Peter, 132, 153

Pardes, Ilana, 115
Paul: anti-Judaism, 7, 7n15, 90n159, 91, 95, 163–64, 171–72, 175; as apostle, 96n178; Arendt on, 178, 183–84, 212–13, 269n54; Buber on, 91–93, 95, 101; Christian eschatology, 173, 178; on deferral, 174; Gnostic interpretation, 86; Heidegger and, 7, 7n15, 163–64, 174–75; on the katechon, 174; life philosophy, 163; political theology, 85, 89, 89n156, 96; prophetic thinking, 87, 87n152, 88, 90, 90n159, 92, 95
Perloff, Marjorie, 217, 241
Peskowitz, Miriam, 113n15
Plato and Platonism, 42n94, 68, 99, 176
Pöggeler, Otto: on Celan, 216, 228–30, 245, 245n103; on Celan and temporality, 234; correspondence with Celan, 244; temporal concepts and, 249
political theology: Arendt on, 162–63, 169n43, 208; Augustine and, 197, 208; Buber and, 47, 50, 94, 98n186; Christian, 40, 85, 93; emptying out (kenosis), 222; German Jewish thinkers and, 7, 9, 272, 274; Jewish, 36n70, 77, 90, 93n166; language and, 126; Nietzschean Lebensphilosophie and, 47; resistance to, 102n199; Schmitt and, 93, 93n166, 94, 96, 98n186, 99, 272
Polt, Richard, 165n26
Povinelli, Elizabeth, 15, 284–85
presentism, 40, 45, 45n2
Presner, Todd Samuel, 163n17

Rabinbach, Anson, 10n18, 19, 22, 117n32
Ragaz, Leonhard, 90
Rancière, Jacques, 214
Rang, Florens Christian: Benjamin and, 75n105; Buber and, 75, 75n104, 76–77; Forte circle, 74, 74n100, 75n105; temporality and, 70
rhythm: Benjamin and, 125–26, 131–39; breathing and, 139n107; graphology and, 136–37; immanent life force (*Lebenskraft*), 135–36; industrial modernity and, 23, 132, 138; language and, 82, 120, 125–26, 128, 131n81; now-time and, 151; as origin, 134–36, 136n96, 137–39; social and political involvement, 135, 137–38; space and, 2n2; time and, 22, 38, 113, 131–37, 140
Rickert, Heinrich, 71n94, 116, 176n70, 178, 190n123
Rilke, Rainer Maria, 41, 240–41, 248, 248n107, 265n35
Robinson, James, 31n55
Roemer, Nils, 20, 38
Rosa, Hartmut, 284
Rose, Gillian, 94n171
Rosenstock-Huessy, Eugen, 74, 81n125
Rosenwald, Lawrence, 82n132
Rosenzweig, Franz: Benjamin and, 81n125; blood lineages and, 79, 79n118; Buber and, 51, 62, 73–75, 75n104, 77–78, 80; critique of idealism, 255; on dialogism, 76–77; finite-infinite relation, 36, 36n71; Hebrew Bible translation, 40, 80–82, 82n132, 83; Hebrew language and, 35, 35n69, 78n116, 80–81; Heidegger and, 237n73; in-betweenness and, 36, 36n70; on immediacy, 80n122; on Jewish community, 79; Jewish Lehrhaus, 49; Jewish revivalism, 73; philosophy of life, 13, 33, 41; presentism and, 45; *Star of Redemption*, 70, 76n107, 77n111, 79n118; temporal concepts and, 77n111, 78–79, 81, 223
Rothberg, Michael, 166n32
Rovelli, Carlo, 24
Rudavsky, Tamar, 31

Sachs, Nelly, 216
Safranski, Rüdiger, 29n46

Sagan, Claire, 284
Santner, Eric, 100, 272–73
Sartre, Jean-Paul, 188, 188n119, 228
Scanlon, Michael, 196
Schmitt, Carl: Buber on, 102; on friend–enemy distinction, 7n15; on the katechon, 94, 94n169; on physical killing, 95, 102; political theology, 93, 93n166, 94, 96, 98n186, 99, 272; *Political Theology*, 84–85, 85n142; on real decision, 84; on sovereignty, 39, 93–94, 98, 100, 228; state of exception, 94, 100, 273
Scholem, Gershom: Benjamin and, 3, 5, 111, 116–17, 120, 125–26, 155, 202; on Buber, 13, 46n6, 61, 61n59, 62, 122; Celan and, 228; collaboration with Buber and Bergmann, 73; cultural Zionism and, 14, 122; on deferral, 3, 15, 35, 35n66, 126, 272n66; on ecstasy, 34; on emptying out (*kenosis*), 222; on Kafka, 143, 202; on lived experience, 118; Nietzsche's philosophy and, 33–34; temporal concepts and, 159, 223
Schopenhauer, Arthur, 33
Schumacher, Eric, 175n66
Schwartz, Yossef, 57
Scott, Joanna Vecchiarelli, 187
Shapira, Avraham, 58n48
Shapiro, Michael, 23
Shapiro, Susan E., 30n49
Shenhav, Ghilad, 115n24
Sieber, Mirjam, 226, 226n28
Simmel, Georg: bare life (*blosses Leben*), 274, 274n75; on being, 176; bridges/doors concept, 50n15; Buber and, 13, 50, 53, 57; on figure of the third, 226n30; historical consciousness, 22; influence of George, 13; influence of Nietzsche, 13; on the intersubjective, 48; life-form (*Lebensform*), 274, 274n75; living time and, 24–25, 259; Nietzschean Lebensphilosophie, 57, 71, 117; *Philosophy of Money*, 21; on social norms, 33; temporal concepts and, 21, 159; translation of Bergson, 117;
Smith, Zadie, 71
Smolin, Lee, 30n48
socialism: Buber and, 52–53, 90, 97, 104; Landauer and, 51–53, 60; Marxist, 38, 97; Nietzsche and, 34; open-ended, 97; religious, 90, 97, 104; secularization and, 37n76; utopian, 97; Zionist, 4, 49, 60
Sorkin, David, 32
Spector, Scott, 4n7, 10n18, 11, 32n58, 63n65, 64n69, 102n199
Spranger, Eduard, 257
Stark, Judith Chelius, 187
Steiner, Uwe, 132n84
Steizinger, Johannes, 133
Stern, Adam Y., 276
Stoermer, Eugene, 278
Susman, Margarete: Buber and, 45; Celan and, 223, 234, 234n61, 250, 259; Forte circle, 74n100; Jewishness and, 234n61; Nietzsche and, 129, 129n74, 259n13
Sutcliffe, Adam, 171
Szondi, Peter, 216, 219

Taubes, Jacob: Buber and, 95n173, 105; on Buber's prophetic past, 90; on Christian eschatology, 89, 89n157; on concept of time, 1–2; Jewish political theology, 90; on Paul's temporality, 90n159;
Taylor, Chloë, 273
Taylor, Marc C., 42n94
temporality: Anthropocene and, 13, 15–16; clockwork metaphor, 25; as critique of power, 172; of deferral, 34–36; egalitarianism and, 4, 39–40, 138, 208, 260, 265, 270; eternal recurrence, 34, 154–55; German Jewish betweenness, 36–37; human language and, 110; identity and, 10, 159; industrialized annihilation of the Jews, 5; infallibility and, 192–93; intuition and, 19; Jewish calendars, 30–31; life-forms and, 256, 283;

temporality (*continued*)
   lived experience and, 13–14; minoritarian perspective, 16; queer, 256, 271; railways and, 19, 22, 22n20, 23; spatial boundaries, 2, 2n2, 39; transience and, 131, 133, 139–40, 182
theopolitics: Buber and, 45, 47, 49, 83–86, 88, 93–97, 99–101; divine presence and, 97; identification of real decision in, 83–84; Jewish, 99; versus political theology, 96; prophetic, 100
Tillich, Paul: Anders and, 261; Buber and, 75n104, 97; concept of time and, 70n93; dialogism and, 69n88, 70; presentism and, 45
Tobias, Rochelle, 242, 242n90
Traverso, Enzo, 264
Troeltsch, Ernst, 86, 173n53
Tsao, Roy, 166, 166n30, 192, 193n132

Underwood, Mary, 190

Varnhagen, Rahel, 165, 165n23, 180–81, 259, 278
Vatter, Miguel, 36n70, 169n43, 208–9, 209n196
Villa, Dana, 165n25, 212n213, 271
Virgil, 172, 200, 208–9
Virilio, Paul, 23
Vischer-Bilfinger, Wilhelm, 141n116
vitalism: Bergson and, 24, 116, 137; German Jewish thinkers and, 4n7, 15, 137, 205n183, 285, 287; neo-Kantian, 69; Nietzschean life philosophy, 15, 34
Volovici, Marc, 65n73, 78n116

Weber, Samuel, 124n58
Weheliye, Alexander, 108–9, 276
Wehle, Kurt, 89n155
Weidner, Daniel, 102n199
Weigel, Sigrid, 123n54
Weizsäcker, Viktor von, 74, 90
Wellhausen, Julius, 86
Wellmann, Janina, 134–35, 135n94
Weltsch, Felix, 63

Weltsch, Robert, 63, 142
Werfel, Franz, 11, 51, 73, 91–92
Wiese, Christian, 267
Wigen, Einar, 284
Windelband, Wilhelm, 137n103, 178
Winters, Joseph, 108–9, 255, 256n3, 276
Wissenschaft des Judentums, 33n60, 265, 265n37
witness doctrine: Augustine and, 6–7, 171, 171n47, 171n48, 175; Christian theologians on, 175n68; Jews as a political minority, 6, 6n13, 36, 171, 171n48, 180
Wittgenstein, Ludwig, 258
Wittig, Joseph, 74, 90
Witton-Davies, Carlyle, 86n144
Wohlfarth, Irving, 132n84
Wolfe, Judith, 173, 177
Wolfskehl, Karl, 141
Wolfson, Elliot, 76n107
Wolin, Richard, 37n75, 132n84, 139n108, 213n216
Wolosky, Shira, 218n6, 242n89, 246n104
Woolf, Virginia, 286
Wycoff, Asher, 61
Wyneken, Gustav, 116

Young, Julian, 141n116
Young-Bruehl, Elisabeth, 193, 203n170

Zanetti, Sandro, 220–21, 221n13, 224
Ziarek, Krzysztof, 234, 238
Zionism: cultural, 8, 34, 37, 48, 53, 55, 60n55, 62–63, 72, 120, 122; nationalism, 37, 51, 101; political, 34, 47–48, 51, 55, 60n55, 67; revivalism and, 47n8; territorial ambitions, 67
Zunz, Leopold, 20
Zweig, Stefan: Buber and, 51, 73, 91–92, 92n164; critique of modern state, 92, 92n164; *Jeremias*, 91; prophetic thinking, 46n5; unpolitical view, 186–87; *The World of Yesterday*, 186

www.ingramcontent.com/pod-product-compliance
Lightning Source LLC
Chambersburg PA
CBHW030520230426
43665CB00010B/695